POLICY ANALYSIS for SOCIAL WORKERS

SOCIAL WORK IN THE NEW CENTURY
Michael Reisch, *Social Policy and Social Justice*

Mary C. Ruffolo, Brian Perron, Ph.D. and Elizabeth H. Voshel,
*Direct Social Work Practice: Theories and Skills for
Becoming an Evidence Based Practitioner*

Lisa E. Cox, Carolyn Tice and Dennis D. Long,
Introduction to Social Work: An Advocacy-Based Profession

POLICY ANALYSIS *for* SOCIAL WORKERS

RICHARD K. CAPUTO
Yeshiva University

Los Angeles | London | New Delhi
Singapore | Washington DC

Los Angeles | London | New Delhi
Singapore | Washington DC

FOR INFORMATION:

SAGE Publications, Inc.
2455 Teller Road
Thousand Oaks, California 91320
E-mail: order@sagepub.com

SAGE Publications Ltd.
1 Oliver's Yard
55 City Road
London, EC1Y 1SP
United Kingdom

SAGE Publications India Pvt. Ltd.
B 1/I 1 Mohan Cooperative Industrial Area
Mathura Road, New Delhi 110 044
India

SAGE Publications Asia-Pacific Pte. Ltd.
3 Church Street
#10-04 Samsung Hub
Singapore 049483

Acquisitions Editor: Kassie Graves
Editorial Assistant: Elizabeth Luizzi
Production Editor: Stephanie Palermini
Copy Editor: Kate M. Stern
Typesetter: Hurix Systems Pvt. Ltd
Proofreader: Kristin Bergstad
Indexer: Jean Casalegno
Cover Designer: Candice Harman
Marketing Manager: Shari Countryman

Printed in the United States of America

Library of Congress Cataloging-in-Publication Data

Caputo, Richard K.

Policy analysis for social workers / Richard K. Caputo, Yeshiva University.

pages cm. — (Social work in the new century)
Includes bibliographical references and index.

ISBN 978-1-4522-0327-0 (pbk. : alk. paper) — ISBN 978-1-4833-1093-0 (web pdf) 1. Social workers. 2. Social work administration. I. Title.

HV40.35.C36 2013
361.3—dc23   2013015905

Brief Contents

Detailed Contents

Lists of Tables, Figures, & Cases in Point

Tables

Figures

Cases in Point

Introduction

This book introduces students to the world of policy analysis. It addresses postmodern challenges to scientific ethos and their implications for social workers seeking to undertake policy analysis in a credible, constructive, and critical manner. The book also provides working knowledge and requisite skills to enable social workers to analyze policies and programs, with client advocacy, professional integrity, and social justice in mind. Before we start, however, consider the following bill (H.R. 45) as introduced in its entirety into the House of Representatives of the U.S. Congress:

113th CONGRESS
1st Session
H. R. 45

To repeal the Patient Protection and Affordable Care Act and health care-related provisions in the Health Care and Education Reconciliation Act of 2010.

IN THE HOUSE OF REPRESENTATIVES

January 3, 2013

Mrs. BACHMANN introduced the following bill; which was referred to the Committee on Energy and Commerce, and in addition to the Committees on Education and the Workforce, Ways and Means, the Judiciary, Natural Resources, Rules, House Administration, Appropriations, and the Budget, for a period to be subsequently determined by the Speaker, in each case for consideration of such provisions as fall within the jurisdiction of the committee concerned

A BILL

To repeal the Patient Protection and Affordable Care Act and health care-related provisions in the Health Care and Education Reconciliation Act of 2010.

Be it enacted by the Senate and House of Representatives of the United States of America in Congress assembled,

SECTION 1. REPEAL OF PPACA AND HEALTH CARE-RELATED PROVISIONS IN THE HEALTH CARE AND EDUCATION RECONCILIATION ACT OF 2010.

(a) PPACA— Effective as of the enactment of the Patient Protection and Affordable Care Act (Public Law 111-148), such Act (other than subsection (d) of section 1899A of the Social Security Act, as added and amended by sections 3403 and 10320 of such Act) is repealed, and the provisions of law amended or repealed by such Act (other than such subsection (d)) are restored or revived as if such Act had not been enacted.

(b) Health Care-Related Provisions in the Health Care and Education Reconciliation Act of 2010— Effective as of the enactment of the Health Care and Education Reconciliation Act of 2010 (Public Law 111-152), title I and subtitle B of title II of such Act are repealed, and the provisions of law amended or repealed by such title or subtitle, respectively, are restored or revived as if such title and subtitle had not been enacted.

SEC. 2. BUDGETARY EFFECTS OF THIS ACT.

The budgetary effects of this Act, for the purpose of complying with the Statutory Pay-As-You-Go Act of 2010, shall be determined by reference to the latest statement titled 'Budgetary Effects of PAYGO Legislation' for this Act, submitted for printing in the Congressional Record by the Chairman of the Committee on the Budget of the House of Representatives, as long as such statement has been submitted prior to the vote on passage of this Act.

Source: Retrieved from http://www.gpo.gov/fdsys/pkg/BILLS-113hr45ih/pdf/BILLS-113hr45ih.pdf

If you were the staff person asked to analyze H.R. 45 as policy, how would you go about it? What challenges would you face in assessing its merits and the likelihood of this bill's being enacted by Congress and signed by the president? Who is likely to support H.R. 45; who oppose it; for what reasons? What underlying assumptions would influence their decision? Aside from self-interests of individual taxpayers and health insurance companies, what public interest arguments might opponents and supporters advance to augment their respective positions? What was happening socioeconomically and politically during the 2000s to prompt passage of the Patient Protection and Affordable Care Act (P.L. 111–148) and health care-related provisions in the Health Care and Education Reconciliation Act of 2010 (P.L. 111–152) in 2010? How might knowledge of those earlier conditions and circumstances affect how you might go about analyzing H.R. 45 now? If the National Association of Social Workers (NASW) were to formally recommend rejecting this bill and were subsequently accused of working against the public interest by increasing health care costs and penalizing those who prefer to do without health insurance, would you be inclined to advocate for or against its passage? Why? How would you assess the merits of arguments for or against H.R. 45? How would passage/defeat of this bill serve social justice? How certain are you about related judgments and conclusions? Given gaps in the related knowledge base, how certain would you have to be to make a reasonable decision about adopting H.R. 45?

Welcome to the world of policy analysis, one that presents formidable challenges to social workers seeking to retain a sense of professional integrity as analysts while fulfilling the mandate to pursue social justice. Both integrity and social justice are two core values of the social work profession (National Association of Social Workers, 2011), and in the world of policy analysis they may come into conflict with one another. Social workers having a requisite set of conceptual, critical, practical, and technical skills are better able to adjudicate competing or conflicting demands of professional integrity and social justice. This book is meant to highlight what such skill sets entail, thereby enabling social workers to effectively meet such challenges and to avoid conflating advocacy for and research about public policies in general and social welfare policies in particular (Manski, 2013). It significantly elaborates an earlier chapter-length formulation of related concerns, concepts, and skills requisite to policy analysis that appears elsewhere in this Sage social work series (Caputo, 2013; Reisch, 2013). This book also draws from and further elaborates on earlier concerns about and approaches to integrating norms and values into evaluations of social policies (Caputo, 1989).

The book highlights how policies are invariably value-laden, so policy analysts must possess conceptual and technical skills to enable them to identify and assess values that underlie policies in question and those that may be ignored or downplayed. Social justice is one such value that social workers use in their assessment of policies and in determining societal priorities. Policy analysis may serve a variety of purposes, contingent upon the context in which it is carried out. As such, its relation to policymakers and others who have a stake or an interest in the particulars of any given policy complicates the role of the policy analyst. A related goal of the book is to show how policy analysis can be done in a way that enables social workers to retain professional integrity. The integrity of policy analysts, in general, and of agenda-driven policy analysts in particular, including social workers guided by the professional mandate to seek social justice, may be severely tested unless safeguards are in place. Another goal of this book is to highlight those safeguards that enhance the integrity and legitimacy of the practice of policy analysis itself.

The book is meant for social workers, both students and professionals. Given the technical nature of policy analysis and the conflicting values associated with making and implementing social welfare policies, some parts of the book are "easier reads" than others. Some concepts are easier to grasp than others, particularly those that lend themselves quite readily to what we know about human behavior and the social environment. I suspect that some of the philosophical and economic concepts introduced in the book might be more challenging and require more sustained attention. The book does require thoughtful reading, and in some places rereading, to achieve the degree of conceptual clarity and understanding essential for undertaking credible policy analysis. The casual reader may too easily get discouraged. As a life-long learner, however, I encourage you to stick with it, even if that entails a second reading of some material or going beyond the text to seek out additional information when further knowledge is desired. The rewards of increasing your knowledge base accordingly are well worth it.

ORGANIZATION OF THE BOOK

The book is divided into four major Sections. Section I has three chapters, which explore the relationship of science, values, and policy analysis. It ends with an introductory segue to the 3Ps of policy analysis, which form the central core Sections II–IV: policy as product, process, and performance. Chapter 1 discusses the postmodern challenge to the scientific ethos and its implications for social workers seeking to undertake policy analysis in a credible, constructive, and critical manner. It also distinguishes value neutrality from value relevance in the social sciences and shows how impartial or objective analysis of relevant issues germane to social workers and other helping professionals is both desirable and possible. Chapter 1 concludes with a discussion of the role of critical thinking in social work practice and policy analysis.

Upon successful completion of the skill building exercises of Chapter 1, students will have mastered the following Council on Social Work Education (CSWE) Competencies and Practice Behaviors:

Chapter 1	CSWE Core Competencies
#	**Description**
2.1.1	**Identify as a Professional Social Worker and Conduct Oneself Accordingly**
	Attend to professional roles and boundaries
2.1.3	**Apply Critical Thinking to Inform and Communicate Professional Judgments**
	Demonstrate effective oral and written communication in working with individuals, families, groups, organizations, communities, and colleagues

(Continued)

Chapter 1	(Continued)
#	**Description**
2.1.9	**Respond to Contexts That Shape Practice**
	Continuously discover, appraise, and attend to changing locales, populations, scientific and technological development, and emerging societal trends to provide relevant services
	Provide leadership in promoting sustainable changes in service delivery and practice to improve the quality of social services

Source: Adapted from Council on Social Work Education (2012). *Educational policy and accreditation standards.* Washington, DC: Author. Retrieved from http://www.cswe.org/file.aspx?id=13780

Chapter 2 discusses the role of government in the economy and society and introduces several basic micro- and macroeconomic concepts in the context of traditional market failures. Public goods, externalities, natural monopolies, and information asymmetry—four commonly recognized market failures—are the subject matter of microeconomics. Business cycles and related issues such as unemployment and inflation are the subject matter of macroeconomics. The chapter also provides an overview of economists' ways of thinking about the role of the market vis-à-vis government when addressing policy-relevant resource allocation or distributional issues. Pareto efficiency—that is, the inability to make someone better off without making someone else worse off—is contrasted with the social welfare function—that is, the allocation of goods that maximizes the greatest good—as a basis for allocating goods. Alternative social welfare functions—namely, *utilitarian, Rawlsian,* and *multiplicative*—are discussed in light of how they would lead to adoption of different policies. Upon finishing the chapter, students will have learned that (1) despite limitations and caveats, economic concepts and ways of thinking are integral to policy analysis, and (2) allocation mechanisms other than Pareto efficiency justify different policy options.

Upon successful completion of the skill building exercises of Chapter 2, students will have mastered the following CSWE Competencies and Practice Behaviors:

Chapter 2	CSWE Core Competencies
#	**Description**
2.1.3	**Apply Critical Thinking to Inform and Communicate Professional Judgments**
	Demonstrate effective oral and written communication in working with individuals, families, groups, organizations, communities, and colleagues
2.1.7	**Apply Knowledge of Human Behavior and the Social Environment**
	Utilize conceptual frameworks to guide the processes of assessment, intervention, and evaluation
	Critique and apply knowledge to understand person and environment

Chapter 2	(Continued)
#	**Description**
2.1.8	**Engage in Policy Practice to Advance Social and Economic Well-Being and to Deliver Effective Social Work Services**
	Collaborate with colleagues and clients for effective policy action

Source: Adapted from Council on Social Work Education (2012). *Educational policy and accreditation standards*. Washington, DC: Author. Retrieved from http://www.cswe.org/file.aspx?id=13780

Chapter 3 examines differing views about the appropriate role of the policy analyst based on several conceptual formulations and empirical studies. It provides a typology of roles, classified as objective technician, client's advocate, and issue advocate, distinguishable by three fundamental values: analytical integrity, responsibility to clients, and adherence to one's conception of Good. Chapter 3 also examines advocacy and ethics as integral components of social work practice and the problems policy analysis pose to the profession. Particular attention is paid to merits and limitations of treating or viewing social problems as a function of claims-making activity. A major argument of Chapter 3 is that in determining what is to be done, failure to assess and obtain agreement about the nature and extent of a social problem, however contested related measures and values might be, makes it exceptionally difficult if not impossible to determine if social justice goals are being met or thwarted by policy actions.

Chapter 3 also discusses criteria about deciding the appropriate type of analysis that a given situation calls for, contrasting what needs to be done and what one would like to be done. It raises such questions as the extent to which any given analysis should aim at root causes or seek pragmatic adjustments; be comprehensive or seek short-term relevance; rely on consensual or confrontational procedures; and/or be subject to rational assessment or democratic processes. Upon completion of the chapter, students will have learned that (1) the roles of policy analysts vary by values associated with analytical integrity, responsibility to clients, and one's conception of Good; and (2) failure to assess and obtain agreement about the nature and extent of a social problem makes it impossible to determine if social justice goals are being met or thwarted by policy actions.

Upon successful completion of the skill building exercises of Chapter 3, students will have mastered the following CSWE Competencies and Practice Behaviors:

Chapter 3	CSWE Core Competencies
#	**Description**
2.1.1	**Identify as a Professional Social Worker and Conduct Oneself Accordingly**
	Practice personal reflection and self-correction to ensure continual professional development
	Attend to professional roles and boundaries

(Continued)

Chapter 3	(Continued)
#	**Description**
2.1.2	**Apply Social Work Ethical Principles to Guide Professional Practice**
	Make ethical decisions by applying standards of the NASW Code of Ethics
	Tolerate ambiguity in resolving ethical conflicts
2.1.3	**Apply Critical Thinking to Inform and Communicate Professional Judgments**
	Demonstrate effective oral and written communication in working with individuals, families, groups, organizations, communities, and colleagues

Source: Adapted from Council on Social Work Education (2012). *Educational policy and accreditation standards.* Washington, DC: Author. Retrieved from http://www.cswe.org/file.aspx?id=13780

Section II has four chapters that explore how to go about analyzing policy products—that is, the laws and bills about which legislative bodies such as the U.S. Congress and state assemblies deliberate and pass. Chapters 4–7 are meant to help social workers think through what distinguishes sound or desirable polices worth advocating for from those that might have adverse consequences or be deemed less than desirable. Priority is given to policy as product based on the assumption that advocacy efforts are enhanced when social workers have a clearer understanding of what they are advocating for and the likely consequences of achieving their objectives. Readers who are initially or primarily interested in the advocacy dimension of policy practice—that is, where, when, and how to intervene in the policy-making process or in how policies are implemented—can go directly to Section III, Policy as Process.

Chapter 4 addresses an elemental task of policy analysis—namely, getting a handle on what the policy states about who gets what and under what circumstances. It identifies and discusses criteria for evaluating policy proposals and asks several basic questions, answers to which provide a descriptive summary of policy products. Upon completion of the chapter, students will have learned that (1) policy analysts need to be alert to which and how criteria for assessing the merits of a policy are used; (2) policy analysts have a responsibility to assist clients in sorting through the relative weights attributed to evaluative criteria, including effectiveness, efficiency, equity, freedom, political feasibility, social acceptability, administrative feasibility, and technical feasibility, and (3) asking and answering such basic questions as "Who gets what?" and "Under what conditions?" will provide a working descriptive summary of the policy under scrutiny, particularly about types of benefits and eligibility requirements. Students will also develop a skill set enabling them to (1) identify and apply criteria for assessing the merit of eligibility rules, including those based on prior contributions, administrative rules and regulations, private contracts, professional discretion, administrative discretion, judicial decision, means testing, and attachment to the workforce, (2) identify and apply criteria for evaluating the merit of linking policies to social problems and eligibility rules, including fit of analysis to the social problem, correspondence between social problem theory and social policy or program theory, correspondence between eligibility rules and target specifications of the social problem analysis, and (3) identify and assess the merit of applying criteria specific to eligibility rules, including stigmatization, off-targeted benefits, as well as trade-offs in evaluating eligibility rules.

Upon successful completion of the skill building exercises of Chapter 4, students will have mastered the following CSWE Competencies and Practice Behaviors:

Chapter 4	CSWE Core Competencies
#	**Description**
2.1.2	**Apply Social Work Ethical Principles to Guide Professional Practice**
	Make ethical decisions by applying standards of the NASW Code of Ethics
	Tolerate ambiguity in resolving ethical conflicts
	Apply strategies of ethical reasoning to arrive at principled decisions
2.1.3	**Apply Critical Thinking to Inform and Communicate Professional Judgments**
	Demonstrate effective oral and written communication in working with individuals, families, groups, organizations, communities, and colleagues
2.1.4	**Engage Diversity and Difference in Practice**
	Recognize the extent to which a culture's structures and values may oppress, marginalize, alienate, or create or enhance privilege and power
2.1.5	**Advance Human Rights and Social and Economic Justice**
	Understand the forms and mechanisms of oppression and discrimination
2.1.7	**Apply Knowledge of Human Behavior and the Social Environment**
	Utilize conceptual frameworks to guide the processes of assessment, intervention, and evaluation
	Critique and apply knowledge to understand person and environment
2.1.8	**Engage in Policy Practice to Advance Social and Economic Well-Being and to Deliver Effective Social Work Services**
	Analyze, formulate, and advocate for policies that advance social well-being
2.1.9	**Respond to Contexts That Shape Practice**
	Continuously discover, appraise, and attend to changing locales, populations, scientific and technological development, and emerging societal trends to provide relevant services

Source: Adapted from Council on Social Work Education (2012). *Educational policy and accreditation standards.* Washington, DC: Author. Retrieved from http://www.cswe.org/file.aspx?id=13780

Chapter 5 focuses on the goodness of fit between proposed policies and social problems they are meant to address. It highlights the importance of ensuring a close correspondence between the theoretical bases of both social problems and policies or programs that are being considered or have been adopted to address them. The chapter also discusses how policies are financed, including both public and private sources, in light of ideological, political, and practical rationales or justifications associated with them. Upon completion of the chapter, students will have learned that (1) causal assumptions embedded in theories about social problems drive or affect policy or program criteria for determining who gets what type of social provisioning, (2) the extent to which eligibility rules do not correspond to concrete indicators of sufficiently defined social problems, the designated benefits and services may get directed to those population groups who are not the main object of the policy or program, (3) certain types of social welfare provisioning are prone to stigmatizing program beneficiaries or clients, and (4) financing social welfare provisioning in the United States includes government revenue generated primarily from income and payroll taxes, and private sector philanthropy and private sources of funds from philanthropies and employers, and (5) the type of financing reflects ideological and political considerations.

Upon successful completion of the skill building exercises of Chapter 5, students will have mastered the following CSWE Competencies and Practice Behaviors:

Chapter 5	CSWE Core Competencies
#	**Description**
2.1.2	**Apply Social Work Ethical Principles to Guide Professional Practice**
	Recognize and manage personal values in a way that allows professional values to guide practice
	Make ethical decisions by applying standards of the NASW Code of Ethics
	Tolerate ambiguity in resolving ethical conflicts
2.1.3	**Apply Critical Thinking to Inform and Communicate Professional Judgments**
	Demonstrate effective oral and written communication in working with individuals, families, groups, organizations, communities, and colleagues
2.1.5	**Advance Human Rights and Social and Economic Justice**
	Engage in practices that advance social and economic justice
2.1.7	**Apply Knowledge of Human Behavior and the Social Environment**
	Utilize conceptual frameworks to guide the processes of assessment, intervention, and evaluation
	Critique and apply knowledge to understand person and environment
2.1.8	**Engage in Policy Practice to Advance Social and Economic Well-Being and to Deliver Effective Social Work Services**
	Analyze, formulate, and advocate for policies that advance social well-being
2.1.9	**Respond to Contexts That Shape Practice**
	Continuously discover, appraise, and attend to changing locales, populations, scientific and technological development, and emerging societal trends to provide relevant services

Source: Adapted from Council on Social Work Education (2012). *Educational policy and accreditation standards.* Washington, DC: Author. Retrieved from http://www.cswe.org/file.aspx?id=13780

Chapter 6 presents two methodological procedures used by policy analysts—namely, cost-benefit analysis and risk assessment. It describes strengths and limitations of each procedure. The chapter also presents several typologies for comparing alternative policies aimed at the same social problem. Upon completion of the chapter, students will know what goes into conducting cost-benefit analyses and risk assessments, while understanding the limitations of using them.

Upon successful completion of the skill building exercises of Chapter 6, students will have mastered the following CSWE Competencies and Practice Behaviors:

Chapter 6	CSWE Core Competencies
#	**Description**
2.1.3	**Apply Critical Thinking to Inform and Communicate Professional Judgments**
	Distinguish, appraise, and integrate multiple sources of knowledge, including research-based knowledge and practice wisdom
	Analyze models of assessment, prevention, intervention, and evaluation
	Demonstrate effective oral and written communication in working with individuals, families, groups, organizations, communities, and colleagues
2.1.4	**Engage Diversity and Difference in Practice**
	Recognize the extent to which a culture's structures and values may oppress, marginalize, alienate, or create or enhance privilege and power
2.1.5	**Advance Human Rights and Social and Economic Justice**
	Understand the forms and mechanisms of oppression and discrimination
2.1.6	**Engage in Research-Informed Practice and Practice-Informed Research**
	Use research evidence to inform practice
2.1.7	**Apply Knowledge of Human Behavior and the Social Environment**
	Utilize conceptual frameworks to guide the processes of assessment, intervention, and evaluation
	Critique and apply knowledge to understand person and environment
2.1.8	**Engage in Policy Practice to Advance Social and Economic Well-Being and to Deliver Effective Social Work Services**
	Analyze, formulate, and advocate for policies that advance social well-being

Source: Adapted from Council on Social Work Education (2012). *Educational policy and accreditation standards.* Washington, DC: Author. Retrieved from http://www.cswe.org/file.aspx?id=13780

Chapter 7 provides a step-by-step illustration of applying cost-benefit analysis to assess the merits of taxing alcohol policies to save lives. Upon completion of the chapter, students will know how to conduct a detailed cost-benefit analysis, while understanding its limitations. Students will also know how to lay out alternative policies in a way that enhances their capacity to make informed choices about the advantages and disadvantages of adopting one policy option among others.

Upon successful completion of the skill building exercises of Chapter 7, students will have mastered the following CSWE Competencies and Practice Behaviors:

Chapter 7	CSWE Core Competencies
#	**Description**
2.1.3	**Apply Critical Thinking to Inform and Communicate Professional Judgments**
	Distinguish, appraise, and integrate multiple sources of knowledge, including research-based knowledge and practice wisdom
	Analyze models of assessment, prevention, intervention, and evaluation
	Demonstrate effective oral and written communication in working with individuals, families, groups, organizations, communities, and colleagues
2.1.6	**Engage in Research-Informed Practice and Practice-Informed Research**
	Use research evidence to inform practice
2.1.7	**Apply Knowledge of Human Behavior and the Social Environment**
	Utilize conceptual frameworks to guide the processes of assessment, intervention, and evaluation
	Critique and apply knowledge to understand person and environment
2.1.8	**Engage in Policy Practice to Advance Social and Economic Well-Being and to Deliver Effective Social Work Services**
	Analyze, formulate, and advocate for policies that advance social well-being

Source: Adapted from Council on Social Work Education (2012). *Educational policy and accreditation standards.* Washington, DC: Author. Retrieved from http://www.cswe.org/file.aspx?id=13780

Section III focuses on policy as process, which encompasses policy making and implementation. Chapter 8 discusses salient aspects of the policy-making process in representative democracies. It focuses on the role of the U.S. Congress, highlighting how laws are made, the sources of legislation, forms of congressional action, and the nature and role of congressional committees. The chapter discusses conceptual frameworks and theories about policy-making processes that have implications for policy analysis, including *elite theory, interest group theory, institutional rational choice theory, path (state) dependence theory, advocacy coalition,* and *social construction frameworks.* The chapter also describes the nature of policy formation and agenda setting, highlighting the roles of the public at large and elected officials. Finally, it presents a typology of political feasibility, suggesting that when deliberating about the likelihood of adopting any given policy product, policymakers and policy analysts should assess such practical concerns as strategic, institutional, psychological, and behavioral feasibility. Upon completion of Chapter 8, students will be able to (1) identify components of political processes associated with policy formation and adoption, and (2) know how to account for political and other self-interest in the policy-making process.

Upon successful completion of the skill building exercises of Chapter 8, students will have mastered the following CSWE Competencies and Practice Behaviors:

Chapter 8	CSWE Core Competencies
#	**Description**
2.1.3	**Apply Critical Thinking to Inform and Communicate Professional Judgments**
	Distinguish, appraise, and integrate multiple sources of knowledge, including research-based knowledge and practice wisdom
	Analyze models of assessment, prevention, intervention, and evaluation
	Demonstrate effective oral and written communication in working with individuals, families, groups, organizations, communities, and colleagues
2.1.4	**Engage Diversity and Difference in Practice**
	Recognize the extent to which a culture's structures and values may oppress, marginalize, alienate, or create or enhance privilege and power
2.1.5	**Advance Human Rights and Social and Economic Justice**
	Understand the forms and mechanisms of oppression and discrimination
2.1.7	**Apply Knowledge of Human Behavior and the Social Environment**
	Utilize conceptual frameworks to guide the processes of assessment, intervention, and evaluation
	Critique and apply knowledge to understand person and environment
2.1.8	**Engage in Policy Practice to Advance Social and Economic Well-Being and to Deliver Effective Social Work Services**
	Analyze, formulate, and advocate for policies that advance social well-being
2.1.9	**Respond to Contexts That Shape Practice**
	Continuously discover, appraise, and attend to changing locales, populations, scientific and technological development, and emerging societal trends to provide relevant services

Source: Adapted from Council on Social Work Education (2012). *Educational policy and accreditation standards.* Washington, DC: Author. Retrieved from http://www.cswe.org/file.aspx?id=13780

Chapter 9 highlights the importance of considering factors affecting implementation of a policy during the policymaking process. It presents a theoretical framework to help enable policy analysts to assess the effectiveness of the means of implementation. Two basic approaches to thinking systematically about implementation, forward mapping and backward mapping are highlighted. An overarching multilevel logic of governance (LOG) framework is presented in detail. The "black box" approach to treating variables highlighted within the LOG framework is discussed. Types of policy outputs are described, to enable policy analysts to make appropriate linkages between statutory and non-statutory factors affecting implementation processes. This chapter also identifies practical considerations about implementation, with particular focus on the potential for unintended consequences of a policy. The chapter concludes with a discussion of how street-level bureaucrats such as mid-level government administrators and in-the-field professionals such as social workers function at times as de facto policy-makers, often at variance with legislative intent when implementing policies.

Upon completion of the chapter, students will be able to (1) develop a logic of analysis of process associated with governance, showing in effect how politics, policymaking, public management, and service delivery are hierarchically linked with one another in the determination of public policy outputs and outcomes; and (2) assess the organizational culture about the use of discretion and how that culture affects the likelihood of street-level bureaucrats taking actions they deem necessary to bring about outcomes they consider fair, despite constraints that would dictate otherwise.

Upon successful completion of the skill building exercises in Chapter 9, students will have mastered the following CSWE Competencies and Practice Behaviors:

Chapter 9	CSWE Core Competencies
#	**Description**
2.1.2	**Apply Social Work Ethical Principles to Guide Professional Practice**
	Tolerate ambiguity in resolving ethical conflicts
	Apply strategies of ethical reasoning to arrive at principled decisions
2.1.3	**Apply Critical Thinking to Inform and Communicate Professional Judgments**
	Distinguish, appraise, and integrate multiple sources of knowledge, including research-based knowledge and practice wisdom
	Analyze models of assessment, prevention, intervention, and evaluation
	Demonstrate effective oral and written communication in working with individuals, families, groups, organizations, communities, and colleagues
2.1.4	**Engage Diversity and Difference in Practice**
	View themselves as learners and engage those with whom they work as informants
2.1.5	**Advance Human Rights and Social and Economic Justice**
	Understand the forms and mechanisms of oppression and discrimination
2.1.7	**Apply Knowledge of Human Behavior and the Social Environment**
	Utilize conceptual frameworks to guide the processes of assessment, intervention, and evaluation
	Critique and apply knowledge to understand person and environment
2.1.8	**Engage in Policy Practice to Advance Social and Economic Well-Being and to Deliver Effective Social Work Services**
	Analyze, formulate, and advocate for policies that advance social well-being
2.1.9	**Respond to Contexts That Shape Practice**
	Continuously discover, appraise, and attend to changing locales, populations, scientific and technological development, and emerging societal trends to provide relevant services

Source: Adapted from Council on Social Work Education (2012). *Educational policy and accreditation standards.* Washington, DC: Author. Retrieved from http://www.cswe.org/file.aspx?id=13780

Section IV focuses on policy as performance, the subject of Chapters 10 and 11, and concludes with a conceptual framework for program evaluation and policy analysis, the subject of the Epilogue. Chapter 10 discusses three main approaches to policy and program evaluation: *pseudo-evaluation, formal evaluation,* and *decision-theoretic evaluation* (Dunn, 2008). It examines the relation between values and evaluation, first by presenting a typology of evaluator valuing roles vis-à-vis stakeholders (Alkin, Vo, & Christie, 2012), and second, by discussing two major categories of evaluation models—namely, *values-distanced evaluation models* and *values-salient evaluation models* (Speer, 2010). Upon completion of the chapter, students will be able to (1) distinguish between and identify appropriate circumstances warranting implementation of *pseudo-, formal, and decision-theoretic evaluations,* (2) understand the logic behind making value-related judgments about the merits of performance-related program or policy evaluations, and (3) distinguish between and know the appropriate uses of explanatory and normative theories when evaluating program or policy outcomes.

Upon successful completion of the skill building exercises in Chapter 10, students will have mastered the following CSWE Competencies and Practice Behaviors:

Chapter 10	CSWE Core Competencies
#	**Description**
2.1.3	**Apply Critical Thinking to Inform and Communicate Professional Judgments**
	Distinguish, appraise, and integrate multiple sources of knowledge, including research-based knowledge and practice wisdom
	Analyze models of assessment, prevention, intervention, and evaluation
	Demonstrate effective oral and written communication in working with individuals, families, groups, organizations, communities, and colleagues
2.1.7	**Apply Knowledge of Human Behavior and the Social Environment**
	Utilize conceptual frameworks to guide the processes of assessment, intervention, and evaluation
	Critique and apply knowledge to understand person and environment
2.1.9	**Respond to Contexts That Shape Practice**
	Continuously discover, appraise, and attend to changing locales, populations, scientific and technological development, and emerging societal trends to provide relevant services
2.1.10	**Engage, Assess, Intervene, and Evaluate With Individuals, Families, Groups, Organizations, and Communities**
2.1.10(b)	*Assessment*
	Select appropriate intervention strategies
2.1.10(c)	*Intervention*
	Implement prevention interventions that enhance client capacities
	Negotiate, mediate, and advocate for clients

(Continued)

Chapter 10	(Continued)
#	**Description**
2.1.10(d)	*Evaluation*
	Analyze, monitor, and evaluate interventions

Source: Adapted from Council on Social Work Education (2012). *Educational policy and accreditation standards.* Washington, DC: Author. Retrieved from http://www.cswe.org/file.aspx?id=13780

Chapter 11 examines the relation between values and evaluation, first by presenting a typology of evaluator valuing roles vis-à-vis stakeholders (Alkin, Vo, & Christie, 2012), and second, by discussing two major categories of evaluation models, namely *values-distanced evaluation models* and *values-salient evaluation models* (Speer, 2010). The chapter also discusses the role of theory in evaluation and policy analysis, distinguishing explanatory from justificatory or normative theories.

Upon completion of the chapter, students will be able to (1) understand the logic behind making value-related judgments about the merits of performance-related program or policy evaluations, and (2) distinguish between and know the appropriate uses of explanatory and normative theories when evaluating program or policy outcomes.

Upon successful completion of the skill building exercises in Chapter 11, students will have mastered the following CSWE Competencies and Practice Behaviors:

Chapter 11	CSWE Core Competencies
#	**Description**
2.1.2	**Apply Social Work Ethical Principles to Guide Professional Practice**
	Recognize and manage personal values in a way that allows professional values to guide practice
	Make ethical decisions by applying standards of the NASW Code of Ethics
	Tolerate ambiguity in resolving ethical conflicts
	Apply strategies of ethical reasoning to arrive at principled decisions
2.1.3	**Apply Critical Thinking to Inform and Communicate Professional Judgments**
	Distinguish, appraise, and integrate multiple sources of knowledge, including research-based knowledge and practice wisdom
	Analyze models of assessment, prevention, intervention, and evaluation
	Demonstrate effective oral and written communication in working with individuals, families, groups, organizations, communities, and colleagues
2.1.4	**Engage Diversity and Difference in Practice**
	View themselves as learners and engage those with whom they work as informants

Chapter 11	(Continued)
#	**Description**
2.1.5	**Advance Human Rights and Social and Economic Justice**
	Understand the forms and mechanisms of oppression and discrimination
2.1.7	**Apply Knowledge of Human Behavior and the Social Environment**
	Utilize conceptual frameworks to guide the processes of assessment, intervention, and evaluation
	Critique and apply knowledge to understand person and environment
2.1.8	**Engage in Policy Practice to Advance Social and Economic Well-Being and to Deliver Effective Social Work Services**
	Analyze, formulate, and advocate for policies that advance social well-being
2.1.9	**Respond to Contexts That Shape Practice**
	Continuously discover, appraise, and attend to changing locales, populations, scientific and technological development, and emerging societal trends to provide relevant services
2.1.10	**Engage, Assess, Intervene, and Evaluate With Individuals, Families, Groups, Organizations, and Communities**
2.1.10(b)	*Assessment*
	Select appropriate intervention strategies
2.1.10(c)	*Intervention*
	Implement prevention interventions that enhance client capacities
	Negotiate, mediate, and advocate for clients
2.1.10(d)	*Evaluation*
	Analyze, monitor and evaluate interventions

Source: Adapted from Council on Social Work Education (2012). *Educational policy and accreditation standards.* Washington, DC: Author. Retrieved from http://www.cswe.org/file.aspx?id=13780

The Epilogue provides general guidelines and an overarching framework for program evaluation and policy analysis. It draws on many of the concepts, themes, tools, and techniques presented in prior chapters. Upon completion of the Epilogue, students will be able to (1) identify and apply general guidelines for conducting program and policy evaluations while retaining professional integrity and keeping social justice in mind, and (2) conduct program and policy evaluations at the appropriate level.

Upon successful completion of the skill building exercises in the Epilogue, students will have mastered the following CSWE Competencies and Practice Behaviors:

Epilogue	CSWE Core Competencies
#	**Description**
2.1.1	**Identify as a Professional Social Worker and Conduct Oneself Accordingly**
	Advocate for client access to the services of a social worker
	Practice personal reflection and self-correction to ensure continual professional development
	Attend to professional roles and boundaries
	Demonstrate professional demeanor in behavior, appearance, and communication
	Engage in career-long learning
	Use supervision and consultation
2.1.2	**Apply Social Work Ethical Principles to Guide Professional Practice**
	Recognize and manage personal values in a way that allows professional values to guide practice
	Make ethical decisions by applying standards of the NASW Code of Ethics
	Tolerate ambiguity in resolving ethical conflicts
	Apply strategies of ethical reasoning to arrive at principled decisions
2.1.3	**Apply Critical Thinking to Inform and Communicate Professional Judgments**
	Distinguish, appraise, and integrate multiple sources of knowledge, including research-based knowledge and practice wisdom
	Analyze models of assessment, prevention, intervention, and evaluation
	Demonstrate effective oral and written communication in working with individuals, families, groups, organizations, communities, and colleagues
2.1.4	**Engage Diversity and Difference in Practice**
	Recognize the extent to which a culture's structures and values may oppress, marginalize, alienate, or create or enhance privilege and power
	Gain sufficient self-awareness to eliminate the influence of personal biases and values in working with diverse groups
	Recognize and communicate their understanding of the importance of difference in shaping life experiences
2.1.5	**Advance Human Rights and Social and Economic Justice**
	Understand the forms and mechanisms of oppression and discrimination
	Advocate for human rights and social and economic justice
	Engage in practices that advance social and economic justice
2.1.6	**Engage in Research-Informed Practice and Practice-Informed Research**
	Use practice experience to inform scientific inquiry
	Use research evidence to inform practice

Epilogue	(Continued)
#	**Description**
2.1.7	**Apply Knowledge of Human Behavior and the Social Environment**
	Utilize conceptual frameworks to guide the processes of assessment, intervention, and evaluation
	Critique and apply knowledge to understand person and environment
2.1.8	**Engage in Policy Practice to Advance Social and Economic Well-Being and to Deliver Effective Social Work Services**
	Analyze, formulate, and advocate for policies that advance social well-being
2.1.9	**Respond to Contexts That Shape Practice**
	Continuously discover, appraise, and attend to changing locales, populations, scientific and technological development, and emerging societal trends to provide relevant services
2.1.10	**Engage, Assess, Intervene, and Evaluate With Individuals, Families, Groups, Organizations, and Communities**
2.1.10(a)	*Engagement*
	Substantively and affectively prepare for action with individuals, families, groups, organizations, and communities
2.1.10(b)	*Assessment*
	Collect, organize and interpret client data
	Assess client strengths and limitations
2.1.10(c)	*Intervention*
	Implement prevention interventions that enhance client capacities
2.1.10(d)	*Evaluation*
	Analyze, monitor and evaluate interventions

Source: Adapted from Council on Social Work Education (2012). *Educational policy and accreditation standards.* Washington, DC: Author. Retrieved from http://www.cswe.org/file.aspx?id=13780

Acknowledgments

I wish to thank Michael Reisch, the editor of the social work series of which this book is a part, and Kassie Graves, Senior Acquisitions Editor, Human Services, Sage Publications, for providing me with the opportunity to write this book. Their continued enthusiastic encouragement and unwavering support throughout the prospectus and full manuscript review processes greatly eased what turned out to be a far more daunting undertaking than I had initially anticipated. I also wish to thank those individuals who reviewed drafts of the prospectus and full manuscript. The reviews were anonymous, at least to me, throughout the entire process until the very last, when several, having the option during the feedback process, identified who they were. Out of respect for all the reviewers and for the integrity of the review process that seems to work best when anonymity is preserved, I will refrain from disclosing anyone specifically. I benefited greatly from each reviewer's comments, incorporating as many as possible given the nature of the book and my particular "take" or viewpoint about the role of policy analysis in social work practice.

The book was several years in the making, and during that time I was very fortunate to work with Dean Sheldon Gelman and his successor Carmine Hendricks, each of whom made it possible for me to devote the time necessary to complete it while carrying out teaching responsibilities, other research efforts, and administrative responsibilities as director of the PhD Program in Social Welfare (a position I happily relinquished effective May 1, 2013). In this last capacity, my competent, gregarious, and sunny-dispositioned secretary, Ann Persaud, made the day-to-day operations of the doctoral program run quite smoothly, enabling me to focus on writing for sustained periods of time; for this and much else, I am deeply grateful to her. I also benefited from students, some of whom provided feedback on the prospectus and others who commented on early drafts of the entire manuscript. My thanks go to: Fabian Egeruoh, Amanda Falk, Rodney Fuller, Hannah Junger, Rebecca Hanus, Yosef Kalinsky, Jaclyn Lieberman, and Adolpho Profumo, each of whom I hope someday—sooner rather than later—to welcome formally into the community of scholars upon completion of their degrees.

Finally, and by no means least, I owe my most heartfelt thanks to my best friend and most loving wife, Mary, who enhances every aspect of my life and to whom I dedicate this book. Her own successful career in the fiercely competitive human relations arena of mergers and acquisitions worldwide is an inspiration to me. I am deeply appreciative of her efforts to ensure that I have the requisite "space," without which I doubt I could write anything of merit.

Dedication

To My Loving Wife and Best Friend, Mary

In Memory

Emily and Salvatore Caputo, My Parents

Philip Caputo, My Uncle and Social Policy Sparring Partner

Arthur Mann, Historian

The World of Policy Analysis

CHAPTER 1

Science, Values, and Policy Analysis

This chapter discusses postmodern challenges to the scientific ethos and the implications for social workers seeking to undertake policy analysis in a credible, constructive, and critical manner. The chapter also distinguishes value neutrality from value relevance in the social sciences and shows how impartial or objective analysis of relevant issues germane to social workers and other helping professionals is both desirable and possible. The chapter concludes with a discussion of the role of **critical thinking** in social work practice and policy analysis.

Upon successful completion of the skill building exercises of Chapter 1, students will have mastered the following Council on Social Work Education (CSWE) competencies and practice behaviors:

Chapter 1	CSWE Core Competencies
#	**Description**
2.1.1	**Identify as a Professional Social Worker and Conduct Oneself Accordingly**
	Attend to professional roles and boundaries
2.1.3	**Apply Critical Thinking to Inform and Communicate Professional Judgments**
	Demonstrate effective oral and written communication in working with individuals, families, groups, organizations, communities, and colleagues
2.1.9	**Respond to Contexts That Shape Practice**
	Continuously discover, appraise, and attend to changing locales, populations, scientific and technological development, and emerging societal trends to provide relevant services
	Provide leadership in promoting sustainable changes in service delivery and practice to improve the quality of social services

Source: Adapted from Council on Social Work Education (2012). *Educational policy and accreditation standards.* Washington, DC: Author. Retrieved from http://www.cswe.org/file.aspx?id=13780

THE POSTMODERN CHALLENGE

An explicit concern of this section of Chapter 1 is the postmodern challenge to the scientific ethos and its implications for social workers seeking to undertake policy analysis while maintaining their professional integrity. A related implicit concern of this section and the chapter as a whole is the longstanding observation that reliance on policy experts by policymakers presents a formidable challenge to democratic governance (Collins & Evans, 2007; Dewey, 1927/1954; Fischer, 1991; Lovett, 1927; Moynihan, 1965; Westbrook, 1991). Given the profession's commitment to social justice, it behooves social workers seeking to conduct policy analysis as part of their professional practice to understand dilemmas associated with both concerns so as to take appropriate steps to resolve them accordingly.

Postmodernist thought is not of one piece and it may be past its prime of influence: it has been written about as a period, strategy, mindset, ambience, paradigm, and style, despite denials or evasions by intellectuals such as Foucault, Baudrillard, and Latour (Mathewman & Hoey, 2006). Nonetheless, postmodernism focuses scholarly and public attention on a common set of contemporary concerns that pose major dilemmas for social workers and social scientists in general and for social policy analysts in particular; that is, can the human mind and social knowledge be relied on to give truthful accounts of the world, whether about anything (the wholesale version) or about some things (the selective version), conceding truth to descriptive claims including mathematical ones while denying it to "evaluative" or moral, ethical, interpretive, or ethical ones (Dworkin, 1996; Olkowski, 2012; Rosenau, 1992). If so, as some postmodernists have argued (e.g., Rorty, 1981), many different stories, each a political act, eclipsed the idea of one single truth and called into question the possibility of objective, value-neutral, or impartial social science. As posed by Cravens (2004), the question becomes: "If there were no longer faith in authoritative expertise but faith in all experts, no matter how credulous their claims might be, then of what use was social science [and by extension policy analysis] in the first instance?" (p. 133). Taylor-Gooby (1994) put the issue this way: "if nothing can be said with certainty, it is perhaps better to say nothing" (p. 393). This suggests that an absence of an agreed-upon method of selecting among competing alternative claims might result in no society-wide policy actions at all.

In addition, the postmodern claim that certain themes of modern society (the nation-state, rational planning by government, and large-scale public or private sector bureaucracy) are obsolete challenges theories of social policy that stress such themes as inequality or privilege and for the practice of social policy that relies on rational analysis to inform policymakers and implementers of social provisions (Taylor-Gooby, 1994). Most social workers are not professionally trained as social scientists. Nonetheless, the knowledge base of social work practice is informed by social scientific theories of human behavior and the social environment, and social workers use methods and procedures gleaned from the social sciences when assessing need, deliberating about the appropriateness of policy options, and evaluating their practice (Hart, 1978). Given the profession's commitment to social justice, the challenges posed by reliance on experts and postmodern thought suggest the need for developing and promoting the idea that participatory policy analysis become a more mainstream component of the policy sciences and analyses than is currently the case, while concomitantly balancing professional mandates for impartiality, objectivity, and advocacy as integral components of social work practice (Benveniste, 1984; Brunner, 1991; Fischer 1993; Hampton, 2004; Haynes & Mickelson, 2010; Hernandez, 2008; Meyer, 2008; Schram, 1993; Thompson, 2001).

A key consideration is how to resolve an inherent tension between what Collins and Evans (2007) view on the one hand as the Problem of Legitimacy—that is, how to introduce innovations in social welfare provisioning in the face of widespread distrust or lack of trust in science and in government to address social problems; how to ensure that analysts' views are not influenced by pressure from their principals or clients or by conflicts of personal interests—and on the other hand the Problem of Extension—that is, knowing when and how to limit increased public participation in the policymaking process. In addition, the postmodern challenge to universal claims (egalitarianism, humanism, liberal democracy) suggests that social workers have a responsibility to contribute to the development of appropriate conceptual and analytical skills to discern when such claims serve as an ideological smokescreen, preventing recognition of trends of some of the most important social problems in modern society such as increasing income inequality (Alderson, Beckfield, & Nielsen, 2005; Rosenau, 1992; Taylor-Gooby, 1994).

Case in Point 1.1: ACA and Health Insurance Coverage of Contraceptives

Think of the Patient Protection and Affordable Care Act (P.L. 111–148, hereafter ACA) passed during the Obama administration's first term in office and the subsequent bill (H.R. 45), introduced in the first session of the 113th Congress, to repeal it. Part of the opposition to the ACA stemmed from those who contend that the new law exemplifies government overreach by infringing on individual liberty: ACA, they contend, forces individuals to purchase health insurance, some of whom may not want to do so. Catholic bishops as a group have opposed a regulation emanating from the law requiring health insurance coverage of contraceptives. The Obama administration proposed that churches and nonprofit religious groups that object to providing birth control coverage on religious grounds would not have to cover or pay for it. Women who work for such organizations could get free contraceptive coverage through separate individual health insurance policies, costs to be incurred by the insurance company, with the rationale that the health insurance company could recoup the costs through lower health care expenses resulting in part from fewer births. The Obama administration refused to grant an exemption or accommodation to secular businesses owned by people who said they objected to contraceptive coverage on religious grounds (Pear, 2013). As you think about the general libertarian objections to ACA and the Catholic bishops' objections to the contraceptive mandate, assess the extent to which such appeals to individual liberty and religious freedom, respectively, are ideological smokescreens to thwart the public interest—namely, as Jean Bucaria (2013), the deputy director of NOW-N.Y.C put it, the "health and individual liberties of the vast majority of American women who will use birth control at some point in their lives." Alternatively, to what extent might Bucaria's appeal to women's rights be a smokescreen to thwart religious freedom or individual liberty as understood by the Catholic bishops and libertarians, respectively?

The approach taken in this chapter and throughout the remainder of the book is in line with Kitcher (1993), who rejected the views of both the logical positivists—who glorify science as conforming to otherworldly standards of purity and rigor—and those contemporary philosophers who reject any idea of scientific truth and condemn scientists for not living up to such standards (Papineau, 1993). **Positivism** refers to a realist ontological belief system (about what entities are "real"—i.e., mind-independent) and an epistemological belief that external realities can be known objectively (Morçöl, 2001). Briefly, "positivism includes the ontological belief in a deterministic universe and the epistemological beliefs that knowledge reflects external realities, the laws of the universe can be known, and science can be unified through a common methodology"—that is, one favoring deductive, inductive, and reductionist/ analytical approaches and quantitative analyses (Morçöl, 2001, p. 382).

Although the approach taken in this text rejects positivism per se, it nonetheless is also consistent with Collins and Evans (2007), who take the position that science, including the social sciences, is a central element of our culture; that is, the norms and culture of evidence-based scientific argument have a central place in modern society and scientifically related expertise requires a logical space independent of politics. Social work reflects these general norms as indicated by its adoption of using research-based evidence to inform practice (see CSWE Core Competency # 2.1.6 in Appendix A). This is not to say that politics does not matter, especially in light of how government, foundations, and **think tanks** have come to sponsor, finance, and use research in many instances primarily for political ends (Medvetz, 2012; Oreskes & Conway, 2010; Lyons, 1969; see Appendix B), nor is to say that human behavior and the social environment are unknowable. That would be foolhardy. Acknowledging that science occupies a central place in our culture is to recognize that scientific expertise is real and substantive, and that politics and science are legitimate, even at times interrelated, domains. Further, the failure to distinguish the two analytically and substantively may all too easily lead to technological populism—in which there are no experts; to fascism in which the only political rights are those gained through supposed technical expertise; and to blunders with little wiggle room for correcting mistakes. In short, "Democracy cannot dominate every domain—that would destroy expertise—and expertise cannot dominate every domain—that would destroy democracy" (Collins & Evans, 2007, p. 18).

For our purposes, acknowledging that science occupies a central place in our culture means equipping social workers with the requisite conceptual and technical skill sets such that when they practice as policy analysts they do so (1) with the proficiency and authority of experts—that is, other things being equal, their judgments are preferred because "they know what they are talking about" (Collins & Evans, 2007, p. 11), and (2) in ways that further public participation in the policy-making process to a reasonable and feasible extent, as the circumstances under which they undertake policy analyses warrant (Hampton, 2004; Sabatier, 1988). Both objectives necessitate a "realist" approach to policy analysis, one grounded in a stratified conception of reality, knowledge, and human interests, where distinctions may be drawn between, on one hand, a realm of "intransitive" objects, processes, and events—those that must be taken to exist independently of human conceptualization—and, on the other hand, a "transitive" realm of knowledge-constitutive interests that are properly subject to critical assessment in terms of their ethical or socio-political character (Bhaskar, 1986, 1989; Norris, 1995; Sprinker, 1987). Logically contraindicative truth-claims are rejected, such as "all truth-claims are fictitious," "all concepts [are] just subjugated metaphors," or science is "merely the name we attach to some currently prestigious language game" (Norris, 1995, p. 121; Brown, 1998). Feminist scholar Sondra Harding (1986), who insisted that the rigor and objectivity of science are inherently androcentric and called for a de-gendered "successor science" (pp. 104, 122), nonetheless acknowledged (p. 138) that it would be difficult to appeal to feminists' own scientific research in support of alternative explanations of the natural and social world that are less false or closer to the truth while concomitantly questioning the grounds for taking scientific facts and their explanations to be reasonable (Brown, 1998, p. 534).

Postmodernists have difficulty reconciling normative positions such as "extolling the virtues of difference and condemning the vice of repressive normalization with their generally relativist theoretical positions denying any non-arbitrary basis to authority" (Calhoun, 1993, p. 96). Social workers cannot with any consistency "speak truth to power" if the ideas of truth or truth-seeking are jettisoned from our mutual understanding of what policy analysis is all about, or in the absence of a way to adjudicate competing claims about facts or the evaluative criteria used to assess the importance of values in a way that the parties involved can agree upon and abide by the outcome. Likewise, social workers cannot convincingly fault policymakers for failing to address structural factors or forces and casting policy recommendations in terms of individual responsibility for their clients' or client groups' plight if such factors are invented by or spring from the minds of analysts rather than as constituent attributes to be uncovered, discovered, or, as Reed and Alexander (2009) contend, "read" (p. 31) during the process of analysis or research. In any event, the positivist wave, such as it ever was, is long gone. Contemporary efforts such as those in political science—for example, under the rubric of a "new perestroika" and "phronetic social science"—that use positivism as a "straw" characterization to justify turning away from legitimate preoccupations with methods in the social sciences (Flyvbjerg, 2004; Schram, 2003; White, 2002) risk throwing out the baby with the bathwater. Otherwise, they may fill the bathtub with too many theoretical and methodological toys and no discernible way to assess the merits of which should be retained and which discarded to prevent overflow (Bennett, 2002; Jervis, 2002; Laitin, 2003; Landman, 2011).

SOCIAL WORK AND COMPETING IN THE POLICY ANALYSIS ARENA

An extensive array of institutional support for the training and employment of policy analysts in academia, foundations, professional associations, and think tanks presents formidable challenges for the profession of social work to compete on anything approximating an equal footing. Appendix B provides an overview of the development of the nature and functions of this institutional support, including that of social work during its formative years and as it matured into a profession. Readers interested in the historical dimensions of how the current social and institutional environment emerged and the varying degrees of success with which issues of activism and objectivity have been handled are encouraged to read Appendix B. As has been the case historically, policy practitioners make up a small percentage of students entering and graduating from accredited social work programs, thereby limiting the overall exposure or reach of the profession. Further, by design policy practice encompasses advocacy and analysis, which need not be inherently problematic to the extent the analysis component is approached in a disinterested or objective manner—which helps to ensure the moral integrity and normative authority of the profession. As Medvetz (2012) suggests, this is no easy task in light of the contested space among such institutions as academia, historically rooted research institutes, and more recently proliferating think tanks, all of which compete for financial support, public attention, and legitimate claim as to who produces and what counts as policy knowledge.

A relative latecomer in this highly competitive process, the National Association of Social Work (NASW) launched its own think tank, the Social Work Policy Institute (SWPI), in 2009, as a division of the NASW Foundation, in order to fill gaps identified by the Social Work Reinvestment Initiative (SWRI) (http://SocialWorkReinvestment.org). SWPI seeks to secure public money in professional social work and to respond to imperatives that emerged from the 2005 Social Work Congress. Such imperatives include participation in politics and policy where decisions are being made about behavioral health and mobilization of the profession to actively engage in politics, policy, and social action. Emphasis is placed on the strategic use of power and influencing the corporate and political landscape at federal, state, and local levels (Haynes & Mickelson, 2010; NASW Foundation, 2010; Social Work Congress, 2005). Whether SWPI can meet its mission of securing resources for the profession's own survival and of political engagement in areas concerning behavioral health while maintaining some semblance of professional integrity for purposes of policy analysis seems unlikely in light of the historical context within which think tanks rose to such prominence and in light of their contemporary activities and overtly declared partisan missions (discussed in Appendix B). To get a better sense of how social workers seeking to conduct policy analysis might do this—that is, retain a sense of professional integrity while relying on their critical thinking—a discussion of value neutrality and value relevance is warranted.

VALUE NEUTRALITY, VALUE RELEVANCE, AND CRITICAL THINKING

This section distinguishes value neutrality from value relevance in the social sciences and shows how impartial or objective analysis of relevant issues germane to social workers and other helping professionals is both desirable and possible. It draws on Max Weber (1946, 1949, & 1962; Bruun & Whimster, 2012), one of the foremost architects of sociological theory and methodology, whose major writings spanned the first two decades of the twentieth century. Weber also had political interests, becoming involved with the Christian-Social movement and its social reform efforts. Despite a passion for political issues, Weber "remained largely detached from partisan passions" and as an academic he cultivated "a value-neutral analysis of political and social trends in which he himself participated" (Coser, 1977, p. 256). That is, he retained pursuit of truth as a viable scientific undertaking and clarified the role of value neutrality as regulative ideal of social inquiry and investigation for purposes of policy analysis.

As will be shown below, Weber's nuanced discussions of the social sciences and their relation to politics and by extension policymaking belies postmodernists' stereotypical characterizations of "modernist" science as a combination of "the detached subject of knowledge, of the reduced and delimited object of knowledge, and of the knowledge process, or, more precisely, the referential semantics of the production of knowledge" (Outhwaite, 1999, p. 9; Gunnell, 2009). This section concludes with a discussion of the role of critical thinking in policy analysis.

Value Neutrality

Value neutrality differs from value relevance and both of these differ from critical thinking, at the least in an analytical sense. There is general agreement that values enter into the selection of problems investigators choose to examine. Weber (2012b) provides one of the clearest and most convincing rationales for value neutrality as a regulative ideal on the part of natural and social scientists (and by extension, for our purposes, policy analysts). Weber readily acknowledges that what particular problems attract scholars and what level of explanation is sought depend on the values and interests of investigators:

The distinctive characteristic of a problem of social *policy* is precisely that it *cannot* be settled on the basis of purely technical considerations applied to settled ends: [that] the regulatory value standards themselves can and *must* be the subject of *dispute,* because the problem projects into the region of general *cultural* questions. . . . It is simply naïve when even professionals occasionally still believe that what is important is above all to set up "a principle" for the practical social sciences and to corroborate its validity [by scientific means], so that norms for the solution of individual practical problems can then be unambiguously deduced from it. (p. 104)

Weber thereby concedes the "subjectivity" of "personal or collective interests that shape investigators' perspectives" (Ringer, 1997, p. 124). The choice of problems and the level of explanation sought are always "subjective" or value relevant. Weber (2012b) further contends: "*There is no* absolutely 'objective' scientific analysis of cultural life or . . . of 'social phenomena'—independent of special and 'one-sided' points of view according to which [those phenomena] are—explicitly or implicitly, deliberately or unconsciously—selected as an object of inquiry, analyzed and presented in an orderly fashion" (p. 113). Although Weber (1962) distanced himself from positivist scientists and defined sociology as the science that aimed at the "interpretive understanding" (***Verstehen***) of human behavior (p. 29), it would be an error to align him with postmodernists such as Rorty (1981) or **social constructivists** such as Spector and Kitsuse (1987) and to conclude that he thereby abandons or is silent about notions of truth, the pursuit of truth, or objectivity. Quite the contrary, for Weber (1962) contends that interpretive understanding of social behavior makes it possible "to gain an explanation of its causes, its course, and its effects" (p. 29). *Verstehen* and causal explanation are correlative rather than opposed principles of method in the social sciences. That is to say, as Coser (1977) states, "Immediate intuitions of meaning can be transformed into valid knowledge only if they can be incorporated into theoretical structures that aim at causal explanation" (p. 221).

The methodological individualism associated with *Verstehen* has been criticized on several grounds, such as ignoring the role of individual agent in historical causality, reducing the social to the psychological, and denying the "existence" or "epistemic usefulness" of "social wholes"—including economic movements and balance of power in social scientific explanations (Flynn, 1997, 2005; Jarvie, 1964). It is not the intent here to adopt Weber's approach to social inquiry whole cloth, since that would also necessitate rejecting Durkheim's first rule of sociological method, namely "*to consider social facts as things*" (Durkheim, 1982, p. 60, italics in original). Durkheim (p. 59) defined social facts as "*any way of acting, fixed or not, capable of exerting over an individual an external constraint;* or: *which is general over the whole of a given society whilst having an existence of its own, independent of its individual manifestations*" (italics in original). It is the intent here to retain the possibility of establishing theoretically grounded causal explanations, whether they emanate from Weber's *Verstehen* approach to social science—which focused on meanings individuals attach to their experiences of events—or Durkheim's approach, which located causality in factors outside or beyond the individual's understanding of events. The "start where the client is" mantra of the profession closely aligns social workers with Weber's *Verstehen* approach. Social workers who work with groups know, however, that group dynamics and processes are not reducible to individual experiences or meanings, providing firm footing for retaining Durkheim's "social facts as things" approach to social inquiry.

Value Relevance

Value relevance in selection of problems and level of explanation need not invalidate the objectivity of the social sciences and by extension of policy analysts. Parsons (1937/1968, p. 594), whose own theory of social action has been faulted for ignoring the role of power (Conklin, 1977), nonetheless provided an apt summary of Weber's view about value relevance:

> Even though a value element enters into the selection of the material of science, once this material is given it is possible to come to objectively valid conclusions about the causes and consequences of given phenomena free of value judgments and hence binding on anyone who wished to attain truth, regardless of what other subjective values he may hold.

> This is possible first because even though in describing a concrete phenomenon what is made the subject of scientific analysis is not the full totality of experienceable fact about it, but a selection, the facts included in the historical individual as it is constructed are objective, verifiable facts. The question of whether a statement of fact is true is clearly distinguishable from that of its significance to value. . . . Secondly, once a phenomenon is descriptively given, the establishment of causal relations between it and either its antecedents or its consequences is possible only through the application, explicitly or implicitly, of a formal schema of proof that is independent of any value system, except the value of scientific truth.

Machamer and Douglas (1998) and Douglas (2000) maintain that distinguishing cognitive or epistemic values associated with scientific practice (such as truth, reliability, evidential support, plausibility, coherence, consistency, accuracy, simplicity, and the like) from social values (such as the desire for a research program to promote political purposes) is untenable. In their understanding, values not only affect problem selection, they also enter into the scientific reasoning process itself, when for example judgments are made about categorizing data. The change in the classification of a dead person from one based on cardio-pulmonary functioning to one based on brain functioning (profound coma, no eye movement, no corneal reflexes), for example, reflected in part a desire or goal of creating better possibilities for organ transplants. In this example, fact and values appear to be indistinguishable. The facticity of death seems to be inextricably linked to the social value of increasing the pool of organs for transplants.

Contra Machamer and Douglas (1998), however, in their example, the determination of criteria for what constitutes the facticity of death lay outside the scientific process. At issue for our purposes is the importance of retaining a distinction between cognitive or epistemic values from social values because adherence to those epistemic values associated with scientific practices increases our ability to adjudicate between competing truth claims about statements of fact, to distinguish those that are true from those that are false or incorrect, albeit with varying degrees of certainty or probability. Machamer and Douglas are correct in moving away from dichotomizing fact/value issues as such and in noting that values may enter at many different points in the "objective" process of science, or, for our purposes, analysis. Showing that something may happen differs from claiming that it must happen or that it always happens. They are incorrect, however, to claim unequivocally that "one cannot distinguish usefully or coherently the cognitive from the social" (p. 35). The distinction is useful and necessary as a basis for adjudicating competing truth claims about statements of fact.

The relativity of value orientations leading to different cognitive choices of problem selection in Weber's formulation of the issue has nothing to do with questions of scientific validity or objectivity (Coser, 1977). Problems are relativized, not findings. Further, objectivity resides in formal principles guiding the relationship between knower (as subject) and thing known (as object) and for the scientist what is known is a conceptual or ideal object resulting from a theoretical consciousness in relation to a real, perceptual world. As an intended object, the scientific object is "constructed" in reference to a theory, not to a set of culturally variable subjective meanings or values, and as such it serves as a filtering device on perceptual findings, which in turn can be shown either to verify its reality or truth (Goddard, 1973)—or as scientist and philosopher Karl Popper (1965, 1959/1968) contends, to falsify them. The merits of any given theory are subject to contestation in light of adequacy, appropriateness, coherence, fruitfulness (generating further research), predictive capacity, testability (verification/falsifiability), and the like, and theories can be subject to critical analysis (e.g., see Hauptmann, 2005).

It should be noted here however that Weber's methodological approach differs from the positivist or behaviorist and covering law models and the phenomenological and other "interpretivist" views of social science. As noted in Appendix B, when discussing the professionalization of the social sciences, social scientists adhering to the former seek to uncover social laws much like "universal" laws in the natural sciences (Hempel, 1942). The latter phenomenological view of social science, as Goddard (1973, pp. 12–13, n. 24) notes, seeks "to describe [a social world] without reference to external interpretive schemata the meaningful character of cultural data" and presupposes only "that the data have internal (subjective) meaning." Although phenomenologists have a set of generally agreed upon methodological procedures that address concerns about objectivity and value neutrality to ensure the integrity of their inquiries and investigations, as do behaviorists, it is important to note on one hand that phenomenology is a branch of philosophy, not of social science per se (Goldstein, 1964; Gurwitsch, 1961; Schmicking, 2005; Schmitz, Müllan, & Slaby, 2011). As such, its role in policy analysis for our purposes is more restricted than is the case for the social sciences in general.

On the other hand, it is important to note that some of the social sciences, such as sociology and psychology, for example, have appropriated phenomenological methods into their studies of human behavior and the social environment to understand "the world [as] an interpreted phenomenon" with the implication that such researchers "may advance different 'reality' assumptions than the individuals whom they study" (Murphy, 1986, p. 331) and that knowledge gleaned in this "interpretive" manner is essential for efforts aimed at social betterment (Taylor, 1985). The notion of truth and the search for it are retained in phenomenological studies, albeit with criteria for what it means and what constitutes an appropriate set of ways to search for it that differ from more traditional approaches to social science. Truth can be attained in a phenomenological sense but "only when the experiential judgments of a researcher and a community are united" (p. 332). Value neutrality cannot be attained because it "fails to illuminate the action domain of a community [which phenomenologists seek to discover during the course of their studies], since the values of science are substituted for the meaning which data convey" (p. 336).

As noted above by Parsons, however, preferring the value of scientific truth need not preclude drawing valid conclusions about cause-effect relations of given phenomena free of value judgments and binding on anyone wishing to attain truth, regardless of other subjective values they hold. This is in part so because more traditional social science studies are more theoretically and methodologically transparent, affording the possibility for replication, verification, and falsification—that is, having generalized agreement about ways of adjudicating competing truth claims. Phenomenological social scientists have a more difficult time demonstrating what would have to occur to enable them to know that they were incorrect, even after several iterations between researchers and those under investigation about meanings of social reality gleaned from their studies. Agreement of ways to adjudicate competing interpretive claims by way of replication, verification, and falsification remain inherently problematic (Schatzki, 2005; Schmitz, Müllan, & Slaby, 2011; Schmicking, 2005).

Furthermore, the phenomenological claim that the social fabric can be known only through the inherent methodological components of reflexivity or self-reflection (Murphy, 1986, p. 331) remains highly contested (Brownstein, 2010). Nonetheless, lest the baby be discarded with the bathwater, Murphy's claim that such a phenomenological sensitivity increases "the social relevancy of policy research" (p. 327) remains warranted, especially when seeking what making, implementing, or evaluating specific policies might mean to policymakers, implementers, or targets, respectively. Penna and O'Brien (1996) make a similar case for postmodernist thinking in general, noting for example that in lieu of presenting a single history of the West in terms of a progressive movement toward humanism in which social policy emanates from enlightened reformers and welfare workers, focusing on the co-existence of different histories—of black people, women, homosexuals, disabled persons, and so on—highlights the rootedness of processes of domination and oppression that many of the more traditional policy sciences (as discussed in Appendix B) too easily ignore.

As noted above, Weber sharply contrasts value relevance and value neutrality, since they refer to two different orders of ideas (Coser, 1977). Ethical neutrality implies that once the social scientist has selected a value-relevant problem, the values that entered into that selection choice must be held in abeyance while following the guidelines that the data reveal. Those values cannot be imposed on the data and the line of inquiry continues whether or not the results turn out to be inimical to what is held dear. **Value neutrality** in this first instance refers to the normative injunction that scientists should be governed by the ethos of science in their role as scientists, but not necessarily in their role as citizens. In the second instance, value neutrality refers to the disjunction between the world of facts and the world of values, the impossibility of deriving "ought statements" from "is statements." Empirical scientists as scientists, Weber (2012b, p. 103) contended, can never advise anyone what he or she should do, although they may help clarify what one can or wants to do under certain circumstances:

> science might want to go further in its treatment of value judgments and, not only let us understand and re-experience the goals that are striven for and the ideals in which they are rooted, but also, and above all, teach us to "judge" them critically. *Such* a critique, however, can only have a dialectical character; that is to say, it can only consist in judging the substance of historically given value judgments and ideas from the point of view of formal logic, i.e., in testing the ideals against the fundamental demand for the internal *consistency* of what we strive for. But in setting this goal, [the "critical judgment"] can aid the striving person to reflect on the ultimate axioms that form the basis of what he is striving for, on the ultimate value standards he applies, or that he should apply in order to be consistent. But to make us *aware* of the ultimate value standards that manifest themselves in a concrete value judgment is as far as [the "critical judgment"] can go without entering the realm of speculation. Whether the individual who makes a value judgment *ought to* subscribe to those ultimate value standards

is purely his own personal affair; it is a question which concerns his striving and his conscience and which cannot be answered by empirical science.

Value Analysis and Objectivity

As the above formulation suggests, "value interpretation" or "value analysis" can be carried out objectively—that is, adhering to the logic of empirical cause-and-effect proof, not in the sense of subjective detachment. Value analysis may serve to articulate the relevance of singular phenomena for one's particular values, while concomitantly exposing the *conceivable* value relations of cultural objects. As Ringer (1997, p. 124) notes, "our understanding of a particular text or institution might initially be vague and unconsciously affected by personal commitments. 'Value analysis' would then transform our inchoate appreciations into explicit judgments of value relatedness. It would clarify the grounds of our interest in certain objects, if only to separate those grounds from the causal analysis of these phenomena." Weber (2012b, p. 105) stated the matter this way:

> There is and remains . . . an eternal, unbridgeable difference as to whether an argument is aimed at our feelings and our capacity for embracing with enthusiasm concrete practical goals or forms or elements of culture; or, if it is a question concerning the validity of ethical norms, [whether it is aimed at] our conscience; *or* finally, [whether it is aimed] at our ability and need to *order* empirical reality *intellectually* in a manner that claims *validity* as empirical truth. And this proposition remains true even though . . . the ultimate "values" underlying our *practical* interest are, and will remain, of decisive importance for the *direction* that the intellectual activity of ordering within the cultural sciences will take in each particular case. For it is, and continues to be, true that a methodically correct proof in the field of social science must, in order to have reached its goal, also be accepted as correct even by a Chinese— or, to put it more correctly: that goal must at any rate be *striven for,* although it may not be completely obtainable because the data are lacking. In the same way, moreover, the *logical* analysis of an ideal with respect to its content and its ultimate axioms, and the demonstration of the logical and practical consequences of pursuing this ideal, must also, if it is deemed to be successful, be valid for [a Chinese]. Even though he may not be "attuned" to our ethical imperatives, and even though he may be, and most probably often will, reject the ideal and the concrete *valuations* flowing from it, this in no way detracts from the scientific value of that intellectual *analysis.*

In Weber's formulation, then, the scientist as scientist can evaluate the probable consequences of courses of action but cannot make value judgments. "Science today [1918, when Weber initially made the statement] is a 'vocation' that is pursued as a profession, in the service of knowledge of oneself and of relationships between facts" (Weber, 2012c, p. 351). Continuing, he admonishes: "it is not a gift of grace, possessed by seers and prophets and dispensing salvation goods and revelations; nor is it a constituent part of the meditation of sages and philosophers on the *meaning* of the world." In effect, the scientist as scientist has a professional obligation to provide no response to Tolstoy's questions of "What shall we do, and how shall we arrange our lives?" Academic prophesy, Weber further admonishes, creates "only fanatical sects but never a genuine community" (p. 352). This is not to say that scientists as citizens or in other roles such as academics, lawyers, ministers, social workers, and the like refrain from subjecting personal or collective (professional, social, or cultural) valuations of value-choices or preferences to vigorous debate.

Weber (2012a, pp. 304–334) explicitly denied the possibility of objectivity and promoted vigorous debates about values (ends or purposes), especially within the academy, with the understanding that academics and other committed professionals could be wrong about the bases or merits of their valuations and that resolution of these debates may include accommodation of opposing views about what might be desired or possible as well as going beyond the opposing views to what might seem at first blush less desirable or impossible (Blum, 1944; Ringer, 1997). Arguing for professional autonomy lest academics become captives of the state, seeking to exclude or stifle expression of opposing views or impose their personal views on unwitting students, professional "thinkers" are, Weber (2012a) quipped, "under a special obligation to keep a cool head when confronted with the dominant ideals—even the most majestic ones—at any given time; and this means that they should continue to be able 'to swim against the current' if necessary" (p. 333). Preceding Popper (1965, 1959/1968), Weber in short contended that the human capacity for error on one hand implies nothing about the duty to search for truth, and on the other hand leaves open-ended the extent to which debates about values (ends or purposes) get resolved by accommodation to existing conditions or by somehow going beyond or transcending the contested values, the conditions, or both. This is not to equate Weber with relativism about values. For Weber, "absolute" values included those of science itself, since it afforded the greatest opportunity for legitimating and institutionalizing independence of thought and of the ethically autonomous, responsibility choosing free human beings (Blum, 1944).

Critical Thinking and Professional Impartiality

To get a handle on the importance of and purpose for making an analytical distinction between value-relevant and value-neutral approaches to policy analysis and to further distinguish these from the role of critical thinking in policy analysis, it is helpful to keep in mind the impartial or objective disposition that guides social work practice in general. Assuming an impartial or objective disposition toward clients (e.g., a physically abused woman, child, or elderly person) and vulnerable population client groups (e.g., low-income women with children) is an essential component of social work practice. Much as the role disinterestedness plays in science as a social enterprise, impartiality is less a matter of individual motivation than an institutionalized pattern of professional control of a wide range of motives that characterize the behavior of social workers (Merton, 1942; Parsons, 1939). Impartiality is essential to the moral integrity of the profession, imparting normative authority to its practices. This is not to claim that social workers somehow jettison attitudes, beliefs, or preferences they may harbor about a whole host of matters, including what constitutes the good life for themselves and for everyone else and how best to pursue it in general, and what constitutes the best practices that might most benefit clients and vulnerable population client groups in particular. The use of self as a cornerstone of social work practice necessitates that social workers know themselves well enough to be able to identify likely cognitive and behavioral biases so that they do not interfere with their assessment of a client's situation—that is, their understanding of "where the client is," or with their determination or judgment of an appropriate intervention (Ornstein & Ganzer, 2005; Seligson, 2004; Yan & Wong, 2005).

Case in Point 1.2: Cognitive and Behavioral Biases

Examples of biases that social workers need to attend to as practitioners in general and as policy analysts in particular include such tendencies as:

1. Anchoring effects—relying too heavily on one trait or piece of information when making decisions;
2. Bandwagon effects—doing or believing things because others do;
3. Confirmation bias—searching or interpreting in a way that confirms one's preconceptions;
4. Outcome bias—judging a decision by its potential outcome rather than the quality of the decision at the time it was made;
5. Pseudo-certainty effects—making risk-averse choices if the expected outcome is positive, but making risk-seeking choices to avoid negative outcomes. (Brown & Rutter, 2006)

Critical thinking is another attribute requisite for social work practice (Gibbons & Gray, 2004). As a quality of thinking to distinguish it from uncritical thinking—for example, daydreaming or stream of consciousness—critical thinking is inherently normative, applying to a greater or lesser degree appropriate criteria and standards of adequacy and accuracy to what we or others say, do, or write, in addition to fulfilling the relevant standards to some threshold level (Bailin, Case, Coombs, & Daniels, 1999). **Critical thinking** includes cognitive activities such as logical reasoning and scrutinizing arguments unsupported by empirical evidence, as well as (1) a willingness to examine and the capacity to acknowledge assumptions underlying one's own beliefs and behaviors, (2) justifying one's own ideas and actions, (3) judging the rationality of these ideas and actions accordingly, (4) comparing them to a range of varying interpretations and perspectives, (5) thinking through, projecting, and anticipating likely consequences of such ideas and actions that are based on these justifications, and (6) testing the accuracy and rationality of these justifications against some kind of objective analysis of the "real" world as we understand it (Brookfield, 1987; Brown & Rutter, 2006). As items 4 and 5 suggest, creativity and engaging others in deliberation are requisite components of critical thinking: new interpretations and perspectives may be offered as a basis of comparison to existing ones; imagination is involved in anticipating possible consequences, generating original approaches, and identifying alternative perspectives; and thinking through likely consequences entails discussion and dialogue with others (Bailin et al., 1999).

Requisite intellectual resources for critical thinking include background knowledge, operational knowledge of standards of good thinking (i.e., of critical deliberation and judgment), knowledge of key critical concepts, and heuristics (e.g., strategies and procedures), as well as developing an appropriate frame of mind. The quality of thinking about a particular problem, issue, or question social workers are able to do is in large part affected by what they already know or are able to find out about it and about the context in which it must be resolved. Context plays a significant role in determining what is likely to count as a sensible or reasonable application of standards and principles of good thinking. Thinking critically when deciding, for example, whether to accept or reject moral judgment requires a clear understanding of the nature of the action or policy being judged, the context in which it is to be carried out, and the array of moral considerations relevant to the judgment (Bailin et al., 1999).

Operational knowledge of the standards that govern critical deliberation and judgment, a requisite for critical thinking, includes standards for judging intellectual products such as arguments, theories, legal judgments, and principles relevant to guiding practices of deliberation or inquiry or justification in specialized areas such as history, law, or any of the social sciences. Variation among intellectual products requires critical thinkers to have knowledge of key critical criteria or standards accordingly. Confronted with a statement requiring evaluation, for example, critical thinking social workers should be able to discern whether it is a value statement, an empirical statement, or a conceptual statement if they are to assess it responsibly. Heuristics or strategies guiding performance of thinking tasks include basic activities such as making a list of pros and cons when deciding which side of an issue to support, or discussing issues with knowledgeable persons, or examining positive and negative consequences in light of alternatives, including those that might be deemed unacceptable at first blush, and double checking factual claims (Bailin et al., 1999).

Finally, some important habits of mind for critical thinking include (1) respect for reasons and truth (commitment to having justified beliefs, values, and actions); (2) respect for high quality products and performances (appreciation for good design and effective performance); (3) open-mindedness (a disposition to withhold judgment and seek new points of view when existing evidence is inadequate and a willingness to revise one's view should the evidence warrant it); (4) fair-mindedness (commitment to understanding and giving fair consideration to alternative points of view, and a disposition to seek evidence or reasons that may go against one's view); (5) independent mindedness (intellectual honesty and courage to seek out relevant evidence and basing one's beliefs and actions on it, despite pressures to do otherwise, and to stand up to one's sufficiently scrutinized and firmly held beliefs); (6) respect for others in group inquiry and deliberation (commitment to open discussion in which all are given a fair hearing); (7) respect for legitimate intellectual authority (appreciation for giving due weight to others who satisfy the criteria for being an authority in a specified area of study or practice); and (8) an intellectual work-ethic (commitment to carrying out relevant thinking tasks in a competent manner) (Bailin et al., 1999).

Following Holonen (1995), critical thinking skills can be classified by cognitive elements. Foundation skills include the cognitive elements of describing behavior, recognizing concepts and theories, interpreting behavior, identifying assumptions, and listening. Higher level skills include the cognitive elements of applying concepts and theories (comparing, contrasting, analyzing, and predicting them), evaluating theories and behavioral claims (questioning and synthesizing them), and generating hypotheses and challenging them. Complex skills include the cognitive elements of problem-solving (diagnosis, research design, systematic qualitative and quantitative data analysis), theory building, formal criticism, decision making, and collaboration.

As critical thinkers, social workers can be committed to points of view that are well informed, rational, and supported by relevant and valid material for a given client-related situation or for circumstances about vulnerable population client groups. Professional impartiality entails only that social workers take measures to minimize potential biasing effects such commitments might have as they approach and undertake the task of policy analysis.

Neither critical thinking nor impartiality need imply a relativistic disposition about epistemological (how we know what we know) or ontological (the nature of human reality or being-in-itself) issues. For the most part, social workers have found a middle ground between positivism and postmodernism (interpretive-constructivist perspective), acknowledging that the world is knowable in a particular way, bolstered by empirical evidence, such that social problems including poverty, child abuse, and discrimination exist, with a generalized consensus of agreement about definitions, albeit subject to ongoing critique and analysis (McNeill, 2006).

Skill Building Exercises

1. Discuss paradoxes of the postmodernist challenge to policy analysis.

2. What distinguishes value neutrality from value relevancy?

3. Discuss the relationship between value analysis and objectivity.

4. Discuss the significance of Weber's and Durkheim's approaches to causal explanations.

5. Discuss the relationship between objectivity as a central concept in the social sciences from the professional attribute of impartiality when dealing with clients or vulnerable groups of people.

6. Discuss the relationship between critical thinking and professional impartiality.

CHAPTER 2

The Purpose of Policy Analysis

To get a better handle on rationales for policy interventions aimed at meeting need or for social betterment—that is, on justifications for doing something rather than nothing—this chapter discusses the role of government in the economy and society in general and introduces several basic micro- and macroeconomic concepts in the context of traditional market failures. Public goods, externalities, natural monopolies, and information asymmetry—four commonly recognized market failures—are the subject matter of microeconomics. Business cycles and related issues such unemployment and inflation are the subject matter of macroeconomics. The chapter also provides an overview of economists' ways of thinking about the role of the market vis-à-vis government when addressing policy-relevant resource allocation or distributional issues. Pareto efficiency—that is, the inability to make someone better off without making someone else worse off—is contrasted with the **social welfare function**—that is, the allocation of goods that maximizes the greatest good—as a basis for allocating goods. Alternative social welfare functions, namely *utilitarian, Rawlsian,* and *multiplicative,* are discussed in light of how they would lead to adoption of different policies. Upon finishing the chapter, students will have learned that (1) despite limitations and caveats, economic concepts and ways of thinking are integral to policy analysis, and (2) allocation mechanisms other than Pareto efficiency justify different policy options.

Upon successful completion of the skill building exercises of Chapter 2, students will have mastered the following CSWE Competencies and Practice Behaviors:

Chapter 2	CSWE Core Competencies
#	**Description**
2.1.3	**Apply Critical Thinking to Inform and Communicate Professional Judgments**
	Demonstrate effective oral and written communication in working with individuals, families, groups, organizations, communities, and colleagues
2.1.7	**Apply Knowledge of Human Behavior and the Social Environment**
	Utilize conceptual frameworks to guide the processes of assessment, intervention, and evaluation
	Critique and apply knowledge to understand person and environment
2.1.8	**Engage in Policy Practice to Advance Social and Economic Well-Being and to Deliver Effective Social Work Services**
	Collaborate with colleagues and clients for effective policy action

Source: Adapted from Council on Social Work Education (2012). *Educational policy and accreditation standards.* Washington, DC: Author. Retrieved from http://www.cswe.org/file.aspx?id=13780

RATIONALES FOR PUBLIC POLICY

In a classic formulation of the issue about social provisioning to meet need in twentieth century society, Towle (1944, 1945/1965) identified passage of the Social Security Act of 1935 as one of only two "significant developments that spell hope for our country"—the other being advances in our knowledge about human behavior. Modern society, such as it was in the aftermath of the Great Depression of the 1930s and in the midst of World War II, had reached a point, in Towle's estimation, that required national level government intervention for ensuring a decent and dignified standard of living and protection against the vicissitudes of market-based economies. Far too many individuals and families had faced unemployment, poverty, and other common-need vulnerabilities that stifled individual and social development. Over time, provisions of the Social Security Act have expanded considerably—as any social welfare policy text about the United States indicates— even as the proper role of government in the economy and society has been continually debated—it was only after much debate about prospects of achieving a full employment economy that Congress formally authorized federal oversight of and intervention in the economy, to use fiscal and monetary policies to manage or prevent unemployment, inflation, and other market maladies with passage of the Employment Act of 1946 (P.L. 79-304) (Caputo, 1994; Santoni, 1986).

Debates about the nature and reach of government involvement in the economy and society have continued into the twenty-first century, forming one of the central issues in the presidential election of 2012 (CNN, 2012) and in the budget and debt debates of the 113th Congress (whose first session convened on Thursday, January 3, 2013). Towle's optimism about national level social welfare provisioning, however, has eroded considerably since the 1970s, as the moral prestige of the market subsequently rose over the next several decades and that of the government fell (Caputo, 2011; Friedman, 2005; Ignatieff, 2012b; Porter, 2012; Rodgers, 2011). National level politics in the United States has become increasingly strident and partisan since the 1994 elections, when the Republican Party took control of both chambers of Congress, shifting the political center to the right well into the first decade of the twenty-first century and favoring greater reliance on market forces to meet human need.

For our purposes here, it is helpful to identify some of the more common concepts about market functioning, knowledge of which can aid social workers as policy analysts as they think about their roles and related tasks that confront them. It should be noted that a focus on market mechanisms tends to privilege individualistic rather than structural explanatory accounts of how the world works. Social work practice, however, is informed by theories about human behavior and the social environment, and social workers are therefore encouraged to think in systemic terms about clients and their circumstances in light of social justice considerations, attending to relations among intra-psychic, interpersonal, and structural dynamics. To the extent that social workers want to do credible policy analysis either on their own, with other social workers, or with professionals such as economists and others who have familiarity with economic concepts and related skill sets, they invariably benefit from knowing how economists think about the market. To that end, what follows is a discussion of select aspects of microeconomics and macroeconomics that are often used to inform social welfare policy debates about what, if anything, should be done in the way of government intervention for allocating resources and why implementation of some allocation-related policy decisions might be more efficient than others. As elaborated in Chapter 4, efficiency is one of several criteria for assessing the merits of alternative policies.

To get a better handle on market considerations and their importance to policy analysis, what the discipline of economics is and what economists mean by the concepts of *scarcity, choice,* and *opportunity costs,* is noteworthy. At the risk of oversimplification, economics is the study of how economic agents (individuals, households, businesses, governments) use their scarce resources to specialize in production and to exchange and consume goods and services according to the prevailing economic system (Gregory, 2004). *Scarce* resources (land and natural resources, labor, and capital, which are called *factors of production*) are those in which the amount that economic agents would want free of charge exceeds the amount available. With this definition in mind, **scarcity** has little to do with wealth or poverty per se. Scarcity exists in rich and poor countries. The only requirement, to the economist's way of thinking, is that there is an imbalance between what is available and what people would want if the good were free. Resources or factors of production represent economic wealth because they ultimately determine how much output can be produced. The limited nature of resources precludes production of infinite amounts of goods and services.

A long acknowledged factor leading to increased material well-being is *specialization* or the division of labor (Gregory, 2004). That is, economic agents increase their material well-being by doing what they do relatively better than others can. *Specialization* dictates exchange, in the absence of which economic agents would be left only with their own goods. The economic system is the set of organizational arrangements and institutions that economic agents use to manage scarcity. Ownership of resources used to produce economic goods is the prime determinant of the type of economic system. For our purposes, market capitalism is characterized by private ownership of resources, with individuals largely making their own economic decisions; in contrast, in more socialist-oriented economies government owns much of the resources and the state makes major economic decisions. Private versus public ownership of the factors of production is a matter of degree, with no modern economy is considered a purely market capitalist or socialist. It is more helpful to think of modern economies as mixed markets—that is, on a continuum with purely or ideal market capitalism and socialism serving as anchor or end points.

The economic problem is how to allocate scarce resources among competing uses: what goods and services to produce, how (what combinations of resources are to be used) to produce them, and for whom (how what gets produced is divided among people) (Gregory, 2004). Friction between unlimited wants (i.e., what people would wish to have if the price were zero) and scarce resources causes the economic problem. There is no single formula for allocating scarce resources, given that allocation entails the apportionment of resources for specific purposes or to particular persons or groups, with each having costs associated with it. Economists measure *costs* in terms of **opportunity costs**—that is, the loss of the next-best alternative. Every time a what, how, or for whom choice is made, alternative courses of action are sacrificed. *Free goods* have *zero opportunity costs*—that is, users can have more, like air, without others having to give up some of the good. *Scarce goods* have *positive opportunity cost*—that is, in order to have more of a scarce good (e.g., electricity), an alternative must be sacrificed—the billion tons of coal, seven trillion cubic meters of natural gas, and the 190 million barrels of petroleum used to produce electricity in any given year could have been used for other things, such as driving more miles or creating more petrochemical products.

Finally, economists study both the economy at large—macroeconomics—and the economy as it operates in smaller entities, such as a household, business, or price of particular goods and services—microeconomics (Gregory, 2004). **Macroeconomists** focus on the economy as a whole and study the determinants of total output. Inflation, unemployment, growth, and changes in the level of business activity are the subject matters of macroeconomics. **Microeconomics** deals with studies of behavior of the individual participants in the economy: how individual businesses behave in competitive environments, and how prices of individual commodities are determined. Economic theories explain how economic facts are related, with economists isolating the most important factors that explain economic phenomenon. Economic theories yield hypotheses or predictions about how things are related. Positive economics focuses on what is—that is, how the facts cohere. If the price of a product falls relative to other prices, what happens to sales? If money supply increases, what happens to the inflation rate? Normative economics focuses on what ought to be. Should we have a more equal distribution of income? Should we sacrifice more inflation for less unemployment? Should we spend public dollars on social welfare or on national defense? Having some basic terminology at our disposal, we now turn to how market considerations fit into this general description of economics.

Case in Point 2.1: Health Care and the Market

Think again of the Patient Protection and Affordable Care Act (here referred to as ACA) as well as H.R. 45, introduced in Congress in 2013 to repeal the ACA. Michael Tanner (2013), a senior fellow at the Cato Institute, contends that ACA is far from the best route to health care reform because among other things, due to expected government regulatory initiatives and mandates, it will fail to control costs and will still leave approximately 40 million people uninsured, thereby failing to achieve universality. (On this latter issue, see also Cohn, 2013; Jacobs et al., 2011; Jost, 2013). To more effectively reform health care in the United States, with the aim of containing costs and achieving universality, Tanner recommends ignoring debates that have traditionally animated health reform as to whether health care is a right or a privilege. Instead, Tanner advises treating health care "simply [as] a commodity, and, in fact, a finite commodity" (p. 7). Grounded in personal experience surrounding the hospital care and death of his father, the basis of an article in *The Atlantic* and subsequent book, David Goldhill (2013a; 2013b; 2009), the CEO of GSN (Game Show Network), recommends providing health insurance for everyone but restricting benefits only for "truly rare, major and unpredictable illnesses." That is, health insurance would cover for example only such things as cancer, stroke, or trauma. As you read through the remainder of this chapter, keep Tanner and Goldhill in mind and identify under what circumstances or conditions and why you might agree or disagree with them. For more about the Cato Institute, see Appendix B.

MARKET CONSIDERATIONS

Markets bring buyers and sellers together to determine conditions of exchange in which prices of goods and services play an import role. It is important to note that it is relative prices that inform consumers what is cheap and what is expensive (Gregory, 2004). Relative prices are to be distinguished from money prices—that is, those expressed in monetary units such as dollars, yen, and euros. Relative prices are expressed in terms of other commodities. The pricing system comprises the entire set of relative prices, which are constantly changing, particularly in light of new products or improvements in current products, and they can move in directions opposite to the general level of money prices. Think of cell phones, with the relative price expressed as a ratio of two money prices: the relative price of cell phone service fell from almost 2.5 to 1.5 that of regular phone service between 1997 and 2000 and for global broadband service by 22 percent versus 8 percent from 2008 to 2010 (Gregory, 2004; Meyer, 2011). Relative prices are important because people substitute one good for another as relative prices change, which is not to say that there is an equally good substitute. Rather, it means only that increases in relative prices motivate economic agents to seek out relative cheaper substitutes.

Political economist Adam Smith's theory of the invisible hand conveys the idea that a capitalist society can function well without government direction by using signals of the price system. This is not the same thing as claiming there is no need for a legal system to ensure economic contracts or agreements are enforced. In general, prices are a function of demand (what consumers are willing to pay), supply (costs of production), and market structure (number of competing firms) (Winter, 2005). The price system is made of the millions of relative prices, informing buyers and sellers what goods are cheap and what goods are expensive. As noted above, relative prices are not to be confused with monetary prices. They are expressed in terms of other goods, as ratios of two monetary prices of goods or commodities that can often be used as substitutes one for the other (Gregory, 2004). As businesses use this information to gain profits and as buyers use this information to determine their best buys, the economy theoretically runs itself without direction from the government or planning from government. The invisible hand ensures that markets will move toward equilibrium—that is, as buyers and sellers adjust to the change in relative price, eventually a balance is struck between quantity demanded and quantity supplied. An equilibrium price is reached when the amount of the good or service people are prepared to buy equals the amount businesses or service providers are prepared to sell (Gregory, 2004).

A related basic assumption about markets is that as an idealized competitive model it produces a Pareto-efficient allocation of goods. This means that the satisfaction- or utility-maximizing behavior of persons and the profit-maximizing behavior of firms will result in a distribution of goods in such a way that no one could be better off without making anyone else worse off (Weimer & Vining, 2011). In the model, Pareto efficiency arises through voluntary actions of buyers and sellers reacting to changes in the relative prices of goods and services, avoiding the need for public policies to reallocate scarce resources. It is commonly acknowledged that in reality resource allocation deviates considerably from the idealized competitive model leading to a balance or price equilibrium, thereby justifying public participation in private or voluntary activities related to the production and consumption of goods. These violations of the model constitute **market failures**—that is, circumstances in which decentralized behavior, the respective maximizing actions of individuals (satisfaction) and firms (profits) does not lead to Pareto efficiency.

Traditional Market Failures

Traditional market failures are circumstances in which social surplus (the total value added by an activity or transaction to all members of society who are affected by that activity) is larger under some alternative allocations than that resulting under the market equilibrium (Social Surplus, 2012). Given the dynamic nature of market economies, and notwithstanding the idea of an "invisible hand" guiding the economy, equilibrium price (Pareto optimality) seems unobtainable. Nonetheless, given two basic assumptions of economic thinking—namely finite or scarce resources and an indeterminately infinite aggregate satisfaction level (insatiable wants, needs, and preferences vying for those resources)—the idea that supply and demand change in relation to each other such that over time, all else being equal, what is demanded is exactly what is produced, that an equilibrium price is obtainable, has analytic or heuristic merit. Public goods, externalities, natural monopolies, and information asymmetry are four commonly recognized market failures or imperfections in the operation of the invisible hand and they are the subject matter of microeconomics. In addition, business cycles pose challenges to a well-functioning economy guided by an invisible hand, particularly in regard to related issues such as unemployment and inflation—which are the subject matter of macroeconomics.

Public Goods and the Problem of Free Riding

What is there about public goods that make them problematic or inappropriately responsive to market signals such as price? One way to address this question is to contrast public goods with private goods. *Rivalrous consumption* and *excludable ownership* characterize private goods. *Rivalrous consumption* goods are those such that what one consumes cannot be consumed by another. *Excludable ownership* goods are those whose use one has control over, with perfectly private goods defined as those over which one has complete excludability. The shoes on my feet are private goods: no one else can wear them (*rivalrous consumption*), and since I own them, I determine who gets to wear them at any particular time (*excludable ownership*).

In contrast to private goods, public goods are characterized as *nonrivalous* in consumption, *nonexcludable* in use, or both. That is, more of the good can be consumed by one person without less being available for others, and nonpayers cannot be excluded from using the good by those who actually pay. The pricing mechanism that buyers and sellers use to base their respective choices about private goods—this invisible hand that in effect determines how those goods are allocated—is noticeably absent when considering public goods. This failure or imperfection in the operation of the invisible hand results in the practical problem of *free riding,* which may warrant government intervention. The *free rider* problem arises in cases, for example, where some people living in a flood zone who do not voluntarily pay their share of flood control insurance or projects benefit from what others pay at their expense. Economically, it is rational for most to try to *free ride,* hoping that others will pay. A solution to the *free rider* problem is for government to provide public goods, paying for them with tax revenues. A related question is why the private market would provide any public goods at all. Cultural and material benefits associated with an educated citizenry, for example, are public goods. Left to its own, the private market would fail to educate a sufficient number of citizens at a level of cognitive or intellectual proficiency to produce such goods from which everyone benefits. Government thereby mandates that everyone receive schooling, in the United States from K-12 grade levels, or up to the age of 18, and education makes up sizable portions of state budgets to ensure a supply of free public schools.

Externalities

Private calculations about what to buy or produce and sell have un-priced consequences that affect others who are not party to such market exchanges. These un-priced consequences either confer benefits (positive externalities as Case in Point 2.2 also illustrates) or impose costs (negative externalities). Positive externalities occur when individuals or firms make decisions that result in society obtaining greater benefits than do the individuals or firms making the decisions. Immunization prevents me from

Case in Point 2.2: Universal Preschool as a Public Benefit

In his 2013 State of the Union Address, President Barack Obama proposed "working with states to make high-quality preschool available to every child in America." He justified the proposal by claiming that every dollar invested in high-quality early education can save seven dollars later on—by boosting high school graduation rates (which among other things better equips the U.S. workforce to compete in a high-tech global economy), reducing teen pregnancy (which in turn among other things lowers teens' exposure to health risks and saves medical-related costs), and reducing violent crime (Obama, 2013). Whether such a proposal will be implemented during Obama's second administration is doubtful given congressional stalemates over the size of the federal budget and debt and the related ideological differences between Democrats and Republicans characteristic of the 112th and 113th Congress (Harward, 2013; Stevenson, 2013). Nonetheless, note that the justification for universal preschool education is based on the idea that everyone benefits, both from a more productive workforce and a reduced crime rate, even those without children, and hence Congress and the populace might be amenable to picking up some of the costs as a public expense.

getting a disease whereas society gains more positive benefits from my not spreading the disease to others; keeping my yard well maintained has the positive effect of helping the value of my neighbor's property. The net result of positive externalities is less produced than would be optimal. A way to get more consumers to consume goods having positive externalities is to subsidize them from revenues obtained from those who benefit from the good. Government can impose a tax on beneficiaries and redistribute the income to those who produced the good—that is, for example, tax income generating adults to subsidize the cost of immunizations (Taylor, 2006). Negative externalities occur when the producer does not pay the full cost of decisions. A classic example of an external cost or negative externality is the owner of a factory that pollutes the river and raises the water-purification costs of downstream factories or reduces the number of fisheries. The owner who takes no external cost into account when making decisions about the factory can produce more output and hence more pollution than if he or she had to pay these external costs. The presence of external costs presents another potential role for government: to use regulation (e.g., limiting the pollution quota) or market-based programs (imposing a fee to offset the external costs others bear) to make sure that those who impose these external costs include them as part of their private calculation (Gregory, 2004).

Natural Monopolies

Monopolies exist when a single individual or firm has the ability to affect market price. A natural monopoly exists as a result of high fixed or start-up costs of a business in a particular industry. High start-up costs discourage competitors from entering the market. Utilities are a good example. The costs of establishing the means to produce power and supply it to each household can be quite large. Capital costs deter competition. Societies benefit from natural monopolies, so it makes economic sense for governments to regulate those in operation to ensure that consumers get a fair deal (Investopedia, 2012d).

Information Asymmetries

Another failure of competitive equilibrium models of market economies has to do with information, which is treated as a scarce good. In a classic formulation of the role of information in the economy Hayek (1945), intending to "shock" readers "out of complacency," extols the virtue of the price system this way:

> The marvel is that in a case like that of a scarcity of one raw material, without an order being issued, without more than perhaps a handful of people knowing the cause, tens of thousands of people whose identity could not be ascertained by months of investigation, are made to use the material or its products more sparingly; i.e., they move in the right direction. (p. 527)

Prices serve as the regulatory mechanism in market economies. Recall that in equilibrium models, economic agents know the relative prices that affect their well-being: wage rates in relevant occupations, relative prices of consumer goods, interest rates on home mortgages. As a scarce good, some people even make their livings by collecting and analyzing information: real estate brokers know locations and prices of homes, investment bankers know where to find large investors for companies that need capital. Such information is costly to acquire. Information costs are the time and money it takes to acquire information about prices today and in the future and on product qualities (Gregory, 2004). Stiglitz (2002) also acknowledges the importance of information in the economy but highlights how economists have long known that imperfections or asymmetries preclude anything resembling movement toward equilibrium in the real world as opposed to in perfectly competitive economies. Asymmetrically distributed information between a firm, as an employer, and its workers has come to replace the traditional view of a firm that hires labor at fixed wages in well-defined labor markets "with one in which firms actively manage long-term employment relations, on average pay wages in excess of those available on the labor market at large, control workers with carefully designed incentive mechanism, and often ration access to jobs" (Greenwald & Stiglitz, 1990, p. 160).

Asymmetric information characterizes many market situations—that is, those in which one party in a transaction has more or better information compared to another (Investopedia, 2012a). Think of the used car salesperson who would know more about the "lemon" she or he wants to unload and thereby perhaps take unfair advantage of the less knowledgeable buyer (Kim, 1985). Such potentially harmful activity justifies intervention to protect those with less or inadequate information. Two main problems associated with information asymmetries justifying government intervention in market economies are *adverse selection* and *moral hazards*. *Adverse selection* occurs when someone takes advantage of asymmetric information before a transaction takes place. Individuals in less than optimal health are more likely than those who feel fine to purchase health insurance, in effect raising payout costs to insurers while depleting sources of revenue to cover expenses.

Moral hazard is an insurance term (Marshall, 1976) that is a central part of the "law and economics explanation of how things as they are came to be" (Baker, 1996, p. 237)—hence its importance as an analytic tool, based on rational choice theory, of policy analysis when pertaining to social responsibility issues. The idea of *moral hazard* finds common currency in light of the government bailout of big banks in response to the financial crisis begun in December 2007 (Dewan, 2012). Essentially, *moral hazards* occur when someone takes advantage of asymmetric information after a transaction takes place (Investopedia,

Case in Point 2.3: ACA and Adverse Selection

To offset the prospect of adverse selection, the Patient Protection and Affordable Care Act (P.L 111–148) (here referred to as ACA) passed in 2010 during the Obama administration's first term mandated that everyone purchase health insurance (Lee, 2010). ACA, however, gives states substantial flexibility in how they structure their respective health insurance exchanges—those marketplaces that are meant to provide affordable, good-quality coverage options to individuals and small businesses. Lueck (2010, p. 1) poses the problem of adverse selection that states and their respective health insurance exchanges should be wary of as follows:

Adverse selection—the separation of healthier and less-healthy people into different insurance arrangements—will occur if a disproportionate number of people who are in poorer health and have high health expenses enroll in coverage through the insurance exchanges, while healthier, lower-cost people disproportionately enroll in plans offered through the individual and small business markets *outside* the exchanges. If that occurs, the cost of exchange coverage will be higher than the cost of plans offered in outside markets. That would drive up costs not only for consumers and small firms purchasing coverage through the exchanges, but also for the federal government, which must provide premium subsidies to enable low- and moderate-income people to afford coverage in the exchanges. Higher premiums would depress participation in the exchanges by individuals and small businesses, particularly by those people and firms that can obtain better deals in outside markets.

That, in turn, could raise premiums even higher in the exchanges and could ultimately result in their failure over time.

To lessen the possibility of adverse selection between plans inside and outside the exchanges, Lueck (2010) discusses four actions states could take that ACA allows but does not mandate: (1) make the rules for any insurance markets outside the exchange consistent with those that apply inside the exchange; (2) require insurers to offer the same products inside and outside the exchange; (3) merge the individual and small-group markets over time; and (4) ensure that risk-adjustment and risk-pooling requirements work effectively.

To lessen the possibility of adverse selection among plans within an exchange, Lueck (2011) discusses four actions: (1) establish consistent health benefits; (2) create a menu of cost-sharing options for each coverage area; (3) require insurers that want to operate in an exchange to offer products in all exchange coverage levels; and (4) conduct strong and ongoing enforcement and oversight.

2012a). If someone has fire insurance they might unintentionally be more careless striking a match to light a gas oven or perhaps would be even more likely to commit arson to reap the benefits of the insurance (Arrow, 1963, 1968; Pauly, 1968). A banker or lender might sell you a mortgage or a bundle of mortgaged properties knowing that it is not in your interest to buy it; likewise, if government bails out financial institutions that face shortages of capital liquidity due to defaults or delinquent mortgage payments, they subsequently might be more likely to take even greater risks, as occurred during the housing-related financial crisis begun in 2007 (Dowd, 2009; Glassman, 2009; Reich, 2008). Increasing the number of student loans that will be forgiven without full repayment, a transaction President Obama (2011a) proposed, might encourage riskier borrowers to enter the system, as some suggested (Goodman, 2011).

As the examples of government bailouts of big banks and concerns about encouraging student loan defaults reflect, *moral hazard* can be used to argue for or against government intervention. Critics of government bailouts of banks in response to the financial crisis of 2007–2009, for example, asked why tax dollars should be used to rescue banks that drove the economy into *recession* (discussed below in the context of business cycles), whereas those same banks in turn subsequently turned to moral hazard arguments to explain why they were hesitant to help people who had difficulty meeting mortgage payments (Dewan, 2012). Moral hazard can be used to justify keeping any social welfare benefits to a minimum, reducing the incentives or payoffs of taking advantage of them, whether by increasing the number of recipients likely to apply for them or of providers who become less attentive to recipients' needs. Moral hazard arguments can be used to cast doubt on well-intentioned efforts to share life burdens and to deny that refusing to share those burdens is mean-spirited (Baker, 1996). Gladwell (2005) contends that individuals take far less advantage of such moral hazard circumstances than is commonly thought, suggesting that policy analysts would be well advised to assess how extensively it has occurred in the case of policies that have already been implemented or how likely it might be for proposed policies under a variety of alternative incentive scenarios and making recommendations to policymakers accordingly.

Business Cycles

Macroeconomic dynamics associated with *economic growth* and *business cycles* are often the central focus of rationales for public policy, although the specifics of related public policies are contested. *Economic growth* is the expansion of the economy's output over the long run. The business cycle measures the short-run fluctuations around the economy's expansion of output (Gregory, 2004). Expanding the economy's output is a function of increases in productive resources (primarily labor and capital) and of advances in technology. Investment adds to the stock of capital whose rate of expansion is contingent upon the amount that is invested. Society makes choices between capital goods (plants, equipment, inventories that add to capital stock) and consumer goods. Economic growth is not smooth: in some periods it is above the long-term trend, at other times below it. In extreme cases output shrinks. Labor force participation is connected to the pace of business activity. Employment opportunities generally expand as output does and the unemployment rate usually decreases. When output contracts, employment opportunities decline and the unemployment rate increases.

The business cycle has four phases: *recession, trough, recovery,* and *peak*. During recession, or downturn, output declines for two consecutive quarters (six months) or more. The unemployment rate rises, corporate profits fall, and economic activity declines, which if prolonged and severe is called a *depression*. The trough occurs when output stops falling—the economy has reached a low point from which recovery begins. In the recovery, or expansion, phase of the business cycle, output rises, unemployment falls, and profits increase, as does economic activity. The peak is the final phase of the business cycle, preceding a recession, as output growth ceases after the peak is reached. The economy is not of one piece but includes different sectors responding differently to business cycles, with the stock market often serving as the leading indicator, as illustrated in Figure 2.1.

Since 1945, the U.S. economy has gone through 11 business cycles; the average trough or recession has lasted 11 months and the average recovery 59 months, with each peak (excluding the last in 2001 which was 1.3 percent lower than the 2007 peak) higher than preceding ones, signifying the long-term growth of the economy (Gregory, 2004; National Bureau of Economic Research, 2010,

| Figure 2.1 | Sector Rotation Model: |

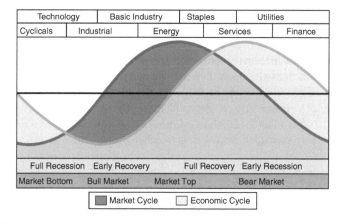

Source: Retrieved, courtesy of StockCharts.com, from http://www.tradingonlinemarkets.com/Beat_the_Market/The_Business_Cycle_Phases.htm

2012). The most recent uninterrupted period of prosperity was the decade of the 1990s, with the mid-1990 to mid-1991 recession playing a major role in the presidential election of 1992: a Democrat, Bill Clinton, was elected for the first time since the 1976 election of Jimmy Carter. The economic growth and prosperity that followed undoubtedly contributed to President Clinton's reelection in 1996. The election of Republican presidential candidate George W. Bush—though controversial, given balloting irregularities in the state of Florida—was nonetheless surprising in light of the economic prosperity at the time. The most recent recession began in December of 2007 and lasted about 18 months, to June 2009 (Center on Budget and Policy Priorities, 2012a; National Bureau of Economic Research, 2012). As noted above, business cycles affect far more than presidential elections, and despite long-term average growth in the economy, the short term does matter. Whether one has a job today matters a great deal; whether interest rates are high right now determines whether one can afford to buy a home right now. Whether a business cycle is at a peak or in a trough affects unemployment rates and wage levels.

The major macroeconomic variables of concern are *output, price,* and *employment* (Gregory, 2004). Since its focus is on the entire economy, macroeconomics requires aggregate measures of these variables. The aggregate measure for the *total output of the economy* is called the *gross domestic product,* or simply GDP; that of *the price level of the economy* as a whole and its rate of change is called *inflation.* The aggregate measures of labor force participation and unemployment rates are used for the whole economy rather than in a particular industry, which is a focus of microeconomics. The most general level of business activity is the total volume of goods and services produced by the economy over a specified period of time. GDP is the market value of all final goods and services produced by the factors of production located in the country in one year's time. It should be noted that to the consternation of feminist economists (e.g., Folbre, 2001; Folbre & Pujol, 1996; Smith & Ingham, 2005), goods and services produced and used within the household are excluded from the determination of GDP (Schneider & Shackelford, 2012). Related concepts are *Real GDP* and *Nominal GDP. Real GDP* measures the volume of real goods and services produced by the economy by removing the effects of rising prices (*inflation*) on nominal GDP. *Nominal GDP* is the value of final goods and services for a given year expressed in that year's prices. *Real GDP* measures the changing volume of output in terms of constant prices of a specific year (Gregory, 2004).

Inflation is a general increase in *prices,* occurring when *prices* in the entire economy are rising on average—*prices* of some goods rise more rapidly than the average, whereas other *prices* fall (Gregory, 2004). *Inflation* need not be inherently problematic: modestly rising *prices* can exert positive pressure on wages; incomes rising at a faster rate than *inflation* signify an increased standard of living. What is considered moderate or excessive, however, is relative: in the 1950s, an *inflation rate* of 2 percent raised alarms, whereas in the 1970s, when *prices* were rising about 10 percent a year, 2 percent annual increases would have been greatly appreciated. Double-digit *inflation* was a contributing factor to the one-term presidency of Jimmy Carter and the 1980 election of Ronald Reagan, whose administration's first-term budget and the Federal Reserve Board's *fiscal policies* and the *monetary policies* in effect broke it (Mussa, 1994; Orphandies, 2006; Poterba, 1994).

Fiscal policy and *monetary policy* are the two main instruments governments use to influence the economy and society for purposes of meeting social welfare needs and general well-being of the citizenry and others residing within their respective geographic areas. Among other things, policy analysts assess the merits of these policies, whether already operational or proposed, and the related programs they authorize. Fiscal policy is the use of government spending and taxation to influence the economy (Weir, 2008). Monetary policy is action by a central bank, board, or other regulatory committee that determines the size and rate of growth of the money supply, which in turn affects interest rates (Investopedia, 2012c). In the United States, the Board of Governors of the Federal Reserve System, which oversees the twelve Federal Reserve Banks, has the responsibility for monetary policy. Annual monetary reports, other publications, and related information about the Board of Governors and its members' activities are available online (www.federalreserve.gov/).

Since *inflation* acts like a tax on fixed money receipts or assets, it adversely affects those on fixed incomes, those whose wages are stagnant or increasing at a lower rate, and those who have invested in fixed-income assets like bonds that fall in value as inflation rises. Further, as *inflation* rises, lenders will be less likely to loan money at interest rates insufficiently high enough to compensate them for the declining value of money (Gregory, 2004).

The Employment Act of 1946 commits the federal government to create and maintain useful employment opportunities for those able, willing, and seeking to work, hence the concern for macroeconomic variables of *inflation* and *employment* (and *unemployment*) (Gregory, 2004). *Unemployed* persons are defined by the Bureau of Labor Statistics as those who at the time of interview (1) did not work at all during the previous week; (2) actively looked for work during the previous four weeks; and (3) are currently available for work. Laid-off persons waiting to be recalled to their old jobs are also considered unemployed, even though they are not looking for jobs. Adults are classified as either *employed, unemployed,* or *not in the labor force.* The *labor force* equals the number of employed persons plus the number of unemployed persons. The last category—*not in the labor force*—includes people such as full-time homemakers, full-time students, and retired persons. The *unemployment rate* equals the number of *unemployed* persons divided by the *labor force* (the sum of *employed* and *unemployed* persons). *Unemployment* associated with the normal changing of jobs in a dynamic economy is called *frictional unemployment,* whereas unemployment associated with general downturns in the economy is called *cyclical unemployment.* Unemployment that results from the decline of certain industries, due to such factors as rising costs, changes in consumer preferences, or technological advances that make the industry's product obsolete, is called *structural unemployment.* In the United States, structural unemployment occurred with the loss of jobs in the oil industry during the mid-1980s, when oil prices declined; in the defense industry in the 1990s due to cuts in defense spending; and in the manufacturing sector, which has steadily eroded over the past several decades (though with a slight uptick in recent years), due in large part to the greater supply of lower-cost labor in other countries such as China and India.

DISTRIBUTIONAL AND OTHER GOALS

Social Welfare Functions

The social welfare function, more commonly referred to as the "greatest good" principle, provides an alternative to Pareto efficiency as a way of allocating goods. Instead of defining efficiency as the inability to make someone better off without making someone else worse off (Pareto efficiency), efficiency is defined as the allocation of goods that maximizes the greatest good (the social welfare function) (Weimer & Vining, 2011). Assuming that individuals have identical utility functions, assigning higher utilities (see below for classic definition) to higher levels of, for example, wealth and assigning smaller increments of utility to successive increments of wealth (i.e., they exhibit positive but declining marginal utility of wealth), then the allocation of wealth that maximizes social welfare is exactly equal shares of wealth for each person. Since individuals have different utility functions about wealth as well as many if not most other things they value, Table 2.1 shows how alternative social welfare functions, namely *utilitarian, Rawlsian,* and *multiplicative,* would lead to adoption of different policies.

Table 2.1 Policies Associated With Alternative Social Welfare Functions

	Individual Utilities From Alternative Policies			Alternative Social Welfare Functions		
	Person 1 U1	Person 2 U2	Person 3 U3	Utilitarian U1 + U2 + U3	Rawlsian Minimum (U1, U2, U3)	Multiplicative (U1 * U2 * U3)/1,000
Policy A	80	80	40	200	40	256
Policy B	70	70	50	190	50	245
Policy C	100	80	30	210	30	240
Choose Policy:				C	B	A

Source: Weimer, D.L., & Vining, A.R. Policy Analysis: Concepts and Practice, 5th Edition, © 2011, pp. 134, 177, 294. Reprinted by permission of Pearson Education, Inc., Upper Saddle River, NJ.

Developed by Jeremy Bentham (1781) in the late eighteenth century and John Stuart Mill (1863) in the mid nineteenth century, *utilitarianism* is the social welfare function that became one of the most commonly used frameworks of thought for policy making by the late twentieth century (Hodder, 1892; Sen, 1972). As classically defined, the principle of utility was "that principle which approves or disapproves of every action whatsoever, according to the tendency which it appears to have to augment or diminish the happiness of the party whose interest is in question: or, what is the same thing in other words, to promote or to oppose that happiness" (as cited in Nussbaum, 2004, p. 62). The term *utility* designated a property in any object "whereby it tends to produce benefit, advantage, good, or happiness, (all this in the present case comes to the same thing) or (what comes again as the same thing) to prevent the happening of mischief, pain, evil, or unhappiness to the party whose interest is considered" (as cited in Nussbaum, 2004, p. 62). Modern adherents such as the 1994 Nobel laureate in economics, John Harsanyi (1977), argue for a utilitarian-based rule of maximizing the expected utility of all individuals. *Utilitarianism* is consequentialist—that is, actions are to be evaluated in terms of the preferences of individuals for various consequences that can be aggregated (Weimer & Vining, 2011). Described at times as "the greatest good for the greatest number," the table above illustrates that *utilitarianism* can be understood as "the greatest good," signified by selection of Policy C, which produces 210 utilities, rather than Policy A or Policy B, which produce 200 and 190, respectively.

Mill had argued that utilitarianism was egalitarian in spirit, in the sense that declining marginal utility with respect to wealth, as well as class-related institutional strictures and customs, justified some level of redistribution from rich to poor persons—for example, to promote universal public education (Jensen, 2001). Shortcomings of utilitarianism are that it offers weak protection for fundamental human rights, since it does not guarantee minimal allocations to individuals and it fails to account for comparisons of levels of welfare prior to comparisons of marginal utilities (Sen, 1972; Weimer & Vining, 2011).

Rawlsianism is a highly equalizing social welfare function (see Table 2.1). The moral and political philosopher John Rawls (1971, 1985) posited two principles of justice, which if carried out would enable redistribution of goods that would be construed as fair. These principles were as follows:

1. Each person has an equal right to a fully adequate scheme of equal basic rights and liberties, which scheme is compatible with a similar scheme for all.
2. Social and economic inequalities are satisfied on two conditions: first, they must be attached to offices and positions open to all under conditions of fair equality of opportunity [meritocracy]; and second, *they must be to the greatest benefit of the least advantaged members of society* [The **Difference Principle** or maximin] (Rawls, 1985, p. 227, italics added).

To obtain agreement with the maximin or Difference Principle, Rawls constructed a thought experiment placing participants in a situation in which they were ignorant of any particulars about themselves (who they were, what their capabilities and talents were, what values they had, their sex, ethnicity, race, or class, etc.—the veil of ignorance) but knowledgeable about human affairs in general (e.g., that talent, race, sex, ethnicity, health, class, etc., contribute to well-being, that people and countries go to war with one another, that people have capacities for greed and hate as well as for altruism and love, etc.).

Rawls charged the participants in this thought experiment to decide on a system of social arrangements without knowing what their own endowments would be in such a society. Ignorance of one's endowments was necessary to ensure that participants would be more likely to think about the overall distribution of opportunities and outcomes. Rawls contended that participants would unanimously exhibit risk aversion and select a social welfare function that raises the position of the least advantaged, leading to greater equality of outcomes. Changes to the initial and subsequent distribution of goods that failed to improve the position of the least advantaged provided grounds for government intervention to rectify such circumstances accordingly. In the table above, Policy B, which produces 50 utilities, would be the policy of choice rather than Policy A or Policy C, which produce 40 and 30, respectively (Weimer & Vining, 2011).

Since his seminal work in 1971 Rawls has been criticized for reducing incentives to create wealth and assuming that those in the original position are overly risk averse or too consensual (Weimer & Vining, 2011). Three decades later, he addressed many of the related philosophical and moral issues (Rawls, 2001). For our purposes, it is worth highlighting some of the empirical research on how subjects respond when placed in a veil-of-ignorance type of setting, given the contested applicability of the Difference Principle to policy formation (Gutiérrez, 2005) and program evaluation (Schweigert, 2007).

Researchers have carried out a number of experiments to address questions related to the original position and the veil of ignorance. In one set of experiments Michelbach, Scott, Matland, and Bornstein (2003) reported that nearly one-fifth (18%) of study participants preferred the Rawlsian maximin allocation principle vis-à-vis others who more clearly preferred a strict egalitarian allocation (13%), moderate egalitarian (15%), mixed equality-efficiency maximizer (22%), moderate equality-efficiency maximizer (18%), and strict equality-efficiency maximizer (14%). Most subjects across studies seem to prefer an allocation that maximizes average utility with some kind of floor constraint, although such findings need to be interpreted cautiously given sensitivity to how redistributive issues are framed and whether changes are seen as gains or losses (Bukszar & Knetsch, 1997; Fronlich, Oppenheimer, & Eavey, 1987; Grout, 1978). Nonetheless, such findings are consistent with the *multiplicative social welfare function* shown in Table 2.1, as it avoids allocations with very low levels of utility to any individuals: Policy A, which produces 256 utilities, would be the policy of choice since it results in the greatest overall utility of the three policy alternatives, but the outcomes of Policy B and Policy C, which produce 245 and 240, respectively, are fairly close to it (Weimer & Vining, 2011).

Having a universally accepted social welfare function would invariably reduce the complexity of the task that policy analysts face in ranking policy alternatives. The necessity of making trade-offs among incommensurable values in effect would be eliminated. Analysts would design policy alternatives and predict their consequences. The social welfare function would mechanically rank the alternatives, thereby relieving the policy analyst from carrying a normative burden. As noted above, the empirical evidence suggests that there is no clear-cut preference for which social welfare function alternative policy makers should adopt, although the *multiplicative* seems most consistent with findings to date. Given the subjective nature of the economic concept of utilities, questions of measurement abound: specificity and validity in particular (Scitovsky, 1951; Sen, 1988). Conceptual validity and accuracy of measurement also need to be taken into account when considering the appropriateness of dimensions of social welfare, other than aggregate income or wealth, such as infant mortality, crime rates, adult life expectancy, educational achievement, and number of smog-free days per year. Regardless of the social welfare indicator, predicting impacts of specific policies on millions of individuals who make up society is inherently problematic, with limitations in information and cognition hindering the practical use of any of the three alternative social welfare functions discussed above as an allocation mechanism (Weimer & Vining, 2011). Finally, for purposes here, as Schweigert (2007) and Nathanson (1998) note, such mechanical schemes are silent about adequately meeting human needs—that is, about identifying a basic floor of consumption below which individuals and families have just claim on society for a downward redistribution of goods.

Human Dignity: Equality of Opportunity and Floors of Consumption

Viewing market failure as a necessary condition for government intervention implies that Pareto efficiency is the only appropriate social value. There are other substantive values, discussed in Chapter 4, to justify government intervention in the economy and society and to inform decision making about adopting alternative policy options. For our purposes here, however, the focus is to provide intellectual clarity on inherent tensions and possible trade-offs when deciding whether government intervention is appropriate when seeking equality of opportunity, providing a floor on consumption below which individuals and families should not fall, and/or increasing equality of outcomes. An operating premise is that individuals have intrinsic value derived from the fact that they are human beings, rather than from any measurable contribution they can make to society. A corollary of this premise is that one's dignity requires him or her to respect the dignity of others (Weimer & Vining, 2011).

Where one goes from here is less clear, given that what constitutes dignity is contested, as well as whether dignity is constitutive of individuals as individuals or as members of groups. In many Western liberal societies, the idea of a good society is one that must have mechanisms for limiting the extent to which any person's choices interfere with the choices of others and that facilitate broad participation in the institutions determining the allocation of private and public goods (Weimer & Vining, 2011). In such societies, the universally abstract idea of human dignity is concretely linked to nonsectarian constitutionally guaranteed *individual rights* as a constituent component of citizenship. In more collectively or communally oriented or governed societies, whether secular or theocratic, individual rights to the extent they are constitutionally acknowledged or embedded would take second place to whatever group is or groups are privileged accordingly. Canada is illustrative: its constitution provides both individual and collective rights not only to First Nation peoples, but also its English- and French-speaking citizens—for example the right of Francophones and Anglophones who are a minority population of sufficient size in any province to attend publicly funded schools that serve their language community. On the other hand, a Francophone living in a predominantly French-speaking city such as Montreal would have no individual or collective right to attend a publicly funded Anglophone school, even though French and English are official languages (Sanders, 1991; Van Dyke, 1980).

In most societies, however, people seem to take it upon themselves to mitigate drastic consequences of extreme allocations of goods—that is, those that threaten survival—through voluntary contributions to charities and individuals. The concern that charity is insufficient to reach vulnerable populations—that is, those who cannot compete in the market—is a widely accepted rationale for public assistance. To the extent that individuals require some minimal endowment of assets to be viable participants in market exchanges, public policies intended to provide remedial education, job training, and physical rehabilitation may be readily justified and socially acceptable. Transfers to ensure floors on consumption is one way of preserving human dignity, although once everyone reaches some minimal level of consumption, preservation of human dignity need not necessarily require further redistribution of goods to increase equality. Further, participation in decisions over the provision and allocation of public goods also warrants consideration as an appropriate value to assess the merits of public policies. Support for adult universal suffrage, for example, recognizes the inherent value of people having some say over the sort of society in which they will live, regardless of whether or not it produces greater efficiencies in the provision of public goods (Weimer & Vining, 2011).

In the United States, equality of opportunity invariably trumps equality of outcomes or results as a policy objective. Nonetheless, equality of outcomes had been assured in 1965 when the official *poverty line* was first determined. Based on how much income families must have to consume a set of basic goods that were considered necessary for survival at the time, the official *poverty line* signified a collective assessment of what constitutes *dignified* survival. This *absolute measure of poverty* was used as the basis of determining eligibility for and as a measure of success of government programs. In 1996, however, the federal government abandoned its commitment to make funds available to low-income individuals and families with young children who were deemed eligible for public assistance by the states, thereby pulling the rug from under the idea that federally funded public policies would ensure some minimum level of consumption to all members of society (Caputo, 2011). The Rawlsian social welfare function would lead to greater equality of outcomes and could form the basis for redistribution of goods or resources—for example, a tax policy that achieved vertical equity. In that case, those with greater wealth would pay higher taxes so everyone would give up the same amount of utility, since wealthy individuals gain less additional happiness from additional units of wealth (Duclos, 2006;Weimer & Vining, 2011). At some point, redistribution entails costs, such as the prospect of less overall wealth, which in turn might erode the amount or levels of resources that could be redistributed—though to what extent is contested (Haveman, 1988; Hughes, 1990). The policy analyst needs to consider what if any equality-efficiency trade-offs might accompany a given level of redistribution, to inquire about how those at the bottom of the economic ladder fare, and to assess how much inequality might nonetheless increase (Ballard, 1988; Browning & Johnson, 1984; Bryan & Martinez, 2008; Weimer & Vining, 2011).

Skill Building Exercises

1. In light of economists' ways of thinking about the role of the market vis-à-vis government when addressing policy-relevant resource allocation or distributional issues, discuss what is meant by each of the following types of market failures.

   a. Microeconomic concepts:
      1. Public goods
      2. Externalities
      3. Natural monopolies
      4. Information asymmetry
   b. Macroeconomic concepts:
      1. Business cycles
      2. Unemployment
      3. Inflation

2. Discuss what distinguishes fiscal from monetary policy.

   a. What types of social problems are likely to be addressed by each?
   b. What types of policy interventions are likely to flow from each?

3. Discuss how adoption of principles or evaluative criteria associated with each of the following frameworks is likely to affect adoption of alternative policies.

  a. Pareto efficiency.
  b. Social welfare functions.
     1. Utilitarian
     2. Rawlsian
     3. Multiplicative

CHAPTER 3

Approaches to Policy Analysis

This chapter examines differing views about the appropriate role of the policy analyst based on several conceptual formulations and empirical studies. It provides a typology of roles, classified as objective technician, client's advocate, and issue advocate, distinguishable by three fundamental values: analytical integrity, responsibility to clients, and adherence to one's conception of Good. This chapter also examines advocacy and ethics as integral components of social work practice and the problems policy analysis poses to the profession. Particular attention is paid to merits and limitations of Spector and Kituse's (1987) formulation of social problems as a function of claims-making activity.

A major argument of the chapter is that when determining what is to be done, failure to assess and obtain agreement about the nature and extent of a social problem makes it difficult if not impossible to determine if social justice goals are being met or thwarted by policy actions. As a corollary, this would be so regardless of how contested related measures and values might be.

The chapter also discusses criteria about deciding the appropriate type of analysis that a given situation calls for, contrasting what is needed and what is desirable to be done. It raises questions such as the extent to which any given analysis should aim at root causes or seek pragmatic adjustments; be comprehensive or seek short-term relevance; rely on consensual or confrontational procedures; and/or be subject to rational assessment or democratic processes. This chapter also presents the initial formulation of the foci of policy analysis, viewing policy as product (the subject of Chapters 4 through 7), process (the subject of Chapters 8 and 9), and performance (the subjects of Chapters 10 and 11). As will be seen throughout the remainder of the book, each focus of policy analysis involves establishing *priorities* and coming to terms with social values.

Upon successful completion of the skill building exercises of Chapter 3, students will have mastered the following CSWE Competencies and Practice Behaviors:

Chapter 3	Council on Social Work Education Core Competencies
#	**Description**
2.1.1	**Identify as a Professional Social Worker and Conduct Oneself Accordingly**
	Practice personal reflection and self-correction to assure continual professional development
	Attend to professional roles and boundaries

(Continued)

Chapter 3	(Continued)
#	**Description**
2.1.2	**Apply Social Work Ethical Principles to Guide Professional Practice**
	Make ethical decisions by applying standards of the NASW Code of Ethics
	Tolerate ambiguity in resolving ethical conflicts
2.1.3	**Apply Critical Thinking to Inform and Communicate Professional Judgements**
	Demonstrate effective oral and written communication in working with individuals, families, groups, organizations, communities, and colleagues

Source: Adapted from Council on Social Work Education (2012). *Educational policy and accreditation standards.* Washington, DC: Author. Retrieved from http://www.cswe.org/file.aspx?id=13780

VIEWS OF THE APPROPRIATE ROLE OF THE POLICY ANALYST

While discussing the role of intellectuals in society, Merton (1968) identifies two types: those who exercise advisory and technical functions within a bureaucracy and those who are not attached to a bureaucracy. Whereas for the latter the clientele is the public, for the bureaucratic intellectual the policymakers in the organization comprise the clientele. Merton formulates the occupational code of these technicians as: "the policy maker supplies the goals (ends, objectives) and we technicians, on the basis of expert knowledge, indicate alternative means for reaching those ends" (p. 267). He suggests, however, that the sharp distinction between means and ends that the code embodied makes it difficult for the technical or policy experts to recognize the technician's flight from social responsibility—that is, policy experts would be more likely to regard an end or goal as the end point of action rather than an occasion for further consequences. Merton makes two other comments about the role of experts in bureaucracies that are relevant here. One is that indeterminacy of appraising achievement in human affairs increases the need for policymakers to rely on the judgment of experts to recruit new expert personnel, thereby increasing the likelihood of likeminded and self-contained cliques of advisors. The second is that whereas policy experts are experts in highly specialized areas or more "picayune affairs," policymakers often view themselves as having considerable knowledge about larger issues by virtue of their years of related firsthand experience. Hence, given these two observations, Merton suggests that the advice of expert policy analysts and advisors may be less relevant to, if not largely ignored by, policymakers.

Smith (1991, pp. 225–226) classifies contemporary policy experts into a rough typology of individuals distinguished by the institutions in which they work, the career paths they have followed, and the nature of the mark they seek to make on public policy. The first are the "scholar-statesmen" experts, those who have held prominent public positions in the federal government, such as on the Council of Economic Advisors. Second are those "policy specialists" who have had long-standing research commitments within a given area of policy and can be found in university-based research centers, well-established policy institutions, and governmental research agencies. Third are those "policy consultants" who work on short-term contracts and on problems defined by a client and in that capacity would generate data, evaluate programs, and monitor social experiments—senior policy analysts at RAND and the Urban

Institute would be examples. Fourth are those "government experts" who are members of the bureaucracy and whose academic training and expertise are made available through such operations as the Congressional Research Service (CRS), the Congressional Budget Office (CBO), congressional committee staff, analytic units in cabinet departments, and independent agencies. Fifth are the "instant experts," "media professors," "quote doctors," "talking heads," or "policy interpreters" who appear on broadcast news programs, interview shows, in op-ed pieces, and the like. Finally are the "policy entrepreneurs" who build institutions, mobilizing resources for a particular proposal, creating coalitions among diverse groups of researchers and activists, fostering the careers of able and committed aspirants to membership in the policy elite, and starting journals or other publishing enterprises.

Other conceptually-based typologies of policy experts were also developed, including the pioneering work of Meltsner (1976), who conceptualized three roles policy analysts play in the policy-making process: technician, politician, and entrepreneur. Jenkins-Smith (1982) and Dye (1992) constructed similar dichotomies: objective technicians versus political actors and policy analysis versus policy advocacy, respectively. Several "postpositivist" scholars suggested an alternative participatory or facilitative role for policy analysts. Kelly and Maynard-Moody (1993) defined the policy analyst as a facilitator of rational deliberations. Jennings's (1987) tripartite classification of policy analysts' roles included policy analysis as science (conducted by analysts and researchers who embrace positivism, objectivity, and value neutrality), policy analysis as advocacy (conducted by those who reject objectivity and value neutrality and define their roles as lawyers in an adversarial policy-making process), and analysts as counsel (participant observers who help interpret political and social reality in the service of change). Togerson (1986) formulated a similar tripartite construction but characterized the participant observer facilitative analyst in a non-antagonistic role.

An empirically based study of 38 analysts and researchers in three states (Durning & Osuna, 1994) that applied Q methodology, a research method used to study people's "subjectivity" (Brown, 2013; also see www.qmethod.org/about) on definitions and descriptions of ideal types of policy analysts' roles and values gleaned from prior literature identified five types of policy analysts: objective technician, client counselor, issue activist, ambivalent issue activist, and client helper. *Objective technicians* scored highest of descriptors indicating that they were not inclined to be actively involved in the policymaking process and preferred to remain uninvolved in internal agency disputes. Objective technicians also indicated they had a responsibility to help formulate political strategies for their recommended policies. Of the five types, objective technicians reported the most concern with analytic integrity rather than the outcomes of policies they analyze or the responsibility to their clients. Objective technicians strongly agreed that they had a responsibility to enable policymakers to look in different ways at the nature of the social problems they have to address and that they contribute to social betterment on the whole by providing unbiased information to decision makers.

Client counselors shared many of the characteristics of the objective technicians, such as providing objective advice, concern for analytic integrity, and enabling policymakers to look in different ways at the nature of the social problems they have to address, but they were more inclined to view themselves as agents of their clients. Although client counselors concurred that their success depended on producing analyses that reflect their clients' interests, they placed limits on how far they were willing to go to help clients get the policies they wanted or favored. They were less enthusiastic than Jenkins-Smith's client advocates and were more inclined to produce "objective" advice than advice that favored their clients' interests. Unlike objective technicians, however, client counselors saw politics and producing policy arguments, at times in an adversarial manner, as part of their job.

Issue advocates strongly rejected value neutrality and disagreed with the idea that value decisions were best left to policymakers. Personal involvement in the political aspects of policy making was deemed appropriate. Of the five types of policy analysts and researchers Durning and Osuna (1994) identified, *issue advocates* expressed the most interest in outcomes of issues that concerned them, with policy analysis as a means not an end. They also sought to steer policy in specific directions they thought were best for society as a whole, and they viewed themselves as advocates for ideas and causes in which they strongly believed. Issue advocates nonetheless rejected shading their analyses to preferred outcomes, although not as strongly as either objective technicians or client counselors. Further, they disagreed that they were more concerned with outcomes than with analytic integrity and responsibility to their clients.

As the label implies, *ambivalent issue advocates* pulled in two directions, one that analysts should provide objective advice and the other that they should act on their own strong opinions about issues. They favored promoting issues and showed a willingness to go further than issue advocates in adapting their analyses to support their preferred outcomes. Finally, *client helpers* scored high on assisting clients (as did client counselors) but leaned more toward activists or advocates (as did issue advocates). Clients were weakly viewed as necessary evils, although client helpers strongly agreed that their future lay in protecting their client's future and that their legitimacy derived from their clients. Client helpers viewed themselves as strategists, providing the best possible case for a client's preferred policy, including ammunition when there were competing policies.

In a study of positivist beliefs among 233 policy professionals (a 15% response rate from 1,509 persons surveyed), Morçöl (2001) relied on Jennings's (1987) and Torgerson's (1986) classifications and had respondents self-select among three roles: problem solver (27.0%), power broker/policy advocate or mediator (13.1%), and facilitator (40.9%). Following Weimer and Vining (1999), Morçöl's study sample included "policy analysts," "policy researchers," and "academic social science researchers" obtained from the *APPAM Membership Directory* (Association for Public Policy and Management, 1996), *Policy Studies Personnel Directory* (Nagel & Quant, 1996), and websites listed in the *Think Tank Directory* (Hellebust, 1996). In addition to respondents' perceptions of the analyst's role in the policy-making process, the other epistemological and methodological assumptions of positivism (see Chapter 1) included in the survey were multi-item 5-point Likert scale measures of objectivism, fact–value dichotomy, rational analysis, politics distinction, and quantification. Although only bivariate analyses (procedures examining relationships between only two variables or measures) were reported, results indicated that positivist beliefs were the strongest overall among all respondents, with fewer than half (47.2%) reporting that truth was a matter of opinion and fewer than one-quarter reporting that there was no such thing as value-free analysis (22.2%) and that analysis is inherently political (19.7%). Differences in positivist beliefs were found to vary by role of policy analysts. Positivist beliefs were stronger among problem solvers and facilitators than among mediator/advocates on most measures. The most notable exception was agreement about whether policy analysts/planners should not allow their own values to bias their analyses and results, with over four-fifths (84.5%) of problem solvers agreeing, and about one-half of facilitators (49.3%) and mediator/advocates (56.3%) agreeing to it.

On the whole, Morçöl (2001) concluded that while not monolithic, there was a considerable degree of support for positivist positions among policy professionals, thereby supporting Torgerson (1986), Ascher (1987), and Fischer (1995), who had argued that the field of policy analysis had been under the influence of positivism, and failing to support Lynn (1999) and Weimer (1999), who contended that positivism was no longer an issue. Nonetheless, Morçöl noted that the postpositive influence was also present in the results. Like positivists, postpositivists assume that reality exists independently of our thinking about it, yet they deny that reality is knowable with certainty, recognizing that observation is fallible and contains error and that all theory is revisable. Although policy professionals were more positivist in their abstract beliefs (objectivism, fact-value distinction), they were more postpositive about their tangible experiences (rational analysis—politics distinction, qualitative or interpretive—quantification analysis, law-like or universal—probabilistic or contextual), confirming Durning (1999), who noted that in their actual work policy analysts were more postpositive but in their beliefs they were more positivist.

A TYPOLOGY OF ROLES

In a more recent formulation of policy analysts' roles, Weimer and Vining (2011, pp. 40–43), acknowledging their indebtedness to Jenkins-Smith (1982), provide three perspectives on the appropriate role of the policy analyst that can serve our purposes: objective technician, client's advocate, and issue advocate. Each of the three roles (as noted below) are characterized by three fundamental values: analytical integrity, responsibility to clients, and adherence to one's conception of good.

Objective Technician

Analytic integrity is the fundamental value of *objective technicians.* Their analytic skills and related tools drawn from disciplines with well-established methodologies such as economics, statistics, and operations research are the main source of legitimacy. Objective technicians view their main task as providing objective advice about the most likely consequences of proposed policies. Clients are "necessary evils," providing resources enabling analysts to work on interesting questions, yet having political fortunes that technicians prefer would remain a secondary consideration for purposes of policy analysis. Objective technicians maintain some distance from their clients, whose political fortunes take second place behind preparation, communication, and uses of analyses. Institutional clients such as a legislative body or standing committee are more likely to be preferred to individual clients such as a member of Congress or state assembly, in part because they provide greater opportunities for preparing and disseminating objective analyses and in part because the pressures associated with reelection every two or four or six years are minimized. Methodological rigor is important, with the hope that researchers in their respective disciplines would approve their work accordingly, given the circumstances in which it is carried out. Objective technicians identify relevant values. Trade-offs among conflicting values, however, are left to clients. In the long run, objective technicians see themselves as contributing to the good of society by consistently providing unbiased advice, even when clients select less personally favored options.

Client's Advocate

Client's advocates place primary emphasis on responsibility to the client and see themselves as deriving their legitimacy as participants in the formation of public policy from clients who hold elected or appointed office or who represent organized political interests. In return for access, client's advocates adhere to the medical ethos of "do no harm" to clients and to lawyers' ethos of vigorously promoting clients' interests. Analytical integrity remains important in much the same way as attorneys view their responsibility in an adversarial system. They do not mislead clients with false statements or omissions of relevant information. Having fully informed clients, such advocates have little or no qualms about interpreting their analyses in the best possible light for their clients. Given that analysis rarely produces definitive conclusions, client's advocates proffer possible rather than most likely consequences of adopting a policy when doing so favors their clients. Analytic integrity, however, prohibits lying, but requires neither full disclosure of information nor public correction of misstatements by clients.

Given that client's advocates relegate their policy preferences to a secondary position once they make commitments to clients, the choice of client matters greatly. Overlapping worldviews mitigate the potential of situations requiring analysts to promote policies that are inconsistent with their own conception of the good. When worldviews are disparate, client's advocates may continue in such relationships for extended periods of time, with the hope of changing their clients' beliefs before switching to new clients.

Issue Advocate

For *issue advocates,* analyses are important for making progress toward their conception of the good society. When conducting analyses, they focus on values inherent in policy outcomes, whether actual or projected, rather than on values such as analytical integrity and responsibility to the client. Issue advocates see themselves as intrinsic players in the policy process, perhaps even as champions of groups or interests such as poor persons, minorities, women, children, and others they believe suffer from underrepresentation in the political process and/or exploitation by economic, legal, or other systems or processes. Issue advocates select clients opportunistically, preferring those willing to promote their personal policy agendas. Loyalty to one's conception of the good trumps that to any particular client. As with client's advocates, issue advocates have little or no qualms about taking advantage of analytical uncertainty. Faced with results that fail to support their policy preferences, issues advocates question simplifying assumptions that inevitably accompany complex issues and, challenge the choice of criteria used to evaluate alternatives. They feel no necessity to point out such analytic shortcomings when findings support or corroborate their policy preferences—that burden falls on opponents. Further, although respect of other analysts is important, issue advocates may be more willing than either objective advocates or client's advocates to sacrifice respect to obtain important outcomes.

ADVOCACY, ETHICS, AND POLICY ANALYSIS

Advocacy and ethics are integral components of social work practice. As the previously discussed typology of roles for policy analysis suggests, the relationship of advocacy and ethics to policy analysis can be problematic. The profession of social work has had long-standing discussions about the relationship between advocacy and practice, given the professional mandate to pursue social justice (National Association of Social Workers, 2011). Levy (1974), for example, acknowledges conceptual confusion resulting from the profession's "borrowing" the concept of advocacy from law and he identifies three types of advocacy that fall well within the parameters of social work practice: justice, distributive justice, and corrective justice. Gilbert and Specht (1976) highlight how the profession grappled with concerns about advocacy in the pursuit of social change, a long-term goal, trumping professional obligations to individual clients, a short-term goal, especially when client determination is not taken into account. As political tacticians, how ethical are social workers, Gilbert and Specht (p. 290), citing Brager (1968), muse, for whom Machiavelli becomes a cultural icon? Earlier, when discussing advocacy as gamesmanship, Levy (1974) suggested there might be ethical space for such problematic professional behavior: "If anyone interprets advocacy as implying the validation of professionally questionable means to achieve certain preferred ends, he is quite right" (p. 48). Justification for the use of professionally questionable means, Levy continues "is the imperative nature of the ends as they relate to greater justice and equity in the distribution of goods and opportunities and compensation for past injustices and inequities." Social workers as policy analysts who assume the role of *client's advocate* or of *issue advocate* face related means-ends challenges accordingly, particularly given the contested nature of social justice.

Concern about the compatibility of ethics or the role of values and policy analysis also has a notable history, as highlighted in Chapter 1 and Appendix B. Amy (1984) contended that professional, political, and institutional factors provide plausible explanations as to why ethics and values might more often than not be shunned when it comes to policy analysis. Basically, too many interests are threatened by ethical analysis. Take the analyst-client relationship, for example. To the extent a prospective analysis might raise questions about the merits of a program or policy, strongly committed administrators to and policymakers of those programs are challenged or threatened accordingly. To the extent that taking ethics into account blurs intellectual or analytic distinctions between professional impartiality and value-laden practices, the very foundations of professional practice might be undermined, thereby threatening the profession's integrity as a whole.

Case in Point 3.1: Promoting Health

Obesity has been identified as a major health problem in the United States, prompting New York Mayor Michael Bloomberg, the Obama administration, public health officials, and others to advocate for measures including a tax on soft drinks or limiting the size of soft drinks that can be sold as part of a health promotion campaign (Urist, 2012). It might seem obvious that identifying health-risk behaviors as part of health promotion is a good idea, even if policies such as taxing soft drinks or limiting the size of soft drinks sold might not be the best way to do so. Massé and Williams-Jones (2012), however, raise ethical dilemmas about which advocates of health promotion should be aware: What if the goal of promoting the public good infringes on the civil rights or shared values of minority cultural communities? How far should efforts go in presenting positive health information campaigns to protect the public health without unduly stigmatizing people or making them feel guilty for noncompliance? Are there conflicts between the goals and practices of health promotion and fundamental social (and social work) values of autonomy (self-determination) or social justice? What are the consequences of the social construction of health as an ultimate social good? These questions highlight the importance of thinking through the objectives and consequences of advocacy efforts and assessing the relative merits of benefits gained and potential losses from adverse consequences.

With some caveats and under certain conditions, Weiss (1991) shows how a balance between policy research and advocacy can be found without loss of professional integrity on the part of the analyst. Provided related research is not distorted and data are available to all sides in a debate, Weiss contends that it is appropriate for partisan policy analysts and others to use research on their behalf and that the give-and-take of multiple interpretations of evidence can aid in the development of consensual policies. Weiss is aware of the uneven distribution of skills and resources for using research and calls for measures to level the playing field. Multiple analytic arguments lose luster in that some interests and values are underrepresented, lending support for the development and training of activist or advocacy women and minority scholars (Garza, 1999). Measures to level the playing field include creation of new policy research centers to represent poorly served groups and of agencies, such as the Congressional Budget Office (CBO), that extensively check and recheck data accuracy and logic of interpretation.

FORMULATION OF POLICY
AGENDAS AND ALTERNATIVES: WHAT SHOULD BE DONE?

The source of ideas for what should be done, whether to address a new problem or issue or an existing problem or issue in a better way than is currently the case, originate in diverse quarters, ranging from journalistic or media exposés and reports, public forums attended by politicians, discussions of problems reflecting interest groups and lobbyists, and pet causes of elected officials. What constitutes a problem or issue that government should address and how that problem or issue gets on the public agenda for formal legislative deliberation and actual policy making are questions that policy analysts address.

In their classic constructivist formulation, Spector and Kituse (1987) view social problems as a function of claims-making activity, defining social problems as "*the activities of individuals or groups making assertions of grievances and claims with respect to some putative conditions*" (p. 75, italics in original). For social workers as policy analysts, Spector and Kituse's formulation on one hand has merit in elevating the importance of politics and values involved in problem formation—since the framing of the problem or issue provides the grounds or justification (not explanation) and shapes the content of the legislation that gets debated and eventually adopted or rejected. Lens (2000), for example, shows how the media helped frame welfare reform debates in 1988 and again in 1996 in terms of individual responsibility, while downplaying social or structural factors that contributed to the plight of low-income single mothers with young children.

On the other hand, Spector and Kituse's contention (1987, p. 78) that the factual basis of assertions should fall outside the scope of sociological inquiry is problematic for social workers in general and as policy analysts in particular given the professional mandate to pursue social justice on behalf of vulnerable populations or groups of people. Although definitions of and claims about what constitutes social justice vary (Caputo, 2000; Reisch, 2002; Sterba, 1999) and are subject to challenge (Sterba, 2001), if nothing else social justice is a matter of better outcomes, as Bannon (1980) has observed and as Meenaghan, Kilty, and McNutt (2004, p. 17) have reaffirmed. Critical questions center on defining those better outcomes in relation to where things currently stand. If we have no understanding of where things currently stand, how would we know if, to what extent, or in what manner conditions improved or worsened either because of or in spite of our policy-related efforts? Failure to assess and obtain agreement about the nature and extent of a social problem, however contested related measures and values might be, makes it impossible to determine if social justice goals are being met or thwarted by policy actions. Spector and Kituse's contention also seems odd in light of calls for value relevancy social science research by sociologists and others over the past several decades (Buraway, 2005; Gray, 1983; Harberger, 1993; Wilson, 2002). Getting beneath the asserted claims of assorted stakeholders and assessing the actual social conditions before, during, and after implementation of social policies go hand in hand with the credibility and relevancy of policy analysts' work.

Structuring problems nonetheless remains an important activity undertaken by policy analysts. Problem structuring refers to that phase of policy inquiry in which analysts search among competing formulations of different stakeholders with the aim of *correctly* identifying and characterizing the problem that needs to be addressed. Methods of problem structuring at the disposal of policy analysts include classification analysis (clarify concepts), hierarchy analysis (identify possible, plausible, and actionable causes), brainstorming (generating ideas, goals, and strategies), multiple perspective analysis (generating insight), assumption analysis (synthesizing conflicting assumptions), and argumentation mapping (assessing plausibility and importance of assumptions) (Dunn, 2008, pp. 95–115).

In addition to structuring policy problems, the question "What should be done?" raises several larger questions that analysts address. Such questions include "Who gets what?" "What type of provision or benefit is suited to address the problem or issue?" "To whose benefit?" "By whom?" "At what cost?" "How financed?" There are a host of related subsidiary concerns and questions such as "With what expected results?"—assessments of which are addressed in Chapters 6 and 10. "Who gets what?" prompts a series of related questions such as "What constitutes need, vulnerability, and oppression?" "Who are needy persons?" "How is risk determined?" and "What constitutes a population at risk?" In turn, they necessitate decisions about such concerns as the appropriateness of cash, of direct services, of in-kind services, and of vouchers, while assessing the merits of values associated with each type. "By whom" prompts such questions as "By government?" and if so, "Which level or levels of government—federal, state, local?" "By the private sector?" and if so, "The profit or nonprofit making sector?" "At what cost" prompts "At what level of aggregate direct expenditure or revenue lost through the tax code?" "At what level or range of amounts for individual beneficiaries?" "With what expected results?" raises issues about realistic versus desirable results, and short-term versus long-term results, among others. Ethical, political, and technical dimensions accompany such questions. To get a better handle on addressing these and related questions for purposes of policy analysis, it is helpful, as the social work saying goes, to partialize the problem. Rather than attempting to address such questions at once and risk becoming overwhelmed, it is more helpful, for analytical purposes, to identify specific dimensions of policy and to break up policy analysis into manageable components. For our purposes, relying on Kraft and Furlong (2010) and Gilbert and Terrell (2010), this means briefly discussing appropriate kinds of analyses and the three P's of policy analysis: product, process, and performance.

DECIDING ON AN APPROPRIATE KIND OF ANALYSIS

Policy analysts face important choices about the kind of assessment that is appropriate for a given study and what approaches to use (Kraft & Furlong, 2010). Before embarking on any analysis, it is helpful to distinguish and consider what needs to be done versus what one would wish to do. The following four contrasting pairs of options (root causes vs. pragmatic adjustment, comprehensive analysis vs. short-term relevance, consensual vs. contentious analysis, and rational analysis vs. democratic politics) are worth considering up front with those requesting an analysis of policy. Such discussion increases the likelihood that analysts have a clearer understanding of what is expected of them and thereby can better assess the merits of alternative ways of conducting the policy analysis and the set of methods or tools to use. No pair is meant to be construed as a mutually exclusive "either-or," and if a case can be made for incorporating aspects of both then all the better. Depending on resources at hand, technical capacity, and the like, however, what is needed to be done and what one would wish to do, to the extent they do not overlap, may be mediated by what is practical to do given how the problem that got on the public agenda was formulated.

Before examining the four contrasting pairs of appropriate kinds of policy analysis, a brief discussion of asking fundamental, or radical, questions is warranted. Lindblom (1972) raised this issue when assessing the merits of integrating the social sciences through policy analysis. He contended that policy analysis as then understood and practiced diverted the social sciences from asking fundamental questions about social organization and human behavior that were central to such thinkers as Plato (What is justice?), Hobbes (How can social order be maintained?), Adam Smith (What are the nature and causes of the wealth of nations?), and, more recently, John Rawls (What is social justice?). As can be gleaned from the historical overview in Appendix B, a policy orientation for social science as a whole precluded anyone asking such questions.

Concomitantly, as noted in Appendix B, academic social sciences also shunned such questions as they became increasingly specialized, methodologically focused, and divorced from social problems. Nonetheless, Lindblom (1972) surmised, someone, if not the social sciences or policy analysts, should be asking such questions as what the effect of life in a milieu of exchange relationships is on personality and culture, or how defects in popular control (through the market system) over corporate leadership compare with those of popular control (through political processes) over political leadership, or whether economists' traditional identification of market relationships with voluntary or free relationships is, in fact, valid in societies in which necessity compels people to enter market relationships. Lindblom argued for an enriched policy analysis, one integrated to the extent it refused to respect disciplinary boundaries and remained distinct from the social sciences, bearing a relationship similar to that of medicine and the natural and biological sciences. He left open the question of whether social scientists or policy analysts should be asking fundamental or radical questions such as those posed above. Lindblom seemed to suggest nonetheless that institutional separation and status of the social sciences and policy analysis left some wiggle room to do so with no loss of academic standing for the social sciences and perhaps elevated standing for the policy sciences. Integration would occur by returning to "valuative" questions germane to the social sciences and to policy analysis (MacRae, 1971, 1972). Examples of those taking advantage of the "wiggle room" Lindlbom suggested are Gil (1992), Meehaghan, Kilty, and NcNutt (2004), Pascal (1986), Schram (1995, 2000), and Stone (1997).

Root Causes Versus Pragmatic Adjustment

Lindblom (1959) provided the classic formulation of this issue: rational comprehensive (root) versus successive limited comparisons (branch analysis). An administrator confronted with policy alternatives to control inflation might proceed by taking advantage of any theory available that generalizes about classes of policies—in this instance comparing all policies in light of the theory about prices. All known alternatives would be taken into account, from considerations of strict control and abolition of all prices and markets on one hand and elimination of all public controls with reliance completely on the free market on the other, in light of whatever theoretical generalizations could be gleaned from such hypothetical economies. Finally, the administrator would choose the alternative that maximized the values held most widely. Alternatively, the administrator could establish a principal objective, such as the goal of keeping prices level. Positing such a goal would eliminate other goals—for instance, reaching full employment that might complicate or compromise achieving level prices. The administrator would then identify a narrower set of policy alternatives, most of which might be familiar due to similar past experiences, and compare them, not in light of a body of theories, but instead on the record of past experiences with small policy steps to predict consequences of similar steps extended into the future. Lindblom contended that most administrators "muddle through" (i.e., use the branch method) and that the root method is not workable for complex policy questions. In rejecting the rational comprehensive approach to decision making, Lindblom was consistent with the literature on bounded rationality characteristic of the humanistic turn in administration and organizational theory (Etzioni, 1967; Janis & Mann, 1977; Lindblom, 1990; Simon, 1957, 1976).

Two decades later Lindblom (1979) reaffirmed his preference for what was characterized and criticized as incrementalism, albeit recast as *disjointed incrementalism,* vis-à-vis the pursuit of conventional scientific or theoretically driven policy analysis (Lindblom, 1958). Unlike simple incrementalism characterized by limiting consideration of alternative policies to those only marginally different from the status quo, *disjointed incrementalism* also entails intertwining of analysis of policy goals and other values with empirical aspects of the problem to be addressed, greater analytical preoccupation with ills to be remedied than positive goals to be sought, a sequence of trial and error and revised trials, analyses exploring some but not all important likely consequences of considered alternatives, and fragmentation of analytical work to many partisan participants in the policy-making process. Lindblom contended that **disjointed incrementalism** as a mode of policy analysis that relies on partisan mutual adjustments was an effective way of improving the political nature of the policy-making process, primarily by curbing the power dimension often associated with politics (Schultze, 1968). In partisan mutual adjustment, participants make heavy use of persuasion to influence each other, and their focus is on finding grounds on which their political adversaries or indifferent participants might be converted to allies. To the criticism that outcomes of such a sequential, incremental process as *disjointed incrementalism* are establishment oriented or conservative, Lindblom (1968) argued that rapid successive incremental steps may bring about greater change than more drastic policy moves, which tend to occur less frequently and with greater difficulty (Cain, 1971). Further, as he later argued (Lindblom & Woodhouse, 1993, p. 32), waiting to act in complex situations until one understands the consequences is a prescription for paralysis.

Kraft and Furlong (2010) highlight a related decision about focusing on root causes of a social problem, presumably to eradicate them, or alternatively examining policy actions that address a pressing problem while leaving underlying causes alone. In an ideal setting it may make sense to do both. Some analysts (e.g., Wilson, 1975) argued against examining root causes as the object of policy analysis, primarily because they cannot be changed (Schuck, 1975; Wolfgang, 1975). Wilson's example was crime—to the extent that younger persons commit more crime than older ones or men more than women, both observations of which have withstood scientific scrutiny or the test of time, little could be done in any practical sense or socially acceptable sense to change those "facts." Rather, it would make more sense to think about what can be done to reduce crime rates or deal with proximate or immediate causes of crime. Rather than inquiring about what needs to get done to identify root causes so as to eradicate the social problem, the focus would be on identifying the conditions one wants to produce (such as reduced crime rates), what indicators inform us that the conditions exist, and what policy tools do we have that might, when applied, result in what is desired at a reasonable cost.

Lindblom (1972, also noted by Kraft & Furlong, 2010) long ago acknowledged that an exclusive focus on proximate causes ignores fundamental questions about social and economic structures and thereby enhances tendencies to maintain current policies and practices—or slightly modify then, even if this proves less than successful in addressing a social problem. Rather than dismiss or rule out examining root causes *a priori,* such analyses may be necessary in some circumstances when deciding about the merits of policy alternatives. Such was the case when President George W. Bush (2005) indicated that his administration's energy bill would help address the root causes of high energy prices, primarily by expanding domestic production of energy. Critics countered that the root cause most in need of changing was the nation's appetite for energy, and that intensive programs fostering energy conservation and more efficient use of energy were needed more than an increase in supply. Both sides, as Kraft and Furlong note (2010, p. 115), were correct to go beyond high prices of energy as the issue by addressing root causes. A policy analyst might assess the veracity of each of the claims about root causes, as well as the likely risks associated with each of the policy prescriptions associated with each claim.

A focus on incremental adjustments that ignores or fails to take seriously root causes need not be ruled out or dismissed *a priori* either, if the desired impact is to make a big difference. Changes to laws regulating driving speed limits and the legal age of alcohol consumption both had substantively notable impacts. In the aftermath of legislation denying a percentage of federal highway funds to states that refused to comply with the minimum age drinking requirement, for example, accident rates were reported to have declined by 26 percent for eighteen-year-olds and 19 percent for nineteen- and twenty-year-olds in Wisconsin (Figlio, 1995). The 24 states that raised their speed limits—70 miles per hour, or more, with the exception of Rhode Island, which raised its from 55 to 65, in 1995 and 1996—were found to have about a 15 percent increase in highway fatalities through 1997 compared to fatality counts for the same months in the six years before the speed limits were changed (Insurance Institute for Highway Safety, 1999).

Whether focusing on root or proximate causes of social problems, it should be noted that demonstrating causality and formulating plausible explanatory accounts that can withstand sustained scrutiny is exceptionally difficult. Reading (1977, pp. 82–83) provides a dozen definitions of *explanation,* listed alphabetically from one without any further descriptors—namely explanation as "accounting for a given phenomenon, *system,* generalization, or law" to teleological as "accounting for a given phenomenon by its being a necessary and sufficient condition for a certain state of affairs." Sandwiched between these two alphabetically anchored definitions are constructive ("accounting for a given phenomenon by reference to *constructs, principles,* or generalizations"), deductive-nomological ("accounting for a given phenomenon by deductive subsumption under general *laws*"), folk ("an explanation offered by a *society* or *community* under investigation"), functional ("accounting for a given phenomenon by reference to its *function*"), genetic ("accounting for a later *system* by setting out the sequence of major events through which some earlier system has been transformed into it"), inductive ("accounting for a given phenomenon by inductive subsumption under *statistical laws*"), nomological ("accounting for a given phenomenon by subsuming it under *laws*"), probabilistic ("accounting for a given event or class of events by subsumption under *statistical laws*"), statistical (probabilistic), and structural ("accounting for a given phenomenon in terms of structural relations among units").

It would be an error to assume that an explanatory account of a social problem based on one of these definitions implies that one is as good or has equal standing as any other. As indicated in Chapter 1, social scientists have ways of assessing the merits of types of statements that make truth claims, as well as adjudicating competing truth claims (for extended discussions, see Baert, 2005; Gellner, 1973; Jarvie, 1964).

Comprehensive Analysis Versus Short-term Relevance

Another consideration for the policy analyst entails the merits of using the most comprehensive or rigorous approaches and methodologies to ensure the credibility of results, even when doing so may extend both the time and costs involved in doing the analysis (Kraft & Furlong, 2010). Alternatively, it might be worth aiming for a less comprehensive or rigorous study that provides pertinent results faster and cheaper, although with greater risk of credible results. Much will depend on the nature of the problem under consideration, the context in which the analysis is to be carried out (who wants to know what, by when, under what circumstances), and the level and types of resources available. Invariably, academics are likely to prefer more comprehensive and rigorous studies, placing a high value on methodological precision that can withstand peer-review scrutiny and that can be thereby judged as contributing to a knowledge base. Such studies, however, might take so long to complete that they may have little to no immediate impact or usefulness on decision making about the policy in question than if results, even if more tentative, might have been known earlier. Further, to the extent more comprehensive and rigorous studies are theoretically driven, findings generally have less practical relevance to the extent policymakers have little or no control over factors found or thought to be causing or otherwise contributing to the social problem at hand, especially when theories focus on scientific issues of disciplinary concern (Cowhig, 1971). Theoretically driven comprehensive analyses are further complicated by the loose relationship between theories about what might be wrong, or what causes or contributes to a social problem, and theories about what might be done to put things right, a problem that has long been known in Research & Development literature (MacDonald, 1986).

Policy analysts outside of academia are more likely than their university-based social science and professional school research counterparts to be interested in applied policy research, aiming their efforts primarily at policymakers and other policy actors. Their studies are likely to be accompanied by an "executive summary" designed to enable busy decision makers to get the gist of the study's findings. Executive summaries are typical of advocacy group or think tank studies (e.g., Bloom, Thompson, & Unterman, 2010; Child Advocacy 360 Foundation, 2010; Muro, Rothwell, & Saha, 2011; National Council on Teacher Quality, 2011) and the more comprehensive studies and reports from special commissions and government agencies (e.g., UNAIDS, 2008; U.S. Department of Education, 2009; U.S. Department of Health and Human Services, 2010). Advocacy organizations such as the Children's Defense Fund, the Child Welfare League of America, the National Council of La Raza, and Public Citizen are inherently political, so they are more likely to emphasize short-term policy relevance. It would be unfair to characterize studies that they conduct or sponsor as necessarily invalid. Nonetheless, given the explicit aim of influencing lawmakers, aides, lobbyists, and journalists by advocacy-oriented think tanks (as discussed in Appendix B), such reports emanating from them warrant critical scrutiny to detect any possible bias (Rich, 2000).

Consensual Versus Contentious Analysis

The consideration here is how closely analysts adhere to consensual norms and mainstream public values vis-à-vis challenging them and proposing alternative values or new ways of thinking about the problem under consideration. Rein (1976) contends that a primary though not exclusive function of policy analysis is to "submit goals to critical review rather than merely treating them as given" (p. 72). He suggests three ways of engaging in values-critical research, with increasing degrees of critical inquiry: using consensual or mainstream approaches, using contentious or value-critical approaches, and using paradigm-changing approaches (Kraft & Furlong, 2010). The "value-critical" approach is contrasted with the "value-decisionist" position rooted in classical positivism, which treats values as arbitrary postulates. Rather than assuming that values are wishes and desires, the value-critical approach postulates that values are "grounded in a fundamental structure which is central to real processes" and thereby become "a meaningful subject of debate" (Rein, 1976, p. 72).

Consider, for example, social justice, one of the core values of the social work profession (National Association of Social Workers, 2011). When affirming social justice as a value, taking a value-critical approach necessitates going beyond determining how to reach it or cataloguing the views of those who support, repudiate, or are indifferent to it. Such inquiry requires examining what social justice means, how it is being used, and why it is worthwhile. In addition, the value-critical approach includes examining specific end values such as social justice in relation to other end values such as integrity, dignity of the person, and the like, "by looking at the consequences of pursuing these aims and by considering the latent goal conflicts among them" (Rein, 1976, p. 72).

In his classic formulation of justice as fairness, Rawls (1971) claims that social justice is served when everyone benefits from changes in social institutions that nonetheless produce greater inequality. Is such a formulation of social justice merely an apology for capitalism? In a growing economy, if the well-being of those on the lowest rung of the economic ladder is improved by greater income inequality, say with the top 1 percent of the earning population increasing their share of the total increase in either income or assets by 80 percent, with the middle 2–99 percent increasing their share by 18 percent, and the remaining 1 percent increasing their total share by 2 percent, but nonetheless remaining destitute, would that be considered acceptable or fair? Nathanson (1998) contends not and argues that consideration of the conditions of the worst off need to be taken into account when assessing the merits of increased inequality that invariably accompanies economic growth.

The importance of critique, whether applied to values endemic to policies, approaches to social science methodologies, or to how society in general goes about identifying and addressing a social problem has a formidable history and is readily acknowledged as a crucial component of social work education and practice. The work of Robert and Helen Lynd, C. Wright Mills, New Left scholars during the 1960s and 1970s and others opened the way for a variety of interpretive approaches to the social sciences and to policy analysis, including critical theory, hermeneutics, post-structuralism, feminism, race-critical theory, and the like (Caterino & Schram, 2006) (as discussed in Appendix B). In part echoing but also going beyond Rein (1976), Flyvbjerg (2001, 2004) more recently advanced a program for the social sciences based on the Aristotelian notion of *phronesis,* with the aim of carving out a first step toward greater theoretical and methodological rigor in the practical employment of social science research.

At times referred to as Perestroika in political science circles (Laitin, 2003; Schram, 2003), Flyvbjerg (2001) called for making reflexive analysis and discussion of values and interests aimed at praxis the core of the social sciences, a prerequisite for an enlightened political, economic, and cultural development in any society. The Perestroika "movement," a recent manifestation of long-standing debates within the social sciences about advocacy, impartiality, objectivity, relevancy, and values, rejected emulation of the natural sciences whether in the guise of rational choice theory, formal modeling, or nearly exclusive reliance on quantitative methods and analysis (Bennett, 2002). Calling attention to how the social sciences in general and by extension the policy sciences in particular can matter or contribute to addressing social problems is important, and to the extent that Flyvbjerg and the Perestroikans do so, they are on firm footing, although their apocalyptic rhetoric occludes more than enlightens. As Landman (2011) notes, methods in political science and by extension the social sciences are necessarily linked to substance: the provision of meaningful answers to real-world problems can only be enhanced by continued attention to how research questions are formulated, how adequate theories are about possible relationships and explanations for observed outcomes, how sound the research designs are, the procedures used to gather and present evidence, and how logical inferences are drawn from that evidence. Such concerns are as important for the natural sciences as they are for the social sciences.

Rational Analysis Versus Democratic Politics

As noted in Appendix B, policy studies trained analysts to engage in rational assessment of public problems and their solutions, often relying on economic analysis, operations research, and other quantitative methods to find logical, efficient, and hopefully effective ways to deal with public problems (Kraft & Furlong, 2010). While critical of such methods that elevated *episteme* or *techné* over *phronesis,* some of the Perestroikans, as others had before them (e.g., deLeon, 1997; Gormley, 1987; Jenkins-Smith, 1990), advocated for fostering democratic political processes, such as citizen involvement. Although formal mechanisms for citizenship participation in the policy-making process have been operative at all levels of government for some time (Advisory Commission on Intergovernmental Relations, 1979), there is renewed interest in finding ways to make government more responsive to meeting those most affected by policies and programs. Schram (2003), for example, provided a vision that would "enable people on the bottom working in dialogue with social researchers to challenge power" (p. 838). Shdaimah and Stahl (2006) provide a case example of and reflections about one such study of public policies affecting low-income homeowners in Philadelphia. Fostering democratic political processes invariably oftentimes conflicts with reliance on experts and their technical scientific analysis deemed essential to reach a defensible position on some issues. Rigorous analysis is valued, yet democracy is expected to prevail unless there is some good reason to limit public involvement.

Storage of nuclear and other hazardous waste materials highlights this conflict (Kraft & Furlong, 2010). Over thirty years ago, Duncan (1978) called on sociologists to study public acceptability of nuclear energy. Over twenty years ago Davis (1986) noted that citizens likely to be affected by site selection demanded to be included in related decisions and that many citizens are reluctant to absorb unilaterally the disadvantages associated with site designation or selection, including adverse health effects of unintentional release of hazardous substances into the environment, declines in real estate values, and perceptions of an overall decrease in their quality of life. The NIMBY (not-in-my-backyard) syndrome associated with citizen participation is amply documented (Kraft & Clary, 1991). Given the social phenomenon of NIMBY, how much weight should be given to more analysis of various risks (to health or, in light of events of September 11, 2001, to the possibility of terror attacks on nuclear waste shipment) and better management by the federal, state, and local governments vis-à-vis to the public's fears and concerns? Further, at what point and in what ways should policymakers turn to more democratic political processes for making requisite choices (Kraft & Furlong, 2010)?

Expert opinion versus political calculation played out in the decision by Health and Human Services (HHS) Secretary Kathleen Sebelius (2011) to override the recommendation of Food and Drug Administration Commissioner Margaret Hamburg to allow emergency contraceptives to be sold over the counter. Known as Plan B One-Step, the contraceptive pill delays ovulation and has no effect on established pregnancies. When used within three days after unprotected sex it cuts the chances of pregnancy by half, roughly from 1 in 20 to 1 in 40. The Plan B One-Step pill has been available without prescription to women 17 and over. Commissioner Hamburg (2011) indicated that the drug was safe, with FDA scientists unanimously endorsing the recommendation by the advisory committee appointed to study the matter. After reviewing the FDA summary review, HHS Secretary Sebelius overturned the recommendation, faulting the failure to include 11-year-old girls in related studies and insisting that they be studied as well as adolescents aged 12 through 17. A day later, President Obama (2011b) endorsed Secretary Sebelius's decision to limit Plan B One-Step, citing his concern (as a parent of two daughters) as to whether 12- or 13-year-old girls could use Plan B One-Step properly, even though he acknowledged that the FDA deemed the pill safe (Calmes & Harris, 2011; Harris, 2011).

Questions were invariably raised as to whether the Obama administration, during the presidential election year of 2012, was placating anti-abortion coalitions, especially "the Catholic Church," placing "the politics of birth control" over "science and sound public policy" as a *New York Times* editorial proclaimed ("Politics and the Morning After Pill," 2011); and, as Dr. Phillip Stubblefield of Boston University School of Medicine suggested, about the practicality of obtaining parental consent for 11-year-old girls to participate in a study assessing the consequences of taking such a pill, about the merits of the pill, or the appropriateness of the recommended change in existing policy for purposes of further study, as Secretary Sebelius required (Calmes & Harris, 2011). At what point and under what circumstances would solicitation of additional "facts" and involvement of parents for purposes of consent and of 11-year-old girls be deemed warranted? Even if the science demonstrated the efficacy of the pill, would that trump parental concerns regardless of the politics involved, whether that of Catholic bishops who oppose changing the policy or of scientific and women's rights groups who support the recommended change?

FOCI OF POLICY ANALYSIS

As the foregoing section about kinds of analysis to consider suggests, prior to undertaking any policy analysis, thoughtful deliberation about what to do and how to proceed is necessary. A staple of social work education and practice is learning how to partialize problems into manageable components, so neither the client nor the practitioner feels overwhelmed. Similarly, the policy analyst need not feel compelled to do everything at once, in order to do meaningful work that benefits others. To that end, the primary focus of this book suggests that approaching policy analysis from the vantage points of policy as product, process, and performance (the 3Ps) provides a meaningful and practical way of focusing on relevant tasks at hand to get the job done. Brief descriptions of the 3Ps are presented below. Sections II–IV further subdivide the 3Ps into ways of thinking about them and the requisite sets of skills to conduct policy analyses accordingly. The Epilogue provides a comprehensive framework that integrates the analytic components of the 3Ps presented in Sections II–IV.

Policy as Product

Policy products include tangible documents such as legislation, bills, policy manuals, administrative guidelines, codified rules, regulations, and the like. When examining policy products analysts function at times like journalists, asking who, what, and why types of questions and providing a descriptive summary of the document's contents based on those questions. Analysts go beyond journalistic description, however, by laying out selective criteria used to evaluate the merits of policies in general and showing how well or to what extent the particular policy product under consideration meets these criteria.

Policy as Process

Policy as process encompasses policy making (*ex ante* or "before the fact") and implementation (*ex post* or "after the fact"). In general, process studies are concerned with understanding how relationships and interactions among political, governmental, and interest group collectivities in society affect policy formation and adoption (Gilbert & Terrell, 2010). Such studies examine policy-making processes—that is, how policies are adopted by legislative bodies. Process studies are also concerned with understanding how adopted or proposed policies are or would be carried out. Such studies examine implementation processes.

Policy as Performance

Performance studies are concerned with identification and evaluation of program or policy consequences, effects, or outcomes (Gilbert & Terrell, 2010). Performance is usually assessed through collection of qualitative and quantitative data and by application of a wide range of methodological tools from the academic disciplines. Research methodology as taught in the academic disciplines and professional schools provides the major technical and theoretical knowledge and requisite skills for undertaking performance-based studies. Fact determination is only one aspect of performance studies, which, as with any evaluation study, have evaluative aspects. Evaluations provide reliable and valid information about policy performance—that is, the extent to which needs, values, and opportunities have been realized through public action (Dunn, 2008). In addition, they entail efforts to determine the worth of a policy or program, focusing on judgments about the desirability or value of policies or programs. A given value such as diminished risk against destitution or better health in old age may be regarded as intrinsic—or valuable in itself—as well as extrinsic, or desirable because it leads to some other end, such as in regard to stress for their for adult children who are caretakers of their aging parents.

Skill Building Exercises

1. Given what you know of and understand to be the value base of social work practice as reflected in the NASW Code of Ethics, which of the policy analysis roles discussed in this chapter would you be likely to adopt?

   a. Under what circumstances would you be more likely to adopt one role rather than another?
   b. Which, if any, of the policy analyst roles would you be least likely to adopt? Why?

2. Discuss how a balance between policy research and advocacy can be can be maintained without loss of professional integrity on the part of the policy analyst.

3. Discuss the merits and limitations of each of these dichotomous pairs of approaches to or kinds of policy analysis:

   a. Root causes versus pragmatic adjustment.
   b. Comprehensive analysis versus short-term relevance.
   c. Consensual versus contentious analysis.
   d. Rational analysis versus democratic politics.

Policy as Product

CHAPTER 4

Evaluating Policy Proposals

This is the first of four chapters devoted to policy as product. It addresses an elemental task of policy analysis—namely, getting a handle on what the policy states about who gets what and under what circumstances. The chapter identifies and discusses criteria for evaluating policy proposals and asks several basic questions, answers to which provide a descriptive summary of policy products. Upon completion of the chapter, students will have learned that (1) policy analysts need to be alert to which and how criteria for assessing the merits of a policy are used; (2) policy analysts have a responsibility to assist clients sort through the relative weights attributed to evaluative criteria, including effectiveness, efficiency, equity, liberty/freedom, political feasibility, social acceptability, administrative feasibility, and technical feasibility; and (3) asking and answering such basic questions as "Who gets what?" "For what reasons?" and "Under what conditions?" will provide a working descriptive summary of the policy under scrutiny, particularly about types of benefits and eligibility requirements.

Students will also develop a skill set enabling them to (1) identify and apply criteria for assessing the merit of eligibility rules, including those based on prior contributions, administrative rules and regulations, private contracts, professional discretion, administrative discretion, judicial decisions, means testing, and attachment to the workforce; (2) identify and apply criteria for evaluating the merit of linking policies to social problems and eligibility rules, including fit of analysis to the social problem, correspondence between social problem theory and social policy or program theory, correspondence between eligibility rules and target specifications of the social problem analysis; and (3) identify and assess the merit of applying criteria specific to eligibility rules, including stigmatization, off-targeted benefits, as well as trade-offs in evaluating eligibility rules.

Upon successful completion of the skill building exercises of Chapter 4, students will have mastered the following CSWE Competencies and Practice Behaviors:

Chapter 4	CSWE Core Competencies
#	**Description**
2.1.2	**Apply Social Work Ethical Principles to Guide Professional Practice**
	Make ethical decisions by applying standards of the NASW Code of Ethics
	Tolerate ambiguity in resolving ethical conflicts
	Apply strategies of ethical reasoning to arrive at principled decisions

(Continued)

Chapter 4	(Continued)
#	Description
2.1.3	**Apply Critical Thinking to Inform and Communicate Professional Judgments**
	Demonstrate effective oral and written communication in working with individuals, families, groups, organizations, communities, and colleagues
2.1.4	**Engage Diversity and Difference in Practice**
	Recognize the extent to which a culture's structures and values may oppress, marginalize, alienate, or create or enhance privilege and power
2.1.5	**Advance Human Rights and Social and Economic Justice**
	Understand the forms and mechanisms of oppression and discrimination
2.1.7	**Apply Knowledge of Human Behavior and the Social Environment**
	Utilize conceptual frameworks to guide the processes of assessment, intervention, and evaluation
	Critique and apply knowledge to understand person and environment
2.1.8	**Engage in Policy Practice to Advance Social and Economic Well-Being and to Deliver Effective Social Work Services**
	Analyze, formulate, and advocate for policies that advance social well-being
2.1.9	**Respond to Contexts That Shape Practice**
	Continuously discover, appraise, and attend to changing locales, populations, scientific and technological development, and emerging societal trends to provide relevant services

Source: Adapted from Council on Social Work Education (2012). *Educational policy and accreditation standards.* Washington, DC: Author. Retrieved from http://www.cswe.org/file.aspx?id=13780

GENERAL CONSIDERATIONS ABOUT POLICY AS PRODUCT

Policy products include tangible documents such as legislation, bills, policy manuals, administrative guidelines, codified rules, and regulations. When examining policy products, analysts function at times like journalists, asking who, what, and why types of questions and providing a descriptive summary of the document's contents based on those questions. Analysts go beyond journalistic description, however, by assessing the merits of policy objectives in light of evaluative criteria and arguing or showing how well or to what extent the particular policy product under consideration meets these criteria. In general, evaluative criteria are used to weigh policy options or judge the merits of existing or proposed policies or programs (Kraft & Furlong, 2010). As policies are argued and debated, evaluative criteria function as justifications or rationales for a policy or government action. They are used to assess the worth of proposals aimed at addressing social problems that warrant public action.

At the very least, according to the classic formulation of political philosopher Charles W. Anderson (1979), to be regarded as "reasonable," a policy recommendation must be justified as lawful and be plausibly argued as equitable and as entailing an efficient use of resources. Such evaluative criteria as authority or lawfulness, the public interest, equitability, efficiency, and justice are not merely personal preferences in the economic or positivist sense of the terms nor norms of conduct, but rather inherently necessary or "obligatory criteria of political judgment" (Anderson, 1979, p. 713). Chosen criteria should fit the policy area and the set of circumstances under consideration: efficiency for example may be inappropriate or less important than equity when deliberating about health care services versus agricultural subsidies. In addition, the stipulation, ordering, and choice of evaluative criteria are invariably influenced, as is the case with policy analysis in general, with "real-world" contingencies related to the political and institutional context at the time of policy debates, as well as by available resources and time.

It should be noted, as do Kraft and Furlong (2010), that at times policymakers, interest groups, and analysts favor the use of one criterion over others without being clear why they do so and at other more partisan or ideologically driven times may explicitly privilege one criterion, claiming for example that self-determination or freedom trump all others. Politically, policymakers and others who seek to shape policies in general and policy analysts who view themselves as advocates use arguments to make their case without necessarily attempting to address every consideration or every criterion, instead focusing on those that support their cause or point of view. When this occurs, the credibility of the policy and related analysis is considerably reduced: the purported benefits of a proposed policy are likely to flow or be inferred from highly dubious assumptions, regardless of how strongly they are held (Manski, 2013).

Case in Point 4.1: Advocacy, Credibility, and Educational Vouchers

Free market theorist and Nobel prize laureate Milton Friedman, who died in 2006 (Noble, 2006), was a long-time proponent of government supplying educational vouchers rather than government operated free public schools. From the outset, he assumed "a society that takes freedom of the individual, or more realistically the family, as its ultimate objective, and seeks to further this objective by relying primarily on voluntary exchange among individuals for the organization of economic activity" and Friedman (1962/1982) provided three reasons for government intervention: "natural monopoly," "neighborhood effects," and "paternalistic concern for children and other irresponsible individuals" (pp. 85-86; see Chapter 2 for these and related economic concepts). For purposes here, a focus on his discussion of neighborhood effects or externalities is sufficient. Friedman (1962/1982) acknowledged the force of arguments for "nationalizing education," namely the otherwise impossibility of providing "the common core of values deemed requisite for social stability" (p. 90). He then asserted that it was not clear that the argument was valid. Friedman provided no evidence to that effect, nor did he call for related research. His argument placed the burden of proof on free public schooling, asserting that supplying vouchers was the preferred policy in the absence of evidence. As Manski (2013) contends (correctly in my view), Friedman's advocacy eclipsed his scientific or objective analysis. An advocate for educational vouchers could easily reverse the burden of proof, arguing that the existing educational system should be retained in the absence of proof. Each scenario is equally faulty, giving rise to dueling uncertainties. A more credible approach would start from acknowledging the limits of drawing any optimal design of education systems and stress that the merits of alterative designs depend on the magnitude and nature of market imperfections and neighborhood effects.

Given cost and time constraints, it would probably be unreasonable to expect policy analysts to account for more than a few criteria, such as effectiveness, efficiency, or equity, for any specific project. Policy analysts in general and social workers in particular nonetheless need to be alert to which and how select criteria are used, which may under certain circumstances become part of the analysis itself, as Case in Point 4.1 above suggests. In addition, as Stone (2011) notes, interpretations of evaluative criteria and their limitations are fraught with ambiguities and paradoxes that need not preclude their use for practical purposes of policy analysis, but underscore the need to be alert to limitations in how they are applied.

Case in Point 4.2: Universal Versus Targeted Approaches to Poverty Reduction

As you read through the remainder of this section about select criteria for evaluating the merits of policy proposals, think of the historical tension in social welfare provisioning that involves a choice between universalism versus selectivity through targeting. Over the past several decades, there has been a marked shift away from universalism, whereby the entire population is the beneficiary of social benefits as a basic right (e.g., Social Security in the United States or health care in Canada), and more toward targeting, usually on the basis of means or income testing (e.g., TANF [Temporary Assistance for Needy Families] in the United States, SA [Social Assistance] in Canada, or Bolsa Família in Brazil). Which of the two approaches might better address the social problem of poverty and how might the criteria for evaluating policy proposals discussed below favor one approach over the other? Thandika Mkandawire (2005), Professor of African Development, Department of International Development, London School of Economics (LSE), and former director of the United Nations Research Institute for Social Development (UNRISD), contends that universalism is the better approach to addressing poverty, particularly in "developing" countries. Speculate about which evaluative criteria discussed below would be more consistent with Professor Mkandawire's ideas, then read his article to verify your hunches and to discern his rationale.

SELECT CRITERIA FOR EVALUATING POLICY PROPOSALS

Kraft and Furlong (2010, pp. 151–161) discuss eight criteria for evaluating public policy proposals: effectiveness, efficiency, equity, liberty/freedom, political feasibility, social acceptability, administrative feasibility, and technical feasibility. Chambers and Wedel (2005) also discuss stigmatization, target efficiency, trade-offs, and substitutability. The relative weight of each criterion is context dependent. Policy analysts are expected to know these criteria. One of the main functions of the policy analyst is to assist clients in identifying which criteria are appropriate for consideration and sort through the relative weight that should be assigned accordingly.

Effectiveness

Effectiveness is the likelihood of achieving policy goals and objectives or demonstrated achievement of them. It is limited by our capacities to estimate uncertain projections of future events and to link the policy and anticipated outcomes in a causal relationship. Identification and development of suitable indicators or measures are requisites for assessing effectiveness of policies or programs in existence—for a proposed policy or program, likelihood estimates that stated goals and objectives would be met if adopted. Determination and agreement about what constitutes appropriate indicators of effectiveness can be problematic for political as well as technical reasons.

Many policies and programs have multiple goals, which are usually broadly stated, and objectives, which may lack the degree of specificity more familiar to researchers when operationalizing variables. This lack of clarity about goals and objectives is in part a function of political processes that enable adoption or increase the likelihood of adoption. In addition, some goals and objectives may succeed, whereas others may fall short. Goals achievable only in the long term, say more than a generation, preclude the efficacy of short-term assessment. Forecasting is inherently problematic, given uncertainties about future events and conditions. Politicians may also exaggerate success or failures of policies and programs to enhance their prospects for remaining or obtaining public office. Acknowledging such difficulties, Congress passed the Government Performance and Results Act of 1993 (GPRA, P.L. 103–62) to encourage agencies to focus on results, service quality, and public satisfaction. GPRA also mandated annual performance plans and reports about each program activity in an agency's budget. Reports of the Board of Governors of the Federal Reserve System (2011), for example, include goals, objectives, performance measures, and resources for monetary policy, its supervisory and regulatory function, and its payment system and oversight function, in addition to a statement about mission, values, and goals of the board as a whole.

Efficiency

Efficiency entails an assessment of achieving program goals or providing benefits in relation to costs. It can mean either least cost for a given benefit or largest benefit for a given cost. Efficiency encourages analysts to think about overall costs and benefits of existing programs and alternative proposals to change them or substitute something different. Efficiency serves as a way of justifying government action on the basis of economic concepts, often expressed in terms of relative virtues of government intervention and the operation of a free market in promoting social welfare. With efficiency in mind, policy analysts consider possible alternative uses of labor, capital, and materials that are forgone or might be lost when costs of a policy or program exceed actual or anticipated benefits. To the extent government underwrites prescription drug expenses under Medicare *more than is needed to gain better health for senior citizens,* for example, it will have fewer resources available for other services, such as public education, low-income households, and national defense. At the state level, the two largest expenditure programs, Medicaid (which targets low-income families and destitute senior citizens in nursing homes) and public education, are often pitted against each other to maintain their respective shares of total expenditures (National Association of State Budget Officers, 2011).

Weighing the costs and benefits of one program's expenditures against the other can be problematic. What constitutes a cost (to whom) and a benefit (for whom) over what period of time, and estimated or assigned values, should be subject to public debate prior to reducing such concerns to technical matters amenable to formulaic calculations. Measuring all costs and benefits is not necessarily easy, nor is it always possible, thereby limiting its usefulness. Determining what constitutes an appropriate measure can also be problematic. This is not to suggest abandoning attempts to calculate costs and benefits, but rather to highlight the need to make costs and benefits of adopting a policy more explicit and understandable so the public at large and policymakers in particular can be better informed than they would be in the absence of such information. Who benefits and who bears the costs of adopting a policy are distributional issues that go beyond efficiency, raising equity issues that warrant critical analysis and public scrutiny.

Equity

Equity refers to fairness or justice in the distribution of a policy's cost, benefits, and risks across population subgroups. In policy debates, equity has two different meanings: process equity, often referred to as procedural justice, and outcomes equity, often referred to as social justice. **Process equity** refers to decision-making procedures or processes—that is, the extent to which they are voluntary, open, and fair to all participants. Adherents of process equity such as Robert Nozick (1974) contend that guaranteeing and protecting individual and property rights are the primary responsibility of government. Process equity adherents are likely to resist government efforts to promote equality beyond ensuring equal opportunity to participate in society's decisions. Adherents of **outcome equity** such as John Rawls (1971) contend that equity or fairness refers to the fair distribution of societal goods, such as wealth, income, or political power. Adherents of *outcome equity* tend to favor government intervention to promote more equitable distribution of society's resources than seems possible when market forces are the primary or final arbiters, even those outcomes resulting from dynamics of process equity. Measuring equity is inherently problematic given disagreements about the composition of the "basket of social goods" that ought to be more equitably distributed than is the case and given the requisite technical challenges that invariably accompany them.

Equity is likely to be central to any consideration of redistributive policies, such as tax reform, access to education and health services, and assistance to low-income persons and families. It invariably arises in any policy area where debate and decisions turn on who gains and who loses as a consequence of adopting a policy and modifying an existing policy. The "who" of the gains/losses refers to different groups or categories of people, that is, the targets of the policy: wealthy, middle class, or poor, whether families, neighborhoods, or individuals; urbanites or suburbanites; tax-filers or non-filers; homeowners or renters, and the like. As a contender for the 2012 Republican nomination for president, Herman Cain advocated a tax plan, known as the 9-9-9 tax plan, that mixed a flat tax and a national sales tax, both of which were viewed as regressive—that is, more adverse to those at the lower end of the economic ladder and disproportionately advantageous to more affluent persons and families (Fletcher, 2011; Kucinich, 2011).

Liberty

Liberty or freedom refers to the extent to which public policy extends or restricts privacy and individual rights and choices. Cash benefits associated with the Temporary Assistance for Needy Families (TANF) program or the Supplemental Security Income (SSI) program maximize individual choice, whereas food stamp, housing, and education vouchers are more restrictive since they must be used for designated purposes. Public money supporting family planning or counseling organizations that include information about abortion services or provide such services affirm women's right to privacy, ensuring access for low-income women on more equitable terms with more affluent women than would be the case otherwise.

Political Feasibility

Political feasibility refers to the likelihood that a policy would be adopted—that is, the extent to which elected officials accept and support a policy proposal. It can be difficult to determine, contingent in part on perceptions of related issues, changing economic and political conditions, and the climate of opinion about related issues. Highly visible programs targeting "deserving" populations such as low-income elderly or children, and those with severe mental or physical health problems usually carry relatively low political risk, since helping such economically vulnerable populations of people projects an image of a social and moral conscience (Chambers & Wedel, 2005). Politicians are also likely to assess the potential for failure/success to reduce the impact of the social problem a policy or program is meant to address. Much of the debate leading up to the welfare reform legislation, for example, focused on how best to end dependence on government benefits and to prevent or reduce the incidence of out-of-wedlock pregnancies, both of which were incorporated into the Personal Responsibility and Work Opportunity Act of 1996 (PRWORA, P.L. 104–93) (Caputo, 2011). Note that one of the two primary purposes of PRWORA was to end dependence on government benefits for low-income persons and families, not to reduce poverty. What constitutes failure/success is debatable and may prove contentious or problematic when discussing existing programs and policies, particularly during election years when candidates want to accentuate differences with their opponents. For new or proposed programs lacking a track record, demonstration or pilot projects (in cities or counties at the state level) or in several states (at the national level) may be more politically feasible than full-scale adoption in a state or for the entire country. Experimental failures, should they occur, are less risky politically, whereas program failures, for which success has been advertised or highly touted, could prove politically disastrous.

Social Acceptability

Social acceptability refers to the extent to which the public at large will accept and support a policy proposal. Whether the public views a policy or program as appropriate and responsive can be difficult to determine, even when public support can be measured. Partisans of an issue may grab media headlines, giving the appearance of greater public support or opposition for their pet cause than is warranted, as can be gleaned from Caputo (2011), Medvetz (2012), and Lens (2000) in regard to PRWORA. Ambivalence, uncertainty, or on many issues even indifference may be more the norm.

Administrative Feasibility

Administrative feasibility refers to the likelihood that a department or agency can implement the policy or deliver the program well. It entails an assessment of a department's or agency's capacity, a projection of available resources and agency behavior that may be difficult to estimate. Chambers and Wedel (2005) note that administrators will invariably favor a benefit that is simple rather than complicated to administer. Cash benefits and subsidies place responsibility on the beneficiaries (or parents and legal guardians when beneficiaries are children or incapacitated adults) for obtaining needed products or services, thereby avoiding *administrative complexities* and perhaps even higher administrative costs of service provision. Lower administrative cost is one of the more consistently persuasive rebuttals against privatizing Social Security, since brokerage fees for fund management of individual private accounts are avoided (Congressional Budget Office, 2004).

Technical Feasibility

Technical feasibility refers to the availability and reliability of technology needed for policy implementation. It is often difficult to anticipate technological change that would alter feasibility. Technological advances in data collection, storage, and retrieval, for example, made it feasible for the federal government to require states to establish case registries to enhance the prospects of successful child support enforcement by enabling authorities to locate and track parents who owed such support, not only within states but between states as well. Title III, Subtitle B of the Personal Responsibility and Work Opportunity Act of 1996 (P.L. 104–93) required states to create and maintain such automated systems.

Stigmatization, Target Efficiency, and Trade-Offs

Acquisition and consumption of many income- or means-tested social welfare benefits that are public or overtly visible to others often carry negative or *stigmatizing* attributions or connotations, such that recipients of such benefits are associated, for example, with "being on welfare" (e.g., see Stuber, 2003). Recipients of in-kind benefits such as food stamps and WIC (Special Supplemental Nutrition Program for Women, Infants, and Children), whether in the form of debit card look-alikes or vouchers, are also often subject to disparaging or stigmatizing comments by cash-paying or debit/credit-card customers when purchasing groceries.

Despite the stigma associated with in-kind benefits, as a policy option they are notable for their *target efficiency*—that is, benefits such as food, education or housing vouchers, or medical subsidies go directly to the specific social problem of concern: nutrition, schooling, shelter, or health. Whereas cash as a type of benefit increases consumer sovereignty, in-kind benefits restrict choice, suggesting there may be *trade-offs* between various evaluative criteria, relaxing or extending social control. Invariably, increasing choice or enhancing self-determination over what to consume, which is often associated with cash benefits, is a worthwhile evaluative criterion, especially to the extent it is accompanied by decreasing the prospect of stigma.

In general, a *trade-off* occurs when some disadvantage occurs in order to get another advantage. Obtaining *target efficiency* with in-kind benefits extends social control, thereby diminishing to some unspecified extent a recipient's self-determination about the nature of the benefit and how to use it. The provision of cash assistance, however, though less visible than in-kind benefits, did little to mitigate the generalized stigma attributed to low-income "welfare" mothers who participated in the Aid to Families with Dependent Children (AFDC) program (established as Aid to Dependent Children in the Social Security Act of 1935 and designed primarily for low-income widows) between the 1960s and 1996, or afterward when the federal government replaced AFDC with TANF, which placed time limits on receipt of federal cash payments and instituted work requirements and other conditions for benefits (Hartzell, 2007; Kim, 2009; Soper, 1979). Economists often debate the likelihood of *trade-offs* between labor force participation and inflation rates: greater labor force participation increases the likelihood of consumption, and the increased demand for goods and services increases the likelihood of greater willingness to pay higher prices. The *trade-off* need not be exact or zero-sum, as the 1994–1998 period of historically low unemployment rates and low inflation demonstrated, but does become a point of contention in related policy debates.

Substitutability

Substitutability refers to the possibility that a public policy or program may be used in such a way so as not to produce desired effects (Chambers & Wedel, 2005). Food stamps, for example, whose recipients are meant to increase their food purchases and consumption, may instead forgo such purchases and consumption and use the money "released" by their availability to purchase other commodities of choice. The net gain is not necessarily food items: some alternative purchases may nonetheless be deemed socially acceptable (such as books or other essential items), but others may not be (such as illegal drugs).

DESCRIPTIVE SUMMARY OF POLICY PRODUCTS

Who Gets What?

One of the first tasks of the policy analyst is to identify who benefits from the policy under consideration, what type of benefits they get, what if any criteria and their accompanying or underlying rationales are used to determine eligibility for those benefits, and how well do the benefits fit with the definition of the problem they are meant to address (Chambers & Wedel, 2005; Gilbert & Terrell, 2005). **Universal benefits** are available to an entire population and for the most part are not *means tested*—that is, they are provided regardless of income levels of recipients, their families, or households. Examples in the United States include the Old Age, Survivor, and Disability Insurance (OASDI) program, commonly referred to as Social Security, primarily for retirees and their dependents, and public education for the young. Fostering social solidarity is a commonly understood rationale for providing universal provisions such as OASDI and public education. **Selective benefits** are available on the basis of individual need, usually determined by a means test. Examples in the United States include the Temporary Assistance for Needy Families (TANF) program, Medicaid (health care for low-income families and destitute elderly or disabled people in nursing homes), and the Supplemental Nutrition Assistance Program (SNAP), commonly referred to as food stamps. Targeting intended beneficiaries and lower costs than universal programs are common rationales for such selective programs. Within these two broad categories of benefits, there are a variety of types.

Types of Benefits

Cash, vouchers, in-kind services, opportunity, and credits

Types of benefits include *cash* (Social Security, TANF, and Unemployment Insurance), *vouchers* (SNAP, the Housing Choice Voucher Program or Section 8 Housing), *in-kind services* such as Medicare's Program of All Inclusive Care for the Elderly (PACE), and *opportunity* or *positive discrimination* directed to protected groups to redress past inequities (Affirmative Action). Benefits can also take the form of *credits.* When government directly pays a hospital, for example, to cover costs of providing care to a low-income individual in need of medical or psychiatric services rather than giving cash to the recipient to pay the hospital, a credit is issued from the public treasury into the recipient's account at the hospital. Credits are like vouchers in that both are payments to a supplier of benefits or services, but they are more restrictive in regard to consumer choice. Vouchers are written authorizations to receive a benefit or service, leaving the choice of purveyor to the beneficiary. A credit is prearranged such that the benefit or service can be received only by the service provider chosen for this purpose by the government or its delegated agency. This type of credit also differs from the benefits of such government programs as the Earned Income Tax Credit (EITC) or the child tax credit administered by the Internal Revenue Service (IRS) as part of the tax system.

The EITC, for example, is an annual lump or monthly sum of money sent by the U.S. Treasury in the form of a check to many workers with children and, to a lesser extent, childless workers whose income falls below official poverty thresholds (Caputo, 2006, 2009). Both the EITC and the child tax credit are "refundable tax credits." That is, unlike other tax preferences that reduce the amount of taxes owed to the government, refundable credits may result in net payments from the government: if the amount of the refundable tax credit exceeds a filer's tax liability before the credit is applied, the government pays the excess to the person or business (Congressional Budget Office, 2013). There are two major groupings of refundable tax credits: earnings-based, such as the EITC and child tax credit, and expenditure-based, such as the health coverage tax credit and adoption tax credit. A third grouping involves those refundable tax credits associated with the Alternative Minimum Tax (ATM). Table 4.1 shows the start dates (i.e., the first year that the credit became refundable) and expiration dates of all types of refundable tax credits.

Subsidy

Another type of benefit is a *subsidy,* a payment to a third party. To encourage hospitals to provide expert services to low-income individuals and families in need of medical or psychiatric care, for example, states may give 50 percent of start-up costs and 70 percent of net operating costs (or some fixed percentage of each) in return for guaranteeing that their facility would serve all or a specified portion of such clients. The state thereby increases the likelihood of getting services to categories of people in need, *indirectly* through such institutional subsidies. Examples of such public subsidies include government payments to purchase computers for educational centers; passenger railroad service operations; national, state, and local highway construction; the operation of community mental health centers and day care centers; the education of developmentally disabled children; and to employers to hire specified groups of workers, such as unemployed veterans and long-term unemployed individuals. More specifically, the Medicaid program, which subsidizes medical expenses for low-income patients, also benefits the hospital industry by picking up costs for services that hospitals cannot deny, services for which they cannot expect low-income patients to pay. Hospital employees, including professionals such as physicians, nurses, and social workers, as well as support staff such as administrators, aides, orderlies, and janitors, also benefit indirectly from such subsidies. Pell Grants, which are made available through the U.S. Department of Education (2003) and awarded primarily to undergraduate students in financial need, are a form of subsidy. The grant goes directly to the student's educational institution, which in turn can credit the student's account for any educational expenses, such as tuition or books. The institution may also pay the student directly by check or cash, for which the school gets a signed receipt.

Table 4.1	Start Dates and Expiration Dates of Refundable Tax Credits	
Credit	**Start Date**	**Expiration Date**
Earnings-Based Credits		
Earned Income Tax Credit	January 1, 1975	None
Child Tax Credit	January 1, 1998	None
Economic Stimulus Payments	January 1, 2008	December 31, 2008
Making Work Pay Credit	January 1, 2009	December 31, 2010
Expenditure-Based Credits		
Health Coverage Tax Credit	December 1, 2002	December 31, 2013
First-time Homebuyer Tax Credit	April 9, 2008	April 20, 2010
COBRA Premium Assistance Credit	September 1, 2008	May 31, 2010
American Opportunity Tax Credit	January 1, 2009	December 31, 2017
Adoption Tax Credit	January 1, 2010	December 31, 2011
Small Business Health Care Tax Credit	January 1, 2010	None
Health Premium Assistance Tax Credit	January 1, 2014	None
Other Credits		
Prior-Year Alternative Minimum Tax Credit—Individuals	January 1, 2007	December 31, 2012
Prior-Year Alternative Minimum Tax Credit—Corporations	April 1, 2008	December 31, 2013

Source: Adapted from Congressional Budget Office. (2013). *Refundable tax credits.* Washington, DC: Author, p. 26.

Positive Discrimination

Positive discrimination is a form of benefit that provides special treatment now to remedy unequal treatment in the past. Examples are health-related benefits for Native Americans through the Indian Health Service and Social Security retirement benefits for Japanese Americans who spent part of their working years in internment camps during World War II. *Positive discrimination* was launched as the concept of affirmative action by an Executive Order of President John F. Kennedy in 1961 and codified in the 1964 Civil Rights Act to ensure nondiscrimination in employment on the basis of race, creed, color, or national origin (Caputo, 1994). Increasingly, affirmative action came to mean and be practiced as giving special treatment to individual members of "protected groups," not only in regard to employment-related hiring and workplace treatment but also in access to education, in part to redress past wrongs. Affirmative action laws that make benefits available to protected groups such as racial and ethnic minorities, disabled persons, and women are controversial in part because membership, which is assigned by policy, is deemed prima facie evidence of past employment-related discrimination (e.g., in hiring or promotions).

On February 16, 2011, the Equal Employment Opportunities Commission (EEOC) held hearings to examine the treatment of unemployed job seekers in light of reports indicating that employers and agencies refused to consider unemployed persons for openings ("The Unemployed Need Not Apply," 2011) and about specific job postings indicating that employers would consider or at least give strong preference only to those currently employed or recently laid off (Rampell, 2011a). Under current law, unemployed persons are not a protected group. President Obama reportedly had endorsed legislation, The Fair Employment Opportunity Act of 2011 (H.R. 2051, introduced on July 7 by Representative Rosa L. DeLauro, D-Conn.), barring discrimination against the jobless (Rambell, 2011b). The District of Columbia has passed such legislation and New York City is considering it, with Christine C. Quinn, speaker of the City Council, reportedly in favor ("We want to do everything we can to help people work"), and Mayor Michael Bloomberg opposed, contending that lawsuits would deter companies from hiring anyone at all (Hu, 2013). If such legislation were more widely adopted and favorably ruled on by local, state, federal, and ultimately the U.S. Supreme Court, as a protected group, unemployed persons would fall under the protective umbrella of positive discrimination. Even in the absence of a finding that unemployed persons are a protected group, judicial decisions and state legislators have grappled with challenges to affirmative action laws, particularly in regard to admission to colleges and graduate schools, with the Supreme Court likely to take up the matter again in the future (Arizona Civil Rights Initiative, 2011; Billups, 2011; Edelman, 2011; Garfield, 2005; Kahlenberg, 2011; Malos, 2011).

Case in Point 4.3: The Supreme Court and Affirmative Action

The term of the Supreme Court beginning October 1, 2012, had affirmative action on the docket. On October 10, 2012, the Supreme Court heard arguments in *Fisher v. the University of Texas*, which challenged affirmative action in higher education. Abigail Fisher, a white woman, charged she was denied admission to the University of Texas on the basis of race. To ensure racial diversity, race is one of several factors the University of Texas takes into account when selecting its incoming class. Nine years ago the Supreme Court had endorsed this approach in a 5-to-4 vote, in *Grutter v. Bollinger*. Writing for the majority, Justice Sandra Day O'Connor, who has since retired, said she expected affirmative action to remain in place another quarter of a century (Liptak, 2012a; Overview, 2013).

Loan Guarantee

A loan guarantee is another type of benefit. A common example is the Federal Housing Administration (FHA) Program, which provides federal government guarantees of mortgage loans for private dwellings. Should a homeowner default, the U.S. government pays off the loan, thereby enabling banks to make loans that they might not have made, or perhaps would have made but at higher interests rates, without the guarantee. The beneficiaries of loan guarantees often result from multiplier effects of the loan. This is to say that benefits go well beyond homeowners, the primary intended beneficiary, to include the home builder, the banker, the materials supplier to the home builder, and so on. Loan guarantees are also given to businesses. In 1990, for example, the government bailed out the U.S. savings and loan (S&L) industry, to the tune of $293.3 billion (in 2008 U.S. dollars). In 2008, the Federal Reserve provided a $30 billion line of credit to ensure the sale of Bear Stearns to JP Morgan Chase. To stem the financial crisis of 2008, in October of that year Congress passed the Emergency Economic Stabilization Act, authorizing the Treasury to spend $700 billion. An additional $280 billion of federal guarantees were extended to Citigroup in 2008 and $142.2 billion in 2009 to Bank of America (Sorkin & Thomas, 2008; Nankin, Umansky, Kjellman, & Klein, 2009). The federal government also makes a number of guaranteed loans to students at relatively low and/or fixed interest rates, including Stafford Loans (which may or may not also be subsidized) made to college and university students to supplement personal and family resources, scholarships, and work-study grants: $31,000 lifetime limit (up to $23,000 unsubsidized) for dependent undergraduates; $57,500 for independent undergraduate students; and for graduate or professional students $138,500 (up to $65,000 unsubsidized) and $224,000 for health professionals (StudentLoanNetwork, 2011).

Eligibility Criteria and Types of Eligibility Rules

All social programs in the United States have eligibility criteria that are inherently exclusionary in some sense, even the universal programs. Social Security benefits, which require an accumulated work history and related percentages of salary contributions from workers and employers (in most cases), for example, apply to retirees or their beneficiary dependents; public education is free to everyone only through high school, not beyond. Child allowances are available to everyone with young children, but granted only to those who file federal income tax returns, thereby excluding many low-income families who are not required or perhaps are reluctant to do so. The Earned Income Tax Credit (EITC) targets low-income workers who must also file federal tax returns to claim the benefit, excluding those who do not file whether by intent or ignorance, as well as some married couples who file jointly and whose combined income lifts them above the eligibility threshold for their family size. It is important to note that eligibility for a service or benefit differs from who actually receives the benefit or service (Gilbert & Terrell, 2005, pp. 125–128). Take-up rates frequently fall well short of those who meet eligibility requirements for many means-tested social welfare programs, as Caputo (2006) has shown in the case of the EITC and as Ratner (2012) has shown for SNAP (or food stamps). Reasons vary, from ignorance among those eligible about the programs to diversionary or exclusionary practices on the part of the service agencies and providers.

Drawing on and elaborating upon Titmuss (1976), Chambers and Wedel (2005) identify eight types of eligibility rules meant to capture the bewildering variety of rules and regulations for determining who gets what, how much, and under what conditions, given the decentralized disarray of social welfare in the United States: prior contributions, administrative rules, private contracts, professional discretion, administrative discretion, judicial decision, means testing (needs minus assets and/or income), and attachment to the workforce.

Eligibility Rules Based on Prior Contributions

Social welfare programs such as Social Security and Unemployment Insurance (UI) are exemples of providing benefits based on prior financial contributions from individual recipients, others on their behalf, or some combination of the two. The rationale behind the method of prior contributions as the basis of benefit receipt is similar to principles that lie behind all private insurance schemes, namely (1) advance payment provides for the future, and (2) protection against the economic consequences of personal disasters or misfortune is better achieved by spreading risk among large numbers of people. The nature and amount of prior contributions vary by the age at which the benefit is drawn and the type of benefit. To draw Social Security benefits, for example, at least 40 quarters of coverage (10 years) are generally required, although for disability benefits 20 quarters in the 10 years prior to determination of the disability are required, with special insurance status for those who are disabled before age 31. Prior contributions come from both the individual workers and the employers, a matched amount expressed as a percentage of workers' wages. As of 2012, the established rates for Social Security and Medicare were 6.2 percent and 1.45 percent of wages (up to $110,100), respectively, paid by both employee and employer (12.4% and 2.9% respectively for self-employed individuals) (U.S. Social Security Administration, 2012). To be eligible for Unemployment Insurance benefits, an unemployed worker must have worked in covered employment for a period of time specified in *state law* (in most states, the first four of the last five completed calendar quarters). Contributions come from a tax on wages paid by employers in covered employment, with funds credited to each state's unemployment trust fund, which the federal government maintains. An individual who has had no contributions made on his or her behalf by a covered employer is ineligible for unemployment cash benefits.

Eligibility by Administrative Rule and Regulation

Administrative rules are meant to clarify eligibility rules laid out in the law. On one hand, they provide social workers and other human service staff a means by which to administer the program benefit or service evenhandedly and reliably, such that people similarly situated are provided with similar benefits. On the other hand, administrative rules restrict social workers' and other human service staffs' discretion or judgment about the need for the benefit or service in individual circumstances. The eligibility rules for the Supplemental Nutrition Assistance Program (SNAP), or food stamps as it is more commonly known, are specified in the law: the exact amount of assets and income is specified by family size in the text of the act, along with definitions of what constitutes a household (U.S. Department of Agriculture, 2012). The administrative rules for TANF (Temporary Assistance for Needy Families), in contrast, are quite numerous and cover many different topics, resulting in tome-like manuals that include state and federal statutes relevant to the program as well as how those laws are to be interpreted by the staff members who sign the eligibility documents. Administrative rules govern how to count assets and income and may specify whether a child's paper route income is to be counted as family income or whether an inherited item such as a piano is to be counted as an asset. Further, TANF gives states more discretion in how to spend federal cash assistance, so state laws and administrative rules and regulations governing the service mix (job training, child care, education, etc.) and noncompliance sanctions vary accordingly. Administrative rules are created with the understanding that they can change over time as circumstances warrant. Changes in administrative personnel may also result in changes to eligibility rules. If devised by administrators, such rules can also be changed by administrators. In addition to discerning what are permissive versus mandatory rules, it behooves the policy analyst to know whether the entitlement or eligibility rule originates with judicial decision, administrative rule, or individual staff discretion, given that the probability of change varies accordingly. Staff decisions, to the extent they can be observed and monitored with any consistency, may be easier to change than formal rules or statutes.

Eligibility by Private Contract

Private contracts are involved in purchase-of-service contracting (POSC). Over the past several decades more and more social welfare services, such as counseling, legal advocacy, special education, day care, and some transportation services (e.g., for the elderly or disabled), are delivered by private agencies and organizations that contract with the public agencies. State, county, or city governments usually pay the bill or some portion of it directly to the private purveyor of the contracted service. State and local governments, as well as private charitable organizations, often insert conditions into the contract—about who can get what services under what conditions (Faith et al., 2010; Martin, 2004, 2000; McBeath, 2006; Wedel, 1991; Wedel & Colston, 1988).

Eligibility by Professional Discretion

Professional discretion by individual practitioners plays an inordinately large role in the determination of eligibility of social welfare benefits. (See Chapter 9 for a discussion of the role of professional discretion in implementing social welfare policies and programs.) Nearly every licensed professional controls part of the process for assessing and determining eligibility for social welfare benefits: medical benefits are contingent upon the discretion of the physician or her or his surrogate; dental care for children in TANF program families in entitled in part by dentists; legal advocacy for low-income persons is determined in part by the judgment of lawyers and judges; foster care for children is decided in part by social workers. The requisite professional judgment in each of these cases is presumed to be based on their expertise about the matter. It is important that social workers and other professionals realize that their judgments can be challenged in an administrative or judicial hearing and that they have a professional obligation to help their clients with any such challenge they deem unwarranted or prejudicial. At times, professional discretion is the leading evidence or final arbiter of very difficult sets of circumstances. Removing children from their parents' care is a case in point, as in child physical abuse, sexual abuse, or neglect cases: judgments of physicians, clinical psychologists, and social workers are commonly used. Social workers and other professionals are advised to be wary of blanket assumptions about the validity of these difficult judgments.

Case in Point 4.4: Child Protective Services and Professional Discretion

In a study of the Norwegian Child Welfare Service (CWS) workers, Christiansen and Anderssen (2010) reported that social workers' long-term back-and-forth processes—that is, experiences with their cases and, in particular, interactions with parents—were determinative in shaping their judgments and reaching decisions about placing children in out-of-home care. In the absence of any national guidelines for how assessments in child welfare cases should be resolved, the Norwegian Child Welfare Act of 1992 provided a wide berth for professional discretion in such matters.

Eligibility by Administrative Discretion

As noted above, discretion is an integral component of professional practice when assessing the eligibility of individuals and families for social welfare services. Administrators also exercise discretion that affects eligibility for services. In many county public welfare offices, staff workers distributing small amounts of cash and credits for food, housing, and utilities for low-income individuals and families as part of the General Assistance program financed by the local government, account for the funds only in a fiscal sense, with little accounting about the requisite judgments and limited if any systematic effort to document accuracy. More generally, organizational policies and administrative rules entail interpretation and application to specific situations, invariably involving significant personal judgment by the staff member. Think of a state patrol officer who while driving past a motor vehicle witnesses an adult spanking a five-year-old child in a car stopped at the side of the highway. Is what the officer witnessed a case of acceptable discipline of a disobedient or otherwise unruly child? Or is the discipline too harsh, perhaps to the point of leaving black and blue marks or breaking the skin of a defenseless child? The discretion in this example is about how to interpret the state's child abuse law. Such statutes seldom reveal rules for interpretation—no mention of how inflamed the bruises must be, or even whether black and blue rather than red bruises count. Nor will such statutes necessarily protect the officer from consequences if the parent claims illegal detainment or false arrest. Social workers and medical personnel face similar situations in emergency rooms, but with a slight difference in the type of discretion exercised. The source of authority differentiates the administrative discretion in the case of the state patrol from professional discretion of the social worker and medical personnel in emergency rooms: professionals exercise discretion on the basis of the authority of their professional preparation and training, whereas administrators exercise authority because they are appointed by their superiors to do so.

At times, administrative discretion has gone amok, with the effect of preventing access to services for individuals and families who are eligible. Chambers (1985) provides a telling example of efforts during the early 1980s Reagan administration to terminate Social Security Disability (DI) and Supplemental Security Income (SSI) benefits for chronically mentally ill individuals. The Social Security Disability Amendments of 1980 (P.L. 96–265), signed into law by President Jimmy Carter on June 6, 1980, had several administrative features that the Reagan administration used to terminate DI/SSI beneficiaries: (1) institution of "Continuing Disability Investigation," which scheduled re-review of all DI/SSI beneficiaries, giving the Social Security Administration (SSA) discretion to set policy guidelines by which state personnel awarded DI/SSI benefits; (2) for the first time permitted SSA to arrange its own private medical consultation for evaluating disablement (thereby making SSA independent of claimants' personal physicians); and (3) gave SSA the right to contest disability decisions even after they were appealed to SSA's own administrative law judges, so SSA could exercise administrative control throughout the disability award process (Chambers, 1985; Congressional Research Service, 2011). The expected termination rate of 20 percent increased to 47 percent by mid-1982; the 40 percent approval rate of 1979 declined to 29 percent in 1981; and the 71,500 beneficiaries terminated by continuing disability investigations in 1980 were reported to have increased to 98,800 in 1981, to 121,404 in the first five months of 1982, and were projected to reach 360,000 per year by 1984. Thousands of appeals ensued, with judicial decisions (e.g., *MHA of Minnesota v. Schweiker,* 1982) overturning about 80 percent of terminations, highlighting the importance of advocacy efforts on behalf of clients and of the judiciary as an influential actor in the policy arena.

Eligibility by Judicial Decision

As noted above in the example of overturning DI/SSI terminations in the early 1980s, judicial decisions affect determinations of eligibility for social welfare benefits. Generally, they occur after a program has been in operation for a period of time and a question arises as to whether the enabling legislation or whether an administrative rule or discretionary judgment was faithful to the spirit and intention of the law under which the program was established. Appeals to the judiciary for clarification of the law are routine and they can become as important as legislative and administrative rules themselves. Paternity determinations, for example, are a source of judicial entitlement to child support payments by non-supporting fathers. Many courts use the human leukocyte antigen (HLA) test, which will rule out, with 97 percent accuracy, whether a given individual is the father of a particular child. Judicial decisions also play a large role in the family court system, particularly in the area of protective services when making determinations about foster care and about child abuse and neglect cases, at times using the expert testimony of social workers and other helping professionals (Calkins & Millar, 1999; Strand, 1994).

A 1969 ruling of the Supreme Court held that residence requirements (i.e., having to establish permanent residence in a state for a specified period, often for one year) to obtain cash benefits under the Aid to Families with Dependent Children (AFDC) program were unconstitutional infringements on citizens' (labor's) right to free movement between states. This ruling still applies to AFDC's successor, TANF, created in 1996 by the Personal Responsibility and Work Opportunity Reconciliation Act (PRWORA, P.L. 104–193). Judicial decisions have for the most part validated PRWORA provisions that made all lawful immigrants who arrived in the United States after August 22, 1996, ineligible for many federally funded social welfare benefits regardless of age, disability, or minor status, in addition to authorizing states to deny Medicaid, TANF, and Social Services Block Grant services to those residing in the United States and receiving benefits as of August 22, 1996 (Kim, 2001).

Case in Point 4.5: ACA and Judicial Decision

Sometimes judicial decisions have a bearing on legislation that barely has had any time for implementation. A prime example is the Patient Protection and Affordable Care Act (ACA, P.L. 111–148), signed by President Barack Obama on March 23, 2010. ACA extends medical insurance to more than 30 million people, primarily by expanding Medicaid and providing federal subsidies to help lower- and middle-income individuals buy private coverage (Health Care Reform, 2011). More than 20 court challenges have been filed against the law, resulting in a series of conflicting appellate decisions over an array of issues, the central one being whether Congress has the constitutional power to require people to purchase health insurance or face a penalty through the so-called individual mandate (Challenges to the Health Law, 2011; Liptak, 2011a). On November 14, 2011, the Supreme Court decided to hear a challenge to the law (Liptak, 2011b) and on June 28, 2012, the Supreme Court, in a 5–4 vote, upheld the law (Liptak, 2012a).

Eligibility by Means Testing

Eligibility by **means testing** is one of the most widely used of all eligibility rules. Income and assets are totaled to determine if they are less than some established standard for what a person or family needs. Those at or below the standard are deemed eligible for benefits. What constitutes countable income and assets for purposes of means testing varies by program and oftentimes also by state. Income, which is often a matter of record and in the form of cash, is more easily determinable than assets, which are usually held in private and whose valuation can thereby be problematic. Programs such as TANF, SNAP (food stamps), and WIC (the Special Supplemental Nutrition Program for Women, Infants, and Children) count almost all wages and assets of household members, whereas SSI counts wages up to $65 a month and half the amount above $65 a month, and assets over $2,000 for an individual/child and $3,000 for an adult. Some forms of income are excluded from consideration. SSI excludes income tax refunds, the value of food stamps, loans that have to be repaid, grants, scholarships, fellowships, or gifts used for tuition and educational expenses, as well as the first $20 of most other income received in a month. What constitutes need also varies by program and by state. Many programs use the official federal poverty thresholds (which establish an absolute minimum level for subsistence) or a multiple percentage of these levels (to establish nutritional adequacy) as a basis for determining need. SNAP sets a monthly income limit at 200 percent of the current poverty level; Medicaid is set at 100 percent plus $25 ($50 for couples), which is disregarded income in Illinois; energy assistance or LIHEAP is at 150 percent; senior employment assistance at 125 percent; and weatherization of housing at 200 percent of the 2009 poverty level (Government Programs, 2012). SSI does not rely on official federal poverty thresholds. Instead, benefit amounts are determined by that which brings an otherwise qualifying person's total monthly income up to a designated amount—up to $674 in 2011 for individuals and up to $1,100 for couples. The primary beneficiary focus also varies by program: the child for TANF; the household for SNAP; the pregnant or postpartum woman, infants, and children up to age 5 for WIC; the individual for SSI. As all this variation in programs suggests, when analyzing means-tested programs, it is helpful to examine them in light of the type of resource counted (wages and/or assets), the basis of need (minimum subsistence or nutritional adequacy), and the beneficiary (child, household, worker).

Establishing Attachment to the Workforce

Labor force attachment, such as being employed or actively seeking work, as a determinant of social welfare benefit eligibility is not to be confused with its desirability as an aim or consequence of a policy or program. Social Security and Unemployment Insurance (UI) both have requirements about minimum work-related contributions. As noted above, Social Security requires 40 quarters of coverage (a minimum of 10 years), although for disability benefits 20 quarters in the 10 years prior to determination of the disability are required, with special insurance status for those who are disabled before age 31. The UI program benefits those who have significant work histories, excluding from benefits those working part-time, only in casual employment, or only for insignificant wages. Specific rules vary by state. Typically, UI requires the worker to have received wages for at least six months and to have received at least $200 in wages during each prior three-month period.

Other programs such as TANF or SNAP (food stamps) tie labor force participation, whether holding a job or looking for work, to benefit receipt. The labor force participation requirements of these types of social welfare programs are meant to ensure that recipients are making concerted efforts to achieve "self-sufficiency," in order to minimize the length of time they participate in the social welfare programs.

Like TANF and SNAP, the Earned Income Tax Credit (EITC) has no specific prerequisite about length of time worked, such as number of quarters or full or part time for eligibility. Instead, having earned income below a specified amount (contingent on tax filing status and age and number of children), whether from wages, salaries, tips, or other taxable employee pay, net earnings from self-employment, or gross income received as a statutory employee, as well as strike benefits paid by a union to its members, is requisite for EITC eligibility. EITC is meant to encourage continued labor force attachment among low-income workers by allowing wage-related earnings to reach levels of 125 percent, or in some cases around 200 percent, of official federal poverty thresholds before phasing out completely (Kneebone & Garr, 2011).

Skill Building Exercises

1. Provide a summary description of legislation currently under consideration by the U.S. Congress, a State Assembly, or a local municipality (county, city, or other local government).

   a. Who gets what, under what circumstances?
   b. How is the proposed bill to be funded?

2. What eligibility criteria were used to determine the beneficiaries of the policy described in skill building exercise #1?

   a. What values are associated with these eligibility criteria?
   b. Assess the merits and/or limitations of the eligibility criteria.
   c. Given your understanding of human behavior and the social environment, what theoretical frameworks undergird these eligibility criteria and the values associated with them.

3. Discuss trade-offs likely to occur when considering modifications to or alternatives of eligibility criteria embedded in the legislation described in skill building exercise #1 and identified in skill building exercise #2.

   a. Given that some trade-offs are likely to be more consistent with the professional mandate to advance social justice, rank each alternative trade-off on a scale of 0–10, with 10 signifying the greatest degree of consistency with the professional mandate for advancing social justice.
   b. Taking the two extreme alternatives as ranked above (i.e., the lowest and highest ranked), provide a rationale for your rankings.

Matching Policy Proposals to Problems

This chapter focuses on the goodness of fit between proposed policies and social problems they are meant to address. It highlights the importance of ensuring a close correspondence between the theoretical bases of both social problems and policies or programs that are being considered or have been adopted to address them. Particular attention is given to the degree of consistency between eligibility rules for obtaining access to benefits of a policy or program and (1) the ideology that guided the analysis of the social problem, and (2) the target specifications—that is, the designation of beneficiaries' characteristics, circumstances, or conditions that were determined on the basis of the analysis of the social problem. The chapter also includes discussion of how policies are financed, both from public and private sources, in light of ideological, political, and practical rationales or justifications associated with them. Upon completion of the chapter, students will have learned that (1) causal assumptions embedded in theories about social problems drive or affect policy or program criteria for determining who gets what type of social provisioning; (2) to the extent eligibility rules do not correspond to concrete indicators of sufficiently defined social problems, the designated benefits and services may get directed to those population groups who are not the main object of the policy or program; (3) certain types of social welfare provisioning are prone to stigmatizing program beneficiaries or clients; (4) financing social welfare provisioning in the United States includes both government revenue generated primarily from progressive income taxes and regressive payroll taxes, and private sector philanthropy; and (5) the type of financing reflects ideological and political considerations.

Upon successful completion of the skill building exercises of Chapter 5, students will have mastered the following Council on Social Work Education (CSWE) Competencies and Practice Behaviors:

Chapter 5	CSWE Core Competencies
#	Description
2.1.2	**Apply Social Work Ethical Principles to Guide Professional Practice**
	Recognize and manage personal values in a way that allows professional values to guide practice
	Make ethical decisions by applying standards of the NASW Code of Ethics
	Tolerate ambiguity in resolving ethical conflicts

(Continued)

Chapter 5	(Continued)
#	**Description**
2.1.3	**Apply Critical Thinking to Inform and Communicate Professional Judgments**
	Demonstrate effective oral and written communication in working with individuals, families, groups, organizations, communities, and colleagues
2.1.5	**Advance Human Rights and Social and Economic Justice**
	Engage in practices that advance social and economic justice
2.1.7	**Apply Knowledge of Human Behavior and the Social Environment**
	Utilize conceptual frameworks to guide the processes of assessment, intervention, and evaluation
	Critique and apply knowledge to understand person and environment
2.1.8	**Engage in Policy Practice to Advance Social and Economic Well-Being and to Deliver Effective Social Work Services**
	Analyze, formulate, and advocate for policies that advance social well-being
2.1.9	**Respond to Contexts That Shape Practice**
	Continuously discover, appraise, and attend to changing locales, populations, scientific and technological development, and emerging societal trends to provide relevant services

Source: Adapted from Council on Social Work Education (2012). *Educational policy and accreditation standards.* Washington, DC: Author. Retrieved from http://www.cswe.org/file.aspx?id=13780

FIT WITH ANALYSIS OF SOCIAL PROBLEM

Whatever the type, a basic question that needs to be raised about benefits is whether or how well they fit with the social problem they are meant to address (Chambers & Wedel, 2005). After-school recreational programs for children who are disruptive in classrooms may be desirable, perhaps providing supervision of children for working parents when no adult is at home, but if a case for linkages to classroom behavior cannot be made, such programs would fail the fitness test. A recreational program tailored to disruptive classroom behavior on the other hand would pass the fitness test in principle—subject to assessing how well it does so in fact.

Correspondence Between Social Problem Theory and Program Theory

What can be subjected to analysis and assessment is how well the social problem theory and its deriva-tive, the program theory or logic, fit. A program theory or logic specifies some set of factors as a preferred outcome and describes what and how to set in motion a chain of events or processes to obtain that outcome. The benefit or service type is included as one or part of the chain of events or processes—that is, identified among the causal antecedents likely to set the chain of events in motion. Rationales and arguments as to why the benefit or service would be expected to have the results would also come under scrutiny for their credibility, plausibility, and logic. For social workers this means a firm grounding in our theoretical understanding about human behavior and the social environment. If a credible, plausible, and coherent argument cannot be made or is not provided, then no fit can be established with any degree of certainty. As with theories in general, program theories can be challenged. Foundational challenges may preclude action or intervention until an agreement can be reached about a satisfactory way to proceed, perhaps suggesting that demonstration projects whose implementation offers a prospect for adjudication between competing causal accounts and claims may be a reasonable political compromise enabling adoption or enactment of a policy or program.

Highlighting the importance of a good fit between problem formulation and program theory, Chambers and Wedel (2005) describe how the social problem analysis of poverty in the 1960s, highlighting individual, personal failures or shortcomings, contributed to the federal policy prescription emphasizing the expansion of personal services in the early 1970s. In doing so, however, the example they use and how they attribute causality highlight the importance for more sustained analysis and more accurate claims. The social problem viewpoint at the time was that the cause of poverty was an interaction between lack of material resources and some personal attribute (attitude, cultural approach to work) and was amenable to change by a service strategy: family, group, and individual counseling; job and parent training; referral agencies; and service coordination to avoid duplication of services. Federal expenditures for personal services aimed at the "rehabilitating" of poor persons increased from $194 million in 1963 to $1.5 billion by 1972. Chambers and Wedel claim, however, that the increased expenditures for personal

> services weren't successful in reducing poverty [suggesting that poverty remained the same or increased during this period]. The money was directed at what was perceived to be the shortcomings of individuals rather than the shortcomings of the economic system. The mistake was to think that these services could somehow substitute for the problem of an economy that created most of the poverty in the first place. (p. 104)

Chambers and Wedel might be correct about the faulty program theory but the logic they used to substantiate the claim can be faulted. They cite no evidence of increasing poverty rates to support their claim. Across several categories, poverty rates declined between 1963 and 1972: from 19.5 percent to 11.9 percent for all persons in the population, from 17.9 percent to 10.3 percent for families, from 47.7 percent to 38.2 percent for families with female householder and no husband present, and from 44.2 percent to 29.0 percent for unrelated individuals (DeNavis-Walt, Semega, & Stringfellow, 2011). These declines may be attributable to a concomitant rise in the Gross Domestic Product (GDP) from inflation adjusted $617.8 billion in 1963 to $1,237.9 billion in 1972, and declining unemployment rates between 1964 and 1969, from 5.2 percent to 3.5 percent, rising to 4.9 percent in 1970, and 5.9 percent in 1971, before declining again to 5.6 percent in 1972 (*Economic Report of the President,* 2011). GDP growth and declines in unemployment rather than increased federal personal services expenditures would indirectly support Chambers and Wedel's claim about the importance of structural factors on poverty, but studies showing the relative influence or correlation of personal services expenditures to poverty trends between 1963 and 1972 when controlling for structural factors of the economy are warranted. The need and justification for personal services along the lines suggested above for the service strategy used in the 1960s and early 1970s still resonate with social work scholars as necessary components to complement structural changes aimed at poverty alleviation (University of Michigan School of Social Work, 2009).

Correspondence Between Eligibility Rules and the Ideology of the Social Problem Analysis

Eligibility rules often reflect general ideological positions that underlie or are associated with viewpoints from which social problems are defined (Chambers & Wedel, 2005). Commitment to the work ethic is a prime example, referring to the common belief that paid work or employment is inherently virtuous and that the virtue of a citizen is related to work effort and work-related productivity. What counts as work has been disputed, particularly by feminist economists who note that unpaid household labor most often performed by women falls outside mainstream, neoclassical economic models of productivity (Bergmann, 2005; Brown, 1984; Dolfsma & Hoppe, 2003), perhaps reflecting in part male-dominated or patriarchal ways of thinking (Lerner, 1997).

Case in Point 5.1: Women, Work, and Wages

Feminist scholars have long taken issue with labor market studies that assume children and housework affect women's opportunity costs but not men's (Brown, 1984). Neoclassic models fall short of explaining significant differences found in the labor force elasticity of wages and income changes of white women, black women, black men, and white men. They account for such differences as reflections of "choices" made to reflect benefits of specialization of roles, with women having invested in household capital, the experts in "home" work, and men having invested in market capital, the experts in "market" work. Feminists claim that such modeling thinly disguises the male-centric or patriarchal traditional division of labor and ignores structural factors such as labor market discrimination, as evidenced by women's relative restrictions in occupational choice and lower aggregate earnings. Policy prescriptions about child care, education, employment, and income security programs that flow from such analyses will vary markedly from analyses that assume women respond to market incentives and opportunities in essentially the same way as men.

Commenting upon the thirtieth anniversary since passage of the Family and Medical Leave Act of 1993, historian Stephanie Coontz (2013) noted that despite cultural shifts in attitudes for greater equality in the workplace and in the home (i.e., sharing breadwinning and caring responsibilities), nonetheless "structural impediments prevent people from acting on their egalitarian values, forcing men and women into personal accommodations and rationalizations that do not reflect their preferences." The net effect is that the gender revolution has "hit a stone wall": "Women are still paid less than men at every educational level and in every job category. They are less likely than men to hold jobs that offer flexibility or family-friendly benefits. When they become mothers, they face more scrutiny and prejudice on the job than fathers do." Noting how the United States falls well behind other affluent nations in areas such as paid family leave, she calls for work-life policies that "enable people to put their gender values into practice."

Much of the political discussion around the welfare reform debates in the 1990s leading up to and incorporated in the Personal Responsibility and Work Opportunity Act (P.L. 104–93) that created TANF in 1996 was steeped in ideological rhetoric that extolled the virtue of labor force participation (Caputo, 2011). Partisan rhetoric was applied not only to welfare recipients, but also to linking work effort to eligibility of unemployed persons to receive food stamps. Such provisions reflected the idea that citizens should expect to work to meet their basic needs and that if they did not, they should show that no work was available or that they were unable to do what work was available.

Another instance of eligibility ideology is "relatives-responsibility"—that is, commitment to the idea that families were and remain primarily responsible for their members. The safety net social welfare provisioning in general in the United States is based on the premise that parents are responsible for the care of their children, whereas adult children are expected to be responsible for the overall care of their aging parents.

Eligibility ideology can be subjected to goodness-of-fit tests with relevant social policy analysis. The field of mental health, for example, reveals an interesting ideological split between prevention and treatment. Sufficient resources may make the apparent trade-off less necessary, but policy options include how resources should be allocated to prevention services and how much to treat already existing conditions, which may be either acute or chronic. Child protective services also pose ideological dilemmas. If the ideological position is such that a child is not to be considered a cause of its abuse or neglect by an adult, the rule that entitles children to protection by state intervention should also entitle them to remain in their own homes while the adult perpetrator is required to leave. However, Chambers and Wedel (2005) contend this is not universally followed as a matter of child protection public policy.

Correspondence Between Eligibility Rules and the Target Specifications of the Social Problem Analysis

To achieve more coherent solutions to a social problem, policy analysts are well advised to ensure that program beneficiaries are included in the group identified with the social problem (Chambers & Wedel, 2005). Identification of concrete indicators or observable signs by which the existence of a problem can be known is an integral part of problem formulation. When analysis of a social problem occurs prior to adopting or implementing a policy or program, the policy analyst should see to it or highly recommend that eligibility and entitlement rules are drawn from those concrete indicators, subtypes, and quantifications identified and elaborated upon during the analysis of the social problem under consideration. When an analysis occurs after a policy or program has been adopted or implemented, policy analysts should check to see if the eligibility and entitlement rules were drawn from those concrete indicators, subtypes, and quantifications. To the extent such eligibility rules do not correspond to those indicators, they will "off-target" program benefits and services.

The idea of "off-targeting" can be tricky or less straightforward than at first blush. On one hand, if poverty is defined as cash income less than a specified amount for a family of a given size, then for purposes of coherency one would expect that at least one of the eligibility rules of a program aimed at poverty reduction would restrict the benefits of a cash assistance program to those at or below that level of income. Yet it is often the case in the United States that programs targeting only or primarily poor persons and/or families tend to be poorly funded and demeaning or stigmatizing of participants. Broadening eligibility to near-poor individuals and families—those with incomes up to twice the poverty thresholds, for example—might increase the prospect for more adequate levels of financial support and for more responsive or enabling service delivery, thereby increasing the participation rate for such programs by those falling at or below the poverty thresholds and lowering the overall poverty rates. Chambers and Wedel (2005) acknowledge the merits of assessing the goodness of fit between eligibility rules and target specification when they contend that a central question is whether the entitlement rules expand or reduce an agency's ability to bring the program to those affected by the social problem. Widening target specification is a way of doing this, albeit at increased financial cost and also with the risk of confounding the causal factors identified when assessing the merits of the correspondence between the social problem theory and program theory.

CRITERIA SPECIFIC TO ELIGIBILITY RULES

Two criteria specific to eligibility rules are stigmatization and off-targeted benefits. Both are unintended, undesirable by-products or side effects of eligibility rules that convey negative connotations about a policy's or program's merits.

Stigmatization

Stigmatized persons are those who are marked as having lesser value, bearing a burden of public disapproval (Chambers & Wedel, 2005). A related, often accompanying concept is alienation, referring to the subjective sense of estrangement from the mainstream of the society. Alienation and stigmatization are serious side effects of eligibility rules, often associated with many negative consequences such as suicide, proclivities toward serious crime, and chemical addiction. Social workers are all too familiar with the negative role that eligibility stigma plays throughout the social service delivery system, evidenced by serving client populations of TANF recipients, mentally ill persons, HIV/AIDS infected persons, child welfare, or protective services recipients, among others (Corrigan, 2007; Corrigan, Watson, Byrne, & Davis, 2005; Dudley, 2000; Ell, 1996; Hodge & Roby, 2010; Lawrence, 2010; Lens, 2010; Mills, 1996). It is important to note that many eligibility rules, such as those for the Social Security retirement or disability program, entail no stigma. Some means-tested programs such as those involved in applying for student loans (Pell Grants or the Direct Loan Program) or for the Earned Income Tax Credit (EITC) also entail no stigma. Applicants for TANF often require something that has to be explained or apologized for, such as lack of a job with sufficient income, or sole support of a child without benefit of, or erratic or limited child support payments. Loan applications, on the other hand, until very recently in light of the financial crisis that erupted in 2008, almost never entail occasions or circumstances that need apologies—to the contrary, they often incur congratulations or positive recognition that one is on the path of valued social regard, such as going to school in the case of loans, or maintaining labor force attachment in the case of the EITC.

Off-Targeted Benefits

As noted above, off-targeted benefits refer to benefits directed to population groups who are not the main object of the policy or program. College and university students who might have taken out a $10,000 loan through the NSDL program in 1981 at an approximately 3 percent annual interest rate, for example, would have netted about $1,400 had they placed the $10,000 loan in a long-term savings account at an approximately 17 percent interest rate ($1,700 annual yield — $300 on the loan = $1,400)—that is, more than $100 a month (Chambers & Wedel, 2005). Such a porous gap resulting from eligibility rules was closed by raising interest rates on such loans to competitive levels. Such use of public financing depletes the level of financial resources for income transfers from those who most clearly are in need of them. In one sense, near-universal programs such as Social Security can be perceived as off-targeting, but in a more positive sense than the case for student loans. All retirees who have met the lifetime work requirements (or if they die, their dependents) get monthly cash allotments regardless of financial need. In addition, over a short time the cash benefits easily exceed the total amount of their and their employers' contributions to the Trust Fund with interest. For universal stigma-free programs such as Social Security, the cost of avoiding stigma is the cost of off-targeting—to the extent that financial need functions as a primary consideration or justification upon which benefit allocation decisions are based.

Case in Point 5.2: Increasing the Federal Hourly Minimum Wage to $9.00

Increasing the minimum wage as an example off-targeting. In his 2013 State of the Union address, President Obama proposed raising the federal minimum hourly wage to $9.00, arguing in part that no one working full time should have to live in poverty (Obama, 2013). Much of the immediate commentary, including those opposed such as Senator Marco Rubio(2013) and those favorably disposed such as the progressive Campaign for America's Future , addressed the likely effects on the hiring practices of businesses, especially small businesses. Obama had earlier proposed a minimum hourly wage hike to $9.50. Related analyses by Sabia and Burkhauser (2008) and by Sherk (2007) highlighted poor target efficiency as an argument against it. They noted that only about 11 percent of beneficiaries would be living in poor households, thereby blunting the impact of the raise to lift poor families out of poverty; if the poverty threshold were increased to 200 percent of the official poverty line, nearly 65 percent of beneficiaries of such a proposed increase would not be living in poor households. Economist and former chair of President Obama's Council of Economic Advisors (CEA) Christina Romer (2013) notes, however, that that about half of all beneficiaries, namely families with less than $40,000 of income, would still benefit from the proposed minimum wage increase to $9.00 per hour, so, while not particularly well targeted, the proposed increase is "not badly targeted, either." Nonetheless, she contends that other anti-poverty measures would be more beneficial: specifically a more generous Earned Income Tax Credit (EITC) or universal preschool education, both of which are "first-rate" policies.

TRADE-OFFS IN EVALUATING ELIGIBILITY RULES

Given that off-targeting can produce desirable and undesirable effects, as the examples of Social Security and TANF, respectively, exemplify, what might policy analysts do to assist policymakers to adjudicate between them? One way of addressing this question is to identify and lay out trade-offs associated with eligibility rules. This presupposes having some decision rules, such as a preference for getting the best value for the money, or a preference for avoiding stigma and increasing costs (as is the case for Social Security), or for lower costs (which makes money available for other social problems) at the expense of creating stigma for beneficiaries (as is the case for TANF). Since almost all policy choices entail trade-offs of one kind or another, settled on value/preference grounds, a value-critical perspective is important. The policy analyst identifies and explicates the trade-offs associated with eligibility rules.

Vertical and Horizontal Equity

The concepts of vertical and horizontal equity are helpful when examining trade-offs. *Vertical equity* refers to the extent resources are allocated to those with respect to the most severe need—the kind of target efficiency discussed earlier in this chapter. *Horizontal equity* refers to the extent resources are allocated to all those in need. In a climate of scarce resources, there is a trade-off between *vertical equity* and *horizontal equity:* a choice between meeting a partial or less than adequate level of need for all those experiencing the problem or more adequately meeting the need of those most seriously experiencing the problem. Other criteria for evaluating eligibility rules involving trade-offs include over- and underutilization, work incentives and disincentives, and a host of family structure and lifestyle criteria.

Overwhelming Costs, Overutilization, and Underutilization

Medicare affords a striking example of trade-offs involving costs and utilization. It is a universal entitlement for U.S. citizens age 65 and over who are entitled to OASDI benefits (40 quarters of work if OASDI taxes are paid, over a minimum of 10 years) and for those with fewer quarters of coverage if they pay Part A premiums. Both the absolute and relative costs of Medicare have risen exorbitantly over the past decade for a host of reasons, including more costly medical technology and drug treatments. A longer-living and an increasingly disproportionate portion of aging persons in the population also contribute to making Medicare an expensive program, consuming about 15 percent of annual federal expenditures in 2010, with Medicaid and CHIP consuming about another 6 percent, and Social Security and the military about 20 percent each (Center on Budget and Policy Priorities, 2011). Bypass operations for heart disease are routine and kidney dialysis is included as an acceptable medical procedure for Medicaid beneficiaries. Some question the long-term benefits of both, with kidney dialysis extending life about ten years and bypass procedures lasting on average about five years before having to be repeated, as well as ethical dilemmas about quality of life germane to both (e.g., Agodoa & Eggers, 2007; Bargman, 2007; Karhunan, Jokinen, Raivio, & Salminen, 2011; Wiedmann, Bernhard, Laufer, & Kocher, 2010). To the extent such services are available and relatively cost-free or low-cost to Medicare recipients—in that full or actual costs are hidden—overutilization is encouraged, reducing financial resources that might be spent on other services, whether to Medicare recipients in need of other services, or others in the population in need of primary, secondary, or tertiary medical services. The United States has yet to answer a basic social policy question that would make for easier judgments about such trade-offs, namely, "On what value premises shall medical care, life, and death, be rationed?"

Many social welfare benefit programs go underutilized. TANF and SSI (Supplemental Security Insurance, a federal program providing cash to aged, blind, and disabled persons to meet basic needs for food, clothing, and shelter), are notable examples, both of whose take-up rates have been reported to run consistently below 60 percent (Arcs & Loprest, 2007; Remler & Glied, 2003). Whereas stigma and administrative diversionary objectives may deter eligible persons from seeking TANF, for which primarily low-income single mothers are eligible, such is not necessarily the case with SSI, for which low-income disabled and aged persons qualify. Much of the underutilization of SSI involves disabled persons. Eligibility rules are complex, in themselves making it difficult to obtain, especially for certain populations of people in need, such as otherwise eligible formerly incarcerated individuals (Bazelton Center for Mental Health Law, 2009). Related procedures initially qualified only those completely and totally disabled for long periods—that is, those "unable to engage in any substantial gainful activity [SGA] by reason of any medically determinable physical or mental impairment expected to result in death or that has lasted or can be expected to last for a continuous period of at least 12 months" (Social Security Administration, 2011, p. 53). Ordinarily disqualified are those with acute or shorter-term episodic mental illness (psychosis, bipolar disorders, or even certain categories of schizophrenia), who might be able to work intermittently throughout a 12-month period, especially with a combination of medication and behavioral/cognitive-oriented counseling or intervention services, accordingly. The often time-consuming and dogged process of documenting medical diagnosis and treatment may also deter many of those with limited income and mobility from seeking SSI benefits. Otherwise eligible mentally ill homeless persons are also known to underuse SSI (Kauff, Brown, Altshuler, Denny-Brown, & Martin, 2009; National Law Center on Homelessness and Poverty, 2008).

Work Incentives, Disincentives, and Eligibility Rules

The relationship between eligibility rules for social welfare provisioning and labor force attachment has been an ongoing concern for policymakers and the general public throughout the development of the social welfare system in the United States and elsewhere. Sorting out deserving from undeserving poor on the basis of ability of work predated the Social Security Act of 1935 (P.L. 74–271), which in effect created the welfare state in the United States, preoccupying state and local officials as well as charitable, philanthropic, religious, and reform minded individuals who sought social responses to meeting need throughout most of the nation's history (Axinn & Stern, 2011). The centrality of labor force participation was evident in the Social Security Act of 1935, which directed the most generous and secure, first-tier, non-means-tested, federally administered provisions to those with a demonstrated work history and second-tier, primarily means-tested, shared federal-state administered and financed provisions to those primarily thought to be detached from the labor force. The second-tier federal-state Aid to Dependent Children (ADC [hereafter Aid to Families with Dependent Children, or AFDC]) program, which targeted at the time primarily widow-headed households with children, was expected to wither away as increasing numbers of widows were to be absorbed by the Social Security Act's first-tier old age survivors' provisions.

Changing sociodemographic characteristics of AFDC recipients from primarily widows with children to increasingly never-married and disproportionately black single mothers, precluded the withering away of AFDC and precipitated several decades of reform efforts aimed at increasing the labor force participation of welfare mothers (Caputo, 2011). The effects of social welfare provisioning on labor force attachment were central to the negative income tax experiments of the 1960s and 1970s and to the

Nixon administration's failed welfare reform bill known as the Family Assistance Plan (Caputo, 2002b). Results of large-scale experimental studies showed some decreases in work effort among those who received guaranteed income versus those who did not. The percentage declines in work effort, however, varied by sociodemographic group, though most were modest: for example, a 31 percent decrease in hours worked for white wives in the New Jersey study, a 1 percent decrease in hours worked for husbands in the rural wage earners study. Two percent of female heads-of-household reduced their work effort in the Gary, Indiana, study and 12 percent of female heads-of-household in the Seattle-Denver study (Burtless & Hausman, 1978; Chambers & Wedel, 2005; Cogan, 1983; Office of Income and Security Policy, 1983; Robins & West, 1980). Efforts to definitively link labor force attachment to second-tier social welfare provision culminated in 1996 with passage of the Personal Responsibility and Work Opportunity Reconciliation Act (P.L. 104–93). This in effect replaced the AFDC open-ended entitlement program with TANF, which limited receipt of federal cash assistance to a lifetime maximum of five years. Henceforth, not only TANF recipients but participants in SNAP (food stamps) and SSI were expected to be labor force participants in some capacity, either preparing for work or actively seeking employment, if not actually obtaining and remaining employed regardless of the pay level.

If any cluster of findings from the social experimentation with guaranteed income contributed to its demise as a viable policy option for addressing poverty, they were those indicating a marked increase in the proportion of marital dissolution among income guarantee recipients (Chambers & Wedel, 2005): at the support level of $3,800, blacks were 1.73 times more likely to dissolve their marriages than were those with no support, 3.12 times for whites; at the support level of $4,800, blacks were 2.02 times more likely to dissolve their marriages than were those with no support, 2.13 times for whites; no statistically significant effects ($p > .05$) were found for Latinos (Hannan, Tuma, & Groeneveld, 1977). Subsequent policy debates about welfare reform shifted from concerns about income maintenance and poverty reduction per se to reducing caseloads and adding work incentives or requiring work as an eligibility requirement for existing social programs.

Procreational Incentives, Marital Instability, and Generational Dependency

Other criteria for evaluating eligibility rules are the extent to which they provide incentives for procreation, marital dissolution, and the dependency of the children in families who receive public benefits, especially cash. The history of social welfare provisioning for low-income families is replete with discussions about the possibility that such women will conceive children in order to become eligible for or to increase welfare benefits. Despite evidence suggesting no discernible reduction in out-of-wedlock births to low-income women in family cap versus non-family cap states (Dyer & Fairlie, 2003), a "family cap" rule is used in over 20 states to deny increased cash assistance to women who have another child while on TANF—15 states had implemented family cap rules prior to the creation of TANF in 1996 (Dinkel, 2011; Levin-Epstein, 2003).

The efficacy of financial incentives on fertility is questionable, as countries that seek to increase fertility rates in light of declining or aging populations such as Canada, Sweden, Russia, and Macedonia can attest (UNFPA, 2011a, 2011b). The wisdom of forming large-scale public policy that links benefits to influence family size warrants scrutiny. The same may be said for claims that public benefits create marital instability, despite the SIME-DIME (Seattle and Denver Income Maintenance Experiments) and other income guarantee experiments of the 1970s that on the surface suggest otherwise. This issue is in part empirical and in part normative. Cash subsidies that enable low-income mothers to dissolve marital relationships that involve abuse or neglect, whether to themselves or their children, can be viewed as empowering, positive outcomes. As Mason and Caputo (2006) contend, social workers are required to consider the best interest of clients rather than adopt whole cloth policies promoting marriage.

Intergenerational transmission of public benefit receipt is also questionable. The argument here is that children who grow up in welfare recipient families lack role models of adults working to make a living and are likely to emulate that behavior, following the pattern set by their parents. Most welfare recipients even prior to TANF had short-term spells (under 4 years) on public assistance—about 12 percent of all beneficiaries received benefits over 4 years cumulatively (Rein & Rainwater, 1978) and situational factors have been found to have much greater explanatory power for welfare receipt than cultural factors (Dolinsky, Caputo, & O'Kane, 1989). The upshot of considerations about procreational incentives, marital instability, and intergenerational dependency is to caution policy analysts about the merits of causal claims, to approach such claims with the aim of getting the facts right and assessing the extent, direction, and magnitude of the effects of public policies, particularly those that provide cash benefits. A major question to be considered is whether large-scale policy responses are warranted when either presumed or actual effects are marginal or limited to small percentages of targeted populations.

As policy analysts, social workers need to be aware of strongly asserted causal relationships and subject them to scrutiny. Manski (2013) contends that stronger assumptions may yield more powerful or firmly held conclusions but they tend to be less credible, given that they may be faulty or "nonrefutable"—that is, when alternative assumptions are also consistent with the available data. Case in Point 5.3 highlights one such example, based on *Losing Ground* (Murray, 1984) and reactions to it.

Case in Point 5.3: Powerful But Less Credible Analysis: *Losing Ground*

As Medvetz (2007, 2012) has shown, the political scientist Charles Murray's *Losing Ground* provided much of the intellectual fodder, based on extensive data analysis, for the idea that government programs do more harm than good, even for their intended beneficiaries. The Manhattan Institute where Murray worked at the time promoted the book (Lane, 1984), which also got much immediate media attention (e.g., Lemann, 1984; Raspberry, 1984; Samuelson, 1984) and whose popularity and contentions survived an onslaught of scholarly criticism (e.g., Ellwood & Bane, 1985; Greenstein, 1985; Miller, 1985), as better endowed free-market oriented think tanks advanced its cause during the welfare reform debates leading up to passage of the Personal Responsibility and Work Opportunity Act (P.L. 93–104) in 1996 (Mone, 2002). See the Epilogue 1.1 Case in Point and Appendix B for more information about the role of think tanks in welfare reform and policy analysis in general. The powerful image was provided by Harold and Phyllis, the fictional couple Murray created to illustrate that social programs led to unemployment and illegitimacy among African Americans by encouraging poor persons to live off welfare rather than work.

HOW IS THE POLICY OR PROGRAM FINANCED?

In the United States, what can be done with revenues generated for social welfare purposes is substantially influenced by how that money is obtained. Along with philanthropy and to a lesser extent other sources of revenue, such as user charges and voluntary contributions, taxes fuel public social welfare programs and related endeavors. Prior to 2000, the distribution of public versus private sources of revenue for social welfare expenditures was more easily identifiable than afterward, primarily because of the rise of for-profit social services, the continuous expansion of the private nonprofit human services sector, and the concomitant increased use of contracting out of services by public agencies, in effect underwriting many nonprofit private service providers and even for-profit organizations such as those for some charter schools and prison systems (Grønbjerg, 2001). Public or government funding as a percentage of all social welfare expenditures was nearly double that of private spending in the early 1970s (66.2% vs. 33.8%) and one and one-half times that in 1994, the last year for which such data were reported by the Social Security Administration (Social Security Administration, 2003). More recent estimates of public versus private social welfare expenditures indicate that the 1.5 ratio still holds: in 2007 public social welfare expenditures amounted to 16.2 percent of GDP whereas private expenditures amounted to 10.5 percent of GDP (Organisation for Economic Co-operation and Development, 2011).

Complicating the private to public social welfare expenditure ratio is the hybrid nature or mixed economy of the welfare state and social welfare provisioning (Gilbert & Terrell, 2005; Hacker, 2002). That is, a major part of funds expended by voluntary agencies is provided by government, with some of the largest social service organizations such as Catholic Charities USA (ranked #2 by total revenue in 2010) receiving over half of its income (67% in 2009 and 62% in 2010), Legal Aid Society (87% in 2010, ranked #95 by total income), and others such as Planned Parenthood Federation of America (ranked # 13) and C.A.R.E (ranked #26) receiving nearly half of their income (39% and 36%, respectively, in 2010) from government grants, fees, or contracts (Catholic Charities USA, 2012; Dennis, 1995; Gilbert & Terrell, 2005; Hrywna, 2011). Public funds invariably come with strings attached, particularly in regard to employment-related discrimination policies and in the case of religious organizations that serve the general public in regard to their mission. As Dennis (1995) notes, in instances where the Salvation Army decided to accept government funds (about 15% of its revenues in the mid-1990s and about 12% in 2010), it stopped requiring church attendance as a condition of its assistance. More recently, the Obama administration's proposed rule that health insurance plans would be required to provide free birth control to female employees at employers' expense, including those offered by Roman Catholic hospitals, universities, and charities, set off an immediate outcry from Catholic bishops and evangelical groups, charging government overreach and an abridgement of their First Amendment right regarding religion (Cooper, 2012; Goodstein, 2012; Pear, 2012; Steinhauer, 2012a) This resulted in a revised ruling, shifting the cost from employers to insurance providers (Cooper & Goldstein, 2012).

This section examines funding sources of social welfare expenditures, knowledge about which is of interest to managers and planners who have to secure resources to sustain their programs, to funders (whether legislators, foundation trustees, or executives of agencies [such as the United Way, Catholic Charities, the Jewish Federation, and Lutheran Social Services]) who make choices among competing interests to achieve their goals, and to direct-service practitioners whose clientele are directly affected by funding decisions of others. Such knowledge is also of interest to the public at large, who are called upon by government through taxation or by philanthropic organizations for financial contributions and who can hold both the public and private sector accountable for the nature, extent, and quality of social welfare benefits and services (Gilbert & Terrell, 2005).

Funding Sources of Social Welfare

Public/Government Funding

Taxes are the main source of revenues for government. They are imposed in a variety of ways: levied on income through personal income taxes, on assets through personal asset taxes (e.g., property taxes), and on corporations through corporate income taxes. For purposes of determining income tax rates for individuals and families, earned income (i.e., wages, salaries, tips, interest from savings accounts) is distinguished from unearned income (i.e., capital gains from stocks and bonds). Different levels of government rely on different forms of taxation to generate revenue for public services, with the federal government relying primarily on individual income taxation and state and local government relying more heavily on property taxes and excise taxes (i.e., on the sale, use, or consumption of particular goods).

Types of Taxes: Progressive, Regressive, Flat, Payroll, Income, Other

Taxes are the main source of revenues for government, with varying distributional or "burden" effects depending on the type of tax (earned [wages, salaries, tips] or unearned [stocks, bonds]) and level of income, and the tax-filing status of the taxpayer (Caputo, 2005; Gilbert & Terrell, 2005). Some, like the *payroll tax* that is used to fund Social Security, are *regressive:* that is, everyone pays the tax at the same rate regardless of their income up to the capped limit ($110,100 for Social Security in 2012) and nothing in excess of that limit regardless of their total income. *Consumption* or *sales* taxes are also *regressive,* as everyone pays the same tax on an item they purchase regardless of income level. As a percentage of total income, *regressive* taxes adversely affect low-income individuals and families more than affluent individuals and families. Other taxes, like the federal income tax, are *progressive* in the sense that individuals and families with higher incomes pay taxes at a higher rate than lower-wage workers.

For calendar year 2012, for example, the following tax brackets (i.e., the rate paid on the last dollar earned, known as the marginal tax rate), were in effect for single wage-earners with taxable income (minus deductions and exemptions): 10% for those with taxable income up to $8,700; 15% between $8,700 and $35,350; 25% between $35,350 and $85,650; 28% between $85,650 and $178,650; 33% between $178,650 and $388,350; and 35% at $388,350 and above (MoneyChimp, 2012). Marginal tax rates are applied only on income above designated thresholds. See Case in Point 5.4 for an example. Keep in mind that below specified levels of income, contingent on tax-filing status, some wage earners need not file tax returns, as Table 5.1 indicates.

Overall federal tax burdens have declined to historic lows for most income groups, particularly middle income families, since the George W. Bush administration cut rates in 2001 and 2003: a family of four in the middle of the income spectrum paid 4.7 percent of its income in federal taxes (this refers

Table 5.1	Filing Requirements for Most Taxpayers for Tax Year 2011	
IF your filing status is . . .	AND at the end of 2011 you were . . .*	THEN file a return if your gross income was at least . . .**
single	under 65	$9,500
	65 or older	$10,950
married filing jointly***	under 65 (both spouses)	$19,000
	65 or older (one spouse)	$20,150
	65 or older (both spouses)	$21,300
married filing separately	any age	$3,700
head of household	under 65	$12,200
	65 or older	$13,650
qualifying widow(er) with dependent child	under 65	$15,300
	65 or older	$16,450

*If you were born on January 1, 1947, you are considered to be age 65 at the end of 2011.
** Gross income means all income you received in the form of money, goods, property, and services that is not exempt from tax, including any income from sources outside the United States or from the sale of your main home (even if you can exclude part or all of it). Do not include any Social Security benefits unless (a) you are married filing a separate return and you lived with your spouse at any time during 2011, or (b) one-half of your social security benefits plus your other gross income and any tax-exempt interest is more than $25,000 ($32,000 if married filing jointly). If (a) or (b) applies, see the instructions for Form 1040 or 1040A or Publication 915 to figure the taxable part of social security benefits you must include in gross income. Gross income includes gains, but not losses, reported on Form 8949. Gross income from a business means, for example, the amount on Schedule C, line 7, or Schedule F, line 9. But, in figuring gross income, do not reduce your income by any losses, including any loss on Schedule C, line 7, or Schedule F, line 9.
*** If you did not live with your spouse at the end of 2011 (or on the date your spouse died) and your gross income was at least $3,700, you must file a return regardless of your age.

Source: IRS *Publication 17 (2011), Your Federal Income Tax,* Table 1.1.2011, from http://www.irs.gov/publications/p17/ch01.html#en_US_2011_publink1000170407

to federal income tax and does not include federal Social Security and Medicare taxes, also known as payroll taxes or OASDI taxes), the third lowest percentage in 50 years. Most of the drop is attributable to the pronounced decline in individual income tax burdens, with the sharpest drops among the highest income households: in 2010, when the 2001–2008 tax cuts were in full effect, households with $1 million or more had their after-tax incomes increased by an average of 7.7 percent, whereas households in the middle fifth of the income distribution had their after-tax income increase by an average of 2.6 percent (Brunet & Cox, 2009; Marr & Brunet, 2011).

Case in Point 5.4: Income Tax Progressivity

Marking the one-hundredth anniversary of the federal income tax, Sam Pizzigati, editor of Inequality.org, and Chuck Collins, who has directed the Institute for Policy Studies (IPS) program on inequality and the common good, attribute much of the income inequality that has come to characterize the advent of the twenty-first century to the erosion of its progressivity. In 1964 Congress reduced the top marginal tax rate from 91 to 70 percent; in the 1980s, the Reagan administration reduced it further, first to 50 percent and then to 28 percent. As can be gleaned from Table 5.2, the top rates increased to their contemporary high at 39.6 percent during the Clinton administration of the 1990s, were temporarily reduced to 35 percent during the G.W. Bush administration, and returned to 39.6 percent when Congress allowed the temporary top rate of 35 percent to expire. Wealthy individuals pay lower rates on income below the designated thresholds. For an individual reporting an annual earned income of $500,000 in 2012, for example, the 10 percent rate would apply only to the taxable income up to the threshold of $8,700, the 15 percent rate on taxable income between $8,700 and $35,350, the 25 percent rate on taxable income between $35,350 and $85,650, and so on, with the highest rate of tax (39.6%) paid only on income above $388,350. To reduce the inequality that resulted in part from the lessened progressivity of the U.S. income tax structure, Pizzigati and Collins (2013) recommend setting the entry threshold for a new 91 percent maximum rate as a multiple of the nation's minimum wage—say twenty-five times, which was roughly the ratio between CEO and typical worker pay for much of the mid-twentieth century, before top corporate pay started to average over 300 times workers' take-home pay in recent decades. What do you think about this recommendation? (For more about IPS, see Appendix B.)

At the federal level, payroll and income taxes are the main sources of revenue that finance public programs; other sources include *corporate* and *excise* taxes. *Payroll taxes* are levied on employees and employers, each contributing 6.2 percent of salaries and wages into a Social Security Trust Fund from which payments are made to the current generation of retirees and those on disability, as well as 1.45 percent each to a trust fund that funds Medicare. (Self-employed or contract workers generally must pay both employee and employer sides of the Social Security and Medicare payroll taxes, submitting these on a quarterly basis—a total of 15.3 percent of income). Social Security and Medicare account for approximately 32 percent of federal expenditures (Center on Budget and Policy Priorities, 2012b). Income, corporate, and excise taxes are used to fund discretionary programs that include military-related expenses (about 20% of federal expenditures), and all other social welfare programs such as EITC, Medicaid, SNAP, SSI, housing assistance, and TANF.

Also keep in mind that tax rates have changed markedly since 1992, as Table 5.2 below indicates. By and large, the federal personal income tax structure, which is the nation's most progressive tax, has adhered to its "ability to pay" ethos: as income rises, so does the tax rate. Nonetheless, despite the heavier "tax burden" the progressive nature of the federal income tax structure imposes on more

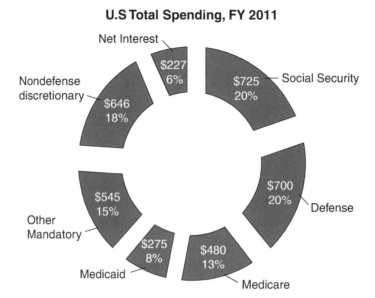

U.S Total Spending, FY 2011

Net Interest
$227
6%

Social Security
$725
20%

Nondefense discretionary
$646
18%

Defense
$700
20%

Other Mandatory
$545
15%

Medicaid
$275
8%

Medicare
$480
13%

Note: Category of Other Mandatory consists of spending on unemployment compensation, federal civilian and military retirement, veterans' benefits, the Earned Income Tax Credit, food stamps, and other programs.

Source: Schwabish, J., & Griffith, C. (2012). *The U.S. federal budget, fiscal year 2011.* Washington, DC: Congressional Budget Office. Retrieved from http://www.cbo.gov/ftpdocs/125xx/doc12577/budgetinfographic.pdf

affluent individuals and families, the relationship between total income and taxes paid is neither simple nor direct: type of income, family size, and spending patterns all influence the amount of tax owed.

During the Republican presidential nomination campaign of 2012, Mitt Romney reported that his effective tax rate was about 14 percent, making headline news in the aftermath of the Occupy Wall Street demonstrations protesting among other things increased income inequality between the top 1 percent of income earners versus the other 99 percent (Confessore, Kocieniewski, & Parker, 2012; Parker, 2012).

Most states also collect income taxes to finance public programs. These are supplemented by *property* and *sales* taxes, which also finance municipal and county governments. *Property taxes* are also *progressive* in that property owners in more affluent neighborhoods are more likely to have higher incomes and therefore pay higher taxes associated with the greater assessed value of their property. Public education expenses are primarily borne by state and municipal governments and financed primarily through local *property* taxes, with many states implementing lottery systems to cover increasing costs and avoid raising property taxes.

Mode of Finance: Categorical and Block Grants, General Revenue Sharing

Federal and state governments use several mechanisms to transfer revenues obtained from taxes, lotteries, fees, and other sources of income to lower units of government, private sector service

Table 5.2	Tax Hikes, Tax Cuts 1992–2013					
1992	**1993–2000**	**2001**	**2002**	**2003–2010**	**2011–2012**	**2013**
			10%	10%		10%
15%	15%	15%	15%	15%		15%
28%	28%	27.5%	27%	25%	Same as 2010	25%
31%	31%	30.5%	30%	28%		28%
	36%	35.5%	35%	33%		35%
	39.6%	39.1%	38.6%	35%		39%

Source: IRS *Publication 17 (2011), Your federal income tax,* Table 1.1.2011, from http://www.irs.gov/publications/p17/ch01 .html#en_US_2011_publink1000170407

providers, as well as to individuals and families. In federally funded and administered benefit programs such as Social Security, Supplemental Security Income (SSI), and SNAP (food stamps), recipients or officially recognized or designated beneficiaries receive checks or wire transfers for deposit into their bank checking/savings accounts or vouchers directly from the federal government. For joint federal-state programs such as TANF, Section 8 housing vouchers, or Medicaid, which share costs but are administered through states or local governments, the three systems of transfer are *categorical grants, block grants,* and *general revenue sharing.* Of the three, *categorical grants* are the most narrowly specified, ensuring that the unit of government providing the revenue substantially controls its expenditure and limits the recipient level of government or service provider to implementing its policies and procedures. Historically, the majority of grant-in-aid programs have been defined narrowly and they remain so, despite emphasis since the 1990s on program flexibility. Categorical grants specify who is served, what benefits they are to receive, and how the delivery system is to be organized. TANF's predecessor, the Aid to Families with Dependent Children (AFDC) program was a prototypical categorical program. Categorical funding had its heyday during the so-called Great Society era of President Lyndon Johnson's administration, which wanted to ensure that money went to programs such as those operated by the Office of Economic Opportunity, serving inner-city populations and bypassing state administrative mechanisms (Caputo, 1994; Gilbert & Terrell, 2005). Since the Great Society of the 1960s, however, the federal aid system has made less use of categorical grants.

The shift from categorical grants accompanied the ascendency of conservative (economic and social) critiques of the welfare state, whose rhetoric against "big government" still resonates for some of the U.S. population and fuels political candidates mostly from the Republican Party—although it was Democratic President Bill Clinton (1995, 1996) who announced that the era of big government was over. A major objection to categorical grants, aside from ideological proclivities of libertarians and some economic and social conservative thinkers, politicians, and pundits, is administrative or managerial: the sheer number of such programs precludes effective coordination, given that many are separately administered. Making such a system work as a whole is a considerable challenge to mayors and governors, even if aware of all the programs that come under their jurisdiction.

In an effort to break the categorical tradition, the Nixon administration initiated *General Revenue Sharing (GRS)* in 1972. *GRS* provided for the first time federal aid without any specification of program priority—that is, it was unconditional with regard to function. Operating as independent policymakers, localities or states could develop their own programs (either creating new ones or expanding old ones), use the money for tax relief, or build new facilities. If creating new or expanding old programs, localities and states could invest in recreation, police, sanitation, or code enforcement. Under General Revenue Sharing the federal government provided more than $6 billion a year for over a decade, with one-third of the money going to states and the remainder to local authorities for unhampered use—basically grant aid for free. Despite its flexibility, General Revenue Sharing was abolished as part of the Reagan administration's efforts to trim the federal deficit in 1987 (Caputo, 1994; Gilbert & Terrell, 2005).

The Omnibus Budget Reconciliation Act of 1981 (P.L. 97–35) collapsed seventy-seven categorical grants-in-aid programs into nine *block grants,* whose degree of specificity of purpose fell between *categorical grants* and *General Revenue Sharing.* Ten separate grants that provided state aid for dealing with different aspects of alcohol and drug abuse and mental health, for example, were combined into one new *block grant,* in effect streamlining administration, reducing paperwork, and increasing state discretion to define programs. *Block grants* enabled states and localities to establish and implement policy within a given functional area. Other block grants created by the Omnibus Budget Reconciliation Act of 1981 that remain to this day include community services, preventive health and health services, primary care, maternal and child health services, social services, and home energy assistance (*Federal Regulations,* 2012). In 1996 the Clinton administration ended the categorical Aid to Families with Dependent Children (AFDC) program and created the Temporary Assistance for Needy Families (TANF) block program, giving states broad discretion as to how to use the lump sum of federal money for low-income parents and their children (Caputo, 2011).

Private Sources of Funding Social Welfare Provisions

Private Giving, Philanthropy: Individuals, Corporations, Foundations, Charitable Service-Oriented Organizations, Agency-Based Fundraising, Community Fundraising

Private sources of revenue for social welfare expenditures are quite varied, ranging from individual donations of varying amounts, to foundations and other nonprofit organizations, to for-profit groups or corporations. It should be kept in mind that philanthropies contribute to a variety of causes, some of which fall outside what are ordinarily considered to be social welfare—such as environmental, arts, culture, religion. The largest U.S.-based foundation is the Bill and Melinda Gates Foundation, which has assets hovering around $34 billion, followed by the Ford Foundation with $10.9 billion, the J. Paul Getty Trust with $9.6 billion, and the Robert Wood Johnson Foundation with $8.5 billion (Foundation Center, 2012).

According to the Giving USA Foundation (2011), in 2010 charitable contributions from individuals, corporations, and foundations amounted to about $290.9 billion, the lion's share (73%) of which came from individuals ($211.8 billion), followed by grant-giving foundations ($41 billion, or 14%), and corporations ($15.3 billion, or 5%). More than one-third (35%) of the expenditures went to religious organizations ($100.6 billion), followed by education ($41.7 billion, or 14%), nonprofit foundations ($33 billion, or 11%), human service organizations ($26.5 billion, or 9%), health and public-society benefit organizations ($22.8 and $24 billion, or about 8% each), and the remainder to arts, culture, and humanities ($13.3 billion, or 5%), international affairs ($15.8 billion, or 5%), environment/animal organizations ($6.7 billion, or 2%), and individuals ($4.2 billion, or 2%). Between 2008 and 2010 philanthropic contributions declined on the whole by 4.2 percent in inflation adjusted dollars and from all contributors except corporations (+21.6%), with the largest decline from bequests (–28.1%), followed by foundations (–4.1%). With the exception of international affairs (+17%), changes to recipients were more modest and evenly distributed: health (+4.1%), arts, culture, and humanities (+2.5%), human services (+1%), public-society benefit (+.2%), religion (–2.1%), education (–2%), and environment/animal organizations (–.1%).

Employment-Related Benefit Funding

Employers constitute another source of funding for social welfare provisions through a variety of legally required and optional programs (U.S. Small Business Administration, 2012a). They are required by law to contribute to the Social Security Trust Fund (FICA) and to the Medicare Trust Fund. In 2012 the FICA rate was 6.2 percent of all wages up to $110,100 and the Medicare rate was 1.45 percent of all wages (for self-employed persons, the rates were 12.4% and 2.9%, respectively). They are also required to carry workers' compensation insurance, providing coverage to employees who have suffered an injury or illness resulting from job-related duties. Coverage includes medical and rehabilitation costs and lost wages for employees injured on the job (U.S. Small Business Administration, 2012b).

Employers must also contribute to the federal-state Unemployment Insurance (UI) program, which provides unemployment benefits to eligible workers who are unemployed through no fault of their own, as determined under state law, and meet other eligibility criteria, also determined by state law. Benefits are based on a percentage of an individual's earnings over a recent 52-week period, up to a state maximum amount, and in most states up to a maximum of 26 weeks for regular state-funded UI programs. Emergency Unemployment Compensation (EUC), made possible by Federal legislation passed in 2008, is available for those who exhaust their UI benefits (up to 14 additional weeks or a maximum of 47 weeks in areas with at least 9% unemployment), and Extended Benefits (EB) are available for those who exhaust both UI and EUC benefits (up to a maximum of 20 additional weeks for those in areas with at least 8% unemployment (Center on Budget and Policy Priorities, 2013). In all but three states the benefit funding is based solely on a tax imposed on employers. Taxable wage bases and rates vary by state. In 2011 for the United States as a whole, employers contributed an estimated 3.24 percent of taxable wages (slightly less than 1% of all wages). Among the 48 contiguous states, the wage base for taxable income purposes ranged from a low of $7,000 (Arizona, California, Florida) to a high of $37,000 (Washington), and the tax rates on taxable wages ranged from a low of 1.43 (South Dakota) to a high of 6.7 (Pennsylvania) (U.S. Department of Labor, Employment and Training Administration, 2012a, 2012b).

Employers also contribute to social provisioning in optional, less visible ways, for example, by providing health care insurance and retirement benefits. Employers pay the lion's share of health insurance premium costs for workers and their families. In 2011 employer contributions were estimated to be 83 percent of total premium costs for single employee coverage and 73 percent for family coverage (Kaiser Family Foundation, Health Research & Educational Trust, & NORC, 2011). Many employers also contribute to employees' retirement or pension plans, either with defined benefits or defined contributions. In a Money Purchase Pension Plan, the employer is required to make fixed annual contributions to the employee's individual account. A 401(k) plan is a defined contribution plan, a cash or deferred arrangement—that is, employees can elect to defer receiving a portion of their salary, which is instead contributed on their behalf to the 401(k) plan. Employers may match these contributions (U.S. Department of Labor, Secretary's Office, 2012). In 2009, private employers spent $116.1 billion for defined benefit pension plans and $118.6 billion in defined contribution plans, inclusive of profit sharing plans, roughly 15 percent of all retirement benefits that year (Employee Benefit Research Institute, 2011). In 2010 corporate employer contributions to defined benefit retirement plans reached nearly $50 billion, over 6 percent of such total contributions, compared to less than 6 perecnt in 2009 and less than 5 percent in 2007 and 2008 (Kozlowsky, 2011).

Social Entrepreneurs: A Hybrid Way of Funding to Meet Social Needs

Social work is noticeably absent from the social entrepreneurship movement that has spread across the globe over the past several decades (Berzin, 2012). Although it defies any single definition, **social entrepreneurship** can be viewed as a process "involving the innovative use and combination of resources to pursue opportunities to catalyze social change and/or address social needs" (Mair & Marty, 2006, as cited in Pless, 2012, p. 317). Social change and addressing social needs fall well within the purview of social work practice. As Berzin (2012) and Dees (2001) note, social entrepreneurs have been around a while and they are in countries around the world, including the likes of economist Muhammad Yunus who in 1976 launched what became the Grameen Bank in Bangladesh to provide joint-liability or microcredit loans to low-income women to operate small businesses. A YouTube video, titled Social Entrepreneurs: Pioneering Social Change, that features Yunus can be found at http://www.youtube.com/watch?v=jk5LI_WcosQ. (In 2011, Yunus was indicted by the Bangladeshi government for violations in handling bank funds, and the case is under appeal.) As a form of social entrepreneurship, microcredit has spread around the globe, albeit with some controversy (Selinger, 2008). As Dees (2001) notes, the blurring of boundaries between the for-profit and not-for-profit sectors of the economy has expanded beyond the more familiar innovative not-for-profit ventures to social purpose business ventures. These include for-profit community banks and hybrid organizations mixing not-for-profit and for-profit entities, such as homeless shelters that start businesses to train and employ their residents. Social entrepreneurship takes a multiplicity of forms, as social entrepreneurs are devising innovative ways to achieve social mission impacts and generating new sources of funds to do so.

In the United States, social entrepreneurship began in the mid-1980s as a way for private nonprofit agencies to fuse market-based enterprise innovation and social purpose. Since then social entrepreneurship has blossomed to include the public sector, encouraging new ways of approaching work in the human services (Keohane, 2013). Much of the public sector emphasis has been on how social entrepreneurs measure, evaluate, and proactively use data collection and analysis to change the work and policy objectives of social welfare agencies. (Measurement and evaluation issues, among other related issues, are the foci of Chapters 7–11.) New York City Mayor Michael Bloomberg's administration has been exemplary in this regard, applying social entrepreneurship in its efforts to improve welfare reform and education, reduce homelessness, and use performance-based contracts.

The Obama administration has also endorsed the idea of social entrepreneurship (Leonhardt, 2011). President Obama created the Office of Social Innovation and Civic Participation (SICP), housed within the Domestic Policy Council, with three mission areas: doing business differently by promoting service as a solution and a way to develop community leadership; increasing investment in innovative community solutions that demonstrate results; and developing new models of partnership (www .whitehouse.gov/administration/eop/sicp). The administration's education program "Race to the Top," designed to encourage innovation and reform in schools, is another example of the administration's commitment to social entrepreneurship.

To enhance prospects of carrying out their social mission, social entrepreneurs seek innovative ways to secure funds. A notable example of market shaping in the face of traditional market failure (see Chapter 2) is the GAVI Alliance (formerly the Global Alliance for Vaccines and Immunization), a public-private global health partnership designed to save children's lives by increasing access to immunization in poor countries (Keohane, 2013). Launched in 2000 and created with a $750 million commitment from the Gates Foundation, GAVI has pioneered new financing mechanisms for public health programs. For example, GAVI helped launch the International Finance Facility for Immunization (IFFIm) "to accelerate the availability and predictability of funds. The IFFIm raises funds by issuing bonds in capital markets and uses long-term government pledges as a financial guarantee and to repay interest" (Keohane, 2013, pp. 59–60).

The use of bonds in capital markets for social purposes has attracted attention in other areas of social welfare provisioning around the globe and in the United States. The Obama administration has discussed the potential for *social impact bonds* (SIBs), a symbol of pay-for-success initiatives, partly on the basis of pilot efforts in the United Kingdom (Keohane, 2013; Liebman, 2011). The concept behind social impact bonds is straightforward: "the government agrees to pay for preventive programs that reduce long-term public expenditures or generate new tax revenue by financing against the expected cost-savings or increased receipts; private investors underwrite these investments up front" (Keohane, 2013, p. 173). Investors are paid only for successful outcomes; hence, they bear all the risk of the investment. Google CEO Eric Schmidt (2012) contends that social impact bonds have promise in the area of prison reform, namely with the objective of reducing recidivism rates, emulating in part the UK's experience (Rosenberg, 2012). The scheme would work as follows: The government would float these bonds to investors— typically foundations—who would bet on the ability of companies, community groups, and other qualified parties to provide services such as educating the many inmates who are high school dropouts. The money raised would fund social programs. And if, after a meaningful period—say, five years—the program showed that it had had a significant positive impact (by, for instance, reducing repeat offenses or raising graduation rates), investors would get their money back with a premium (Schmidt, 2012, p. 64).

Despite Berzin (2012), a word of caution is in order about social work joining the social entrepreneurial movement. Reliance on social entrepreneurship may undermine principles of social justice based on rights-based eligibility, especially for universal social welfare benefits. Cook, Dodds, and Mitchell (2003) contend, for example, that pursuing social justice aims is likely to violate conditions required for efficiency, one of the goals of social entrepreneurial efforts. How social entrepreneurs balance resource allocations between profit-making and welfare provisioning is problematic. Further, there's the issue of moral hazard, raised in Chapter 4: governments would have a moral obligation to prevent an entrepreneur from failing, thereby distorting the risk and return choices entrepreneurs face, effectively enabling them to ignore the downside risks of any development plan.

Skill Building Exercises

1. Identify a major social welfare policy or program, such as TANF, Medicaid, or SSI. What are the theoretical or causal links, either as advocated by policy proponents or as can be inferred from identifiable provisions of the policy, or both, between the policy or program and the social problem(s) it is meant to address?

   a. What ideological assumptions are driving or justifying the purported or stated link between the targeted beneficiaries of the program?
   b. Assess the relative merits of these justifications.
   c. What can be gleaned from the assumptions about the cultural and political environment in which the policy or program was originally adopted and about contemporary society?
   d. Based on these assumptions, what changes if any would you propose to advance social and economic justice?

2. Identifying the eligibility criteria of the policy or program in skill building exercise #1.

   a. Discuss, when appropriate, how each conveys negative connotations about a policy's or program's merits.
   b. What does this tell us about the cultural and political environment in which the policy or program was originally adopted and about contemporary society?

3. Discuss trade-offs likely to occur when considering modifications to or alternatives of eligibility criteria embedded in the legislation described in skill building exercise #1 and identified in skill building exercise #2.

   a. Assess the relative merits of the trade-offs.
   b. Which trade-offs are most consistent with social work ethics, sound practice, and advancing social justice?
   c. Why?

4. Discuss the differences between income and payroll taxes, between progressive and regressive taxes, and between earned income and non-earned income taxes in light of who is likely to pay them, who to benefit from them, and how they are likely to do so.

   a. What changes in the tax code would you like to have Congress pass?
   b. Discuss policies or programs that might benefit from greater private sources of financing than from public and vice versa.
   c. Discuss policies or programs that might benefit from hybrid sources of funding, such as might be suitable to social entrepreneurship or *social impact bonds*.

Costs, Benefits, and Risks

This chapter presents two methodological procedures used by policy analysts, namely cost-benefit analysis and, in less detail, risk assessment. It describes strengths and limitations of each procedure. The chapter also presents several typologies for comparing alternative policies aimed at the same social problem. Upon completion of the chapter, students will know what goes into conducting cost-benefit analyses and risk assessments, while understanding the limitations of using them.

Upon successful completion of the skill building exercises of Chapter 6, students will have mastered the following Council on Social Work Education (CSWE) Competencies and Practice Behaviors:

Chapter 6	CSWE Core Competencies
#	**Description**
2.1.3	**Apply Critical Thinking to Inform and Communicate Professional Judgments**
	Distinguish, appraise, and integrate multiple sources of knowledge, including research-based knowledge and practice wisdom
	Analyze models of assessment, prevention, intervention, and evaluation
	Demonstrate effective oral and written communication in working with individuals, families, groups, organizations, communities, and colleagues
2.1.4	**Engage Diversity and Difference in Practice**
	Recognize the extent to which a culture's structures and values may oppress, marginalize, alienate, or create or enhance privilege and power
2.1.5	**Advance Human Rights and Social and Economic Justice**
	Understand the forms and mechanisms of oppression and discrimination
2.1.6	**Engage in Research-Informed Practice and Practice-Informed Research**
	Use research evidence to inform practice
2.1.7	**Apply Knowledge of Human Behavior and the Social Environment**
	Utilize conceptual frameworks to guide the processes of assessment, intervention, and evaluation
	Critique and apply knowledge to understand person and environment

(Contiued)

Chapter 6	(Continued)
#	Description
2.1.8	**Engage in Policy Practice to Advance Social and Economic Well-Being and to Deliver Effective Social Work Services**
	Analyze, formulate, and advocate for policies that advance social well-being

Source: Adapted from Council on Social Work Education (2012). *Educational policy and accreditation standards.* Washington, DC: Author. Retrieved from http://www.cswe.org/file.aspx?id=13780

DEVELOPMENT OF COST-BENEFIT ANALYSIS

Cost-benefit analysis (CBA) is a widely used tool of applied economics to address real-world problems. It has a checkered history, given accusations of technical wizardry that fails to account for the less quantifiable though nonetheless salient aspects of human behavior, abuses associated with manipulation of net benefit data, a tight focus on project-by-project evaluations that rule out a broad defense of longer time horizons and spatial boundaries, and an emphasis on overall net benefits/costs to the exclusion of distributional effects (Persky, 2001). Advocates and opponents of public works projects have nonetheless long weighed costs against measures of economic usefulness, albeit with varying degrees of formality. French engineers' rough-and-ready cost computations preceded the 1789 Revolution and flourished in the mid-nineteenth century with contributions of Jules Dupuit, who developed the first modern cost-benefit approach to markets and contributed to the theoretical groundwork for the marginal utility basis of economic demand (Ekelund & Hébert, 2002; Houghton, 1958; Lamontagne, 1947; Leonard, 2000; Persky, 2001). In the United States, the Army Corps of Engineers (Shallat, 1989) advanced and promoted cost-benefit analysis (CBA), which has been characterized as a "distinctive achievement of American political culture" that government agencies including Congress champion and use as "a defense against meddling outsiders and [as] a strategy for controlling far-flung or untrustworthy subordinates" (Porter, 1995, p. 194). The appeal of cost-benefit analysis is due in part to its transparency about criteria used to determine measures of costs and benefits, albeit contested, while concomitantly ensuring uniformity to limit discretion and ensuring autonomy of the agency or program using it.

Cost-benefit analysis lacks a precise or standard definition beyond the idea that both positive and negative consequences of a proposed action are summarized and then weighed against each other (M. Schmidt, 2012). It has nonetheless pushed economic thinking into public debates and brought public scrutiny to technical deliberations of economists (Persky, 2001). As used in the business sector, where metrics of success such as profit and market share are more readily quantified than is the case in the government and social service sectors, cost-benefit analysis seeks to predict the financial impact and other consequences of an action. Cost-benefit analysis also provides the dominant economic approach by which not only economists talk to one another, but also with government bureaucrats and to the general public about the desirability of public programs and investment projects (Persky, 2001). Fundamental questions that must be answered by the policy analysts who undertake CBA include how costs and benefits are defined in practical terms, which costs and benefits are to be included in the analysis, and what metrics (whether financial or other) are important for decision makers and policy planners.

COST-BENEFIT ANALYSIS AS ORGANIZED COMMON SENSE

Consider how you decided to select the school or program in which you are currently enrolled and the course in which a book such as this might be assigned. Chances are you identified several plausible alternative schools or programs that seemed attractive, perhaps on the basis of what others had told you or what you came to know about them from a variety of other sources, and that warranted further time and effort to assess the likelihood of getting accepted and of the goodness of fit in the event you were accepted. It would probably be a good guess that to aid your deliberations you also made a list of the advantages and disadvantages of each of those options that warranted further exploration. One college or university was sufficiently rigorous, but its costs fell beyond what you either could afford or wanted to pay. Another college was affordable but lacked the rigor or array of programs you wanted. The options also varied by the range of campus activities, housing availability, sports facilities, technical capacity (wireless Internet availability, up-to-date computer hardware and software, online courses, distance learning, and the like), campus location (urban vs. suburban vs. rural), average class size, auspices (public vs. private, nonprofit vs. for-profit), and the like. How did you decide? Perhaps with the help of parents and a counselor, you deliberated about the advantages and disadvantages of each option, assigning some weight or value to your preferences and comparing the options accordingly. In perhaps a roundabout way, you carried out many of the steps or procedures associated with cost-benefit analysis.

STEPS TO COST-BENEFIT ANALYSIS

Theoretically, conducting cost-benefit analysis is relatively straightforward: identify all important long-term and short-term costs and benefits; measure tangible benefits in monetary terms; use a discount rate (i.e., adjust for changes in value over time to ensure that all are expressed in commensurate terms); total the costs and benefits, showing either net benefit (benefits minus costs) or the ratio of benefits to costs (the benefits divided by the costs). As discussed below, each step, however, poses a series of questions and judgments that invariably influence conclusions drawn and recommendations on the relative merits or weights of costs to benefits. The evaluation of adult literacy programs (Holtman, 1970) will be used here to get a handle on merits and limitations of cost-benefit analysis in light of other studies concerning returns on investments in education and to show how cost-benefit analysis can be conducted.

Illiteracy, the inability to perform basic tasks such as totaling an entry on a deposit slip or identifying a piece of specific information in a brief news article, is a long-standing social problem that affects about 14 percent of the adult population. During the 1990s, this was about 32 million persons, in the United States (Kirsch, Jungeblut, Jenkins, & Kolstad, 2002). About 21–23 percent of adults—some 40–44 million persons in the 1990s—scored in the lowest level of prose, document, and quantitative proficiencies—that is, totaling entries on deposit slips and identifying specific information in brief news articles were the most complex proficiency tasks they could perform. Low levels of literacy are strongly correlated with poverty, unemployment, diminished labor force attachment, and low-wages jobs—all of which translates into lost income and tax revenues and increased training costs for business and industry. More recent estimates indicate that over 90 million adults in the United States lack adequate literacy and only 38 percent of twelfth graders in the United States are at or above proficient in reading (National Research Council, 2012).

Policymakers are confronted with choices about the amount and types of resources they should allocate to different educational programs. Since nearly all related choices are likely to generate some social benefits and since resources are limited, policymakers must determine which programs are likely to contribute the most to society given limited resources. The role of cost-benefit analysis is to aid in this necessary matter of choice (Holtman, 1970). Given basic economic assumptions, a main objective of cost-benefit analysis of adult education programs is to show their value in contributing to the net consumption value for the entire population, and to show who will be the main beneficiaries under current institutional arrangements and who will bear the costs. Some of the identifiable benefits and costs will be quantifiable (higher wages over one's life course and less leisure when attending literacy classes), others will be qualitative (love of learning, openness to new experiences).

The approach taken here is that cost-benefit analysis need not be an all-or-nothing task. Benefits defying quantification or not readily quantifiable such as love of learning or openness to new experiences need not preclude the use of cost-benefit analysis; rather, they pose challenges to identifying important or significant benefits that are quantifiable or for which suitable quantifiable measures can be used as proxies, assessing the relative importance of those that are with those that are not, and making a decision or taking an action on the basis of such assessments. Thinking about cost-benefit analysis this way enables us to avoid the trap of viewing education in general and adult education in particular solely in terms of returns on investment (ROI). This may be appropriate for some students under some circumstances but not for all under every circumstance (Edmundson, 2012).

Identifying Important Benefits and Costs

Benefits

One benefit that immediately comes to mind about adult literacy programs is the increased productivity that can be attributed to a worker's ability to read and write. A readily quantifiable measure is the increase of a worker's wage attributable to being able to read and write. The assumption here is that such a wage increase is a valid measure of the value added to the consumption of society. As straightforward as this relationship between literacy and productivity as measured by wages might seem, there may be attributes associated with achievement of a primary education that distinguish such achievers from illiterates and it may be these other attributes (e.g., natural ability, home environment) that contribute to increased earning ability rather than the ability to read and write and, perhaps, do basic arithmetic.

Another difficulty arises when increased productivity associated with literacy is channeled outside the market: a stay-at-home parent is likely to be more productive if literate, but since there is no paid compensation for related activities such as child rearing, there is no market value for the benefit, a long and continuing bone of contention among feminist economists (e.g., see Himmelweit, 2010; Wood, 1997). A value for such activity will need to be estimated or determined. Another benefit associated with literate parents is the ability they gain when educating their children: for example, improved parent-child relationships and better understanding of the schooling process. Part of the return on the child's education is attributable to early investments in time and energy made in the home. Estimates of the effects of such investments are thereby warranted. Literacy also increases future options that warrant consideration: literate individuals, for example, have the option of continuing their education, whether in the form of formal schooling or on-the-job training (OJT). The value of on-the-job training has long been known to increase substantially with increased education (Mincer, 1962). Literacy itself is also likely to have value to an individual as a consumer good—that is, a person might be willing to purchase education even if it does not increase his or her productivity, say to expand one's appreciation for or horizons in the liberal arts (history, literature, music, philosophy). To the extent the consumption benefits of education are ignored, dwelling instead primarily or only on the economic returns to investments (ROI) in education, the costs of such investments are overestimated.

As noted in Chapter 4, public provision of education is often justified because of external benefits (the benefits to others in society in addition to the benefits accruing to the individual). Widespread literacy throughout the population lowers the cost of collecting taxes to support all government services. Other benefits have attributes similar to public goods, making it difficult to determine one's willingness to pay, since by the nature of the good one cannot be excluded from receiving it. Think of instructional written documents for getting something done in an efficient or fair manner: a literate population reduces the time and energy it takes for people to understand what might be expected of them. The United Nations includes adult literacy as a principal component in determining an index of power equality in a country, with greater literacy positively associated with power equality, something from which everyone benefits (United Nations Development Programme [UNDP], 2011). External benefits associated with literacy preclude an efficient allocation of resources if competitive or market forces are solely relied upon for allocating resources. This is because allocation efficiency of a market economy rests on the assumption that individuals consider their own satisfaction when consuming goods. When goods and services consumed by one individual affect the welfare of others in society, individual utility satisfaction need not necessarily be consistent with social utility maximization. Public support for financing primary education, for example, rests on this premise—namely that it is a public good, thereby necessitating cost-benefit analyses to evaluate the provision of the service.

On the whole, benefits from adult literacy are quite extensive, for individuals, families, fellow workers, and society in general; even future generations benefit from an individual's literacy. Many such benefits are measurable, which is not to suggest that all such benefits have been enumerated. Other benefits such as better health and lower mortality are associated with greater degrees of literacy and when used with wage data, for example, expected gains from reduced mortality can be estimated (Weisbrod, 1962).

Costs

The direct costs of producing adult literacy are similar to producing other types of education: the value of teachers' services, the value of capital equipment necessary to provide the education, the value of books and Internet access, the value of extra consumption necessary to attend school. Such values are readily determined by the cost of acquiring them in the market. *Opportunity costs* (i.e., costs associated with alternatives forgone or lost), however, may be overlooked because a market price is not paid for the service even though it has market value. Time spent in a training course is one such input or opportunity cost associated with adult literacy programs. To the extent someone might have done something else such as working for an income, using this time is the value of the production that would have been produced. Cost would be estimated by multiplying one's wage by the amount of time necessary to obtain the education. If the time is taken from leisure time, then an attempt to value that leisure time is warranted. Wages might be used as a proxy to estimate the value of the leisure time forgone to attend adult literacy courses, keeping in mind that the leisure-work substitution breaks down beyond some point (Gramm, 1987; Perlman, 1966). In short, opportunity costs in general are benefits given up to pursue an activity (Holtman, 1970).

Costs are not restricted to what resources might be withdrawn from the market but from other government use—perhaps even other educational programs or activities. This need not be viewed as problematic to the extent the prices government pays for these goods and services represent opportunity costs. It becomes problematic when the pricing system within government is less than efficient or when government has been given these resources. Take the example of volunteers working in public education projects. Market forces can be substituted for similar types of work, or the value of the inputs of other government uses can be estimated using linear programming techniques. If government resources are required to encourage illiterate individuals to attend adult literacy classes, these too would be considered part of the program costs.

Another problematic issue has to do with identifying ways of accounting for changes in values over time—that is, of determining the appropriate *discount rate* or value of present versus future consumption (Holtman, 1970). Under conditions of perfect competition, the market rate of interest can serve as the *discount rate.* Given the assumption of maximizing net consumption under such conditions, future benefits and costs of a program are discounted and the difference in their present value is thereby maximized. These matters are not straightforward, as the choice of a *discount rate* can markedly affect results. Consider, for example, the present value of $100 earned a hundred years from now with varying assumptions of a *discount rate.* At a 1 percent *discount rate,* $100 is worth $36.97; at 2 percent, $13.80; at 3 percent, $5.20; and at 5 percent only $0.76. As these rates illustrate, distant benefits may have minimal value in current dollars and a cost-benefit analysis can yield vastly different results depending on the *discount rate* selected (Kraft & Furlong, 2010).

Further complicating matters, there is no one market rate reflected in the private sector. Interest rates observed in the marketplace reflect a variety of risk factors, some of which may be inappropriate for adult literacy programs (Holtman, 1970). Also, a private rate of discount may not be the same as a public rate of discount (the social rate of substitution of present vs. future consumption). Collective preferences can differ from private preferences. Unemployment and growth also complicate determination of an appropriate *discount rate.* The appropriate discount rate invariably depends on decision makers' value judgments. To the extent there is uncertainty about how widespread those value judgments are in the population at large, *sensitivity analysis* is warranted to estimate the degree of consensus around such values. If a consensus is lacking, a way needs to be found to achieve it so a proper discount rate can be determined. The bottom line here is that determination of a discount rate is inherently problematic: rates varying over time preclude the use of one rate and multiple rates are difficult to manage, further complicating the matter (Bruce, 1996; Bruce, Aldridge, Beesley, & Rathje, 2000). Any further elaboration of the discount rate is better left for more technical discussion and explication, which can be found elsewhere, along with other investment-related criteria such as the internal rate of return (the discount rate that would yield a zero present value if all future benefits minus costs were discounted by this rate) (e.g., see Hirshleifer, 1958; Sandmo, 1971).

The preceding discussion of cost-benefit analysis is based on the assumption that the value of consumption in society is the goal of society. There are other goals society may want to pursue through government projects such as adult literary education. Redistribution of income among class (e.g., the 99% vs. the top 1% of the Occupy Wall Street movement), racial, or regional groups come to mind. Society may want to implement a program to stimulate economic growth and ensure a self-sufficient economy, or to help correct an imbalance of payments problem. There is nothing inherently incorrect about introducing these and other values, nor is it necessary that such projects be less efficient than other means of achieving some of these goals. Literacy programs, for example, may be a more efficient means of redistributing income, given certain political constraints, than a program of taxes and subsidies. Alternative goals in all likelihood would have different degrees of importance or value, so ways would need to be found to weigh them to produce a rank ordering if possible. Some type of formal *sensitivity analysis* (SA) procedure, discussed later on in this chapter, may be necessary to come up with appropriate weighting criteria upon which policymakers can base their decisions about allocating resources for the most desirable programs under the circumstances.

Illustrating Benefits and Costs to Schooling

Cost-benefit analysis has been used to determine the rate of return to primary levels of schooling. This section shows how cost-benefit analysis is done and highlights policy implications that flow from such analyses. In a study about education in India (Gounden, 1967), for example, the following rates of return on investments (ROI) in schooling were reported. The top half of Table 6.1 shows the marginal or incremental rates of return on each separate level of schooling, while the bottom half shows the average rates for each level of schooling relative to the status of illiteracy. No allowances were made in the study for the spells of unemployment or duration of active economic life of persons with different levels of education or for survival rates at different ages—such factors would depress the rate of return. On the other hand, the cross-sectional data used in the study to construct the life-cycle income stream did not reflect the increase of earnings resulting from economic development—a factor that would have enhanced the rate of return. Unspecified was the extent to which these two factors offset each other. Nonetheless, the unit cost of education—that is, the total input cost required to educate one student for one year at different levels and types—was estimated.

Ideally, inputs would have included costs of (1) teachers, school administrators, supervisors, librarians, office assistants, and auxiliary staff; (2) supplies and consumable stores necessary to maintain the institutions; (3) land, buildings, and equipment; (4) books and stationery purchased by the students; and (5) students (imputing the income forgone by students age 14 and above). Returns were broadly classified into (1) private monetary (e.g., salary and the "financial option"—the value of the opportunity to obtain still further education); (2) private nonmonetary (i.e., "opportunity options," e.g., the greater employment choice that education makes available, protection against vicissitudes of technological change, and psychological benefits); (3), social monetary; and (4) social nonmonetary. Social returns (i.e., benefits obtained by persons other than the one receiving the education) accrue to the student's relatives, in improved housing and employment, as well as to the entire society over time. Intangible human costs and benefits such as overall well-being, aesthetic preferences, and learning for learning's sake are exceptionally difficult to measure and many analysts, including Gounden (1967), omit them (noting the omission).

Relying on cross-sectional data, Gounden (1967) used adjusted earnings differentials, classified by various levels of educational attainment, as the measure of the social return on education. Educational expenditures were classified as direct (salaries and allowances, among other items) or indirect (outlays for buildings, equipment, and scholarships, among other items) and a 10 percent per annum depreciation rate was estimated and applied accordingly.

Table 6.1	Internal Rates of Return to Educational Investment

Marginal Internal Rates of Return to Increment of Schooling

Increment of schooling	Percent internal rate of return
Literate over illiterate	15.9
Primary over literate	17.0
Middle over primary	11.8
Matriculates over middle	10.2
Bachelor over matriculation	7.0
Engineering degree over matriculation	9.8
Engineering degree over Bachelor	9.7

Average Internal Rates of Return to Levels of Schooling Relative to Illiteracy Studies

Level of schooling	Percent internal rate of return
Literacy	15.9
Primary	16.8
Middle	13.7
Bachelor	8.9
Engineering	9.6

Source: Gounden, A.M.N. "Investment in education in India." Originally published in the *Journal of Human Resources* 2.3 (Summer 1967): 347–358. © 1967 by the Board of Regents of the University of Wisconsin System. Reproduced by the permission of the University of Wisdonsin Press.

Several policy implications follow from the rates of return reported in Table 6.1. As Holtman (1970) noted, the data suggest that more of India's educational expenditures should be allocated to lower levels of education. Invariably reflecting India's level of economic development at the time, much higher rates of return are reported for fundamental skills associated with literacy and primary education rather than those associated with high level training. The higher rate of return for primary education over literacy alone implies that dropouts are not as economically productive as competitors. Although such information is less than perfect, it nonetheless provides a reasonable basis on which to redistribute and allocate resources to achieve policy goals that account for economic efficiency and social justice concerns. It is important to keep in mind that rates of return on educational investments will vary by level of development of a country's economy and by sociodemographic factors such as family background, ethnicity/race, sex, and regions within countries. Related studies illustrating some methods of calculating rates of return on educational investments and highlighting differences by such factors include

Agnarsson and Carlson (2002), Blaug (1967), Ferber and McMahon (1979), Krueger (1972), Sen (1966), Vijverberg (1993), and Ziderman (1973).

Measurement in Monetized Terms

As noted above, intangible human costs and benefits are difficult to measure. As Weimer and Vining (2009) note, the purpose of monetizing is to value all impacts in the same metric, with willingness to pay as one of the most common. Willingness to pay can be thought of in several ways. For our purposes, imagine a policy with one impact and no expenditure. Assume also truth in response from each person with standing (i.e., those whose costs and benefits were deemed to warrant inclusion in the calculation) about the maximum amount she or he would be willing to pay to have the policy in place. The algebraic sum of those amounts would represent society's willingness to pay for the policy and assign its total dollar value. The algebraic sum is used because some of those with standing would be willing to pay, whereas others would want to be paid for accepting the policy. The algebraic sum corresponds to a measure of change in social welfare known as compensating variation. Alternatively, if the initial question is posed about how much people would have to be paid to return to the status quo after the policy were implemented, the negative value of the algebraic sum of those amounts would signify the willingness to pay.

It should be noted that a determination of standing—that is, of those whose costs and benefits should be counted—is less than a straightforward matter. Cost-benefit analysis takes a social perspective, so what is deemed a society's extent is a consideration (Weimer and Vining, 2009). A national perspective is most often appropriate on economic and political grounds, given that nations have monetary and fiscal policies and rules (laws, constitutions) for collective decision making. In light of externalities such as pollution that go beyond geographic borders, Trumbull (1990) argues that all individuals affected by a policy or project should be taken into account. Weimer and Vining (2009) note that in federal systems such as the United States, the national jurisdiction as the basis of standing is also problematic. Who, for example, has standing in regard to a $100 million grant to a city from the federal government? A cost-benefit analysis from the national perspective would show no net benefit, but from the city perspective the net benefit would be substantial. In practice, where potential program funds come through individual state budgets, the pressure is to consider costs and benefits from the state perspective. Similarly, even federal and state agencies tend to prefer analysts to consider only fiscal impacts that appear in their own budgets. Although policy analysts should note such impacts, they should nonetheless be clear that such exercises overly limit the definition of society for cost-benefit analysis purposes. Weimer and Vining (2009, p. 32) contend that analyses from such limited perspectives are strictly speaking not cost-benefit analyses.

Determination of standing is further complicated by who should be assigned standing within jurisdictions (Weimer & Vining, 2009). Citizens and legal residents are likely to be included. Children born within the jurisdiction to parents who are neither citizens nor legal residents might garner more mixed support, given the practical difficulties associated with separating impacts of other family members. Impacts on illegal immigrants may be problematic. Incarcerated persons constitute another difficult group. Other questions about standing are raised in regard to future generations and those already benefiting from programs. Trumbull (1990) recommends taking future generations into account but excluding those in current programs, since this would entail treating identifiable persons or letting them die. In general, to the extent such issues remain highly contested or preclude confident resolution, prudent analysts might conduct their analyses under other resolutions of standing.

Estimating Willingness to Pay

Economists and others use a variety of approaches to estimate willingness to pay (e.g., see King & Mazzotta, 2012). Social surplus analysis and computable general equilibrium models rely on economic models that go beyond the scope of this book. For our purposes, social surplus analysis refers to change in quantity or price in a private good traded in operational markets—that is, accommodating individual preferences (Grafton & Permaloff, 2001; Weimer & Vining, 2011)— and to changes in quantity or price of resources traded in operational markets. Computable general equilibrium models refer to changes in quantities and prices in multiple goods and resources traded in operational markets. Table 6.2 summarizes other monetization models that economists and others use to estimate willingness to pay.

Contingent Valuation Method (CVM)

One of the most common monetization models, known as the *contingent valuation method* (CVM), is used to estimate intangible or nonmarket values and include them in cost-benefit analysis. Essentially, *contingent valuation methods* are questionnaires or interviews with individuals, designed to allow an estimate of the dollar value of, for example, the time spent in traffic, the preservation of lakes or forests, or some

Table 6.2 Monetization Models to Estimate Willingness to Pay

	Circumstance	Comment
Travel Cost Method	Change in non-traded private good with differential cost of access	Price paid by users approximated by travel costs to facility such as job training center or mammography site
Avoided Cost Method	Change in quantity of an externality with identifiable dimensions of harm	Example: Cost of crime based on victim injury and property loss and criminal justice system costs
Hedonic Methods	Change in non-traded private good relevant to other markets	Example: Statistical value of life based on wage and risk trade-offs
	Change in the quantity of an externality capitalized into land value	Example: Cost of noise based on land values and noise level
Contingent Valuation Method (CVM)	Change in non-traded private good	Example: Cost of commuting time as a fraction of the prevailing wage rate
	Change in quantity of pure public good	Example: Existence and option values of environmental goods

Source: Weimer, D.L., & Vining, A.R. (2009). *Investing in the disadvantaged: Assessing the benefits and costs of social policies.* Washington, DC: Georgetown University Press, p. 36.

other public good (Kraft & Furlong, 2010; Mitchell & Carlson, 1989). Contingent valuation (CV) surveys differ from other surveys on public policy issues in two important ways. First, the public good (or goods) of interest is described in detail. Second, the elicitation of preference for the good is more extensive and nuanced than in a typical opinion survey, entailing the elicitation of a monetary measure of welfare, either the maximum willingness-to-pay (WTP) to obtain a desired good not currently possessed, or minimum compensation, that is, willingness to accept (WTA), to voluntarily give up a good currently possessed.

Carson and Hanemann (2005, p. 825) characterize contingent valuation (CV) surveys this way:

> CV surveys are generally organized in the following manner which reflects current practice: (1) an introductory section identifying the sponsor and general topic, (2) a section asking questions concerning prior knowledge about the good and attitudes toward it, (3) the presentation of the CV scenario including what the project was designed to accomplish, how it would be implemented and paid for, and what will happen under the current *status quo* situation if the project were not implemented, (4) question(s) asking for information about the respondent's WTP/WTA [willingness-to-pay/willingness-to-accept or minimum compensation]for the good, (5) debriefing questions to help ascertain how well respondents understood the scenario, and (6) demographic questions.

Bateman et al. (2002) provide a helpful manual for practitioners who would like to learn the particulars about and use of contingent valuation methods. Quite a bit has been written about contingent valuation methods, including numerous papers from over one hundred countries (Carson, 2012), making a summary here too burdensome a task. For purposes here, it will suffice to note that Carson and Hanemann (2005) provide (1) a historical overview of contingent valuation methods, (2) the theoretical foundations of contingent valuation methods, (3) a discussion of advantages and limitations of relying on observed versus stated or revealed preferences to obtain valuations of public goods, with particular attention to the incentive structure within which preferences are determined, (4) highlights of the major controversies about using contingent valuation methods, (5) a comparison of contingent valuation methods results and actual behavior, and (6) some thoughts about where contingent valuation methods may be headed. All in all, the contingent valuation method does provide useful estimates of the value people attach to intangibles.

Travel Cost Method (TCM)

Although the contingent valuation method has enjoyed widespread use, particularly in evaluations of health care services (Johansson, 1997), its reliance on stated preferences to hypothetical questions rather than revealed through actual behavior has attracted controversy (Diamond & Hausman, 1994; Portney, 1994). Clarke (1998) used the Travel Cost Method (TCV) as an alternative to the contingent valuation method in the evaluation of two different methods of delivering mammographic screening services in rural areas. Travel cost method for the most part originated as a means of valuating benefits from National Parks, since the nominal fees charged to use them failed to generate sufficient variation to estimate demand curves, without which estimates of the benefits that recreationists gain from using the parks are not possible. In developed countries with health care services, fees charged at point of entry do not reflect the market value of the good. In the absence of user fees it has long been well known that the demand for health services is sensitive to non-monetary factors such as travel time (Action, 1975; Sugden & Williams, 1978). In the study of ten towns in Australia, Clarke (1998) found that the level of welfare benefits depended on the distance the town was from the nearest fixed screening unit: the economic benefits of mobile screening outweighed the economic costs if the rural town was situated 29 km (about 18 miles) or more from a fixed mammographic screening unit. At 50 km (about 31 miles), for example, the benefit-cost ratio was 1.8 (every dollar of benefit cost 8 cents), whereas at 160 km (about 99 miles) it was 3.3.

Sensitivity Analysis (SA)

The use of **sensitivity analysis** (SA) can minimize to some extent the weaknesses inherent in cost-benefit analysis (Kraft & Furlong, 2010). Broadly, SA is a technique used to determine how different values of a causal factor or an independent variable will impact a particular outcome or dependent variable under a given set of assumptions (Investopedia, 2012e). For example, based on returns on investments (ROI) in education, an analyst might create a return on investment model that would value aggregate earnings of adults 25–54 years old measured as annual median income, given annual expenditures for formal schooling during that period of time when the cohort was of school age (an independent variable), and annual expenditures per enrolled pupil (another independent variable) at that time. The analyst could then create the state's or society's predicted expenditure per pupil and a corresponding value of aggregate earnings based on different values for each of the independent variables. When calculations are sensitive to a basic assumption such as the discount rate, the analyst can report on several different rates, and the analyst's clients or others can choose or judge the assumptions that seem most reasonable.

Sensitivity analysis is helpful, with a formidable history of use in operations research (OR), but it is not problem free, nor is it meant to be presented in that light (Wagner, 1995). Many operations research applications use deterministic optimization models in which managers' views about parameter values can be incorporated to provide reasonable estimates of a limited number of measures. Under conditions of uncertainty, however, problems of applying sensitivity analysis are more formidable and highly quantitative (Saltelli, Tarantola, & Camplongo, 2000; Wallace, 2000) and go beyond the scope of this chapter. Nonetheless, given the use of sensitivity analysis, for example by the United Nations in the development of composite indicators such as its technology achievement index (Saisana, Saltelli, & Tarantola, 2005), practitioners are encouraged to learn about and acquire the requisite skill sets associated with both contingent valuation methods and sensitivity analysis (Boardman, Greenberg, Vining, & Weimer, 2010; Gramlich, 1998).

MONETIZING IMPACTS AND SHADOW PRICING

Vining and Weimer (2009) provide an overview and summary of cost-benefit analysis studies that monetized impact measures in many social policy areas. For readers interested in particular substantive policy areas, here are some of them: childhood education (Barnett & Masse, 2007; Temple & Reynolds, 2007), elementary and secondary education (Aos, Miller, & Mayfield, 2007; Belfield, Nores, Barnett, & Schweinhart, 2006; Levin, Belfield, Muenning, & Rouse, 2007; Stern, Dayton, Paik, & Weisberg, 1989), health for disadvantaged persons (Clarke, 1998; Devaney, Bilheimer, & Score, 1992; Lai & Sorkin, 1998; Lu, Lin, Prietto, & Garite, 2000), mental health (Culhane, Metraux, & Hadley,

2002; Weisbrod, 1981), substance abuse (Daley et al., 2000; Fleming et al., 2002; French, McCollister, Sacks, McKendrick, & De Leon, 2002; Logan et al., 2004), juvenile justice (Aos, Lieb, Mayfield, Miller, & Penucci, 2004; Caldwell, Vitacco, & Van Rybroek, 2006; Fass & Pi, 2002), prisoner reentry (Aos, Miller, & Drake, 2006; Friedman, 1977; Roman, Brooks, Lagerson, Chalfin, & Tereshchenko, 2007), affordable housing (Johnson, Ladd, & Ludwig, 2002; Turner & Malpezzi, 2003), work incentives (Long, Mallar, & Thornton, 1981; Schochet, McConnell, & Burghardt, 2003), and welfare-to-work (Greenberg & Cebulla, 2008). On the basis of their examination of these studies Vining and Weimer (2009) see potentially large payoffs from cost-benefit analysis projects, explicitly attending to weaknesses in valuation that might be strengthened with future research. They recommend institutionalizing cost-benefit analysis at state and local levels. As a model for strengthening future research they cite the Washington State Institute for Public Policy (WSIPP) as the only state agency investing in a cost-benefit analysis capacity. Established in 1983, WSIPP, whose board of directors is representative of the governor, state legislature, and public universities, has produced cost-benefit analysis studies in the areas of criminal justice (Aos, Miller, & Drake, 2006) and child development (Aos, Lieb, Mayfield, Miller, & Penucci, 2004).

In the area of education and schooling, Vining and Weimer (2009) recommend building on the work of others, summarized by Card (2001), who identified return on investment (ROI) "shadow prices"— that is, benefits other than productivity gains reflected in higher earnings, and nonmonetary labor market remuneration such as improved children's cognitive development and improved health, families' fertility decisions, and communities' external gains such as reduction in crime. Dee (2004) reported that education contributed to voter participation and support for free speech, suggesting that civic returns from education may be operationalized in monetary terms. Vining and Weimer (2009) contend that shadow prices are desired for two types of schooling gains. First, for various levels of education, the shadow price for each additional year would be useful in estimating benefits of programs that increased attendance—analysts could compare shadow prices for those without a high school diploma and those without a college degree. Second, shadow prices for educational benchmarks, which may have important signaling roles for employment opportunities, would be useful in estimating benefits of programs that increased chances of students reaching those benchmarks.

Vining and Weimer (2009) also note that prenatal, nutritional, and early education interventions all have the potential for increasing children's cognitive development, which can be measured in several ways including intelligence quotient (IQ), Peabody Picture Vocabulary Test, Peabody Individual Achievement Test, NEPSY (the Neuropsychological Assessment), and the Cognitive Assessment System (CAS), among others (e.g., Jarratt, 2005; Starkman, Butkovich, & Murray, 1976; Yoshikawa & Seidman, 2001). Cognitive development is known to contribute to other desirable outcomes, such as increased school readiness, higher achievement in school, more years of completed schooling, and higher graduation rates. It may also contribute to better social skills that in turn may reduce delinquent and criminal behaviors, teen pregnancy, and substance abuse. Vining and Weimer recommend development of shadow prices of cognitive development measures that capture all likely future effects. For example, cost-benefit analysis can be applied to longitudinal studies such as those associated with the Perry Preschool Program or the Carolina Abecedarian Project so that shadow prices of IQ points could be estimated. It would then be possible to apply cost-benefit analysis to promising interventions without waiting the ten to twenty years necessary to begin to make assessments about teenage and adult outcomes. IQ gains would be related to schooling gains, which in turn would be shadow priced to account for productivity and non-productivity benefits. Vining and Weimer contend that the efforts needed to create such shadow prices would be worth it if for no other reason than assessing whether such gains could potentially be large enough to affect the sign (+ or –) of the net benefit.

DISTRIBUTIONAL EFFECTS AND WEIGHTS OF COSTS TO BENEFITS

As Vining and Weimer (2009) have emphasized, cost-benefit analysis compares alternative policies in terms of one social goal, namely efficiency. It takes the initial distribution of resources or wealth as a given and ignores distributional consequences of the alternatives it compares. The decision rule is to adopt a combination of policies that maximize net benefits without consideration of who receives the benefits and who bears the costs, as many social policy interventions explicitly seek to improve the circumstances of economically and otherwise disadvantaged people. What, if any, social benefit from such improvements should be counted in the cost-benefit analysis? Economists have addressed this issue in proposals for distributional weighted cost-benefit analyses. The primary rationale for distributional weighting is declining marginal utility of money—an additional dollar of income to a poor person produces greater marginal utility than an additional dollar of income to a rich person. Application of the rationale poses the practical problem of determining empirically the ratios of marginal utilities of income at various wealth levels to some base level of wealth. Attempts to develop weights based on politically determined tax rates and expenditure patterns are viewed as supplemental to rather than replacements of standard approaches to cost-benefit analysis.

An alternative approach to finding the social value of improvements to the circumstances of the least advantaged acknowledges that people are altruistic in economically meaningful ways—that is, they are willing to pay something to help the most disadvantaged (Vining & Weimer, 2009). One way to approach this is a hypothetical or contingent comparison between two states of affairs: the current situation and an alternative to it that differs only in terms of the number of disadvantaged people. Imagine, for example, an alternative state as having one less family with income below the official poverty line. If an individual were willing to pay a certain amount to bring about the alternative rather than the current state of affairs, then that amount would signify the person's willingness to pay to have one less family in poverty. The sum of such willingness-to-pay amounts over the entire population would provide a shadow price for valuing changes in the number of families in poverty resulting from alternative policy interventions. As noted above, contingent valuation methods could provide data for estimating these shadow prices. Dickie and Messman (2004) show how contingent valuation methods can be used to estimate altruistic value: they assessed parents' willingness to pay to relieve both their own acute illness and that of their children. Parents of three-year-olds were estimated to be willing to pay three times as much to relieve their children's symptoms as they were to relieve their own. Extrapolations were used to estimate about ten times as much for newborns, whereas the ratio fell to unity at eighteen-year-olds—that is, parents valued relief of their own symptoms equally to that of their adult children. Developing shadow prices for a population's altruistic value of improving the circumstances of the least advantaged would make an important contribution to the application of cost-benefit analysis to social policy.

RISK ASSESSMENT

Reducing risks benefits the public and related benefits are often part of the calculation in cost-benefit analysis. **Risk** refers to the probability that an event or exposure will occur and the consequences that follow if it does (Kraft & Furlong, 2010). It is often expressed by the equation $R = P \times C$. The higher the probability of the event or exposure (P), or the higher the consequences (C), the higher is the risk. **Risk assessment** is the use of different methods to identify, estimate, and evaluate the magnitude of the risk to citizens from exposure to various intermittent situations such as terrorism, natural hazards (e.g., hurricanes and earthquakes), exposure to toxic chemicals, as well as to various daily life situations such as driving a car, drinking alcohol, and flying in an airplane, among others. **Risk evaluation** refers to the determination of the acceptability of the risks or a decision about what level of safety is desired. In general, higher levels of safety, or lower risk, cost more to achieve. *Risk management,* widely used in corporations and financial markets (see Crouhy, Gailai, & Mark, 2006 for a non-mathematical treatment of this subject for corporations managing financial risks), generally refers to what governments or other organizations do to deal with risks, such as adopting public policies and regulatations to reduce risks.

As will be seen in Chapter 7, when applying cost-benefit analysis to alcohol tax policy, many risks involve a difficult balancing act as far as government intervention and personal choice (Kraft & Furlong, 2010). Think of risks associated with bioterrorism (U.S. General Accounting Office, 1999), particularly in light of the anthrax scare in 2001 (Buettner, 2008; Kolata, 2002). Although for all practical purposes small-pox had been eradicated from the world as a communicable disease (Barrett, 2007), small stocks of the virus still exist and might fall into the hands of terrorists. Is it a good idea to vaccinate the U.S. public against smallpox, even in the absence of evidence that such an attack is likely to occur? Does the small risk of exposure warrant mass vaccinations, or is a more appropriate policy waiting until the prospect of such an attack is almost 100 percent certain, according to the best available intelligence, or until one verified case appears before starting a population wide medical campaign? Monetary cost, perhaps in the hundreds of millions of dollars (William, 2011), is not the only factor entering into such a decision. Alarming the U.S. public and subjecting people to the risk of the vaccine's serious side effects are also concerns that need to be taken into account. Prior to 1972, when the smallpox vaccination was still mandatory in the United States, it killed several children each year and left others with brain damage. Estimates, as cited by Kraft and Furlong (2010, p. 171), suggest that if the entire nation were vaccinated, between two hundred and five hundred people would die from the vaccine, and thousands more would become seriously ill (see also Kemper, Davis, & Freed, 2002). In 2002, public health scientists recommended and policymakers decided to vaccinate on a voluntary basis only health care and emergency workers most at risk of exposure to the virus; the general public would be vaccinated only if an outbreak occurred (May, Aulisio, & Silverman, 2003; U.S. General Accounting Office, 2003). Part of the rationale was to minimize the public's risk of adverse reaction to the vaccine, though they would remain unprotected initially. Given the limitations and benefits of the recommendation and adopted policy, the question remains whether or not it was a good idea.

Risk assessment and risk management have come to play large roles in federal regulatory decision making about environmental and health related issues (Presidential/Congressional Commission on Risk Assessment and Management, 1997). Four federal agencies have primary authority to regulate activities and substances that pose chronic health risks, and many of their activities prompted Congress in 1980 as part of appropriations legislation for agriculture and rural development (P.L. 96–528) to authorize what became in 1983 a National Research Council report. Referred to as the Red Book, it systematically formulated definitions and concepts about human health risk (Committee on the Institutional Means for Assessment of Risks to Public Health, 1983, hereafter NRS Committee). Subsequently, as part of the Federal Crop Insurance Reform and Department of Agriculture Reorganization Act (P.L. 103–354), in 1994 Congress required the United States Department of Agriculture (USDA) to conduct risk assessments and cost-benefit analyses on any proposed rule designated as major legislation and designed to "regulate issues of human health, human safety, or the environment" (Ahl, 1999). In Title III of the Food Quality Control Act of 1996 (P.L. 104–170), Congress mandated such analyses of pesticide use to ensure the health of infants and children (Congressional Research Service, 1996).

Although much of risk assessment and management is technical in nature, with step-by-step guides and templates readily available (e.g., see Health and Safety Executive, 2012, about workplace safety issues), limitations are readily acknowledged given the pervasive uncertainty associated with the availability of appropriate data and ethical considerations that prevent human experimentation with potentially fatal substances, events, and circumstances (NRS Committee, 1983). These and other limitations are readily explicated below when applying cost-benefit analysis to tax policies on alcohol, aimed at saving lives. Such limitations need not preclude the use of cost-benefit analysis and risk assessments for purposes of policy analysis as some assert (e.g., see Gardiner, 2011; Heinzerling & Ackerman, 2002, for pointed and thorough critiques), but rather as long ago acknowledged (Williams, 1972), they are worthwhile tools that when used appropriately within definable limits make us more informed about how to frame recommendations based on such analysis and reach reasonable decisions about what actions to take under specified circumstances and with explicit social goals in mind.

Skill Building Exercises

1. Reconstruct what went into your decisions to pursue social work education rather than some other profession and to attend the college or university in which you enrolled to pursue this course of study.

   a. Use the steps of cost-benefit analysis to help arrange or organize your reconstruction of these decisions.
   b. Which measures or indicators of costs and benefits were easily quantifiable and which were more qualitative?
   c. How did you go about assigning relative weights or degree of importance to you to each of the costs and benefits you identified?

2. Cost-benefit analysis has been criticized for failure to account for distributional effects when examining alternatives to a policy or program.

   a. What makes this a shortcoming of cost-benefit analysis?
   b. How might this shortcoming be remedied?

3. What distinguishes cost-benefit analysis from risk assessment?

CHAPTER 7

Applying Cost-Benefit Analysis

This chapter provides a step-by-step illustration of applying cost-benefit analysis to assess the merits of taxing alcohol policies to save lives. Upon completion of the chapter, students will know how to conduct a detailed cost-benefit analysis, while understanding its limitations. Students will also know how to lay out alternative policies in a way that enhances their capacity to make informed choices about the advantages and disadvantages of adopting one policy option among others.

Upon successful completion of the skill building exercises of Chapter 7, students will have mastered the following Council on Social Work Education (CSWE) Competencies and Practice Behaviors:

Chapter 7	CSWE Core Competencies
#	**Description**
2.1.3	**Apply Critical Thinking to Inform and Communicate Professional Judgments**
	Distinguish, appraise, and integrate multiple sources of knowledge, including research-based knowledge and practice wisdom
	Analyze models of assessment, prevention, intervention, and evaluation
	Demonstrate effective oral and written communication in working with individuals, families, groups, organizations, communities, and colleagues
2.1.6	**Engage in Research-Informed Practice and Practice-Informed Research**
	Use research evidence to inform practice
2.1.7	**Apply Knowledge of Human Behavior and the Social Environment**
	Utilize conceptual frameworks to guide the processes of assessment, intervention, and evaluation
	Critique and apply knowledge to understand person and environment
2.1.8	**Engage in Policy Practice to Advance Social and Economic Well-Being and to Deliver Effective Social Work Services**
	Analyze, formulate, and advocate for policies that advance social well-being

Source: Adapted from Council on Social Work Education (2012). *Educational policy and accreditation standards.* Washington, DC: Author. Retrieved from http://www.cswe.org/file.aspx?id=13780

AN ILLUSTRATION OF COST-BENEFIT ANALYSIS: TAXING ALCOHOL TO SAVE LIVES

Some General Considerations

Alcohol is a problematic commodity with formidable challenges for effective policy interventions (Chesson, Harrison, & Kassler, 2000; Grossman & Markowitz, 1998; Mullahy & Sindelar, 1996; Peterson, Hawkins, Abbott, & Catalano, 1994): on one hand alcohol consumption is inextricably linked in Western society with the good life (think for example of "cocktail parties" among prosperous and better educated persons and medical benefits of moderate red wine consumption), whereas on the other hand its prevalent abuse is a source of harm in the form of injuries, early death, unfulfilled potential, family strife, and violence (think of binge drinking among college youth, Mothers Against Drunk Driving (MADD), and the alcoholic parent, spouse, or significant other). In 1978 Congress charged the National Academy of Sciences to assess alternative strategies for reducing the burden of alcohol abuse, and since then the systematic knowledge base of the "alcohol-abuse" problem and policy responses to this problem have developed accordingly. Much of the related literature has been summarized and reviewed by Cook (1997) and Weimer and Vining (2011), who make use of cost-benefit analysis, the former for purposes of making policy recommendations and the latter for purposes of illustrating how cost-benefit analysis can be implemented. This section of the chapter draws on their work to exemplify how cost-benefit analysis can be carried out on a relevant social problem, while highlighting its strengths and weaknesses so beginning policy analysts get a clearer sense of how to think about conducting such analysis and a better understanding of its appropriate use. At the outset it should be noted that on the basis of the available evidence Cook (1997) concluded that higher taxes and additional restrictions on marketing would save lives and pass the cost-benefit test.

One of the first things to think about when evaluating the economic efficiency of any particular tax increase is how to identify and monetize the external effects—in the example under consideration here, of alcohol consumption. Some preliminary thinking has to be done about how distortions to market economies such as taxes, monopoly power, and externalities might immediately rule out the use of the tax system to achieve social policy aims. This broad policy discussion has been taken up elsewhere (e.g., see Caputo, 2011) and need not concern us at this time. Suffice it to say that for our purposes, alcohol is deemed one of those commodities that complement leisure and substitute for investments in human capital, for example, like purchasing this book. The reduction in take-home pay due to taxation that may "distort" decisions about how much to work or to invest in education and training are more than offset by related losses to productivity and human capital due to alcohol consumption. Hence, taxes on labor income support efficiency arguments for higher taxes on alcohol (Cook, 1997).

One important, unfortunate effect of alcohol consumption are highway fatalities. How many such fatalities would be avoided if people consumed less alcohol *because* increased taxes raise the retail price? To what extent, if at all, can such lives be monetized? To some, the idea of monetizing life is a horrible thought, violating one's sense of humanity. After all, as such reasoning goes, who is to say how much a life is worth? Policymakers are faced with related questions such as how much public money is to be spent to reduce the number of alcohol-related deaths, what are appropriate and effective types of interventions, how shall alcohol-death-reduction efforts be financed, and to what level of reduction, among others. Getting a handle on these types of questions allows policy analysts and policymakers to deal indirectly with questions about the value of lives and to move forward with deliberations about alternative interventions to improve social conditions that in principle can be tested—that is, assessed empirically, in some manner.

Reliance on Prior Studies

The work of Phelps (1988), for example, on which Weimer and Vining (2011) relied for their illustration of CBA, estimated the impact of tax increases on the highway fatality rates of young drivers. Noting that the youth study only considered costs imposed on adult drinkers from a higher tax and accounted for no benefits through reduced fatalities, Phelps nonetheless concluded that even with these conservative biases taxes of at least 25–40 percent were easily justified for values of lives at $1 million (about 1.95 million in 2013 dollars) or more. Acknowledging that such tax increases would fall considerably on lower income groups, Phelps highlighted the much larger external burden imposed on other groups—namely the victims of drunk drivers, many of whom would be dead and thereby unable to speak out in favor of higher taxes. Phelps ends the study with a statement about "unfair burden": "No less fair burden can be described than the sudden death of an innocent victim of a drunk driver" (p. 20). Whether or not one concurs with Phelps's findings and implications for increased taxes on alcohol, the upshot for our purposes is that CBA has value in providing ways to discuss options about what can and by extension subject to debate might be done to what effect, rather than rejection outright of the notion that no value can be placed on a human life, which all too often considerably narrows or closes off discussion of policy options.

Estimating the Effects of a Tax on Alcohol

To estimate the effects of a tax on alcohol for illustrative cost-benefit analysis purposes, Weimer and Vining (2011) consider these impacts: social surplus losses in the alcohol markets (the major cost of the tax), reductions in fatalities caused by young and older drivers (benefits), reductions in the number of nonfatal highway accidents (benefits), and reduction in health and productivity losses (benefits). They discuss yearly effects with specific reference to a 30 percent tax on the retail prices of beer, wine, and liquor. The scenario they set up to estimate social surplus losses is such that the entire tax burden is borne by consumers—for instance, they assume that the beer industry would supply about the same amount of beer at the same price—in economic jargon, the supply schedule is flat or "perfectly elastic," with "elasticity" signifying the percentage change in the quantity of a commodity divided by its price such that the further the resulting value is from 0, the greater its elasticity, whether in a positive (+) or negative (–) direction.

In 1988 the retail price of beer averaged about $0.63 per 12-ounce drink across the United States and at that price 54 billion drinks were consumed annually. A 30 percent increase in tax of $0.19 per drink raises the retail price that consumers see to $0.82 per drink. The economic modeling and related technical procedures used to estimate how consumers would respond go beyond the scope of this book and need not concern us here. Suffice it to say, Phelps (1988) had estimated a 1 percent increase in the price of beer would lead to a 0.5 percent reduction in the quantity demanded. Using Phelps's estimate, increasing the price to $0.82 reduces consumption to 47.4 billion drinks per year. This decline of 7 billion 12-ounce drinks of beer in a given year at a cost of $0.82 each amounts to a $9.54 billion loss in consumer surplus (equal to the sum of tax revenue and *deadweight loss*) in the beer market. *Deadweight loss* is an economic term that refers to the costs to society created by market inefficiencies or distortions—that is, the opportunity costs of consumer surplus forgone by distortions in prices, incentives, or as a result of regulatory policies (Munger, 2000). In the case of beer, such losses would be due to the tax increase that prevents people from engaging in purchases they would otherwise have made or that it is estimated they would have made on the basis of economic models because the final price of the product is above the equilibrium market price (Investopedia, 2012b).

Estimating the Social Surplus Losses in the Wine and Liquor Markets

Weimer and Vining (2011) used similar procedures to estimate the social surplus losses in the wine and liquor markets. Adding the effects across beer, wine, and liquor markets, they estimated that the 30 percent tax in retail prices reduces the consumption of alcohol drinks by 17.6 percent, inflicts a consumer surplus loss of $16,739 billion, generates tax revenue equal to $15,343 billion, and results in deadweight losses of $1,396 billion. Either the deadweight losses can be reported as the net cost of the policy in alcohol markets or the total consumer surplus losses can be reported as a cost and the total tax revenue as a benefit. Although the choice of reporting approach will not alter the estimate of net benefits, the latter approach preserves information that may be relevant when deciding whether the federal government wants to count this as a tax benefit, thus reducing the amount of the federal deficit.

Estimating Reductions in Fatalities Caused by Young Drivers and Older Drivers

The next impacts Weimer and Vining (2011) consider separately are the reductions in fatalities caused by young drivers and older drivers. Grossman, Coate, and Arluck (1987) and Coate and Grossman (1988) examined the effects of alcohol beverage prices and legal drinking ages on alcohol consumption among youth aged 16 to 21. Such research was important given that policymakers have two alcohol-control instruments that they can directly influence—namely, raising taxes to increase prices and raising the legal drinking age to increase the risk of incurring legal sanctions among younger consumers of alcohol products. Coate and Grossman reported that the frequency and intensity of drinking were highly sensitive to price. They estimated that a 7 percent increase in the price of beer and liquor (though not wine) would have about the same effect as increasing the minimum legal drinking age by one year. These estimates made possible the calculation of the probabilities of drinking at given levels and frequencies for any set of assumed alcohol prices. To calculate the number of driver fatalities, the probability of a young driver dying in an automobile accident conditional on drinking level is required. That is, what is the probability that a youthful driver will be killed, given that she or he has had x-number of drinks? Several states do autopsies, which measure blood-alcohol levels, on all highway fatalities. Data from these states enable estimation of the probability that a young driver killed in a highway accident was drinking at a level x.

Phelps (1988) used conditional probabilities of death and the probabilities of drinking frequencies estimated by Grossman, Coate, and Arluck (1987) to calculate the reduction in the number of young drivers who would die as the tax on beer increased. A 30 percent tax was estimated to result in 1,650 fewer drivers 16 to 21 years of age dying in highway fatalities per year, due to decreases in both the intensity and frequency of drinking. Because 77 non-driver fatalities are associated on average with each 100 driver fatalities, the 1,650 avoided driver deaths would result in an additional 1,270 lives saved per year. Thus, the 30 percent tax would reduce the number of highway fatalities by young drivers by about 2,920 per year.

At the time of their writing, Weimer and Vining (2011) found no comparable studies to Grossman, Coate, and Arluck (1987) for quantifying the behaviors of older drinkers in the United States. They did the best they could with available information, a common practice among those who use cost-benefit analysis. Specifically, Weimer and Vining relied on an ad hoc procedure reflecting that adults on average exhibit much less elastic demand for alcohol than youth, and for any given intensity of drinking, adults on average are also less likely than their youth counterparts to be involved in a fatal accident. Ignoring adults' less elastic demand for alcohol and using that of youth would overestimate alcohol-related highway fatalities. Instead, given the greater proportion of adults in the population than youth, Weimer and Vining surmised that the aggregate market demand for alcohol would provide "reasonable approximations" for the elasticity of drinkers older than 21 years of age. To estimate the effect on highway fatalities of a 30 percent tax increase on alcohol, they created a ratio of the weighted averages of the elasticity of beer, wine, and liquor to the youth elasticity, producing a value of 0.3. Applying that ratio to their sample of 3,240 adult drivers saved yielded an adjusted estimate of 972 per year.

Given the lack of relevant data, it was more difficult to adjust further for the lower propensity of older drivers to be involved in fatal accidents at any given drinking level. What was known was that while younger drivers constituted about 13 percent of licensed drivers, they accounted for about 26 percent of all alcohol-related accidents. Using only that piece of information Weimer and Vining (2011) assumed that drivers over 21 years of age were only 50 percent as likely to have fatal accidents as younger drivers. Adjusting for this factor reduced the estimate of adult drivers saved to 486. Applying the victim-to-driver ratio of 0.77 yielded another 375 lives saved. Weimer and Vining estimated that the total number of lives saved due to changes in the behavior of drivers over 21 as a result of a 30 percent tax increase on alcohol was 861 per year. Similar procedures were followed to estimate reductions in injuries and property damages and gains in health and productivity (e.g., reductions in absenteeism and workplace accidents). Assuming some proportionality between consumption and costs, Weimer and Vining estimated $4.29 billion in annual health savings and $6.61 billion in annual productivity savings from the 30 percent tax.

Determine Whether Quantified Effects Belonged in the Calculation of Net Benefits

Up to this point, Weimer and Vining (2011) measured *in dollars* all effects except lives saved. The next step, however, was not assigning a dollar value to lives saved in light of the information they had analyzed. Instead, they had to determine whether all the quantified effects they had identified belonged in the calculation of net benefits. In particular, did any of the measured effects involve double counting? To get at this question meant thinking about and making some decisions about which fatalities to include and how to count them, as well as figuring out how to go about monetizing lives saved. Estimated lives saved fell into four categories: young drivers, victims of young drivers, older drivers, and victims of older drivers. Victims of alcohol-involved drivers can be thought of as suffering an externality of drivers' alcohol consumption. The costs borne by victims are not reflected in alcohol markets. The costs borne by the drivers, however, may be reflected in their demand for alcohol. It is reasonable to expect that someone fully informed about the risks of driving under the influence of alcohol would consider these risks in deciding when and how much to drink. In economic jargon, other things equal, the higher the implicit values drivers place on their own lives or the higher the probabilities of having fatal accidents after drinking, the less alcohol drivers will demand at any given price. To the extent drivers are uninformed about the risks of driving under the influence of alcohol, their demand for alcohol will not fully reflect their risk of being an alcohol-involved driver fatality.

Alcohol markets are considered primary markets, whereas markets for victim and driver fatalities are considered as secondary. In "fatality markets," people demand personal highway safety as a function of the "price" of safety, which can be thought of as the monetary equivalent of the level of effort expended on avoiding accidents. The external effects of alcohol consumption clearly distort the market for victim fatalities. Effects in the "victim market" warrant inclusion in our cost-benefit analysis. To the extent drivers fully realize the increased risks they face from their alcohol consumption, the "driver market" is not distorted. If the operating assumption or belief is that drivers are fully informed and not alcohol-addicted, then reductions in their fatality rate would not be counted in cost-benefit analysis—they are already counted in the alcohol market. If the operating assumption or belief is that drivers do not fully take into account increased risks, or that they are physically addicted to alcohol, the "driver market" is distorted by what economists refer to as information asymmetry and they thereby warrant being counted in all or part of the avoided fatalities as benefits.

Estimating Benefits Under Different Assumptions About How Well Young/Older Drivers Are Informed About the Risks of Drinking and Driving

Given the above, Weimer and Vining (2011) estimated benefits under three different assumptions about how well young and older drivers are informed about the risks of drinking and driving. Assuming that all drivers are uninformed, they counted all avoided driver and victim fatalities as benefits; the estimated benefits under this assumption were considered an upper boundary of true benefits. Under the second assumption, that all drinkers are fully informed, they counted only avoided fatalities as benefits; the estimated benefits under this assumption were considered a lower boundary on benefits. And third, making a "best guess" about the extent to which young and older drivers are informed, they assumed that young drivers are about 10 percent informed, and they counted 90 percent of avoided young-driver fatalities as benefits; they assumed that older drivers are about 90 percent informed and counted 10 percent of avoided older-driver fatalities as benefits. In all other cases, they counted all avoided victim fatalities s benefits.

Assigning a Dollar Amount to Avoided Fatalities and the Value of Life

The *prima facie* "crass" question Weimer and Vining (2011) then faced was what dollar amount to assign to avoided fatalities. Many, if not most, of us would be willing to spend everything we have to save a loved one. Nonetheless, we implicitly put finite values on lives when deciding about risks to ourselves and loved ones: wearing a seat belt, making passengers buckle up, having smoke detectors in every room in our houses, having a working fire extinguisher, driving within legal speed limits. Failure to take such actions implies placing less than an infinite value on life, signifying a willingness to accept greater risks of fatality in order to avoid small related costs.

Actual Versus Statistical Lives

To aid our thinking about placing a value on life, Weimer and Vining (2011) and others (e.g., Viscusi, 1992) distinguish between actual and statistical lives. That is, when assessing the benefits of risk reduction for our purposes of national level policy regulations or interventions, the pertinent value is the willingness to pay for the risk reduction. The related tax dollars do not purchase the certainty of survival. Rather, they pay for the incremental reduction in the probability of an adverse outcome that might otherwise have affected a random member of the country. Put another way, at stake are statistical lives, not certain identified lives (Viscusi, 1992). Weimer and Vining (2011) contend that people seem willing to spend great sums to save the lives of specific persons—say to rescue trapped miners—yet they seem much less willing to take actions that reduce the probability of accidents. As a society, we do not take all possible precautions to prevent miners from becoming trapped, and at times miners knowingly accept higher risks by ignoring inconvenient safety rules. When dealing with probabilities rather than certainties, people seem to be willing to consider trade-offs between dollars and lives. Observing such trade-offs enables us to impute a dollar value to a statistical life, the problem confronting a cost-benefit analysis of the alcohol tax.

Measuring How Much People Implicitly Value Their Lives

One common way of measuring how much people implicitly value their lives is to find out how much additional wage compensation they demand for working riskier jobs, an approach pioneered by Thaler and Rosen (1976). Take two jobs with identical characteristics except that one involves a 1/1,000 greater risk of fatal injury per year. If observed that people were willing to take the riskier job for an additional $2,000 per year in wages, it can be inferred that they are placing an implicit value on their (statistical) lives of $2,000 / (1/1,000), or $2 million. The validity of the inference depends on the jobs' differing only in terms of risk and workers fully understanding the risk. Researchers use econometric techniques to control for a wide range of worker and job characteristics. Reviews of major studies of wage-risk tradeoffs suggest estimates of the value of life ranging from about $1.3 million to over $16.8 million (in 2012 dollars) (e.g., see Boardman, Greenberg, Vining, & Weimer, 1997; Viscusi, 1983; Viscusi & Aldy, 2003). About $2 million, near the lower end of the aforementioned range, would be a conservative estimate of the value of life.

Determining How Much of Injuries/Damages Count as Benefits Under Different Demand Assumptions

Uninformed Demand

The same line of argument about deciding which avoided fatalities to count is used to determine how much of the injury, property damage, health, and productivity effects to count as benefits under uninformed demand, informed demand, and best guess cases. In the *uninformed demand* case, for example, it is assumed that people do not consider the accident, health, and productivity costs of drinking. The entire savings in these categories count as savings.

Informed Demand

In the *informed demand* case, it is assumed that drinkers fully anticipate and bear these costs. Reductions in such costs are not counted as benefits. For example, it is assumed that drinkers pay for the property damage and injuries they inflict on others through higher insurance premiums or loss of coverage. Workers who are less productive workers due to consuming alcohol bear most of the related costs of lost productivity in the form of lower wages. To the extent insurance and wage rates fall short of reflecting accident propensities, health risks, and productivity losses due to drinking, cost-benefit analysis underestimates benefits—an approach Weimer and Vining (2011) note is consistent with treating the informed demand case as a lower boundary on benefits.

Best Guess

In the *best guess* case, costs are apportioned under the assumption that young drinkers are about 10 percent informed and older drinkers are about 90 percent informed of the health, productivity, and accident costs associated with their alcohol consumption. Given that the majority of health and productivity losses accrue to older drinkers, 10 percent of the total savings in these categories are counted as benefits. In regard to accidents, counted benefits include all the costs avoided by non-drivers, as well as 90 percent of costs avoided by young drivers and 10 percent avoided by older drivers. Weimer and Vining (2011) contend that in the absence of better information adoption of these ad hoc assumptions "probably provide a reasonable intermediate estimate of benefits" (p. 419).

Estimate Net Benefits Under Uninformed, Informed, and Best Guess

The next step in the cost-benefit analysis process is to estimate net benefits under each of the three cases. If the same pattern of costs and benefits is expected to persist over time, examining the net benefits in a single year is sufficient. If substantial changes over time are expected, then estimates of net benefits for a number of years into the future and discounting them back to the present are warranted. Table 7.1 highlights the costs and benefits of a 30 percent tax on alcohol.

Table 7.1 Costs and Benefits of a 30 Percent Tax on Alcohol (Billions of Dollars)

	Uninformed Demand	Informed Demand	Best Guess
Lives Saved ($2 million/life)			
Young drivers	3.24	0	2.98
Victims of young drivers	2.54	2.54	2.54
Older drivers	0.98	0	0.10
Victims of older drivers	0.74	0.74	0.74
Subtotal	**7.56**	**3.28**	**6.36**
Injury and Property Damage Avoided			
Young drivers	1.00	0	0.94
Older drivers	0.30	0	0.04
Subtotal	**1.30**	**0**	**0.98**

Table 7.1 (Continued)	Uninformed Demand	Informed Demand	Best Guess
Health and Productivity Costs Avoided			
Health	8.58	0	0.86
Productivity	13.22	0	1.32
Subtotal	**21.80**	**0**	**2.18**
Tax Revenue			
Beer, wine, and liquor	**30.68**	**30.68**	**30.68**
Consumer Surplus Change			
Beer, wine, and liquor	−33.48	−33.48	−33.48
Net Benefits	**27.90**	**0.48**	**6.72**

Source: Adapted from: Weimer, D.L., & Vining, A.R. (2011). *Policy analysis* (5th ed.). Boston, MA: Longman, p. 420.

At first blush, the tax appears to offer positive net benefits in each of the three categories. Cautious interpretation, however, is warranted. Consider first the net benefits in the *informed demand* case. The reported annual net benefits of $0.48 billion are quite small when compared to the size of the costs and benefits. If the consumer surplus losses were underestimated by as little as 2 percent, then the true net benefits under the *informed demand* case would be negative instead of positive. Given the conservative bias in counting benefits in this case, a reasonable conclusion is that the 30 percent tax policy at least breaks even. Next consider the *uninformed demand* case. The reported annual net benefits amount to $27.9 billion. Almost 80 percent of the net benefits come from those under "avoided health and productivity costs." The estimates underlying these benefits, however, were pulled somewhat uncritically from the literature. Lack of time and access to primary data necessitated taking at face value the yearly health and productivity costs estimated by other analysts. Uncertainty about the accuracy of these estimates warrants concern. Their disproportionate representation in the estimation of net benefits adds to the uncertainty of those estimates. Such problems are not as serious in the *best guess* case, where the reported net benefits amount to $6.72 billion annually, a substantial amount when compared to the large consumer surplus losses of $33.48 billion. Health and productivity benefits make up less than one-third of net benefits, reducing the uncertainty of the estimates. Whether the estimate of net benefits under the *best guess* case is close to the true value of net benefits depends on the reasonableness of the previously discussed assumptions.

For a variety of reasons including public acceptability and political feasibility of adopting an alcohol tax policy, as well as whether or not the 30 percent rate offers the largest net benefits, policymakers may be interested in knowing estimates of net benefits at other tax rates. Table 7.2 shows net benefits for lower and higher rates for each of the three cases.

Table 7.2	Net Benefits of Alcohol Taxes (Billions of Dollars)		
Tax Rate (tax revenue)	**Uninformed Demand**	**Informed Demand**	**Best Guess**
.10	12.48	1.26	4.18
(11.46)			
.20	21.44	1.30	6.24
(21.60)			
.30	27.90	0.48	6.72
(30.68)			
.40	35.98	0.40	9.36
(38.92)			
.50	42.20	0.06	11.58
(46.44)			

Source: Adapted from: Weimer, D.L., & Vining, A.R. (2011). *Policy analysis* (5th ed.). Boston, MA: Longman, p. 421.

Under the *informed demand* case, net benefits peak at the 20 percent tax rate. To the extent that this is viewed as most likely or if policymakers prefer conservative estimates, this is the one to recommend. Under either the *uninformed demand* or *best guess* case, net benefits continue to rise to the 50 percent tax rate, the highest analyzed, suggesting that even higher rates may be optimal. Again, caution is warranted when interpreting these estimates and making policy recommendations based on them. The further from current policy, the less confidence analysts have in predicting effects—reasonable assumptions made for small price changes may not apply for larger changes. At some point, higher taxes become prohibitive, portending more radically different behavioral responses. People responded to Prohibition in the 1920s, for example, in part by smuggling alcohol into the country from other countries and forming criminal organizations to supply an illegal market, offsetting benefits associated with reduced per capita alcohol use and alcohol-related harm (Hall, 2010). To the extent such unanticipated effects are not or cannot be taken into account when relying on cost-benefit analysis, caution is warranted about advocating very high tax rates on the basis of cost-benefit analysis alone.

Summary of How Alcohol Taxation Illustrates the Basic Craft and Art of Cost-Benefit Analysis

The analysis of alcohol taxation illustrates the basic craft and art of cost-benefit analysis. Basic concepts for measuring costs and benefits constitute the craft; drawing together fragmentary evidence from disparate sources to predict and monetize effects constitutes the art. The conclusion that a 30 percent tax offers positive net benefits appears fairly robust to changes in assumptions about the measurement of benefits. Weimer and Vining (2011) are "fairly confident in concluding that it would increase economic efficiency if adopted," even if they "remain highly uncertain about whether 30 percent is close to the optimal rate" (p. 423). On the whole, cost-benefit analysis provides a framework for evaluating the economic efficiency of policies. Calculation of net benefits answers the question: Does the policy generate sufficient benefits so those who bear its costs could at least potentially be compensated, thereby making some people better off and not others worse off? To calculate net benefits, decisions about which effects are relevant and how they can be made commensurable are necessary. The general concepts of opportunity cost and willingness to pay guide the application of the craft of cost-benefit analysis. Making reasonable inferences from data that are usually fragmentary and incomplete constitutes the art, which also lies in realizing when inadequate data or social values other than efficiency make the narrow cost-benefit approach inappropriate.

IDENTIFYING ALTERNATIVES

A 30 percent tax on alcohol is not the only policy that government can adopt to reduce the adverse effects of alcohol consumption on individuals and society. The use of cost-benefit analysis above provided estimates of effects of varying the level of taxation on alcohol. Cost-benefit analysis would in all likelihood be appropriate to help assess the relative merits of alternative actions, such as increasing the age of legal purchase and public consumption of alcohol. Of interest in this section, however, is how to think about identifying alternative policies that could in principle achieve similar objectives or serve public purposes as those that are currently available or commonly known. Generating alternatives is part of the design stage of the policy-as-product process, all too often neglected and less understood, given that many alternatives are found, adapted, or remodeled from other experiences—that is, borrowed or tinkered with more as a matter of convenience than resulting from more rigorous scrutiny or analysis, as might be the case for other aspects of polices as product, process, or performance (Alexander, 1979, 1982; May, 1991; Weimer, 1993).

The initial aim is to identify enough alternatives so there will be choice among several good ones, rather than evaluating in detail many marginal alternatives, such as the case above when using cost-benefit analysis to assess the merits of taxing alcohol at different rates. There are varying opinions about the merits of proposing alternatives that veer too far from the status quo. MacRae and Wilde (1985) suggest a wide variety of alternatives should be considered initially, to ensure that the analyst is less likely to overlook important options and so more options are available during the compromise stage when policy recommendations are made politically feasible (Marmor, 1986; Patton & Sawicki, 1993). Others such as Braybrooke and Lindblom (1970)—who described and advanced the strategy of "disjointed incrementalism" as the way that actual or real-time policy-related evaluations occur and decisions get made—long ago acknowledged that considerations of incremental change restrict variety. They also contended that dramatically divergent alternatives are often politically irrelevant and that policy analysts often lack the information or ability to evaluate such alternatives.

Political context invariably plays an important role when considering how far alternatives should veer from the status quo. Policymakers might be more receptive to ideas that are consistent with prevailing views and concepts than those that challenge them, preferring incremental to wholesale change. Nonetheless, demand for change in light of dissatisfaction with the status quo may necessitate embracing new or more comprehensive ideas further from the mainstream (Hall, 1993). Practically, a sensible approach is to consider policies that require incremental changes from the status quo but also including options that appear radically different, even unacceptable, to obtain an idea of what might be possible under changing circumstances (Patton & Sawicki, 1993).

Decision makers have been found to consider the following criteria when deliberating about alternative policies: cost affordability and effectiveness, stability of objectives under changing circumstances, flexibility, riskiness, merit in that on its face it appears to address the problem at hand, ease of implementation, compatibility with existing norms and procedures, reversibility if the option falls short of intended goals, and robustness or likely success in widely different future environments (Walker, 1988; Patton & Sawicki, 1993). Identifying alternatives to which these criteria can be applied is a different task than that which is of concern here. Generally, if some technical, economic, or administrative difficulty or some organizational constraint is likely to prevent implementation of an alternative, it is probably not worth pursuing its adoption, given due deliberation about what it might take to obviate such difficulties and constraints in the long term (Walker, 1988). Sources for alternatives include existing policy proposals, pre-packaged or generic solutions that others have adopted, and tailor-made solutions, as well as reliance on experts, parallel cases, and analogies. Research analysis (survey, comparative analysis, and the like) and experimentation when possible are also good sources of alternatives, though they do take time and effort to undertake. Ideas about alternatives can also be gleaned from brainstorming, literature reviews, comparisons of real-world experiences, and comparison with an ideal. Below are brief descriptions of what is entailed in several particular approaches to identifying alternative policies that make use of social work skill sets amenable to group processes and professional capacities for critical thinking and problem solving.

Development of Typologies

Developing typologies is a list-making approach where the analysts identify affected groups, the probable reactions of these groups to considered alternatives, and finally, develop specific means of making promising alternatives more acceptable to those groups. If the concern is making child care available to working parents, an analyst might classify affected groups by family type, such as single parent and couple parents, and further divide each of these types by class, using official federal poverty thresholds as a criterion of eligibility. Several class-related cut-offs can be proposed—namely, those whose annual income falls below the official poverty line, or twice the poverty line, or higher, and the likely responsiveness of cash or in-kind benefits, for example, on each type of parent in need (Patton & Sawicki, 1993).

Comparison With Ideal

It is often helpful to specify an ideal alternative even if the likelihood of adopting it appears beyond reach. Constraints can always be added to see if an acceptable alternative can be agreed upon, while thinking about constraints may lead to ways of eliminating them, or if they are not possible to remove, perhaps coming up with other alternatives. The value of conceptualizing ideals lies less in stating goals to be attained and more in encouraging thought about alternative means to move toward the ideal. Such alternatives can compete with the status quo and with other more realistic or practical alternatives and be assessed on their prospective merits of solving the problem or set of problems being addressed (Patton & Sawicki, 1993).

Feasible Manipulations

The **feasible manipulations** approach to policy alternatives entails identifying policy-relevant variables, the modifications of which form the basis for developing coherent strategies that can be subsequently revised as the problem the policies are meant to address is redefined and evaluation criteria shift (May, 1981). It requires a sense of what can be done and what should be done. What can be done is a function of what an organization or level of government can influence, so context is important. It makes little sense for a small social service agency to tackle a city's level of unemployment by itself. What can be influenced or manipulated can be considered policy variables. Think of early-retirement options facing many in the Baby Boom cohort, those born between 1948 and 1964, or of "top-heavy" senior tenured faculty whom university administrators would like to have retire so junior untenured faculty can be hired. Patton (1975) took such an approach to defining policy alternatives in a seven-day, quick analysis of early-retirement options for the University of California system that is worth showing here (despite the fact that numbers provided reflect data from that time period). Table 7.3 adapts and highlights Patton's strategies to encourage faculty members to retire early, which included incentive annuities based on the faculty member's own earnings history, early annuities based on the average earnings of the faculty member's peers, and early annuities combined with partial employment.

Table 7.3   Results of Patton's Feasible Manipulations of Early-Retirement Options

Early Retirement Frees Some Funds but Usually Not Enough for the Hiring of a Replacement

| | | | Funds Freed by Each Alternative | | | |
| Age Group | Years of Service | Alternative 1 (Individual-based annuity) | Alternative 2 (Group-based annuity) | | | Alternative 3 (Partial employment plus annuity)[a] |
		Average[b]	Low third[c]	Mid third[d]	High third[e]	Average[b]
56–60	11–15	8,326	2,650	8,326	14,002	3,312
56–60	16–20	5,903	475	5,903	11,332	1,985
56–60	21+	3,400	-1,820	3,400	8,350	588
61–65	11–15	15,188	8,901	15,188	21,423	5,556
61–65	16–20	12,967	10,139	12,967	19,047	4,449
61–65	21+	10,883	4,898	10,883	16,412	4,593

[a] Early retiree reemployed at one-half time.
[b] Average amount of funds freed by retiring a person within the age-service group.
[c] Funds freed by retiring a person whose salary is in the lowest third for the age-service group.
[d] Funds freed by retiring a person earning the mean salary for the age-service group.
[e] Funds freed by retiring a person whose salary is in the top third for the age-service group.

(Continued)

Table 7.3	(Continued)

Early Retirement Under These Options Produces Larger Annuities Than Regular Early Retirement

Age Group	Years of Service	Early-Retirement Income as Percentage of Normal Early-Annuity Income				
		Alternative 1 (Individual-based annuity)	Alternative 2 (Group-based annuity)			Alternative 3 (Partial employment plus annuity)[a]
		Average[b]	Low third[c]	Mid third[d]	High third[e]	Average[b]
56–60	11–15	216%	270%	216%	180%	309%
56–60	16–20	192	240	192	159	251
56–60	21+	174	217	174	148	208
61–65	11–15	131	163	131	109	264
61–65	16–20	122	135	122	102	219
61–65	21+	116	145	116	100	173

[a] Early retiree reemployed at one-half time.
[b] Benefits to all early retirees within the age-service group.
[c] Benefits to an early retiree whose salary is in the lowest third for the age-service group.
[d] Benefits to an early retiree earning the mean salary for the age-service group.
[e] Benefits to an early retiree whose salary is in the highest third for the age-service group.

Source: Adapted from Patton, C.V. (1975). A seven-day project: Early faculty retirement alternatives. *Policy Analysis, 1,* 743, 746.

The effectiveness of the alternatives was determined by computing the impact on faculty members of various ages with a range of years of service in terms of funds freed, number of early retirements generated, increase in the size of the early-retirement annuity, and relationship of the early-retirement annuity to preretirement salary. In a later work, Patton (1979) devised more alternatives in the same way and used other evaluation criteria, including political, legal, and administrative feasibility, though the relative effectiveness of the alternatives remained the same: namely that early retirement frees insufficient funds to hire replacements and it produces larger annuities than regular retirement (Patton & Sawicki, 1993).

Modifying Existing Solutions

Modification of existing solutions to problems is a time-tested approach of generating new ideas about how to problem-solve. Osborn (1957) devised a number of ways to generate new solutions by modifying existing ones, including magnifying, "minifying," combining, and rearranging existing options. Patton and

Table 7.4	Ways to Modify Existing Solutions to Generate New Policy Alternatives
Magnify	**Make larger, higher, and/or longer. Add resources. Apply more often. Duplicate. Multiply. Exaggerate. Add new components.**
Minify	Make smaller, shorter, narrower, lower, and/or lighter. Omit, remove, split apart. Understate.
Substitute	Switch components and/or order. Offer different types of benefits. Change location.
Combine	Blend two approaches. Combine units, purposes, and/or sponsors.
Rearrange	Reverse. Invert. Change sequence. Alter speed. Randomize. Place in a pattern.
Location	Single vs. multiple locations; Scattered sites; Permanent vs. temporary; Mobile, rotating, dense, sparse, mixed, or segregated; Adaptive reuse.
Timing	Accelerate, lag, stagger, sequence, concurrent. Lengthen or shorten time. Time sharing.
Financing	Provide or purchase. Institute tax or user fee. Subsidize, partially or fully. Use marginal or average cost pricing. Use sliding fee scale or ability to pay. Copayments or deductibles.
Organization	Centralize, decentralize. Mandate vs. permissive. Vary use of incentives. Strict vs. loose enforcement. Inform. Implore.
Decision sites	Existing or new organizations; elected or appointed; technical or political; advisory or binding; appealable or not.
Influence points	Pressure from users, providers, intermediaries; other beneficiaries; others harmed or neglected.
Risk management	Encourage adoption through guarantees, insurance, or remedial correction after-the-fact.

Source: Patton, C., & Sawicki, D. *Basic Methods of Policy Analysis and Planning,* 2nd edition, © 1993. Reprinted by permission of Pearson Education, Inc., Upper Saddle River, NJ.

Sawicki (1993) modified Osborn's categories and produced ways of creating or generating policy options that appear in Table 7.4.

Once policy variables that can be manipulated are identified and a determination made in what ways and to what extent the variables can be manipulated, they can be recombined into competing alternatives or, as May (1981) conceptualized them, strategies. This is an iterative process of combining and repackaging creatively in light of assessments aimed at, after some screening to narrow options for plausibility, a reasonable set of alternatives that more completely satisfy the evaluation criteria and that the analyst could propose to policymakers.

Methods of Dealing With Multiple Criteria for Identifying and Selecting Among Alternatives

Analysts rely on a number of comparative techniques or methods when faced with the need to select among alternatives. Some methods summarize the pros and cons of the options into a single value; others incorporate quantitative and qualitative information into a scorecard or matrix. Variations on these methods employ weighting schemes that give more consideration to certain criteria than others. Some are intended for use by an analyst–decision maker team, others for use with larger groups incorporating citizen input. Relying on Patton and Sawicki (1993), several methods classified as either basic or matrix are described below, highlighting strengths and limitations.

Basic Comparison Methods

Paired Comparisons

When there are few options, they can be compared in pairs. First, compare two options to determine the superiority of one over the other. Then compare the superior of the two to the third option, and then the superior of these two to the fourth, and so forth. This process can become cumbersome if there are too many options. It should be noted that the result is not a ranking of alternatives, only the identification of the surviving alternative. The appeal of the method is its assessing each alternative holistically and avoiding the use of summary measures or only key components of the alternatives. Yet the *paired comparison* approach may result in overlooking important considerations that might be revealed if the focus were on individual policy-relevant variables.

Satisficing

Satisficing refers to a rule-of-thumb way of making a satisfactory, but not necessarily the best choice. The notion comes from Simon (1955, 1976, 1979), whose work showed the limitations of economic theorizing about maximizing behavior and of administrative decision making in organizations. It is a form of practical reasoning that has also found favor among political theorists and normative ethicists (Shoemaker, 2006). After identifying criteria, satisfactory levels are then defined. A selection can then be made among the policy options that attain at least these levels for all criteria. If no option is at least satisfactory on all criteria, reducing requirements might be warranted. If several options exceed meeting the satisfactory criteria, increasing requirements might be warranted. At issue is determining what level of achievement would really be adequate or "good enough" for a given criterion, and whether a better alternative might be found if the search is continued, given additional costs such as time and effort associated with continuation of the search. The search stops when the first satisfactory alternative is identified.

Lexicographic Ordering

In **lexicographic ordering** alternatives are ranked, one criterion at a time, starting with the most important first. If two or more alternatives occupy the highest ranking on the most important criterion, then they are compared on the second criterion. The surviving alternatives are compared on the third most important criterion, and so forth. The approach to identifying alternative policy options is appealing because of its apparent straightforward simplicity, but it requires agreement by participants on the ordering of the criteria and the assumption of no interaction effects when considering two or more criteria simultaneously.

Matrix Display Methods

Matrix systems have been designed to display the pros and cons of options, overcoming limitations of approaches that use a single summary value. One such method, the Goeller scorecard, which will be illustrated here by Patton's early-retirement study reported above, describes the impacts for each alternative in "neutral" units—that is, in monetary terms, physical units, other quantified terms, or in qualitative terms. Each row of the scorecard represents an impact and each column represents an alternative. What is known about the impact of each alternative is shown in the respective cells in numerical or written (text) form. A column shows all the impacts for an alternative; a row shows each alternative's value for a given criterion. Shading, coloring, or other notation can be used to indicate the extent to which the alternatives meet each criterion. In Table 7.5, for example, darker shading indicates more beneficial impacts and lighter shading more negative impacts.

This scorecard presents both quantitative and qualitative information deemed relevant from the university's perspective. The analysis was intended for use by various decision makers in different settings: individual faculty members, faculty governance groups, and administrators in the University of California system, as well as university administrators across the country. Each group of decision makers was able to apply its own weights to the criteria. The scorecard makes it possible to reach overall agreement even if decision-making groups assign different weights to specific criteria (a frequent outcome of faculty and administration deliberations).

Table 7.5 Scorecard Evaluation of Selected Early-Retirement Criteria

| Selected Criteria | Selected Early-Retirement Options | | |
	Group-Based Annuity	Individual-Based Annuity	Partial-Employment-Individual Annuity
Funds Freed to the University	$9,076	$10,343	$7,927
Employee Replacement Rate	0.61	0.69	0.53
Retirement Income Level	$24,380	$27,784	$30,200
Administrative Feasibility	Benefit schedule encourages lower-valued persons to retire	Problems estimating number of voluntary return	Reemployment may be cumbersome
Legal Feasibility	Precedent exists	Precedent exists	Precedent exists
Political Feasibility	Lower-paid given larger benefits	Individuals concerned about employment	Employee remains on payroll
Key:	Best	Intermediate	Worst

Source: Adapted from Patton, C.V. (1979). *Academia in transition: Early retirement or mid-career change.* Cambridge, MA: Abt Books, as cited in Patton and Sawicki (1993), p. 352.

There are other types of matrices that need not be considered here. Patton and Sawicki (1993) discuss the Alternative-Consequence Matrix, the Goals-Achievement Matrix, and the Planning Balance Sheet. Interested readers are encouraged to seek information in Patton and Sawicki (1993) or in other sources such as Chapin and Kaiser (1979), Hill (1968), and Miller (1980).

Skill Building Exercises

1. Using the cost-benefit analysis of taxing alcohol to save lives as a model, develop an outline of what would go into implementing a cost-benefit analysis about setting time limits on receipt of federal cash assistance to alleviate poverty among low-income parents with young children.

2. Identify and discuss alternative social welfare policies also aimed at alleviating poverty among low-income parents with young children.

3. How would you go about assessing the relative merits of each alternative policy aimed at alleviating poverty among low-income parents with young children?

Policy as Process

CHAPTER 8

Making Policy

Policy as process encompasses policy making and implementation. In general, process studies are concerned with understanding how relationships and interactions among political, governmental, and interest groups affect policy formation and adoption of policy products. Process studies examine how policies are adopted by legislative bodies, the subject of Chapter 8. Process studies are also concerned with understanding how adopted or proposed policies are or would be carried out. Studies aimed at understanding the current or prospective ways of carrying out mandates of policy products examine implementation processes, the subject of Chapter 9.

In this chapter, we consider salient aspects of the policy-making process in representative democracies. For illustrative purposes, it focuses on the role of the U.S. Congress, highlighting how laws are made, the sources of legislation, forms of congressional action, and the nature and role of committees. We discuss conceptual frameworks and theories about policy-making processes that have implications for policy analysis, including *elite theory, interest group theory, institutional rational choice theory, path (state) dependence theory, advocacy coalition,* and *social construction frameworks.* We also delineate the nature of policy formation and agenda setting, highlighting the roles of the public at large and elected officials. Finally, we present a typology of political feasibility, suggesting that when deliberating about the likelihood of adopting any given policy product, policymakers and policy analysts should assess such practical concerns as strategic, institutional, psychological, and behavioral feasibility. Upon completion of the chapter, students will be able to (1) identify coherently meaningful components of political processes associated with policy formation and adoption, and (2) know how to account for political and other self-interest in the policymaking process.

Upon successful completion of the skill building exercises, students will have mastered the following CSWE Competencies and Practice Behaviors:

Chapter 8	Council on Social Work Education Core Competencies
#	**Description**
2.1.3	**Apply Critical Thinking to Inform and Communicate Professional Judgments**
	Distinguish, appraise, and integrate multiple sources of knowledge, including research-based knowledge and practice wisdom
	Analyze models of assessment, prevention, intervention and evaluation
	Demonstrate effective oral and written communication in working with individuals, families, groups, organizations, communities, and colleagues

(Continued)

135

Chapter 8	(Continued)
#	**Description**
2.1.4	**Engage Diversity and Difference In Practice**
	Recognize the extent to which a culture's structures and values may oppress, marginalize, alienate, or create or enhance privilege and power
2.1.5	**Advance Human Rights and Social and Economic Justice**
	Understand the forms and mechanisms of oppression and discrimination
2.1.7	**Apply Knowledge of Human Behavior and the Social Environment**
	Utilize conceptual frameworks to guide the processes of assessment, intervention, and evaluation
	Critique and apply knowledge to understand person and environment
2.1.8	**Engage in Policy Practice to Advance Social and Economic Well-Being and to Deliver Effective Social Work Services**
	Analyze, formulate, and advocate for policies that advance social well-being
2.1.9	**Respond to Contexts That Shape Practice**
	Continuously discover, appraise, and attend to changing locales, populations, scientific and technological development, and emerging societal trends to provide relevant services

Source: Adapted from Council on Social Work Education (2012). *Educational policy and accreditation standards.* Washington, DC: Author. Retrieved from http://www.cswe.org/file.aspx?id=13780

MAKING POLICY AND RESPONDING TO SOCIAL PROBLEMS

As social problems are formulated and recommended policies and programs proposed, deliberative or legislative processes aimed at adopting appropriate responses are also set in motion. As can be seen in Table 8.1, characteristics of representative political systems such as democracies suggest that making public policy is based on policymakers' considerations other than a careful weighing of social costs and social benefits, as important as these are.

Many of these considerations are a function of the nature and types of interests that are brought to bear on proposals for or changes to any given policy or set of polices, general election incentives of representatives, and electoral incentives of district-based representatives. Accounting for political self-interest in the policy-making process is one of the contributions that policy analysts can make to the social good by helping to craft politically feasible alternatives that are better than those that might otherwise be adopted. As Weimer and Vining (2011) demonstrate, the analysis of policy adoption entails consideration of what constitutes the "big picture"—that is, frameworks and theories—as well as practical approaches to assessing and influencing political feasibility. Before considering conceptual and theoretical issues, it is helpful

Table 8.1	Divergence Between Social and Political Accounting
Nature of Interests in Policy	Concentrated interests have strong incentive to monitor and lobby—too much weight likely to be given to their costs and benefits
	Diffuse interests generally have weak incentives to monitor and lobby—too little weight likely to be given to their costs and benefits
	Organized diffuse interests often overcome collective action problem in monitoring and lobbying—too much weight given to their costs and benefits
	Mobilization of diffuse interests through intermittent media attention—too much weight given to their costs and benefits
General Election Incentives of Representatives	Attempt to realize tangible benefits before elections—too much weight to short-run benefits and too little weight to long-run costs
	Emphasize potential costs of opponents' policy proposals to take advantage of loss-aversion—too much weight given to potential costs
Electoral Incentives of District-Based Representatives	Seek positive net benefits for district—positive net benefits for majority of districts may nonetheless result in negative net social benefits
	Seek support from factor supplies in district—expenditures within district may be viewed as political benefits despite being economic costs

Source: Weimer, David; Vining Aidan R., *Policy Analysis: Concepts and Practice,* 5th Edition, © 2011, pp. 134, 177, 294. Reprinted by permission of Pearson Education, Inc., Upper Saddle River, NJ.

to have a general overview of how laws get made in democracies such as the United States. Equipped with such an overview, prospective policy analysts will be in a better position to identify what part or parts of the process they want to focus on for purposes of analysis. That is, they will be able to partialize the problem of analyzing political processes of policy formation and adoption into coherently meaningful components, as social workers are trained to do as a matter of practice.

Making Laws

This section examines federal lawmaking processes. It relies on the most recent related report of the U.S. House of Representatives (2007), which since 1953 has provided periodically updated basic outlines of the numerous steps of the federal lawmaking process from the source of an idea for a legislative proposal through its publication as a statute. This section also draws on Oleszek (1996), who provides a more extensive description and summary of congressional procedures than that provided in the House report. What follows is an overview of the process of policy making at the national level of government, with a full understanding that "behind the scenes" bargaining or "horse trading" goes on—and it does so well below the radar screen of public visibility—making systematic analysis and public accountability problematic.

It should be noted that legislative histories provide a good source of information about the dynamics of legislative policy deliberation by national and state governments (e.g., Mendez, 2006). Although what follows focuses on the legislative branch of government, it is also important to keep in mind that executive and judicial branches of government are involved in the policy-making process and as such can be the subject of policy analysis during the adoption stage of the policy process, as well as in the implementation stage of the policy process (discussed further below).

Congress

In the United States, the federal legislative or lawmaking body is Congress, which consists of two chambers or Houses, the Senate and the House of Representatives. The Senate is composed of 100 members, two from each state, elected by the people in accordance with the Seventeenth Amendment of the Constitution, with each senator having one vote and the vice president of the United States serving as tie-breaker, in the unusual event that the Senate vote is tied. At the start of the 113th Congress on January 3, 2013 (each Congress lasts two years, with the first year referred to as the first session and the second year referred to as the second session of that Congress), the House of Representatives had 433 Members (due to vacancies, 2 shy of the full 435), each elected for a two-year term. Each member of the House of Representatives serves the people of a specific congressional district, and proportionately represents the population of the 50 states. The decennial U.S. Census is the basis for the apportionment of congressional districts, and as of the 2010 Census, the average population of a congressional district was about 750,000 people, with the largest number of people in the Montana congressional district and the smallest number in the Rhode Island district. In addition, there are five (non-voting) delegates representing the District of Columbia, the Virgin Islands, Guam, American Samoa, and the Commonwealth of the Northern Mariana Islands, and a resident commissioner representing Puerto Rico, also in a non-voting capacity.

The U.S. Constitution authorizes each chamber to determine the rules of its proceedings. Pursuant to that authority, the House of Representatives adopts its rules anew each Congress, ordinarily on the opening day of the first session. The Senate operates under continuous standing rules that it amends from time to time. Unlike some other parliamentary bodies, both the Senate and the House of Representatives have equal legislative functions and powers with certain exceptions. For example, the Constitution provides that only the House of Representatives may originate revenue bills (i.e., tax legislation), though in practice the Senate Finance Committee and other Senate committees also develop tax legislation. By tradition, the House also originates appropriations bills, which allocate (or appropriate) federal monies to executive departments and agencies and groups of programs in each area of government, such as defense, environmental protection, and education.

Sources of Legislation

Sources of ideas for legislation are essentially unlimited and quite varied, including a legislator's own concerns and those of immediate constituents during and after campaigns and by petition, those generated and proliferated by think tanks, as well as those developed and proposed through "executive communication." Although the president, the president's cabinet, and heads of independent agencies cannot directly introduce legislative proposals to Congress, they can nonetheless send a message, letter, or draft of a bill to committee chairs or any sympathetic member of Congress who can then seek other supporters and introduce it. Many such communications follow the State of the Union Address the president delivers to Congress, the Cabinet, the Supreme Court, and guests, as well as the nation (through the media) annually. These communications are referred to congressional standing committees or to other committees having jurisdiction over the subject matter. The committee chairperson or ranking minority member of the relevant committee usually introduces the bill, either in its original form or a modified version of it with desired changes. The most important "executive communication" is the annual message from the president transmitting the proposed budget to Congress. The president's budget proposal, together with testimony by officials from departments, agencies, and commissions of the executive branch of government before the Appropriations committees of the House and Senate, provide the basis of the appropriations bills that are drafted by the Appropriations committees of the House and Senate. Each year Congress passes a set of 12 appropriations bills, which collectively fund government programs from October 1 of one year to September 30 of the next (also known as the fiscal year, as distinct from the calendar year). In practice, in recent decades Congress has often been unable to agree on funding of programs, and appropriations bills have not been passed. In these years, short-term continuing resolutions are passed instead, which allow funding at the level of the previous year for a limited period of time.

Much of government spending is on mandatory programs, whose establishment and continued existence have been authorized by Congress. Such programs—including Social Security and Medicare—do not require a new appropriation of funds each year but grow according to rules within the authorizing legislation. In this sense, funds for Social Security and Medicare rise automatically and do not require congressional approval. These ongoing, congressionally authorized programs are also referred to as entitlement programs because all eligible recipients are entitled to benefits from these programs. Changing these mandatory programs requires Congress to pass legislation. It is for this reason that presidents often say that most of the budget (approximately two-thirds) is not within their control.

The House and Senate Appropriations committees are powerful: the determination about the level of discretionary funding (about one-third of total U.S. spending) to allocate to specific provisions in passed legislation is subject to political influence and pressures. Even though two-thirds of federal outlays go to entitlement programs such as Social Security and Medicare that are for the most part outside annual appropriation deliberations and as such make fundamental changes in social welfare provisioning more difficult, the budget process nonetheless warrants analysis despite claims otherwise (Patashnik, 2001; Pierson, 2001). Many clients of social workers and populations of people in need about whom social workers are concerned as a matter of social justice are affected by annual budget allocation decisions, such as low-income individuals and families, women, and minorities.

When Republicans regained control of the Congress in 1994 for the first time in forty years, they used the House Appropriations Committee to advance their policy agenda (Aldrich & Rohde, 2000; Kiewiet & McCubbins, 1985). The National Association for the Repeal of Abortion Laws (NARAL) Pro-Choice America (2012a, 2012b) also notes that anti-choice legislators continually use these "must pass" bills as vehicles to deny coverage for abortion services to millions of women whose health care is subject to federal control. Since 1980, restrictions on use of federal Medicaid funds for abortion services have been imposed through the Hyde amendment, which was attached to the annual Labor, Health and Human Services, and Education appropriations bill (P.L. 94–439). The Hyde amendment was named after Congressman Henry

Hyde (R-IL), who initially introduced it in 1976; it was then routinely attached it as a "rider" to annual appropriation bills. Between 1981 and 1993 the Hyde amendment prohibited federal Medicaid dollars from being used to provide abortion services except to preserve a woman's life. In 1993, the exception was expanded to include situations where the pregnancy resulted from rape or incest (P.L. 103–12). In 1997, Congress adopted language to make it clear that the Hyde amendment applied to Medicaid recipients enrolled in managed care plans. Congress also passed a permanent Hyde amendment in the Budget Reconciliation Act of 1997 (P.L. 105–33), which applies to the State's Children Health Insurance Program.

Forms of Congressional Action

Proposals initiating the work of Congress can take one of four forms: the bill, the joint resolution, the concurrent resolution, and the simple resolution. The bill is the most customary form used in both chambers of Congress. Over 10,000 bills were introduced in the 111th Congress (the vast majority of which were not acted upon; about 10% getting some action, and about 3% being passed), 100 each of House concurrent, joint, and simple resolutions, and 78 Senate concurrent resolutions, 42 Senate joint resolutions, and 100 Senate simple resolutions (Library of Congress, 2012; Tauberer, 2011). With one exception, bills may originate in either chamber of Congress. Bills for raising revenue are constitutionally mandated to originate in the House of Representatives and may be amended or concurred on by the Senate. By tradition, general appropriations bills originate in the House of Representatives. Public bills are those that affect the public generally. Private bills are those that affect specified individuals or private entities rather than the public at large. Bills originating in the House of Representatives have the designation "H.R." followed by a number that each bill retains throughout its parliamentary stages. A Senate bill is designated by "S." followed by its number. Companion bills are those that originate in one chamber of Congress but are similar or identical to one originating in the other chamber.

Bills agreed to and passed in identical form by both chambers of Congress become law only after (1) presidential approval (by signature); or (2) failure by the president to return the bill with objections to the congressional chamber in which it originated within ten days (Sundays excepted) while Congress is in session, an action referred to as a "pocket veto"; or (3) the overriding of a presidential veto by two-thirds vote of each chamber of Congress.

An enacted bill or enrolled bill (the final copy of a bill or joint resolution passed by both chambers of Congress in identical form) is referred to as a Public Law (in matters governing the relation between individuals and the state) or Private Law (in matters governing relations between individuals), followed by its number, with the number of the Congress (as in the 113th Congress) coming first and then the number of the law following, and these running in sequence as they become law. For example, Public Law 112–1, or P.L. 112–1, signifies the first Public Law of the 112th Congress.

Joint resolutions may originate in either chamber of Congress; they are similar to bills and are often used interchangeably. Unlike bills, however, joint resolutions may include a preamble preceding the resolving clause. Preambles are "whereas" clauses indicating the necessity for or desirability of the joint resolution. Statutes introduced as bills may be amended by joint resolutions and vice versa. Both are subject to the same procedures, except in the case of a joint resolution proposing an amendment to the Constitution. When such an amendment is approved by two-thirds of the members of each chamber of Congress, it is not presented to the president for approval. Instead, such a joint resolution is sent directly to the archivist of the United States for submission to the states, where

Case in Point 8.1: The Comprehensive Child Development Act—Vetoed

On September 9, 1971, the U.S. Senate adopted S. 2007, the Economic Opportunity Amendments of 1971, which, among other things, incorporated under Title V major provisions of S. 1512, the Comprehensive Child Development Act of 1971 (Child Development Plan Vetoed, 1972). S. 1512 had been introduced in 1970 by Senators Walter Mondale (D-MN), Jacob Javits (R-NY), Gaylord Nelson (D-WI), and Richard Schweiker (R-PA), along with twenty-nine co-sponsors. S. 2007 passed both houses of Congress and involved a comprehensive approach to child development, beginning with prenatal care and ending with after-school centers for young teens. On December 9, 1971, President Richard Nixon vetoed the bill, citing, in regard to the "most deeply flawed provision of this legislation . . . Title V, 'Child Development Programs,'" costs (estimated at $20 billion a year), a new army of bureaucrats to administer it, and, his distaste for communal approaches to child rearing (Nixon, 1971). The next day the Senate sustained the veto. Gilbert Steiner (1976), director of Government Studies at the Brookings Institution (see Appendix B) advised advocates that seeking comprehensive and innovative legislation was impractical after Nixon's veto, advice rejected by a member of the Arkansas bar Hillary Rodham (1977), later Hillary Rodham Clinton, Secretary of State, New York Senator, and First Lady. More recently, *The New York Times* columnist Gail Collins (2013), noting Nixon's 1971 veto, reported how delighted Walter Mondale was upon hearing President Obama's 2013 State of the Union address in which he called for high quality pre-school for all 4-year-olds.

ratification by the legislators of three-fourths of the states within the period of time specified in the joint resolution is necessary for the amendment to become part of the Constitution. Joint resolutions originating in the House of Representatives have the designation "H.J. Res." followed by a number they retain throughout its parliamentary stages; one originating in the Senate is designated by "S.J. Res." followed by its number.

Concurrent resolutions are concerned with matters affecting the operations of both chambers of Congress. They are used to express facts, principles, opinions, and purposes of both chambers. As such concurrent resolutions are not legislative in character nor are they presented to the president for approval. They may originate in either chamber. Those originating in the House of Representatives are designated as "H. Con. Res." followed by their original number; a Senate concurrent resolution is designated as "S. Con. Res." followed by its number. On approval of both chambers of Congress, concurrent resolutions are signed by the clerk of the House and the secretary of the Senate and sent to the archivist of the United States for publication in a special part of the Statutes at Large volume covering that session of Congress.

Simple resolutions refer to matters concerning the rules, the operation, or the opinion of either chamber of Congress alone. Those affecting the House of Representatives are designated "H. Res." followed by their number, while a Senate resolution is designated "S. Res." together with its number. Simple resolutions are considered only by the body in which they were introduced. Upon adoption, simple resolutions are attested to by the clerk of the House of Representatives or the secretary of the Senate and are published in *The Congressional Record,* a complete reporting of legislative activity in Congress and available in most libraries. Online access to The Congressional Record (including legislation being considered in the current congressional session, as well as past congressional sessions from 1989—and in summary form from 1973) may be found at the Library of Congress Web site known as THOMAS (http://thomas.loc.gov/home/thomas.php).

Introduction and Referral to Committee

Any member, delegate, or the resident commissioner from Puerto Rico in the House of Representatives may introduce a bill at any time while the House is in session by simply placing it in the "hopper," a wooden box provided for that purpose located on the side of the rostrum in the House Chamber. Permission is not required to introduce the measure. The member introducing the bill is known as the primary sponsor. In the Senate, a senator usually introduces a bill or resolution by presenting it to one of the clerks at the Presiding Officer's desk, without commenting on it from the floor of the Senate. However, a senator may use a more formal procedure by rising and introducing the bill or resolution from the floor, usually accompanied by a statement about the measure. After some formal processes of getting a bill officially on record, it is sent to a committee whose clerk enters it on the committee's legislative agenda for deliberation and action. Congressional committees provide intensive consideration to a proposed measure and by way of hearings they serve as the forum where the public is given an opportunity to be heard. Each chamber of Congress has a standing committee structure and also makes use of ad hoc committees as warranted.

As of the first session of the 113th Congress, the Senate had 20 standing committees, including the Armed Services Committee, the Banking, Housing and Urban Affairs Committee, the Budget Committee, the Health, Education, Labor and Pensions Committee, and the Finance Committee; the House of Representatives had 21 standing committees, including the Appropriations Committee, the Budget Committee, the Education and Workforce Committee, and the Ways and Means Committee. Under these large committees are sixty-eight subcommittees that focus more narrowly on specialized aspects of the larger committees' work and usually make recommendations about issues and bills to the larger committees. There are also four joint (House-Senate) committees (U.S. Senate, 2013). Both chambers of Congress have members on four standing committees without legislative jurisdiction, including the Joint Economic Committee and the Joint Committee on Taxation. Committees generate reports and summaries made available to the public through the Government Printing Office, in hard or electronic copies, many of which are freely available. Such reports provide a wealth of information about issues, facts, and opinions raised during deliberations about what actions to take on specific bills. Committee membership, which generally reflects a member's qualifications and interests, is proportional to party affiliation in each chamber of Congress, with seniority in accordance with the order of their appointment to the full committee and the ranking majority member with the most continuous service often elected chairperson. Each committee is provided with professional staff, of up to 30 people for standing committees, to assist it in the many substantive and administrative matters involved in the consideration of bills within the committee's area of oversight or responsibility. The majority party is allowed a larger staff than the minority party, and the committee's chief of staff is generally appointed by the chair of the committee.

There are many rules and regulations that guide how and in what form bills get from committees to the floor of each chamber of Congress for debate, further modification, and voting. The particulars are beyond the scope of this text, although the dynamics of committee and subcommittee meetings as well as public hearings (if called for) are the subject of extensive scholarly observation, analysis, and comment as part of the policy-making process. Oleszek (1996) provides a useful description of the congressional environment, budget process, preliminary legislative action, scheduling of legislation in both chambers of Congress, procedures guiding discussion, debates, and amendments to bills in both chambers of Congress, resolution of House-Senate differences, and legislative oversight of how effectively the executive branch of government is carrying out congressional mandates. Suffice it to say that most bills die in committee or subcommittee, never reaching the floor of either chamber of Congress for deliberation by that legislative body, and even if introduced never being reintroduced in the next legislative session if not acted upon favorably. For those that do make it to the floor of either or both chambers of Congress, one can follow proceedings and learn about the status of bills in current and prior legislative sessions through *The Congressional Record,* available in libraries and online through the Library of Congress service, THOMAS (http://thomas.loc.gov/home/thomas.php). In addition, committees voting to report out a bill must prepare a report that describes the purpose and scope of the bill and the reasons for its recommended approval; changes to existing laws must be indicated and the text of laws being repealed set out. Such reports provide information about the rationale for the law, as well as its intended aims and objectives.

Case in Point 8.2: Affordable Care Act (ACA) Repeal Bill H.R. 45 Referred to Congressional Committees

Think again of the Affordable Care Act and H.R. 45 introduced in Congress by Representative Michele Bachmann on January 3, 2013, to repeal it. After H.R. 45 was introduced, it was referred to the House Energy and Commerce Committee, Subcommittee on Health and has been referred to the House Education and Workforce Committee, the House Ways and Means Committee, the House Judiciary Committee, the House Rules Committee, the House Administration Committee, the House Budget Committee, and to the House Natural Resources Committee, Subcommittee on Indian and Alaska Native Affairs. Research all congressional actions since January 31, 2013, when H.R. 45 went to the Subcommittee on Indian and Alaska Native Affairs and how H.R. 45 fared in the 1st session of the 113th Congress by going to The Library of Congress Web site, THOMAS, URL: http://thomas.loc.gov/

Another source of information that policy analysts will find useful is provided by the Congressional Research Service (CRS), a legislative branch agency within the Library of Congress, which serves as shared staff to congressional committees and to members of Congress, issuing nonpartisan reports on major policy issues, providing expert congressional testimony and responses to individual inquiries.

The major research divisions of the Congressional Research Service are American law, domestic social policy, foreign affairs, defense and trade, government and finance, and resources, sciences, and industry. The domestic social policy division of CRS has six research sections: children and families, domestic security and immigration, education and labor, health insurance and financing, health services and research, and income security (Social Security, income for disabled persons, unemployment compensation, and retirement savings and pensions). Unfortunately, CRS does not provide direct public access to its reports, although citizens can request them from members of Congress. Unaffiliated sites, however, do make some CRS reports available to the public. The Digital Library at the University of North Texas, for example, provides integrated, searchable access to many of the full-text Congressional Research Service reports that have been available at a variety of different Web sites since 1990 (http://digital .library.unt.edu/explore/collections/CRSR/), covering such topics as abortion (45 reports between 1970 and 2012), job training (15 such reports between 1980 and 2009), federal and state budgets (379 between 1990 and 2012), economic policy (489 between 2000 and 2012; see e.g., Labonte, 2009, for a discussion about the role and size of government), religion (65 between 1970 and 2011), and welfare (199 reports between 1970 and 2012), among others such as energy (675 reports between 2000 and 2012) and environmental protection (428 reports between 2000 and 2012).

Conceptual and Theoretical Considerations

This section highlights relevant conceptual frameworks and theories about policy-making processes that have implications for policy analysis. These include *elite theory, interest group theory, institutional rational choice theory, path (state) dependence theory, advocacy coalition,* and *social construction frameworks* (Dye, 1978, 2001; Sabatier, 1999, 2007; Weimer & Vining, 2011). Each framework has its own internal consistency and none is constructed to capture all relevant aspects of the policy-making process. In each framework some aspects of the policy-making process operate in the foreground while others are in the background or ignored completely.

Elite Theory

Elite theory has been developed with contributions from notable social scientists such as Vilfredo Pareto (Higley, 2009), Robert Michels (1917/1962; 1927; Beetham, 1977a, 1977b), and C. Wright Mills (1967; Horowitz, 1981), among others (e.g., Domhoff, 1967). It has its own set of controversies, in part due to its implication for democracy as a sustainable form of electorally responsive self-governance (Ghiloni & Domhoff, 1984) and to methodological and substantive issues associated with building over time a credible body of empirical research (Domhoff, 2007; Dusek, 1969; Kerbo & Fave, 1979; Mintz, Freittag, Hendricks, & Schwartz, 1976; Polsby, 1968; Quadagno, 2007). It is distinct from pluralist or interest group theory in its unique starting point of viewing power rooted first and foremost in organizations, not in individuals or voluntary associations, or for that matter in class (Domhoff, 2007), although it should be noted that membership networks or "people-by-institutions" matrices are used for analytical purposes (Domhoff, 1983). Organizations are seen as the power bases for those at the top.

For purposes here, the **elite theory** of public policy portrays policy as a function of a governing elite whose preferences and values influence how social problems and policy responses get formulated by virtue of their control over and leadership roles among large corporate and financial institutions. Elites are the principal decision makers in the largest or otherwise most pivotally situated organizations in society (Field, Higley, & Burton, 1990). The national policy outcomes they affect are the basic stability or instability of political regimes, the more specific democratic or authoritative forms regimes take, as well as the regime's main policies. Elites affect political outcomes substantially in the sense that without their support or opposition, the outcome (responsive to their interests) would be noticeably different. Elected officials, the "proximate policy makers" whose actions give official sanction to policy decisions, knowingly or unknowingly respond disproportionately and primarily to the values of the elite. Figure 8.1 highlights the hierarchical formation of the elite theory or top-down policy formulation process.

Although members of the governing elite may disagree over the specifics of any given public policy, this model assumes that they generally share a consensus over the major goals and direction of society, as well as appropriate means of working toward those goals and the desired direction. This is not to say that the elite has no factions or is ideologically monolithic, or is stagnant. Nor does the model suggest that government is "captured" by elites or vice versa, given that much of the related literature makes clear that sustainable democracy as a complex socio-political structure requires some degree of elite autonomy from government intervention per se (Domhoff, 1974; Etzioni-Halvey, 1990; Medvetz, 2012; Slann, 1988). The model posits that elites sponsor and finance associations and political action committees, and they underwrite the formation of organized interest group activities such as direct lobbying (testifying at committee hearings, contacting government officials directly, presenting research results, and assisting in writing legislation), litigation, filing amicus curiae briefs, and making campaign contributions (directly and through political parties, political action committees, and, more recently, SuperPacs). Such activities are directed at government officials and are meant to influence policy outcomes in such areas as welfare, health, education, defense, trade, immigration, law enforcement, taxation, international relations, and the like.

Elites also influence public opinion through their leadership of influential media institutions, national TV networks (ABC, CBS, NBC, CNN, FOX), national newspapers (*Washington Post, New York Times, Wall Street Journal, USA Today*), and broad-circulation news magazines (*The Atlantic, Newsweek, The New Republic, Time, U.S News & World Report Weekly, Economist*). Such media institutions not only report newsworthy political interest stories and events but also, through commentary, interpret events and attempt to influence public attitudes about social problems and related policy interventions. Figure 8.1 suggests a downward flow of influence on policy outcomes. It is worth noting, however, as Jenkins and Eckert (2000) show in their study of the influence of business elites on economic policy, that social, industrial, and regional differences create policy divisions and political pressures from below that condition the dominance of elites.

Interest Group Theory

Interest group politics entail those situations, as Figure 8.1 suggests, where both costs and benefits are concentrated, providing the relevant actors with incentives to participate in policy making, and policy analysts with a way of readily identifying and predicting their reactions to policy proposals (Lowi, 1972). In entrepreneurial politics (diffuse benefits and concentrated costs) and client politics (concentrated benefits and diffuse costs), analysts often face the problem of identifying and mobilizing diffuse interests on their own behalf (Weimer & Vining, 2011; Wilson, 1980). More diffuse interests require mobilization or the creation of representative organizations. They become effective by framing issues broadly or in terms of widely held values, or by creating sensational public events to attract attention. Analysts perform a valuable service by identifying those groups who would bear

Figure 8.1   Top-Down or Elite Policy Formation Process

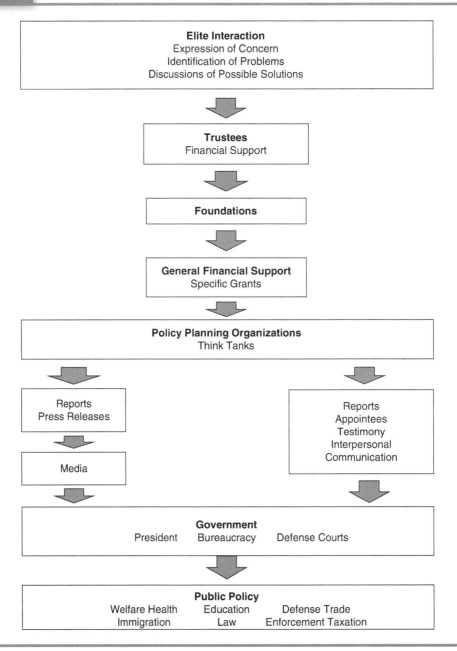

Source: Dye, T.R. (2001). *Top down policymaking.* New York, NY: Chatham House Publishers, p.40.

diffuse costs from policies if they were adopted. For example, failure to take into account diffuse costs associated with the Medicare Catastrophic Coverage Act passage in 1988, with support from both houses of Congress, resulted in its repeal in 1989, when strong opposition from wealthy elderly persons to progressive fees became apparent (Himelfarb, 1995; Oliver, Lee, & Lipton, 2004; Weimer & Vining, 2011).

Institutional or Rational Choice Theory

Analysts who rely on *institutional rational choice theory* focus on the role of institutions, defined roughly as "fairly stable sets of commonly recognized formal and informal rules that coordinate or constrain the behavior of individuals in social interactions" (Weimer 1995, as cited in Weimer & Vining, 2011, p. 267). The focus on rules differentiates *institutional rational choice theory* from *elite theory*, which, as previously discussed, focuses on the constitutive power bases for those at the top of substantively influential organizations. In *institutional rational choice theory*, four levels of rules that cumulatively affect actions taken and outcomes obtained in any setting but are most appropriate for policy analysis are considered (Ostrom, 2007). At the first or *operational level*, operational rules shape the actions of individuals who usually initiate public policy that has to do with situations concerned with provision, production, distribution, appropriation, or assignment of related goods and services. Such rules may be formal, as the rules and regulations adopted by a state, or informal, as conventions or norms about acceptable behavior. The main considerations here are individuals' actions that directly affect policy-relevant variables (those that can be manipulated or are subject to government or influence).

Other types of rules that cumulatively affect actions and outcomes entail collective choice situations—that is, individuals' actions that directly affect rules affecting operational definitions. Related rules are generated at the *collective choice level*—for our purposes, primarily by government bodies according to their legislative and executive authorities. Such rules may also be set at the *constitutional level*, which sets rules about collective choice. Finally, rules may be set at the *meta-constitutional level*—that is, actions taken that directly affect rules that affect constitutional situations.

It is important to keep in mind that there are formal and informal collective-choice arenas between and within which influences on the monitoring and enforcement of public policy actions occur. National, regional, and state/local formal collective-choice arenas include legislatures, regulatory agencies, and courts. Informal collective-choice arenas include private associations, civic institutions, and the like that provide information. At each level of rules, policy analysts examine the formal and informal processes by which a particular set of rules is decided upon and how they get communicated to those to whom they apply, while remaining aware that modifications of rules can be a source of policy changes within or across levels. For example, throughout the early 2000s in many states those opposed to same-sex marriage attempted to constrain their legislatures through constitutional bans via ballot initiatives, while proponents of marriage equality have often looked to the courts to pursue their policy goals. More recently, the issue went to polls in states including Maryland and Maine and was taken up by state legislators such as in Maryland, which approved same-sex marriage in 2013 (Same-Sex Marriage, 2013).

Path Dependence Theory

Path dependence refers to how past policy decisions affect the content and likely adoption of proposed policy alternatives; **state dependence** refers to how current policies affect the content and likely adoption of proposed policy alternatives (Weimer & Vining, 2011). In general, the identification of path dependence involves both tracing a given outcome back to a particular set of historical events, and showing how these events are themselves contingent occurrences that cannot be explained on the basis of prior historical conditions (Mahoney, 2000). Because the presence or absence of contingency cannot be established independent of theory, the specification of path dependence is always a theory-laden process. For example, economists assume that utilitarian mechanisms of cost-benefit analysis underpin processes of institutional reproduction—that is, an institutional pattern once adopted delivers increasing benefits with its continual adoption, and over time it becomes more difficult to transform the pattern or to select previously available options even if they are deemed more efficient. Sociologists and other social scientists identify additional theoretically related mechanisms or causal factors that can underpin institutional reproduction, including functional relationships, power relationships, and legitimation or authority-related mechanisms.

Policy feedback is integral to both path and state dependence—changes in administrative capacity and the identities and resources of social groups make political processes dependent upon previous policy adoption. In addition, as Mettler (2002) shows in regard to the G.I. Bill for the World War II veterans, as Soss and Schram (2007) suggest about welfare reform efforts during the 1990s, and as Pierson (1993) and Mettler and Soss (2004) contend for politics in general, policy feedback may affect public opinion and civic engagement and thereby contribute to policy and political change, at times advancing it and other times reaffirming the status quo (Caputo, 2010). Path dependence calls for historical analysis examining the roads taken, by whom, as well as in what ways past efforts to change policy and influence future opportunities were successful or not. By contrast, a focus on state dependence requires only an assessment of the status quo. Path analysis highlights the importance of the timing of events and relates to when things happen, and to how they happen.

Case in Point 8.3: Ending the Aid to Families with Dependent Children Program

Caputo (2011) observes that ending the entitlement nature of the Aid to Families with Dependent Children (AFDC) program had not been the intent of welfare reform legislation introduced by the Clinton administration, nor was it part of prior welfare reform efforts. Rather, once Republicans took control of Congress in 1994, the path to replacing AFDC with its successor, the time-limited and federally capped Temporary Assistance for Needy Families (TANF) program, was, while not inevitable, much more politically feasible and probable.

Advocacy Coalition Framework

The **advocacy coalition framework** assesses the learning that occurs among coalition members and its relationship to policy change within *policy subsystems* over time (Sabatier & Jenkins-Smith, 1999; Sabatier & Weible, 2007; Weimer & Vining, 2011). *Policy subsystems* are collections of individuals and organizations, such as advocacy or professional groups, who seek to influence public policy within a substantive domain such as health, education, or housing. Key elements of this framework include the policy subsystem as the unit of analysis, the focus on two or more relatively stable and opposed coalitions of actors within the subsystem, the belief systems of the coalitions, and the processes through which learning by the coalitions and policy change occur. Figure 8.2 shows a diagram of the framework.

Within the *advocacy coalition framework,* external events such as changes in the economy or in other subsystems of society, and electoral changes are acknowledged as contributors to policy change. The distinctive contribution of the *advocacy coalition framework,* however, is the focus on the relatively stable belief systems of the coalitions and the extent to which policy learning can affect those beliefs (Sabatier & Weible, 2007; Weimer & Vining, 2011). Coalitions may share deep core beliefs about the relative importance of fundamental values and human nature. Core beliefs span a variety of broad-based issues and concerns, such as the appropriate roles of markets and governments, the causes and seriousness of social problems, and the acceptability of policy instruments for dealing with those problems. Secondary policy beliefs are narrower in scope, concerning either specific issues about a policy or policies and processes in specific locales. For example, a coalition may have core beliefs about the causes of and proper responses

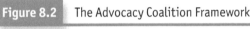

Figure 8.2   The Advocacy Coalition Framework

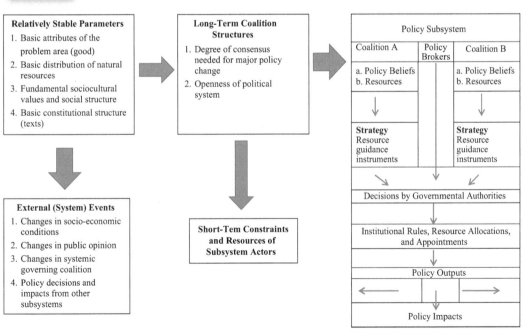

Source: Sabatier, P.A., & Weible, C.M. (2007). The advocacy coalition framework: Innovations and clarifications. In P.S. Sabatier (Ed.), *Theories of the policy process* (2nd ed.), pp. 189–220. Boulder, CO.: Westview Press, p. 202.

to substance abuse in general, but secondary beliefs about specific policies appropriate in a particular geographical area. Changes in secondary beliefs tend to be more amenable to change than core beliefs. Further, successful experiences of change at the local level may serve as the basis among coalition members to facilitate change in core beliefs.

Social Construction Framework

The **social construction framework** relies on the notion that interpretive frameworks used to interpret our observations of the world can to some extent be altered by arguments, thereby providing an avenue for changing the political support for various policies (Weimer & Vining, 2011). It applies this notion to the distribution of benefits and burdens among the groups who are targets of public policies. As can be seen in Table 8.2, this framework identifies four target groups in reference to their social construction and political power (Schneider & Ingram, 1993). The four-fold classification, developed by Ingram, Schneider, and deLeon (2007), is not intended to produce sharp lines among the groups but rather conceptualizes a policy space, with groups slotted appropriately, contingent on time and context. Illegal immigrants in the United States, for example, are often portrayed by some as the backbone of the low-paying sector of its economy, whereas others often portray them as lawbreakers who take jobs from citizens and exploit the welfare system (Fox, 2009; Newton, 2002, 2005).

The *advantaged* are those groups with positive social constructions and strong political power, such as senior citizens, small businesses, homeowners, and the military; policies targeting these groups are viewed as benefits, not burdens. *Dependents* include groups with positive social constructions but weak political power, such as children and mothers; policies targeting these groups tend to be viewed as benefits, but they are smaller and less secure than those provided to the advantaged. *Contenders,* such as big business and labor unions, have negative social constructions but strong political power relative to other groups; the benefits they receive are not always obvious to the public and the burdens they bear (e.g., corporate taxes and linking wage increases to productivity gains, respectively) are often less severe than the rhetoric surrounding them would suggest. Finally, *outsiders,* such as welfare recipients and substance abusers, have negative social constructions and weak political power; they tend to be subject to burdens (least generous cash or in-kind benefits, stigma, social opprobrium) and have almost no influence on the policy-making process.

Table 8.2 The Social Construction Framework of Target Populations

Social Construction	Political Power	
	+	−
+	Advantaged	Dependents
−	Contenders	Outsiders

Source: Adapted from Ingram, H., Schneider, A.L., & deLeon, P. (2007). Social construction and policy design. In P.A. Sabatier (Ed.), *Theories of the policy process* (2nd ed.), pp. 93–126. Boulder, CO: Westview Press, p. 102.

Maintaining and changing social constructions of target populations depends on framing, a process of selecting aspects of perceived reality and making them more salient in such a way as to promote a particular problem definition, causal interpretation, moral evaluation, or policy alternative (Entman, 1993; Weimer & Vining, 2011). In the public sphere, framing refers to the use of organizing concepts or storylines by the media or politicians to create specific meaning for events (Scheufele, 1999). Those seeking to highlight issues in public discourse choose language and metaphors that resonate with the frames shared by groups of individuals. For example, gaining support for public policies that impose burdens to reduce risk appear to be most effective when the issue is framed as involving risk that is involuntary (imposed rather than sought out), universal (affecting all of us rather than some others), environmental (external rather than internal to the individual), and knowingly created (burdens can be assigned to a culpable party) (Lawrence, 2004).

Practical Considerations

General Concerns

Practical considerations to take into account when analyzing policy-making processes include identifying the relevant actors, understanding their motivations and beliefs, assessing available resources, and identifying the arena or level at which rules governing the policy-making process occur (Weimer & Vining, 2011). Analysts need to pay attention to how populations targeted by policies are framed. For example, when children of illegal immigrants are cast as draining public coffers and services meant for children of U.S. citizens, the political feasibility of punitive policy alternatives increases among certain segments of and political constituencies within the U.S. population, whereas when they are cast as innocent victims of their parents' illegal behavior and hardworking students, the political feasibility of more empowering legislation is increased among other segments of and political constituencies within the U.S. population (Eligon, 2012; Fox, 2009; Steinhauer, 2011).

Each arena or level of the policy-making process has its own set of rules about how decisions are made and about which analysts should be aware. For example, legislatures have rules of order and agencies have administrative procedures. Unwritten traditions and standard practices about how decisions are made also need to be considered and understood. When choosing an arena, political strategies to consider include the use of co-optation, compromise, heresthetics (strategies that attempt to gain advantage through manipulation of the circumstances of political choice, by manipulating the context and structure of the decision-making process), and rhetoric. Assessing and influencing political feasibility requires the ability and opportunity to use tools and techniques of data collection and analysis and to make appropriate inferences for recommending actions.

A Typology of Political Feasibility

Although some of the more technical related content is beyond the scope of this book, De Wispelaere and Noguera (2012) provide a useful theoretical framework of practical matters to consider when assessing political feasibility of policy proposals. Table 8.3 presents a typology or matrix of constraints and agency, yielding four types of political feasibility.

Table 8.3	Typology of Political Feasibility	
	Prospective Constraints (achievability)	**Retrospective Constraints (viability)**
Discreet Agency	A. Strategic Feasibility	B. Institutional Feasibility
Diffuse Agency	C. Psychological Feasibility	D. Behavioral Feasibility

Source: De Wispelaere, J., & Noguera, A. (2012). On the political feasibility of universal basic income: An analytic framework. In R.K. Caputo (Ed.), *Basic income guarantee and politics: International experiences and perspectives on the viability of income guarantee.* New York, NY: Palgrave Macmillan, p. 21.

Strategic and institutional feasibility share a focus on discrete agency, which refers to political agency addressed at readily identifiable actors with distinctive interests, roles, capacities, and intentions. However, where strategic feasibility requires a direct engagement to further a policy, institutional feasibility directs our attention to preexisting sets of rules and regulations that may affect the performance of a policy over time. Similarly, psychological and behavioral feasibility both concentrate on diffuse agency with the general public, which refers to political agency addressed at an amorphous set of actors, a "collective" in the loosest sense of the term, with little or no apparent coordination or collective intention. The former addresses the psychological processes that affect popular support of a policy in advance of implementation, while the latter is mostly concerned with how behavioral changes after the event affect the performance or continued survival of a policy (De Wispelaere & Noguera, 2012). For purposes here, the bottom line about the practical considerations for policy analysts charged with the responsibility of providing useful advice to policymakers about the policy-making process is to pay attention to the political environment and account for the interests of actors in the relevant political arenas.

Policy Instruments at the Disposal of Government

As a practical matter, analysts focusing on the policy-making process should be aware of the policy instruments that governments have to help policymakers assess the merits of appropriate instruments, given the problem or set of problems a policy is meant to address. Such instruments include regulation, tax and spending mechanisms (fiscal policy), market mechanisms, educating and persuading the public (using the bully pulpit), subsidy through tax credits or direct payments, contracting out, charging fees, and conducting or supporting research. In addition, national level governments exert control over their money supply. In the United States, the Federal Reserve Board, which has oversight responsibility for the rate of inflation and price stability in the nation, sets the interest rates on big banks—that is, the prices banks pay for the money they want to make available for investors and to meet the levels of cash reserves banks are required to have on hand to ensure depositors can withdraw their money (Orphanides, 2006).

In the policy-making process, the policy analyst can examine and lay out the political feasibility of relying on alternative instruments. Libertarian-oriented policymakers are more likely than Keynesian-oriented policymakers to seek and support policies that rely less on direct government involvement per se and more on market mechanisms, even if government intervention in the form of incentives is required for the market to work. In an acknowledged oxymoronic twist, Thaler and Sunstein (2008) argue for "libertarian paternalism"— that is, for efforts by institutions in the private sector and *also by government* (emphasis added), to make people's lives better as judged by themselves in their own eyes.

Skill Building Exercises

1. Describe how a congressional bill becomes a law.

    a. Identify key areas in the process that might be amendable to influence, whether by social work advocates or others who want to influence what eventually gets enacted into law.
    b. How would you go about influencing the policy-making process?

2. Describe how your analysis of a given policy would vary by adopting each of the following theoretical frameworks:

    a. elite theory
    b. interest group theory
    c. institutional rational choice theory
    d. path (state) dependence theory
    e. advocacy coalition theory
    f. social construction framework

3. Assess the political feasibility of Congress passing and the president approving legislation adopting an unconditional guaranteed annual income for each citizen in the United States, given that the State of Alaska already provides each of its citizens such income, the level or amount of which is based on a percentage of profits from the annual sale of oil divided by the number of citizens, regardless of labor force attachment, current income, or total wealth of recipients.

    a. Specify prospective constraints (achievability)
    b. Specify retrospective constraints (viability)

C H A P T E R   9

Implementing Policy

This chapter highlights the importance of considering factors affecting implementation of a policy during the policy-making process. It presents a theoretical framework to help enable policy analysts to assess the effectiveness of the means of implementation. Two basic approaches to thinking systematically about implementation, forward mapping and backward mapping, are highlighted. An overarching multilevel logic of governance (LOG) framework is presented in detail. The "black box" approach to treating variables highlighted within the LOG framework is discussed. Types of policy outputs are described, to enable policy analysts to make appropriate linkages between statutory and non-statutory factors affecting implementation processes. This chapter also identifies practical considerations about implementation, with particular focus on the potential for unintended consequences of a policy. The chapter concludes with a discussion of how street-level bureaucrats such as mid-level government administrators and in-the-field professionals such as social workers function at times as *de facto* policymakers, often at variance with legislative intent when implementing policies.

Upon completion of the chapter, students will be able to (1) develop a logic of analysis of process associated with governance, showing in effect how politics, policymaking, public management, and service delivery are hierarchically linked with one another in the determination of public policy outputs and outcomes, and (2) assess the organizational culture about the use of discretion and how that culture affects the likelihood of street-level bureaucrats taking actions they deem necessary to bring about outcomes they consider fair, despite constraints that would dictate otherwise.

Upon successful completion of the skill building exercises in Chapter 9, students will have mastered the following Council on Social Work Education (CSWE) Competencies and Practice Behaviors:

Chapter 9	CSWE Core Competencies
#	**Description**
2.1.2	**Apply Social Work Ethical Principles to Guide Professional Practice**
	Tolerate ambiguity in resolving ethical conflicts
	Apply strategies of ethical reasoning to arrive at principled decisions
2.1.3	**Apply Critical Thinking to Inform and Communicate Professional Judgments**
	Distinguish, appraise, and integrate multiple sources of knowledge, including research-based knowledge and practice wisdom
	Analyze models of assessment, prevention, intervention, and evaluation

(Continued)

Chapter 9	(Continued)
#	**Description**
	Demonstrate effective oral and written communication in working with individuals, families, groups, organizations, communities, and colleagues
2.1.4	**Engage Diversity and Difference in Practice**
	View themselves as learners and engage those with whom they work as informants
2.1.5	**Advance Human Rights and Social and Economic Justice**
	Understand the forms and mechanisms of oppression and discrimination
2.1.7	**Apply Knowledge of Human Behavior and the Social Environment**
	Utilize conceptual frameworks to guide the processes of assessment, intervention, and evaluation
	Critique and apply knowledge to understand person and environment
2.1.8	**Engage in Policy Practice to Advance Social and Economic Well-Being and to Deliver Effective Social Work Services**
	Analyze, formulate, and advocate for policies that advance social well-being
2.1.9	**Respond to Contexts That Shape Practice**
	Continuously discover, appraise, and attend to changing locales, populations, scientific and technological development, and emerging societal trends to provide relevant services

Source: Adapted from Council on Social Work Education (2012). *Educational policy and accreditation standards.* Washington, DC: Author. Retrieved from http://www.cswe.org/file.aspx?id=13780

SOME GENERAL CONSIDERATIONS

Given that the chosen method of implementation affects the achievement of intentions behind the policy, the issue facing analysts once a policy has been enacted is what happens to it after it has been adopted (Patashnik, 2008). The task at hand for the policy analyst is to assess the effectiveness of the means of implementation (Brigham & Brown, 1980). Effectiveness of the means of implementation is to be distinguished from the effectiveness of the policies they are intended to serve, the subject of Chapter 10, Approaches to Evaluation. To assess the effectiveness of the means of implementation, some preliminary thinking is in order.

Ideally, systematic thinking about implementing a policy should have occurred with transparent documentation during the policy-making process. In a comparative state-level study of policies affecting hazard-zone areas, May (1993) shows how policy designers can enhance implementation efforts by altering key mandates. Having some record of how implementation was thought about during the policy-making process or policy design stage enables an analyst to examine the logic of the policy in light of plausible if not anticipated outcomes. The logic of a policy can be thought of as a chain of hypotheses about factors affecting success and failure that guided the design of the policy (Weimer & Vining, 2011). For example, think of a state government's efforts intended to identify promising approaches to narrow the racial achievement gap in K–8th grade education. For such efforts to be successful, the following hypotheses must be correct: school districts with good ideas apply for funds; the state department of education selects the applications offering the most promise given the current state of knowledge about academic achievement; the funded schools implement the programs or plans they propose; the "experiments" produce valid evidence on the effectiveness of the approaches being tested; and finally, the Department of Education is able to recognize which successful approaches can be replicated in other school districts. Any of these hypotheses may be incorrect and to the extent that is the case, the less likely it is that the state's efforts will produce useful information about how to go about narrowing the racial achievement gap in K–8th grade education. If the string of hypotheses, the logic of factors affecting success and failure, cannot be found from existing documentation or from the policymakers, it may have to be constructed after the fact.

To help the analyst, Weimer and Vining (2011), drawing from Elmore (1979–1980), recommend two basic approaches to thinking systematically about implementation, forward mapping and backward mapping. Table 9.1 highlights the three-step approach to forward mapping: (1) write a scenario linking policy to outcomes, (2) critique the scenario from the perspective of the interests of those who have to implement the policy, particularly in regard to the scenario's plausibility, and (3) revise the scenario so it is more plausible. Scenarios take the form of stories, so it is helpful for the analyst to have good writing and communication skills and a firm grasp of the appropriate use of narrative in policy analysis (in contrast to its rhetorical use in policy advocacy) (Jones & McBeth, 2010; Kaplan, 1986; Lawler, 1996).

Table 9.1	Forward Mapping
Scenario:	Write a narrative that describes all the behaviors that must be realized for the policy to produce the desired outcome. Specify who, what, when, and why.
Critique 1:	Is the scenario plausible?
	For each actor mentioned:
	Is the hypothesized behavior consistent with personal and organizational interests?
	If not, what tactics could the actor use to avoid complying?
	What counter-tactics could be used to force or induce compliance?
Critique 2:	Thinking of the direct and indirect effects of the policy, what other actors would have an incentive to become involved?
	For each of these actors:
	How would the actor interfere with hypothesized behaviors?
	What tactics could be used to block or deflect interference?
Revision:	Rewrite the narrative to make it more plausible.

Source: Weimer, David; Vining Aidan R., *Policy Analysis: Concepts and Practice, 5th Edition,* © 2011, pp. 134, 177, 294. Reprinted by permission of Pearson Education, Inc., Upper Saddle River, NJ.

Forward mapping of a federal policy, for example, might begin with a statement about congressional intent. An outline of federal agency regulations and administrative actions consistent with the intent would follow, as would an elaborate division of responsibilities between central and regional offices of the federal government, or in many instances of social welfare policies among federal, state, and local administrators, such that each implementing unit had a clearly defined mission. The forward mapping would then specify an outcome, usually in terms of observable effects on a target population, consistent with the initial intent of the policymakers (Elmore, 1979–1980). If implementation depends on technical capacity or the adoption of some form of technology, the analyst can describe what is required at each stage. Such analyses can be elaborated by describing alternatives under varying assumptions of organizational, political, and technological factors, keeping in mind and taking into account that organizational, political, and technological processes affecting implementation often elude policymakers' control, as highlighted below in the discussion of street-level bureaucrats.

With the backward mapping approach, an analyst thinks about polices by looking at the behavior policymakers want to change and asking such questions as what interventions could effectively alter the behavior, and what decisions and resources are needed to motivate and support those interventions (Elmore, 1979–1980; Weimer & Vining, 2011). Policies to be considered are then constructed from alternative sets of decisions and resources that can bring about interventions and be controlled by the policymakers. Backward mapping is similar to using a model of the policy problem to suggest alternative implementation solutions and iteratively returning to adoption. In addition, backward mapping enables analysts to uncover less centralized or more bottom-up approaches to implementation that might be otherwise overlooked. Meyers, Glaser, and Mac Donald (1998) and Fulton and Weimer (1980) provide examples of backward mapping, the former in their study of the welfare workers in California's Work Pays demonstration program and the latter in their development of an implementation plan for neighborhood sticker parking in San Francisco.

At the least, whether forward mapping or backward mapping, in a general sense policy analysis of implementation processes in part entails identification and examination of indicators about the nature, quality, and quantity of the work of the agency, organization, or administrative body charged with the responsibility of carrying out adopted policies. From a system's perspective, implementation processes are viewed here as the "black box" between adopted policies and intended or actual outcomes. The role of the analyst is to assess what is taking place within that "black box." This is important because the actions of administrators and other professionals responsible for managing and implementing policies not only affect the likely outcomes, but they may also make policy in the process of doing so. Lipsky (2010) has shown how social workers and other "street-level" professionals invariably create policy, at times consistent with policymakers' intent and other times not, given the ambiguities associated with mandates that fail to cover the particular circumstances of their clients.

THEORETICAL CONSIDERATIONS

Robichau and Lynn (2009) add a theoretical overlay about government performance that features the influence of administrative systems and processes on outputs and outcomes with major public policy theories (discussed in Chapter 8). They draw on Lynn, Heinrich, and Hill (2001) who, while seeking to find ways to account for differences in performance across multiple administrative sites

Case in Point 9.1: Implementing Job Training and Workforce Legislation

Welfare-to-work initiatives during the 1990s that culminated in the passage of the Personal Responsibility and Work Opportunities Act of 1996 (P.L. 104-193), which created the TANF program, and the Workforce Investment Act (P.L. 105-220, WIA), passed by Congress in 1998, presented formidable challenges to linking performance measures of those responsible for administering or implementing job-training and workforce initiatives with outcome performance measures (Bordon, 2011; Bloom, Hill, & Riccio, 2001). One difficulty is getting agreement about performance measures, given fragmentation and inconsistent data across program sites and a generalized reluctance by administrators to buy into any system that challenges their perceptions of performance. Another difficulty occurs when performance measures are tied to funding, thereby creating incentives for administrators to cream clientele—that is, to ensure that the job-training program accepts those most likely to succeed (e.g., more highly educated people, or those with some skills in hand who would be more likely to find employment without benefit of the program or services), a selection bias at odds with a program goal to get the most net benefits for costs.

and to induce underperforming administrations to function like the best, developed a multilevel logic of governance (LOG) framework, as shown in Table 9.2. This framework rested on the postulate that politics, policymaking, public management, and service delivery are hierarchically linked with one another in the determination of public policy outputs and outcomes.

Table 9.2	Logic of Governance (LOG) Levels and Variables

Citizen preferences and interests expressed politically

1. Expression of citizen preferences and interests

2. Activities of private firms and organizations

3. Activities of interests groups

Public choice and policy designs

1. Socio-economic context

2. Level/type of government

3. Political atmosphere

4. Fiscal situation/budget constraints

5. Type of ownership (public, nonprofit, proprietary)

(Continued)

| Table 9.2 | (Continued) |

6. Mandates by internal government agencies

7. Mandates by elected executives

8. Mandates by legislators

9. Court decisions

10. Other

Public Management

1. Initiation of administrative structures

2. Use of management tools (policy planning, total quality management [TQM])

3. Management values and strategies

Service Delivery

1. Initiation of program design features

2. Fieldworker/office discretionary behavior

3. Fieldworker/office beliefs and values

4. Initiation of administrative processes and policies

5. Client influence, behavior, and/or preference

6. Use of resources

Outputs/outcomes

1. Outputs (means to an end)

   a. By government/public sector

   b. By market/firms/private sector

   c. By individuals/society

2. Outcomes or ends

   a. By government/public sector

   b. By market/firms/private sector

   c. By individuals/society

Stakeholder assessments of policy, agency, or program performance

Source: Adapted from Robichau R.W., Lynn, L.E. (2009). The implementation of public policy: Still the missing link. *The Policy Studies Journal, 37,* p. 23.

One of the striking findings from empirical studies Lynn, Heinrich, and Hill (2001) examined was that many had "skipped" levels in the LOG, in particular mediating effects of management or service delivery on what actually gets delivered, how benefits are delivered, and the effects of what gets delivered. As the LOG framework in Table 9.2 suggests, when conceptualizing the implementation process, policy analysts are well advised to take into account management actions and processes as initiation of management structures, management tools, and values, as well as service delivery actions and processes such as fieldworker discretion and values and the carrying out of administrative rules and regulations. To get a handle on how to go about doing this, it is helpful to think of the relevant "black box" variables that policy analysts need to consider. These "black box" variables fall into three broad categories. As can be seen in Table 9.3, these relate to the tractability or technical difficulties involved, how well the statute laid out the implementation process, and the net effect of factors that can influence intended outcomes.

Consistent with the lower two rows in Table 9.3, Hjern (1982) contends that a legalistic perspective and organizational structuring are important considerations in implementation analysis. Such considerations are important so implementation processes remain distinct for purposes of analysis from the internal processes of politics per se and of public administration per se. Macro-level legal or statutory and political variables structure processes of implementation, and policy analysts are well advised to take them into account when linking implementation processes to policy outcomes (Ingram & Schneider, 1990). Figure 9.1 illustrates the structuring influence of statutes on implementation processes and policy outcomes.

Table 9.3	Theoretically Relevant "Black Box" Variables
Tractability	Assessment of technical difficulties, the diversity of target group behaviors, the size of the target group in relation to the total population, and the extent of behavioral change required
Ability of statutes or other basic policy decisions to structure the implementation process favorably	Assessments of the clarity and consistency of purported objectives, incorporation of an adequate causal theory, initial allocation of financial resources required, hierarchical integration within and among implementing institutions, decision rules of implementing agencies, recruitment of implementing officials, and formal access by outsiders to control for partisan biases for/against the policy and to ensure impartial independent evaluation studies of performance
Non-statutory variables affecting implementation	Socioeconomic conditions and technology, public support, the attitudes and resources of constituency groups, support from sovereigns (i.e., those institutions that control the policy's legal and financial resources), and the commitment, leadership skill, and actions of implementing officials

Source: Adapted from Mazmanian, D.A., & Sabatier, P.A. (1989). *Implementation and public policy.* Lanham, MD: University Press of America, p. 22

Figure 9.1 Statutory Element in Policy Context

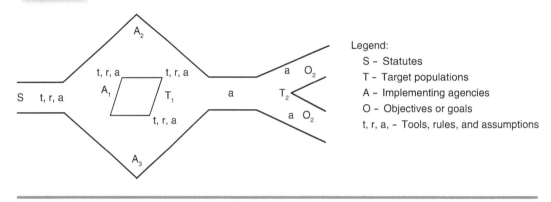

Legend:
S - Statutes
T - Target populations
A - Implementing agencies
O - Objectives or goals
t, r, a, - Tools, rules, and assumptions

Source: Adapted from Ingram, H., & Schneider, A. (1990). Improving implementation through framing smarter statutes. *Journal of Public Policy, 10,* p. 73.

Several types of outcome or dependent measures during implementation warrant conceptual clarity. These include policy outputs, compliance with policy outputs by target groups, actual impacts of policy outputs, perceived impacts of policy outputs, and in the final analysis major revisions in the policy or statute (Mazmanian & Sabatier, 1989). Policy outputs or decisions of implementing agencies that take the form of statutory objectives get translated into substantive regulations, standard operating procedures for processing individual cases, adjudication procedures to handle ambiguous or conflicting objectives and/or means of obtaining those objectives, and mechanisms to enforce adjudicatory decisions. The policy analyst focuses on discrepancies that invariably arise between statutory objectives and policy decisions. These include the nature of and extent to which objectives are ambiguous, assigned agencies are unsympathetic to the policy and are reluctant to give it a high priority, incentives are insufficient to overcome resistance of recalcitrant officials or personnel responsible for implementation, financial resources are less than sufficient to conduct technical analyses and process individual cases, or somehow otherwise biasing the decision rules and access points against program objectives.

Compliance with policy outputs by target groups is in part a function of incentives and sanctions inherent in the policy and the perceived legitimacy of the policy and its governing rules. Broadly construed, incentives include grants (e.g., cash or in-kind social welfare provisions), exemptions, and facilitative measures that seek to induce a "voluntary" change in behavior; whereas sanctions involve unpleasant consequences imposed by a legally constituted authority for a violation of a law or failure to comply with a policy or administrative mandate (Brigham & Brown, 1980). The Temporary Assistance for Needy Families program (TANF), which replaced the AFDC program in 1996, is an example (Bloom & Winstead, 2002). Many states imposed sanctions more stringent that those required by federal law—for example, terminating cash benefits to entire families for parents who missed scheduled appointments with caseworkers regardless of the reason (Goldberg & Schott, 2000). Other jurisdictions improperly screen such that victims of domestic violence who are not legitimately labor force participants are nonetheless denied assistance (DC Coalition Against Domestic Violence, 2012). A better understanding of how sanctions are used and their effects on recipients participating in programs such as TANF is important for policy analysis (Maine Equal Justice, 2011).

The use of incentives and disincentives also needs further analytical scrutiny, not just for purposes of assessing compliance but also for gaining a greater understanding of the dynamics of social control by government or others, making incentives part of voluntary exchanges with vulnerable or less powerful individuals or groups (e.g., offering cash benefits to low-income families in exchange for ensuring that children attend school) and for unintended consequences that may work against the achievement of intentions behind the policy (Grant, 2002). Sandel (2012) notes, for example, that introducing cash incentives into traditionally nonmarket settings can pervert the intended social aims of a policy: in one reported study, a schedule of fines meant to discourage parents from arriving late to pick up their children from daycare centers not only had the opposite effect, with an increase of late pick-ups, but also eroded a sense of guilt or shame for inconveniencing teachers and instilled a sense among parents that late pick-up was a service for which they were willing to pay (Ignatieff, 2012a; Lehmann, 2012). The idea that pecuniary incentives crowd out moral motives has received more extensive treatment elsewhere (Grant, 2011). Given that use of incentives to shape behavior have become increasingly adopted and promoted since the 1990s and that incentives and sanctions form integral components of contemporary social welfare policies such as TANF (Goodin, 1991; Thaler & Sunstein, 2008; Wolfe, 2002), a study of their role and effectiveness in implementation as part of any policy analysis is warranted (Grant, 2006).

PRACTICAL CONSIDERATIONS

During the course of implementation, adaptations or modifications to the original policy or program design invariably arise to meet unplanned or unintended consequences of the policy or program and/or changes in the environment in which policy or program development occurs (Browne & Wildavsky, 1984b). Purposive legislative actions are invariably accompanied by unplanned or unintended consequences that policy analysts who focus on implementation can highlight, account for, and incorporate into a feedback loop to those responsible for carrying out a policy or program. Program administrators, for example, usually have reporting requirements to monitor expenditures, revenues, and activity levels (types of clients served) built into program designs. Periodic reporting requirements of such routinely gathered information provide executive and legislative oversight to help spot anomalous performance and, perhaps, take corrective action (Weimer & Vining, 2011). Systematic analysis of side effects and changing circumstances over time and the accompanying greater awareness this produces enhance the prospects for evaluative assessment and social learning from implementation-related experiences among the public in general and policymakers and implementers in particular (Browne & Wildavsky, 1984a).

The role of implementers as purposive evaluators, as learners in the process, also warrants attention by policy analysts (Browne & Wildavsky, 1984a). Implementers are often confronted with situations about which they have incomplete knowledge, some conditions over which they have only partial if any control, and outputs and outcomes that may be ambiguous or at cross purposes. Given such situations and conditions, the delegated authority over the implementation process that implementers have allows for discretion about what has to happen to achieve intentional or desired policy outcomes. Incomplete knowledge and ambiguous or conflicting objectives of policy interventions increase the likelihood that those with statutory authority to implement policy may thwart policy effectiveness by interpreting their mandates to fit their own goals (Ingram & Schneider, 1990). On a more positive note, administrators learn from mistakes and failures about how things might be done differently to achieve outcomes consistent with legislative intent or statutory mandates. How more successful administrators go about doing so and the extent to which they do so would be a subject for analysis, keeping in mind that implementation is a dynamic process entailing identification variables, many of which lie outside the actual control of policymakers and implementers and are subject to limited statistical controls by researchers and evalators.

THE ROLE OF STREET-LEVEL BUREAUCRATS

Street-level bureaucrats include police, teachers, social workers, nurses, doctors, lawyers, and other service providers such as lower court judges, corrections officers, and prison guards, all of whom occupy positions that have relatively high degrees of discretion and relative autonomy from organizational authority (Lipsky, 1969, 2010). What they do affects how policies are implemented.

Case in Point 9.2: Street-Level Bureaucrats, TANF, and Medicaid Programs

Investigating several welfare offices in Michigan and Texas, Kim (2009) observed systematic variation or wide discretion in manipulating information (whether providing or collecting) by caseworkers assessing applicants for TANF and Medicaid programs. In the more liberal state of Michigan, caseworkers spent more time explaining benefits and less time emphasizing clients' responsibilities than in the more conservative state of Texas. In both states, rural caseworkers provided clients with more information than their metropolitan counterparts. White clients received more information than black clients; black clients were also stigmatized (subjected to degrading and humiliating comments; asked personal questions) more than white clients.

Two TANF-related studies (Lens, 2008; Riccucci, 2005) highlight the role that discretion plays in creating a gap between officially expected actions and anticipated decisions by street-level bureaucrats and what they actually do in practice. A third study highlights how conceptual frameworks or worldviews of street-level bureaucrats shape service delivery outcomes that are compatible with their sense of social justice (Kelly, 1994).

In one of the two TANF-related studies, Riccucci (2005) examines three local county TANF sites in Michigan that had a centralized model of administration and where the work-first immediate job placement official policy goal had priority over human capital investment. The street-level bureaucrats working in work-first and welfare offices in each of the three county sites were found to identify priorities that differed significantly from the official state policy and from each other. Variation was found on measures such as caseload reduction, accurate eligibility determination, requiring and encouraging work, helping people achieve self-sufficiency, diverting applicants from welfare, preventing out-of-wedlock births, ensuring that all eligible receive medical benefits, and the like.

In the other TANF-related study, Lens (2008) explored front-line workers' discretionary use of sanctions on TANF clients for failure to comply with work rules in a suburban county in New York. Findings suggested that workers interpreted and applied sanction rules narrowly, failing to distinguish procedural violations from substantive ones. Workers were also found, among other things, to overlook rules requiring them to show that a client's action was willful prior to imposing sanctions.

Kelly (1994) tested the following hypothesis: Individuals' justice beliefs affect policy implementation at the street level but such influence depends in part on organizational norms about the use of discretionary authority. Open-ended interviews were conducted with twenty-eight school teachers and fifteen field office workers from the California Employment Development Department (EDD). Teachers facing constraints on resources that precluded desirable outcomes for their students, for example, reported they were likely to rely on alternative sources for obtaining resources (often their own) to bring about fair outcomes. EDD workers were less likely than teachers to have their sense of justice affect service delivery outcomes—that is, to orchestrate outcomes that they thought were fair. This was due in part to the greater reliance on rule-bound behavior characteristic of large bureaucratic public agencies such as EDD. Nonetheless, though constrained by rules, EDD workers also reported going out of their way to assist clients—for example, breaking some rules such as doing less than the required amount of paperwork to spend more time with clients. On the whole, however, EDD's rule-governed behavior limited the ability of field workers to orchestrate outcomes that reflected their sense of social justice. In yet another study (Weissert, 1994), one accounting for differences in intrastate Medicaid spending despite a highly centralized rule-governed administration, the personal values of the street-level bureaucrats and the community values about the proper role of government pry open discretionary space that shapes program outputs measured as expenditures, even when controlling for a number of other county-level factors such as per capita income, percentage of births to teens, caseloads, and Medicaid doctors.

The two TANF-related studies (Lens, 2008; Riccucci, 2005) as well as other social welfare studies (e.g., Brodkin, 1997; Glass, 1990; Keiser & Meier, 1996; May & Winter, 2007) suggest that what goes on inside the "black box" of implementation influences the overall impact or effects of policies and programs. They enable us to identify the extent of gaps between officially anticipated actions and performance outcomes (to be discussed in Chapter 11), and what contributes to the size of such gaps, whether narrowing them such that a greater correspondence results or moving anticipated from actual results further apart in either desired or undesired directions. The third study (Kelly, 1994) highlights the importance of taking into account for purposes of implementation analysis the organizational culture and its rules and norms regarding discretion, and how that culture affects the likelihood of street-level bureaucrats taking actions they deem necessary to bring about outcomes they consider fair, despite constraints that would dictate otherwise.

Skill Building Exercises

1. Describe a "backward mapping" approach to analyzing a currently existing social welfare program, such as TANF.

   a. What behaviors would policymakers want to change?
   b. What interventions could effectively alter the behavior?
   c. What decisions and resources would be needed to motivate and support those interventions?

2. Using a multilevel logic of governance (LOG) framework, develop a legislative proposal for reducing income inequality between the top 10 percent of wage earners and the lowest 10 percent of wage earners in the United States that you would like Congress to pass.

3. Imagine you are a social worker assigned to determine eligibility for TANF or to determine whether a reported incident of child abuse/neglect should result in placement of a child in foster care. Think of your intervention as if it were a "black box" in a causal relationship between adoption of a policy and outcomes of a policy.

   a. Identify potential but nonetheless plausible scenarios that are not fully covered or specified in the laws and regulations guiding professional practice under these circumstances, given the nuances of your client's situation.
   b. How might what you do as you implement the policy or deliver the program service affect the likely outcomes of the policy in a way or ways that differ from what was intended by policymakers?
   c. What might you learn about your practice for purposes of improving it?

Policy as Performance

Approaches to Evaluation

Three main approaches to policy and program evaluation are considered in this chapter: *pseudo-evaluation, formal evaluation,* and *decision-theoretic evaluation* (Dunn, 2008). Upon completion of the chapter, students will be able to identify and differentiate appropriate circumstances warranting implementation of *pseudo-, formal,* and *decision-theoretic* evaluations.

Upon successful completion of the skill building exercises in Chapter 10, students will have mastered the following Council on Social Work Education (CSWE) Competencies and Practice Behaviors:

Chapter 10	CSWE Core Competencies
#	**Description**
2.1.3	**Apply Critical Thinking to Inform and Communicate Professional Judgments**
	Distinguish, appraise, and integrate multiple sources of knowledge, including research-based knowledge and practice wisdom
	Analyze models of assessment, prevention, intervention, and evaluation
	Demonstrate effective oral and written communication in working with individuals, families, groups, organizations, communities, and colleagues
2.1.7	**Apply Knowledge of Human Behavior and the Social Environment**
	Utilize conceptual frameworks to guide the processes of assessment, intervention, and evaluation
	Critique and apply knowledge to understand person and environment
2.1.9	**Respond to Contexts That Shape Practice**
	Continuously discover, appraise, and attend to changing locales, populations, scientific and technological development, and emerging societal trends to provide relevant services
2.1.10	**Engage, Assess, Intervene, and Evaluate With Individuals, Families, Groups, Organizations, and Communities**
2.1.10(b)	*Assessment*
	Select appropriate intervention strategies

(Continued)

Chapter 10	(Continued)
#	**Description**
2.1.10(c)	*Intervention*
	Implement prevention interventions that enhance client capacities
	Negotiate, mediate, and advocate for clients
2.1.10(d)	*Evaluation*
	Analyze, monitor and evaluate interventions

Source: Adapted from Council on Social Work Education (2012). *Educational policy and accreditation standards.* Washington, DC: Author. Retrieved from http://www.cswe.org/file.aspx?id=13780

GENERAL CONSIDERATIONS

Performance studies are concerned with identification and evaluation of program or policy conse-quences, effects, or outcomes (Gilbert & Terrell, 2010). The social entrepreneurship movement—discussed in Chapter 5 in the context of market-friendly private and public efforts aimed at identifying and creating opportunities for seeking out new revenue sources for purposes of social change—has also heightened the emphasis on measurement and evaluation (Keohane, 2013). Performance is usu-ally assessed through collection of qualitative and quantitative data and by application of a wide range of methodological tools from the academic disciplines. Research methodology as taught in the aca-demic disciplines and professional schools provides the major technical and theoretical knowledge and requisite skills for undertaking performance-based studies. Fact determination is only one aspect of performance studies, which (as with any evaluation study) have evaluative aspects. When done cor-rectly and with acknowledged methodological limitations (Rossi & Wright, 1977), evaluations provide reliable and valid information about policy and program performance—that is, the extent to which needs, values, and opportunities have been realized through public action (Dunn, 2008).

In addition to providing reliable and valid information about policy and program performance, evaluations entail efforts to determine the worth of a policy or program, focusing on judgments about the desirability or value of policies or programs (Hurteau, Houle, & Mongiat, 2009; Stake & Schwandt, 2006). Determinations of worth or merit entail ethical or normative deliberation about values associated with the aims and goals of policies enacted to benefit society as a whole, as well as specified recipients of related benefits and services. More than half a century ago, political scientist Harold Lasswell (1951, 1957; Lasswell, Brunner, & Willard, 2003) argued that one the most important impacts of the behavioral sciences was the clarification of the primary norms of society and the concomitant deliberation about the choice of sanctioning norms. Like policy analysis in general, evaluation of policy and program per-formance entails consideration of norms and values about their relative merit or worth. Although many of the theories, methods, procedures, and frameworks used for purposes of evaluation of policy and pro-gram performance are based in the behavioral sciences, the merit, worth, or weight of conclusions based on evaluations depend in part on the evaluator's role in deliberations about values and in part on the type of evaluation study conducted, a major focus of this chapter.

The types of inferences about the relationship between policy and program outcomes that are drawn from reliable and valid information generated through evaluations are a function of evaluation designs. For the most part, however, in the absence of truly experimental designs such as those discussed in this chapter, for all practical purposes, inferences are more likely to be statistical (probabilistic) or what Scriven (2012), drawing on the vocabulary of jurisprudence, describes as *probative*. A **probative inference** to a conclusion refers to one that has been established such that those making the claim are prepared to support it as beyond reasonable doubt. Challenges about the effects of a policy or program based on *probative inferences* are invariably part of the evaluation process, just as they are in courts of law. Nonetheless, for such challenges to be credible there must be specific alternative explanations or claims about the relationship between a policy or program and outcomes. This includes their desirability or merit, and the opportunity for rebuttal or counterarguments based on evidence and sound reasoning subject to what are deemed acceptable rules of evidence and argumentation about facts, judgments, and values—that is, identifiable data and backing (Manski, 2013; N.L. Smith, 2007). In the absence of successful challenges based on identifiable data and backing, *probative inferences* to a conclusion are construed as assertions beyond a reasonable doubt, and they can form the basis of adopting or modifying policies and programs.

Although values play an integral role in social work practice, social scientists, policy analysts, and program evaluators are coming to terms with how to operationalize them in light of their respective practices and professional obligations (Hitlin & Piliavin, 2004). The merit or worth of

Case in Point 10.1: Measuring Performance of the Workforce Investment Act

In 1998, Congress passed the Workforce Investment Act (P.L. 105–220), consolidating multiple workforce development programs that had evolved primarily since the 1960s, to ensure that job seekers and employers benefited from more efficient use of federal funds (Caputo, 2011; Cottingham & Besharov, 2011). In a major departure from prior job training programs that focused primarily on low-income individuals, the Workforce Investment Act (WIA) gave every adult access to basic job- and career-related services through a One-Stop system. It was viewed as a way to enable TANF recipients to achieve self-sufficiency by integrating them into the larger workforce development initiatives. How well the Workforce Investment Act works cannot be answered all that readily. As Caputo (2011) and many of the contributors to Besharov and Cottingham (2011) note, outcome studies varied by quality, replication proved difficult, and performance measures varied by program. As you read through this chapter, you will notice that the strength of claims linking effects to interventions will be moderated by the approach to evaluation that is taken and the tools, techniques, and measures that are used. Design and management problems are plentiful whether considering the Workforce Investment Act in the United States or other programs designed to encourage employment, such as the demand-driven employment creation program in India mandated in 2005 by the Mahatma Gandhi National Rural Employment Guarantee Act (Zepeda, McDonald, Panda, & Kumar, 2013).

taking values into account, whether to control for their biasing influence or to explicate them as guides for practice objectives, is no longer in doubt, although their proper role and appropriate weight are contested in specific contexts. A given value such as diminished risk of destitution or better health in old age may be regarded as intrinsic or valuable in itself as well as extrinsic or desirable because it leads to some other end, such as infirm aging parents causing less stress for their adult children caretakers. As noted in Chapter 5, evaluative criteria include effectiveness, efficiency, equity, liberty/freedom, political feasibility, social acceptability (appropriateness and responsiveness), administrative feasibility, and technical feasibility, each of which entails a judgment about values and worth.

THE MAIN APPROACHES TO EVALUATION

Following Dunn (2008), this section discusses three main approaches to evaluation, namely *pseudo-evaluation, formal evaluation,* and *decision-theoretic evaluation.*

Pseudo-Evaluation

Pseudo-evaluations use descriptive methods to produce reliable and valid information about policy outcomes. A basic assumption is that measures of work or value are self-evident or uncontroversial—that is, any given outcome is taken for granted as an appropriate objective. In such evaluations, policy analysts typically use a variety of methods (e.g., quasi-experimental designs, questionnaires, random sampling, or statistical techniques) to explain variations in taken-for-granted policy outcomes in terms of policy input and process variables. Major forms include basic approaches to *monitoring* programs such as *social experimentation, social systems accounting, social auditing,* and *research and practice synthesis,* and major techniques include graphic displays, tabular displays, interrupted time-series, control-series analysis, and regression-discontinuity analysis.

Approaches to monitoring vary by types of controls over policy actions and by types of information required. Only *social experimentation* involves direct control over policy inputs and policy processes, which are measurable (quantifiable) and can be manipulated prior to anticipated outcomes. *Social systems accounting, social auditing,* and *research and practice synthesis* "control" inputs and processes by determining after the fact how much of observed variation in outcomes is due to inputs and processes, as compared to extraneous factors that are not directly connected to policy actions. In regard to information required, *social experimentation* and *social auditing* require collection of new information. *Social systems accounting* may or may not require new information. *Research and practice synthesis* relies exclusively on available information.

Despite differences, the four approaches to *monitoring* or *pseudo-evaluation* share common features. First, each is concerned with monitoring *policy-relevant* outcomes—that is, indicators of policy outputs and outcomes, some of which can be manipulated and others of which cannot. Variables that cannot be manipulated include preconditions, which are present before actions are taken (e.g., average age or cultural values of a target group), as well as unforeseen events that occur during the course of policy implementation (e.g., sudden staff turnover, strikes, natural disasters). It should be noted that what has *policy relevancy* or normative interest at one point in time may not years later—hence the need to re-evaluate periodically. This could be due to any number of factors, including the emergence of new or more pressing social problems, changes in elected officials who bring the priorities of their campaign issues and promises with them, and shifts in sociodemographic and/or cultural trends. Second, each approach is also *goal-focused:* policy outcomes are monitored because they are believed to enhance or inhibit, as the case may be, some need, value, or opportunity satisfactorily.

Third, each approach is *change-oriented:* each uses techniques and procedures enabling it to analyze change in outcomes over time, compare such changes across two or more programs, projects, or locations, or some combination of both. The social systems accounting approach is oriented toward macro-level changes in societies, states, regions, or communities, whereas the social auditing and social experimental approaches are primarily oriented toward micro-level changes in programs and projects.

Fourth, each approach permits *cross-classification* of outputs and impacts by other variables, including those used to monitor policy inputs and policy processes. For example, per pupil educational expenditures may be cross-classified with input variables (e.g., teachers' salaries) and those intended to measure processes (e.g., class size as in indicator of the quality of student-teacher interaction). Outputs and impacts could also be cross-classified by types of preconditions (e.g., average income of community residents) and unforeseen events (e.g., frequency of strikes). Finally, each approach can use objective as well as subjective measures of policy actions and outcomes. Taken together, these common features contribute to a general definition of monitoring as the process of obtaining policy-relevant information to measure changes in goal-focused social conditions, both objective and subjective, among various target groups and beneficiaries.

Social Systems Accounting

Social systems accounting is an approach and set of methods that enable analysts to monitor changes in objective and subjective social conditions over time. The 1933 two-volume report *Recent Social Trends in the United States,* highlighted in Appendix B, is an exemplary compendium of policy-relevant, *social systems accounting* information.

Social systems accounting work continued throughout the 1960s and 1970s and produced its major analytic element, namely the *social indicator.* The *Annals of the American Academy of Political and Social Science,* for example, devoted its May 1967 two-volume edition, under the title *Social Goals and Indicators for American Society,* to an exploration of objectives and of data availability and data needs; and its January 1978 issue, under the title *America in the Seventies: Some Social Indicators,* to highlighting trends in specific areas such as education, health, work life patterns, family, public safety, social mobility, and the like (Taeuber, 1978). Since 1985, the Institute for Innovation of Social Policy, currently housed at Vassar College, has examined and published reports on social indicators at the national, state, and international levels to provide a description and obtain a better understanding of social conditions (e.g., see Miringoff & Opdycke, 2007). The Institute for Innovation in Social Policy (2012) has also published an annual summary index of social health in the United States since 1970. The Office of Management and Budget (2012) includes social and economic indicators in its annual analysis of the federal budget. Friedman (2012) takes a global perspective and uses social indicators of health, safety and security, education, democracy and political participation, and equity and equality (including social and economic mobility and gender advancement) to assess the relative position of the United States on these measures as compared to competitor countries. Table 10.1 shows some representative social indicators.

Table 10.1	Some Representative Social Indicators
Area	**Indicator**
General	
Health and illness	Persons in state mental hospitals
Public safety	Persons afraid to work alone at night
Education	High school graduates aged 25 and older
Employment	Labor force participation rate for women
Income	Percentage of population below poverty line
Housing	Households living in substandard units
Leisure and recreation	Average annual paid vacation by industry
Population	Actual and projected
Social mobility	Change from parent(s)' occupation
Physical environment	Air pollution index
Civic engagement	Individual charitable giving per capita
Vulnerable Groups	
Children	Infant mortality, child abuse, child poverty
Youth	Teenage suicide, drug abuse, school dropouts
Adults	Unemployment, average weekly wages, health insurance coverage
Aging	Poverty rates among those 65 and over, out-of-pocket health care costs for those 65 and over
All Ages	Homicides, alcohol-related traffic fatalities, food stamp coverage, income inequality

Sources: Dunn, W.N. (2008). *Public policy analysis: An introduction* (4th ed.). Upper Saddle River, NJ: Pearson Education, Inc., p. 285. Institute for Innovation in Social Policy (2012). *The index of social health.* Poughkeepsie, NY: Vassar College. Office of Management and Budget. (2012). *Analytical Perspectives: Fiscal year 2012 budget of the U.S. government.* Washington, DC: Author, Table 10–2, p. 99.

Note that indicators include objective measures such as poverty and infant mortality rates and subjective measures such as persons afraid to walk alone at night. They relate to outputs and impacts of public policies. The labor force participation rate of women aged thirty-five to sixty-four, for example, may reflect the impact of equal employment opportunity or affirmative action policies, while the air pollution index may reflect the impact of Environmental Protection Agency programs.

A word of caution is warranted, however, about causal inferences between policies and indicators. It would be incorrect to assume that a policy was the cause of changes in indicators, as other factors may be influencing the social condition. In the absence of experimental controls and perhaps even with second-best statistical controls, the strongest inference that can be drawn about the relationship between policies and indicators is correlational. To the extent underlying assumptions can be subject to refutation, they make inferences more credible than otherwise would be the case (Manski, 2013). A related limitation of using social indicators is that they provide little information about how or in what ways policy inputs are transformed into policy outcomes. Claims about variations in policy outputs and outcomes are based on observed correlations between policy inputs and outcomes, rather than on knowledge about the processes by which resource inputs are transformed into outputs and impacts. Finally, analysts need to be mindful of choice of indicators as well, since any given choice invariably reflects particular social values rather than others and may thereby convey political or other biases.

Social Experimentation

Social experimentation entails the systematic manipulation of policy actions in a way that permits more or less precise answers to questions about the sources of change in policy outcomes. It has many forms, including laboratory, field, and quasi-experimentation. *Social experimentation* is considered an advanced way to find solutions for social problems by deliberately maximizing the differences between types of policy actions in a small and carefully selected group of programs and assessing their consequences prior to making large-scale investments in untested programs. As Table 10.2 shows, social experimentation adapts procedures used in classical laboratory experiments in the physical sciences.

Table 10.2 Classical Experimental Research Procedures

Procedure	Description
Direct control over experimental treatments	Analysts directly control policy actions and attempt to maximize differences among them in order to produce effects that differ as much as possible.
Comparison (control) groups	Two or more groups are used: the experimental group receives the policy action or experimental treatment, while the control groups are not subjected to policy action (receive no treatment) or are subject to a different policy option than that of the experimental group.
Random assignment	To eliminate potential sources of variation in policy outcomes other than those produced by the experimental treatment or policy action, a specific randomization procedure is used such that each participating eligible member of the target population has an equal chance of being assigned to the experimental or control group.

Source: Adapted from Dunn, W.N. (2008). *Public policy analysis: An introduction* (4th ed.). Upper Saddle River, NJ: Pearson Education, Inc., p. 288.

There have been advocates for social experiments and quasi-experiments to monitor outcomes of social policy since the New Deal during the Franklin Delano Roosevelt administration of the 1930s, particularly post-World War II, in the areas of public health, compensatory education, welfare, criminal justice, substance abuse, nutrition, highway safety, and housing (Stephan, 1935; Weiss & Rein, 1969). Two of the most well-known experiments in the United States took place in the 1960s and 1970s to assess the merits of a guaranteed annual income (GAI) policy or negative income tax: the New Jersey-Pennsylvania Graduated Work Incentives Experiment and the Seattle-Denver Income Maintenance Experiment (SIME-DIME), the largest of four such experiments (Caputo, 2012; U.S. Department of Health and Human Services, 1983). Throughout the 1980s and 1990s, related questions surrounding reform of social welfare programs designed for low-income families were addressed by numerous workfare and welfare-to-work demonstration programs, with varying degrees of rigor, resulting in the termination of the open-ended federally financed and state administered AFDC (Aid to Families with Dependent Children) program and the launch of the TANF (Temporary Assistance for Needy Families) program, which capped federal spending and had time limits for receipt of federal cash assistance by economically needy families (Caputo, 2011; Teles, 2001).

More so than other ways of monitoring observed policy outcomes, social experimentation has the potential of showing in precise terms whether certain policy actions, such as provision of income maintenance, result in certain outcomes, such as family economic well-being (Dunn, 2008). The capacity of experiments and quasi-experiments to produce valid causal inferences about the effects of actions on outcomes is referred to as *internal validity,* a concept covered in basic social work research courses. The greater the internal validity, the more confident one can be that policy outputs result from, or are a consequence of, policy inputs. Table 10.3 highlights the threats to internal validity—that is, the special conditions of persons, policies, or context, or methodological features of the experiment itself that compromise or diminish the validity of claims about policy outcomes.

Table 10.3 Threats to Internal Validity

Procedure	Description
History	Unforeseen events occurring between the time a policy is implemented and the point at which outcomes are measured; a sudden shift in public opinion, for example, may represent a plausible rival explanation of the causes of variation in policy outcomes.
Maturation	Changes within members of groups may exert an independent effect on policy outcomes; over time, for example, individual attitudes may change, learning may occur, or geographical units may grow or decline.
Instability	Fluctuations in a time series may produce unstable variations in outcomes that are a consequence of random error or procedures for obtaining information.
Testing	Conducting an experiment and measuring outcomes may sensitize members of experimental and control groups to the aims and expectations of the experiment; policy outcomes may then be a result of the meaning attributed to policy actions by participants and not result from the actions themselves.

Table 10.3 (Continued)	
Procedure	**Description**
Instrumentation	Changes in the system or procedures for measuring an outcome, rather than variations in the outcome itself, may account for the success or failure of a policy.
Mortality	Loss of participants in experimental and/or control groups regardless of reason before the experiment is completed.
Selection	In many situations, random sampling is not possible, requiring a quasi-experimental design that does not eliminate bias (i.e., distributes biases evenly between groups) in selecting respondents.
Regression artifacts / Regression toward the mean	When members of experimental and control groups are selected on the basis of extreme characteristics (e.g., poor children selected for an experimental reading program may be high achievers), artificial changes in reading scores may occur as a result of *regression toward the mean*—the statistical phenomenon where extreme values of some characteristic of a population automatically tends to regress toward or "go back to" the average of the population as a whole.

Source: Adapted from Dunn, W.N. (2008). *Public policy analysis: An introduction* (4th ed.). Upper Saddle River, NJ: Pearson Education, Inc., pp. 290-291.

Research designs vary in their capacity to increase the internal validity of social experiments and quasi-experiments, including reliance on procedures such as random selection, repeated measures of outcome measures over time, and measurement of the pre-program outcome measures for some of the experimental and control groups but not others. Classic (Campbell & Stanley, 1963; Cook & Campbell, 1979; Kerlinger, 1973) and more contemporary texts (Bloom, Fischer, & Orme, 2009; Rubin & Babbie, 2008; Shadish, Cook, & Campbell, 2001) provide excellent descriptions of such designs and show how well they reduce threats to *validity,* both *internal validity* (as given in Table 10.3) and *external validity.*

Social experimentation is less successful when controlling for external validity, which refers to the generalizability of causal inferences outside. This is due in part to "artificiality"—that is, the atypical conditions under which many social experiments are carried out. Conditions in New Jersey and Pennsylvania differ from those in San Francisco, Seattle, and Anchorage, as well as from those in Alabama, Mississippi, and Tennessee, making generalizations problematic. Also problematic for social experimentation is monitoring policy processes, including patterns of interaction among staff and clients, and their changing attitudes and values. Further, the complexity of social problems often requires oversimplification of policy processes for social experimentation to be carried out. For example, social experimentation is not particularly suitable for broad-aim programs that involve high levels of conflict among stakeholders, or contexts where the same inputs of personnel, resources, and equipment are perceived in quite different ways by various groups (Weiss & Rein, 1969). Information about such processes, which invariably entail subjective judgments of stakeholders, and about atypical conditions, may be more appropriately obtained and analyzed by using various qualitative methods, such as social auditing (discussed below), case studies, participant observation, and the use of logs or diaries of group sessions that rely on the Delphi technique, a process of having experts formulating solutions to problems in structured interactive or feedback sessions (de Meyrick, 2003; Jenkins, 1996; Schensul & LeCompte, 1999; Scholz & Tietje, 2002; Yin, 2003).

Social Auditing

Social auditing explicitly monitors relations among inputs, processes, outputs, and impacts, in an effort to trace policy inputs from the points of disbursement to the point at which they are experienced by the intended recipients of those resources (Dunn, 2008). The two main types of processes audited are *resource diversion* and *resource transformation.* In *resource diversion,* original inputs are diverted from intended target groups and beneficiaries as a result of the passage of resources through the administrative system. For example, the total expenditures for two TANF related job-training programs may be equal, yet one program may expend a higher percentage of funds on salaries and other personnel costs, resulting in fewer staff members per dollar and a diversion of services from beneficiaries. In *resource transformation,* resources and their actual receipt by target groups may be identical, yet the meaning of these resources to program staff and target groups may be altogether different. If the meaning of the resources is different, they in effect are transformed in such a way as to enhance (or retard) their impact on beneficiaries. Qualitative methods designed specifically to provide information about the subjective interpretations of policy actions by stakeholders who affect or are affected by the implementation of policies would be most suitable for assessing the nature and extent of *resource transformation.* Studies by Shdaimah (2009a, 2009b) are exemplary: "black box" descriptive qualitative studies of processes about how judges, lawyers, and social workers harbor varying views of housing as a resource for child protective services families.

Research and Practice Synthesis

Social auditing and *social experimentation* require collection of new information about policy actions and outcomes; social systems accounting, while based chiefly on available information, also requires new data insofar as information about subjective social conditions is out of date or unavailable (Dunn, 2008). By contrast, *research and practice synthesis* involves the systematic compilation, comparison, and assessment of results of past efforts to implement public policies. The two primary sources of available information relevant to *research and practice synthesis* are case studies of policy formulation and implementation, and research reports that address relations among policy actions and outcomes. Case-survey methods encompass a set of procedures used to identify and analyze factors that account for variation in the adoption and implementation of polices (Yin & Heald, 1975). Table 10.4 shows a case-coding scheme with representative indicators and coding categories.

Applying the *research and practice synthesis* to available research reports makes use of the *research survey,* research synthesis, or evaluation syntheses—that is, a set of procedures used to compare and appraise results of past research on policy actions and outcomes (Rothman, 1974). The research survey method provides several kinds of information: empirical generalizations about sources of variation in policy outcomes, summary assessments of the confidence researchers have in these generalizations, and policy alternatives or action guidelines that are implied by these generalizations. Sample results of one such undertaking are illustrated in Table 10.5.

Table 10.4	Case-Coding Scheme: Representative Indicators and Coding Categories	
Type of Indicator	**Indicator**	**Coding Categories**
Input	Adequacy of resources	[] Totally adequate
		[] Mostly adequate
		[] Not adequate
		[] Insufficient information
Process	Involvement of policy analyst in defining problem	[] Totally adequate
		[] Mostly adequate
		[] Not adequate
		[] Insufficient information
Output	Utilization of results of policy research	[] Totally adequate
		[] Mostly adequate
		[] Not adequate
		[] Insufficient information
Impact	Perceived resolution of problem(s)	[] Totally adequate
		[] Mostly adequate
		[] Not adequate
		[] Insufficient information

Source: Dunn, W.N. (2008). *Public policy analysis: An introduction* (4th ed.). Upper Saddle River, NJ: Pearson Education, Inc., p. 295. © 2008.

The main limitations of research and practice synthesis are related to the reliability and validity of information (Dunn, 2008). Cases and research reports vary in quality and depth of coverage, and with the partisan nature of many contemporary think tanks, they are too often self-confirming (as discussed in Appendix B). Many available cases and research reports contain no explicit discussion of the limitations and weaknesses of the study and they often express only one point of view. Nonetheless, for the analyst with an awareness of these limitations, research and practice synthesis are a systematic way to accumulate knowledge about policy actions and outcomes in many areas. Given the reliance on available information, research and practice syntheses are less expensive and time consuming than social auditing, social experimentation, and social systems accounting. Each approach to monitoring has its own advantages and limitations, with the strengths of one often the weakness of another. Hence, the most persuasive generalizations about policy outcomes are those having multiple foci (inputs, processes, outputs, impacts),

Table 10.5	Sample Results of the Research Survey Method: Empirical Generalizations, Action Guidelines, and Levels of Confidence in Generalizations	
Generalization[1]	**Action Guidelines**[2]	**Confidence in Generalizations**[3]
1. Current resource expenditures are strongly associated with past resource expenditures.	In determining the receptivity to new policies and programs, analysts should seek out situations where substantial resource expenditures have occurred in the past.	3
2. Policy outcomes are associated with the level of economic development of the municipality, state, or region where policy actions are undertaken.	In determining the receptivity to new policies and programs, analysts should focus attention on wealthy, urban, and industrial areas.	4
3. Outputs of educational policies in municipalities with professional city managers (reform governments) are greater than in municipalities without professional managers (non-reform governments).	Analysts should adjust recommendations according to information about the type of municipality where policy actions are intended to take effect.	2

Notes:

[1] Empirical generalizations are based on available research reports, including scholarly books, articles, and government reports.

[2] Action guidelines are derived from empirical generalizations. The same generalization frequently implies multiple action guidelines.

[3] The numbers used to express the degree of confidence in a generalization are based on the number of reliable and valid studies that support generalization.

Source: Rothman, J. (1974). *Planning and organizing for social change.* New York: Columbia University Press, pp. 254–265, as cited in Dunn, W.N. (2008). *Public policy analysis: An introduction* (4th ed.). Upper Saddle River, NJ: Pearson Education, Inc., p. 296. © 2008.

using different types of controls (direct manipulation, quantitative analysis, qualitative analysis), and based on a combination of available and new information about objective and subjective conditions.

FORMAL EVALUATION

Formal evaluations use descriptive methods to produce reliable and valid information about policy outcomes that have been formally announced as policy-program objectives (Dunn, 2008). A basic assumption is that formally announced or promulgated goals and objectives of policymakers and administrators are appropriate measures of worth or value. The analyst uses many of the same methods as those highlighted above in pseudo-evaluation and the aim is the same: to produce reliable information about variations in policy outputs and impacts that may be traced to policy inputs and processes. The major difference is that in *formal evaluation* policy, analysts use legislation, program documents, and interviews with policymakers and administrators to identify, define, and specify formal goals and objectives. The appropriateness of the formally stated goals and objectives is taken as given, with effectiveness and efficiency used most frequently as evaluative criteria. The two major types of formal evaluations are *summative* and *formative*. **Summative evaluations** involve an effort to monitor the accomplishment of formal goals and objectives after a policy or program has been in place for some period of time. They are designed to appraise products of stable and well-established public policies and programs. **Formative evaluations** involve efforts to monitor continuously the accomplishment of formal goals and objectives. The difference between these two main types is one of degree, since the main distinguishing characteristic of *formative evaluation* is the number of points in time at which policy outcomes are monitored.

Formal evaluations also differ in regard to whether they exert direct or indirect controls over policy inputs and processes. To the extent evaluators can directly manipulate expenditure levels, the mix of programs, or the characteristics of target groups, formal evaluations share many of the characteristics of *social experimentation* as an approach to monitoring. In the case of indirect controls, policy inputs and processes, since they cannot be directly manipulated, must be analyzed on the basis of actions that have already occurred. Table 10.6 summarizes the four types of formal evaluation—each based on a different orientation toward the policy process (summative vs. formative) and type of control over action (direct vs. indirect).

Developmental evaluation refers to evaluation activities that are explicitly designed to serve the day-to-day needs of program staff. It is useful for alerting staff to weaknesses or unintended, usually undesirable, consequences, and for ensuring proper operation of the program or policy by those responsible for implementing it (Rossi & Wright, 1977). *Developmental evaluation* entails some level of direct control over policy actions. It has been used to test new teaching methods and materials in public television education programs, such as *Sesame Street* and *The Electric Company,* both of which have been systematically monitored and evaluated by showing them to audiences composed of children within specified age limits and revised accordingly (Rossi & Wright, 1977, p. 22).

Table 10.6   Types of Formal Evaluation

	Orientation Toward Policy Process	
Control Over Policy Actions	*Formative*	*Summative*
Direct	Developmental evaluation	Experimental evaluation
Indirect	Retrospective process evaluation	Retrospective outcome evaluation

Source: Dunn, W.N. (2008). *Public policy analysis: An introduction* (4th ed.). Upper Saddle River, NJ: Pearson Education, Inc., p. 357. © 2008.

Retrospective process evaluation refers to monitoring and evaluation of programs after they have been in place for some time (Dunn, 2008). Such evaluations often focus on problems and bottlenecks encountered in the implementation of policies and programs. *Retrospective process evaluation* does not permit the direct manipulation of inputs (e.g., expenditures) and processes (e.g., alternative delivery systems). Instead, it relies on after-the-fact or retrospective descriptions of ongoing program activities, which are subsequently related to outputs and impacts. *Retrospective process evaluation* requires a well-established internal reporting system that permits the continuous generation of program-related information (e.g., the number of target groups served, the types of services provided, and the characteristics of the personnel employed to staff programs). Management information systems can be used for *retrospective process evaluations* to the extent that they contain reliable and valid information on processes as well as outcomes.

Experimental evaluation refers to monitoring and evaluation of outcomes under conditions of direct controls over policy inputs and processes. The gold standard is the "controlled scientific experiment," often referred to as randomized controlled trials (RCTs), where all factors that might influence policy outcomes, except one (the particular input or process variable), are controlled, held constant, or treated as plausible rival hypotheses. Participants in *experimental evaluations* are randomly assignment to treatment and control groups. *Experimental evaluations* must meet exacting requirements, including a clearly defined, directly manipulable, and operationalized set of "treatment" variables, sufficient controls for internal and external validity, and a monitoring system that produces reliable data on complex interrelationships among preconditions, unforeseen events, inputs, processes, outputs, and side effects. A much praised example is that of Banerjee and Duflo (2011), who relied on hundreds of randomized controlled trials in their research on global poverty and whose work was credited with transforming the field of international development (Keohane, 2013; Kristoff, 2011).

Given that the requisite conditions for designing and implementing randomized controlled trials are rarely met, experimental evaluations generally fall short of truly controlled experiments and they are more appropriately labeled "quasi-experimental" evaluations. MDRC, founded in 1974 as the Manpower Demonstration Research Corporation and officially registered simply by its initials since 2003, is a nonpartisan research organization that over the decades has carried out many experimental and quasi-experimental evaluations of public education, low-income children, low-wage workers, and those facing barriers to employment, including TANF recipients (e.g., see Bloom, 1999; Bloom, Hill, & Riccio, 2001; Butler et al., 2012; Riccio, Friedlander, & Freedman, 1994; Sherwood, 1999). Several MDRC publications also address evaluation-related methodological issues, such as random assignment (e.g., see Bloom, 2006, 2010; Somers, Zhu, & Wong, 2011), related implications for policy (e.g., see Gueron, 2000), and qualitative research (e.g., see Gardenhire & Nelson, 2003). A long-recognized ethical limitation or problem with experimental evaluations entails the potential denial of a second chance for service or intervention to those randomly assigned to the control group (Fetterman, 1981). This situation arises when control group participants are given a placebo or no treatment (e.g., placed on a waiting list for service). To offset this limitation, control group participants may later receive the service or benefit against which the new intervention is being compared or tested.

Retrospective outcome evaluations refer to the monitoring and evaluation of outcomes but with no direct control over manipulable policy inputs and processes (Dunn, 2008). Three approaches to monitoring discussed above—social systems accounting, social auditing, and research and practice synthesis—may be considered as forms of retrospective outcome evaluation, as can cost-benefit analysis (discussed in Chapters 6 and 7). At best, controls are indirect or statistical: analysts attempt to isolate the effects of many different factors by using quantitative methods. The two main variants of retrospective outcome evaluations are cross-sectional and longitudinal studies. Cross-sectional studies monitor and evaluate multiple programs at one point in time: the goal is to discover whether the outputs and impacts of various programs differ significantly from one another, and, if so, what particular actions, preconditions, or unforeseen events might explain or account for the difference. By contrast, longitudinal studies evaluate changes in the outcomes of one, or multiple programs at two or more points in time. The Head Start Program and the Early Head Start Program, for example, both provide decades of retrospective outcome evaluations (e.g., see Caputo, 2003, 2004; Currie & Thomas, 1995: Pizzo, 1998; Vogel, Xue, Moiduddin, Kisker, & Carlson, 2010).

DECISION-THEORETIC EVALUATION

Decision-theoretic evaluations use descriptive methods to produce reliable and valid information about policy outcomes that are explicitly valued by multiple stakeholders (Dunn, 2008). Their use provides a way to overcome several limitations of pseudo-evaluation and formal evaluation: underutilization and non-utilization of performance information, ambiguity of performance goals, and multiple conflicting objectives. A basic assumption of *decision-theoretic evaluation* is that formally announced as well as latent goals and objectives of stakeholders are appropriate measures of worth or value. Basic tasks of policy analysts doing decision-theoretic evaluations include identification of relevant policy or program stakeholders and uncovering and making explicit the latent goals and objectives of those stakeholders. Basic assumptions are that the goals and objectives of policies and programs cannot be satisfactorily established by focusing on the values of one or several parties (e.g., Congress, a dominant client group, or chief administrator) and that multiple stakeholders with conflicting goals and objectives are present in most situations involving evaluations. Major

Table 10.7	Steps of Evaluability Assessment
Steps	**Description**
Policy-program specification	What federal, state, or local activities and what goals and objectives constitute the program?
Collection of policy-program information	What information must be collected to define policy-program objectives, activities, and underlying assumptions?
Policy-program modeling	What model best describes the program and its related objectives and activities, from the point of view of intended users of performance information? What causal assumptions link actions to outcomes?
Policy-program evaluability assessment	Is the policy-program model sufficiently clear to make the evaluation useful? What types of evaluation studies would be most useful?
Feedback of evaluability assessment to users	After presenting conclusions about policy-relevant evaluability to intended users, what appear to be the next steps that should (not) be taken to evaluate policy performance?

Source: Dunn, W.N. (2008). *Public policy analysis: An introduction* (4th ed.). Upper Saddle River, NJ: Pearson Education, Inc., p. 361. © 2008.

forms of such evaluation include *evaluability assessment* and *multi-attribute utility analysis.* Major techniques for data acquisition include *brainstorming, argumentation analysis, Delphi,* and *user-survey analysis.*

Evaluability assessment is a set of procedures designed to analyze the decision-making system that presumably benefits from performance information, in part by clarifying the goals, objectives, and assumptions against which performance is to be measured. A basic determination is whether a program or policy can be evaluated at all, having clearly articulated policy-program specifications, clearly specified goals or consequences, and a set of explicit assumptions that link policy actions to goals or consequences. The policy-program model must be sufficiently unambiguous to make such evaluations useful in principle and should include a feedback loop, so conclusions about the *evaluability assessment* can be presented to users and next steps identified. Table 10.7 highlights the series of steps analysts follow to clarify a policy or program from the standpoint of the intended users of performance information and the evaluators themselves.

Multi-attribute utility analysis is a set of procedures designed to elicit from multiple stakeholders subjective judgments about the probability of occurrence and value of policy outcomes. Major steps in multi-attribute utility analysis include stakeholder identification, specification of relevant decision issues (courses of action or inaction about which there is disagreement), specification of policy outcomes, identification of attributes of outcomes (all relevant attributes that make outcomes worthy or valuable), attribute ranking in order of importance, and attribute scaling, scale standardization, and outcome measurement (see Dunn, 2008, p. 362, for mathematical formulas), and finally evaluation and presentation (specification of policy outcome with greatest overall performance and presentation to relevant decision makers). When these steps are carried out as part of a group process involving relevant stakeholders, *multi-attribute utility analysis* is a useful way for analysts to deal systematically with conflicting objectives of those multiple stakeholders. It is essential for efficacy of this method that stakeholders who affect and are affected by a policy or program are active participants in the evaluation of policy performance.

Skill Building Exercises

1. What distinguishes pseudo-evaluations, formal evaluations, and decision-theoretic evaluations?

2. Discuss the merits and limitations of using social indicators.

   a. Create a framework for assessing the relative position of the United States on six social indicators relevant to social justice and amenable to social worker intervention, such that the framework incorporates the width, length, and depth of each measure.
   b. Provide a rationale for your choice of indicators.
   c. How does the United States fare on each measure compared to its major economic competitors in the European Union, as well as in Asia?
   d. Identify an appropriate social work intervention and/or public policy to improve the U.S.'s global standing of those social justice relevant measures found to be deficient.
   e. How would you go about advocating for adopting and implementing these interventions and/or policies?

Evaluation, Values, and Theory

In this chapter, we examine the relation between values and evaluation, first by presenting a typology of evaluator valuing roles vis-à-vis stakeholders (Alkin, Vo, & Christie, 2012), and second, by discussing two major categories of evaluation models, namely *values-distanced evaluation models* and *values-salient evaluation models* (Speer, 2010). We also discuss the role of theory in evaluation and policy analysis, distinguishing explanatory from justificatory or normative theories.

Upon completion of the chapter, students will be able to (1) understand the logic behind making value-related judgments about the merits of performance related program or policy evaluations, and (2) distinguish between and know the appropriate uses of explanatory and normative theories when evaluating program or policy outcomes.

Upon successful completion of the skill building exercises in Chapter 11, students will have mastered the following Council on Social Work Education (CSWE) Competencies and Practice Behaviors:

Chapter 11	CSWE Core Competencies
#	**Description**
2.1.2	**Apply Social Work Ethical Principles to Guide Professional Practice**
	Recognize and manage personal values in a way that allows professional values to guide practice
	Make ethical decisions by applying standards of the NASW Code of Ethics
	Tolerate ambiguity in resolving ethical conflicts
	Apply strategies of ethical reasoning to arrive at principled decisions
2.1.3	**Apply Critical Thinking to Inform and Communicate Professional Judgments**
	Distinguish, appraise, and integrate multiple sources of knowledge, including research-based knowledge and practice wisdom
	Analyze models of assessment, prevention, intervention, and evaluation
	Demonstrate effective oral and written communication in working with individuals, families, groups, organizations, communities, and colleagues

(Continued)

Chapter 11	(Continued)
#	**Description**
2.1.4	**Engage Diversity and Difference in Practice**
	View themselves as learners and engage those with whom they work as informants
2.1.5	**Advance Human Rights and Social and Economic Justice**
	Understand the forms and mechanisms of oppression and discrimination
2.1.7	**Apply Knowledge of Human Behavior and the Social Environment**
	Utilize conceptual frameworks to guide the processes of assessment, intervention, and evaluation
	Critique and apply knowledge to understand person and environment
2.1.8	**Engage in Policy Practice to Advance Social and Economic Well-Being and to Deliver Effective Social Work Services**
	Analyze, formulate, and advocate for policies that advance social well-being
2.1.9	**Respond to Contexts That Shape Practice**
	Continuously discover, appraise, and attend to changing locales, populations, scientific and technological development, and emerging societal trends to provide relevant services
2.1.10	**Engage, Assess, Intervene, and Evaluate With Individuals, Families, Groups, Organizations, and Communities**
2.1.10(b)	*Assessment*
	Select appropriate intervention strategies
2.1.10(c)	*Intervention*
	Implement prevention interventions that enhance client capacities
	Negotiate, mediate, and advocate for clients
2.1.10(d)	*Evaluation*
	Analyze, monitor, and evaluate interventions

Source: Adapted from Council on Social Work Education (2012). *Educational policy and accreditation standards.* Washington, DC: Author. Retrieved from http://www.cswe.org/file.aspx?id=13780

VALUES AND EVALUATION

As highlighted throughout this volume, values have long been acknowledged to play an important role in social science in general and policy analysis in particular, entering into deliberations about the relevancy of social problems that policymakers want to address, the appropriateness of means to address them, and the goals or ends to be achieved (see also Caputo, 1989; Fischer, 1980; Harding, 1978; Kuitunen, 1993). Lasswell and McDougal (1943) and more recently deLeon and Weible (2010) have advocated for professionals who undertake policy analysis in such a way as to ensure that the public interest and democratic values in society are met while concomitantly maintaining the integrity of their research and evaluations. Further, understanding the rational basis of values and values clarification have long been viewed as appropriate roles for policy analysts (Chalip, 1985; Easton, 1950; Lasswell, Brunner, & Willard, 2003). This section of Chapter 11 explores the relationship between evaluation and values, first as highlighted in Table 11.1, by presenting a typology of evaluator valuing roles (Alkin, Vo, & Christie, 2012), and second, as highlighted in Table 11.2, by laying out an ordinal gradient or "relative distancing" by which various approaches to evaluation take values into account—categorized as *values-distanced evaluation models* and *values-salient evaluation models* (Speer, 2010).

It should be noted here that evaluation as a field of practice has concerns broader than policy analysis per se, since its related theories, methodologies, and tools are applied in a variety of program and practice settings. Social work students are introduced to evaluation of practice as part of the curriculum; related texts such as Bloom, Fischer, and Orme (2009) are illustrative of single-subject designs that are applicable to direct practice. More qualitatively-oriented practitioners can find appropriate evaluation methodologies in Padgett (2008) and Patton (2002). Educators and others interested in educational outcomes and processes have long been accustomed to evaluation, as the 1942 special issue of the *Journal of Educational Research* reflects, addressing issues associated with evaluation in general (Tyler, 1942; Woody, 1942), evaluation methodology (Wrightstone, 1942), as well as substantive areas about general college education (Eurich, 1942).

It should also be noted that for many decades evaluation was off-limits from consideration as a scientific activity due in part to its ideographic or case focus, and to its concerns with weighing valued outcomes against one another (Scriven, 2012). It seemed to violate the premium placed on "value-free" social inquiry that characterized much of the development of the social sciences (as discussed in Appendix B). Even today, evaluation is often excluded from applied social science texts, and in some universities evaluation studies are deemed unsuitable as doctoral-level dissertations on the grounds that they are atheoretical or idiographic—that is, lacking the requisites for making deductive or statistical inferences, and thereby too limited or simply unable to contribute to a knowledge base. Nonetheless, single-subject science (e.g., single-subject designs in social work and time-series analyses in other disciplines such as behavioral medicine) and idiographic sciences (e.g., obtaining the meaning of life events of individuals in social epidemiology) are more acceptable now (Conner, Tennen, Fleeson, & Barrett, 2009; Molenaar, 2004; Robinson, 2011; Velicer, Hoeppner, & Palumbo, 2012), and evaluation has become a business of sorts (O'Hara & McNamara, 1999). The increasing demands for evidence-based practice and policy in schools of social work and elsewhere (e.g., Urban Institute, 2008), particularly for demonstrations of "what works" by the public at large and by social entrepreneurs in particular (e.g., Keohane, 2013; Liebman, 2011), suggest that the theoretical and methodological developments of the discipline will be adopted or adapted and put to use.

Evaluation has its own history of theoretical and methodological developments whose tree-like genealogical contours can be found in Christie and Alkin (2013). Briefly, the three roots of the evaluation theory tree—*social responsibility, systematic social inquiry,* and *epistemology*—serve as the foundation for evaluation work. The central branch is *systematic social inquiry,* whose emphasis is on research methodology, specifically the techniques used to conduct evaluation studies, and whose pioneering figure is Donald T. Campbell (1957, 1969; Campbell & Stanley, 1963; Shadish & Luellen, 2013). One of the two side branches is *social responsibility,* where the explicit concern is with who uses evaluation information and how it will be used; its pioneering figure is Daniel Stufflebeam (1983). The second of the two side branches is *epistemology,* which focuses on the role of valuing in evaluation, and its pioneers include Michael Scriven (1960, 1967, 1971–1972) and Robert Stake (1967, 1975). The *epistemology* branch is split between objectivists and subjectivists, with both perspectives informing the valuing process. Subjectivists argue that value judgments should be based on "publicly observable" facts. They reason that since subjective factors govern human action, a unique characteristic of human behavior is its "subjective meaningfulness." Subjectivists contend that any science ignoring meaning and purpose is not social science (Deising, 1966). Objectivists contend otherwise. They are more compatible with positivist philosophical ideas, which inform the methodologists inhabiting the central or *systematic social inquiry* branch of evaluation.

Before discussing contemporary views about the evaluator's role in valuing, four broad views of the evaluator's role warrant brief mention. According to Wise (1980), three views of the evaluator fed earlier discussions about what evaluation is for and what evaluators do, as scientists, assistants, and judges, to which was added a fourth—namely, educators. Table 11.1 highlights these views and some of the major the tasks and responsibilities associated with them.

Table 11.1   Evaluator Roles and Responsibilities

Views of Evaluator's Role	Responsibilities and Tasks
As Scientist	Studying the effects of interventions (programs, treatments, service delivery systems)
	Testing causal relationships between intervention and outcomes
	Measuring changes in the intervention's target population and assessing whether these changes can be attributed to the intervention
	Assessing whether the causal relationship holds true beyond the particular setting in which it is implemented.
As Assistant	Assisting a particular client in making choices
	Framing the decision to be made
	Relying on decision makers to establish the requisite criteria for gathering and presenting information necessary to make decisions
	Willingly bend methods of science to practical programmatic and ethical constraints as circumstances warrant
As Judge	Assesses standards to set and then to award credit about how well the program meets those standards
	Applying those standards without regard to the client's situation or purposes

Table 11.1	(Continued)

Views of Evaluator's Role	Responsibilities and Tasks
	Avoiding any interest in the program that would jeopardize full disclosure
As Educator	Studying the program to understand it
	Seeing that those responsible for the program come to a fuller understanding of the program than they otherwise would

Source: Adapted from Wise, R.I. (1980). The role of evaluator as educator. *New Directions for Program Evaluation, 5,* 11–18.

Evaluator Valuing Roles

In a broad sense, the evaluator's role in valuing is "to activate, facilitate a structure, be engaged in, and contribute to the process of determining merit or worth" (Alkin, Vo, & Christie, 2012, p. 39). Gaining an understanding of the making of judgments about the merit or worth of a policy or program can be approached in a variety of ways, given that who makes such judgments and how they do so is context-dependent. This particular definition of the evaluator's role, which is sufficient for purposes here, is a distillation of the varied valuing roles that evaluation scholars have offered over the years when discussing the role of the evaluator in the evaluation process. It reflects the *evaluator context*—that is, the theoretic dispositions that may influence the way in which evaluators go about the valuing process. Table 11.2 presents a typology of evaluator valuing roles upon which this distilled definition is based.

Table 11.2	Typology of Evaluator Valuing Roles

Valuing by	Description
Stakeholders	Stakeholders establish standards before the evaluation begins
	Evaluator provides data to identified stakeholders
	Evaluator provides data for use by broad audiences
Stakeholders and Evaluator	Evaluator guides stakeholders by establishing a framework for valuing
	Evaluator guides stakeholders by guiding the valuing process iteratively
	Evaluator participates with stakeholders in valuing
Evaluator	Evaluator valuing strongly based on the promotion of evaluator values (morals)
	Evaluator valuing based upon evaluation expertise

(Continued)

Table 11.2	(Continued)
Valuing by	**Description**
	Evaluator valuing based primarily on program expertise
	Evaluator valuing based upon scientific appraisal

Source: Adapted from Alkin, M.C., Vo, A.T., & Christie, C.A. (2012). The evaluator's role in valuing: Who and with whom. *New Directions for Evaluation, 133,* p. 33.

Table 11.2 suggests the ways that value judgments are reached by stakeholders alone, by stakeholders and evaluators consorting or collaborating with one another, and by the evaluator only, illuminating the nature of engagement in each of the three categories. **Stakeholders** are those who have a concern in an evaluation and may include (as discussed below in regard to *empowerment evaluation)* the presumptive or targeted beneficiaries for whom policies are made and programs implemented, as well as the policymakers and others with economic, pragmatic, moral, and ethical interests in programmatic outputs and outcomes. Stakeholders may or may not rely on evaluators when determining standards about the merit or worth of a particular program. They may hire evaluators to provide data to consider when making their value judgments. In more collaborative efforts between evaluators and stakeholders, evaluators can set the framework for valuing, guide the valuing process, or serve as active co-contributors to the determination of merit or worth. Some roles might call for more direct engagement of the evaluator in the determination of merit or worth based on the evaluator's evaluation expertise, program experience, or scientific appraisal. On the whole, Table 11.2 suggests that there are varying degrees of distancing of values and evaluation depending on the evaluator context and how values are taken into account.

The Relative Distancing of Values and Evaluation

House (1978) provides an earlier typology of evaluation models and how they relate to values within the tradition of political liberalism, with its emphasis on individual free choice and "subjectivist ethics" about what constitutes the good life and what one's preferences and needs are. That typology is important in part for its distinction between types of evaluation that are of less concern here, such as the accreditation model that schools of social work use and that have a general consensus among professionals about what constitutes acceptable standards, and those evaluation models referred to as systems analysis, decision making, and behavioral objectives, whose assumptions about the appropriateness of using valid and reliable procedures and the proper place for ethical considerations are of concern here. Figure 11.1 highlights the earlier typology.

Table 11.3 below provides a summary of more recent main approaches to or models of evaluation and how they take values into account that will suffice for purposes here. Two major groupings are suggested: values-distant (those that distance themselves from values by introducing a variety of methodological controls to minimize the influence of bias) and values-salient (those that seek to incorporate values explicitly for a variety of purposes, ranging from edification and clarification of stakeholders' perspectives to empowering all stakeholders, including those who are the presumptive beneficiaries of policies and programs).

Figure 11.1	Major Evaluation Models in Relation to Philosophy of Liberalism

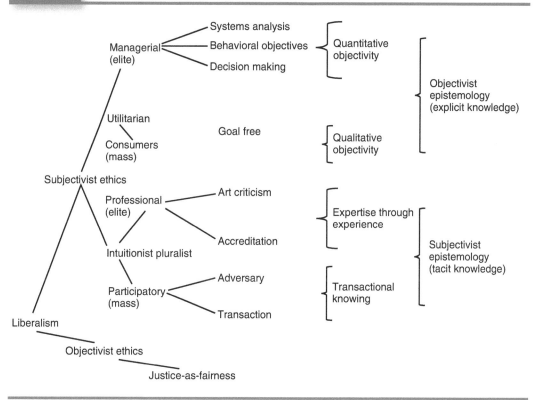

Source: House, E.R. (1978). Assumptions underlying evaluation models. *Educational Researcher, 7*(3), 12

Table 11.3	Evaluation Models and How They Take Values Into Account

Values Consideration	Generic Name of the Evaluation Model	Synonyms
1. Values-distanced	Objectives-focused	Effectiveness evaluation
	Experimental design focused	"Gold standard"
	Quasi-experimental design focused	Econometric evaluation
	Cost-benefit focused	Efficiency analysis
	Context mechanism focused	Realistic evaluation
	Program theory focused	Theory-driven evaluation

(Continued)

Table 11.3 (Continued)		
Values Consideration	**Generic Name of the Evaluation Model**	**Synonyms**
2. Values-salient		
a. Values-relativistic	Issues focused	Responsive evaluation
	Dialogue focused	Constructivist/fourth generation evaluation
b. Values-prioritizing	Decision focused	Accountability oriented evaluation
	Utilization focused	Pragmatic evaluation
	Stakeholder interests focused	Deliberative democratic evaluation
c. Values-positioned	Self-organization focused	Empowerment evaluation

Source: Adapted from Speer, S. (2010). Economics and evaluation. In J. Vaessen & F.L. Leeuuw (Eds.), *Mind the gap: Perspectives on policy evaluation and the social sciences.* New Brusnwick, NJ: Transaction Publishers, p. 71.

Value-Distant Evaluations

Major foci of **value-distant evaluations** include objectives-focused, experimental design (the gold standard), quasi-experimental designs, cost-benefit or efficiency analysis, context-mechanism or realistic evaluation, and program-theory or theory-driven evaluation (Speer, 2010). Objectives-focused evaluations, experimental design, quasi-experimental designs, and cost-benefit or efficiency analysis rely predominantly on quantitatively oriented methodologies and analysis. They tend to focus on goals and outcomes but not on processes. As such they are most appropriate for summative evaluations. Sole reliance on these approaches to evaluation, however, can result in weaknesses or shortcomings for evaluation purposes. They tend to ignore, or relegate to background information, the evaluation context and related processes, discussed in Chapter 10.

Despite bypassing the focus on processes, value-distant evaluations are quite useful and informative because of their direct link to evidence and the persuasiveness of statements about causes of observed outcomes. The idea of "evidence-based" policy, much like evidence-based practice in social work, has found favor among policymakers and social scientists (Thaler, 2012), and the use of randomized controlled trials for new policy initiatives have been encouraged whenever possible. In the U.K., for example, the Cabinet Office "Behavior Insight Team" issued a white paper extolling the virtues of randomized controlled trials as "the best way of determining whether a policy is working" (Haynes, Service, Goldacre, & Torerson, 2012). Over twenty years ago, the U.S. General Accounting Office (1991, now called the Government Accountability Office) noted that the true experimental design with its random assignment feature provides the most persuasive statements about the cause of observed outcomes, contending that despite the difficulty of administering such designs when there are no ethical or administrative obstacles to random assignment, the true experiment is the design of choice. As noted above, MDRC has conducted true experiments in natural settings for many job training, education, and welfare demonstration programs for decades.

Values-Salient Evaluations

Values-salient evaluations are grounded in what is deemed the practical philosophy approach to social inquiry (Schwandt, 1996), seeking to infuse moral discourse in evaluation practices (Schwandt, 1989). They encompass both descriptive and normative undertakings by analysts who engage and incorporate the perspectives and judgments of policy and program participants at all levels in the evaluation process. An aim of practical philosophy is to enable practitioners to refine the rationality of their practice for themselves. Analysts who undertake values-salient evaluations include among practitioners not only themselves but a variety of stakeholders who have a concern in an evaluation, including the presumptive or targeted beneficiaries. Various forms of action inquiry, collaborative inquiry, and feminist inquiry embrace this view.

General characteristics of a practical philosophy of social inquiry include establishing a dialogical relationship of openness with participants in the inquiry, viewing the participants (managers, line workers, clients) as engaged in performing practical acts, and encouraging practitioners to reflect critically on and reappraise their commonsense knowledge as an end in itself (not for purposes of replacing common sense or practical knowledge with theoretical or scientific knowledge) (Schwandt, 1996). The guiding ideal of social inquiry as practical philosophy is democracy, a moral ideal vis-à-vis a set of formal procedures more characteristic of value-distant evaluation approaches. Viewing political science as the policy science *par excellence,* Lasswell (1956) raised this issue of promoting democracy over five decades ago when discussing the role of the political scientist in a democratic society (Farr, Hacker, & Kazee, 2006). It should be noted, as Taylor (1985, pp. 77–81) contends, however, that Lasswell's promoting democracy as a legitimate purpose of political science, and by extension of evaluation, collapses the demarcation between facts and values that for purposes of professional integrity policy analysts need to keep distinct, while remaining mindful of the possibility of imposing their values when inappropriate. Democracy as a moral ideal for purposes of evaluation entails creating an environment of ongoing deliberation, whose integrity is ensured by the active and intentional solicitation of contributions from all concerned members or stakeholders about what is occurring (descriptive) and what should be occurring (normative or judgmental), in the policy-making and implementation processes.

Given the salience of judgment in policy and program evaluation, it is worthwhile at this point to distinguish legitimate from justified judgment. In a broad sense, *legitimate judgments* take the form of "a statement, appraisal, or opinion concerning the merit, worth, or significance of a program, and is formed by comparing the findings and interpretations regarding the program against one or more selected standards of performance" (Hurteau, Houle, & Mongiat, 2009, p. 308). Figure 11.2 highlights the procedural logic in the development of judgments.

Figure 11.2 Procedural Logic in the Development of a Judgment

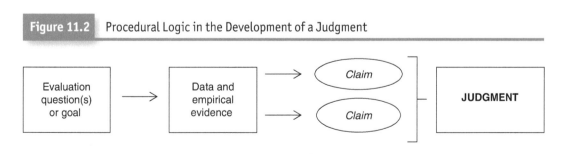

Source: Adapted from Hurteau, M., Houle, S., & Mongiat, S. (2009). How legitimate and justified are judgments in program evaluation? *Evaluation, 15*, p. 310.

The requisite characteristics of legitimate judgments about the merits of a program or policy include specific evaluation questions/goals, criteria of support for those goals, and standards of acceptable performance. *Legitimate judgments* are also subject to justification, that is, they are linked to evidence gathered and consistent with the agreed-upon values or standards of stakeholders. Justification entails argumentation, the idea that evaluative reasoning should be taken into consideration. This type of reasoning promotes judgments based on valid claims, which in turn are deemed defensible, accurate, warranted, acceptable, and justified—hence they are referred to as *justified judgments*. Figure 11.3 highlights the procedural logic that underlies argumentation of a judgment.

Values-Relativistic Evaluations

Major foci of **values-relativistic evaluations** include issues-focused or responsive evaluation (Korzenik, 1977; Stake, 1976) and dialogue focused or constructivist evaluation (Guba & Lincoln, 1989). These approaches, and those associated with *values-prioritizing evaluations* and *values-positioned evaluations*, are incorporated in what is known as fourth generation evaluation and share several features that distinguish them from previous generations (Carney, 1991; Lincoln & Guba, 2013). The other three generations of evaluation deal with measurement (e.g., IQ testing), description (formative evaluation of programs), and judgment (e.g., merit or worth constructions). Constructivist evaluators contend that the fourth generation obviates the major problems of the first three generations: a tendency to privilege management (an evaluation approach that favors the point of view of the client or funder and thereby disempowers other stakeholders, such as the frontline workers or street-level bureaucrats, who implement programs and directly deliver services, and the recipients of services), a failure to accommodate value-pluralism, and on over-commitment to a positivist approach to inquiry. It should be noted that fourth generation evaluation is not meant to displace or supersede previous generations but rather to complement them and even to draw upon them as appropriate—as when, for example, the ability to generalize is requisite for making more persuasive claims about the efficacy of a policy or program (Stake, 1981b). At issue in part is how best to incorporate values in the evaluation process while maintaining the integrity of the process of evaluation and the credibility and persuasiveness of evaluation reports (Page & Stake, 1979). Given the emphasis that fourth generation evaluation places on deliberation among

Figure 11.3 Procedural Logic Underlying the Argumentation of a Judgment

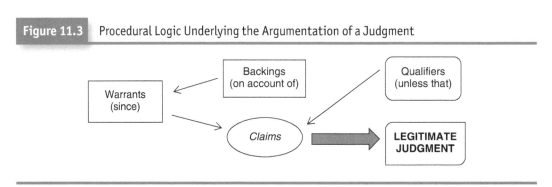

Source: Adapted from Hurteau, M., Houle, S., & Mongiat, S. (2009). How legitimate and justified are judgments in program evaluation? *Evaluation, 15,* p. 311.

stakeholders who have different values and perspectives about the nature and importance of the program, policy, and evaluation, social workers with knowledge of group processes and group facilitation skills are ideally suited for undertaking such evaluations as part of their practice.

The major innovation of fourth generation evaluation is a consensual methodology (Heap, 1995) that is undergirded in part by a political commitment to identify and obtain the viewpoints of stakeholders—those who have important concerns about a program or policy—and to consider carefully and incorporate those viewpoints in deciding what the design of an evaluation should be (Stake, 1981a). Three basic assumptions gird constructivist and responsive evaluations (Guba & Lincoln, 2001; Stake, 1976). First, the basic ontological assumption is relativism—that is, human sense-making (semiotic) that organizes experience so as to render it understandable is an act of construal and is independent of any foundational reality. The idea of objective truth is rejected. Second, the basic epistemological assumption is transactional subjectivism: assertions about truth and reality depend solely on the meaning sets (information) and degree of sophistication available to the individuals and audiences in forming those assertions. Third, the basic methodological assumption is "hermeneutic-dialecticism": a process of discovery and assimilation by which constructions entertained by several involved individuals or groups are first uncovered and plumbed for meaning, and then confronted, compared, and contrasted in encounter situations.

Fourth generation evaluation relies on negotiated co-creation of social reality: that is, those who are the stakeholders of the program or policy, including the beneficiaries and line workers, actively and conscientiously participate in the evaluation process, thereby "owning" the implementation process and the findings of the evaluation (Guba & Lincoln, 2001; Lincoln, 2003; Seafield Research and Development Services, 2012; Stake, 1970, 1976). The idea is to elicit the claims, concerns, and issues that each stakeholder deems or judges important and to provide a context and methodology through which those claims, concerns, issues, and value judgments can be understood, critiqued, and taken into account. Ascertaining and understanding stakeholder value judgments about what the program or policy should do are central components of the evaluation process—that is, they are treated as data for purposes of analysis. To the extent that there are different groups of stakeholders, the analyst seeks to "cross-fertilize" the claims, concerns, issues, and related value judgments, including those drawn from the literature, from other sites, and from the analyst's own experiences, subjecting everything to critique and criticism. This is what is meant by the "hermeneutic-dialecticism" process, in which the evaluator plays a dual and at times conflicting role of advocate and educator. The objective is to generate consensus about the many constructions and related claims, concerns, issues, and value judgments. Analysts oversee the process of negotiations among stakeholders and they develop reports informing stakeholders about their claims, concerns, and issues in light of those raised by others and about resolutions that are of interest to each of the stakeholder groups. This evaluation process is recycled to take up unresolved constructions or understandings and their attendant claims, concerns, and issues.

Fourth generation or constructivist evaluators rely on two major groupings of criteria to assess the quality of their evaluations: "parallel" or foundational and authenticity (Guba & Lincoln, 2001). Parallel or foundational criteria include *credibility, transferability, dependability,* and *confirmability. Credibility,* which is roughly equivalent to the notion of internal validity associated with the more positivist-oriented *value-distant evaluations,* is established by prolonged engagement at the site, persistent observation, peer debriefing, negative case analysis (a process of reworking hypotheses), progressive subjectivity (continuous checking of constructions against records of constructions that were expected prior to data collection), and member checks, continuous testing of hypotheses, data, preliminary categories, and interpretations with stakeholders. *Transferability,* which is roughly equivalent to external validity, is established by the reviewers of analysts' reports, who make judgments about the degree to which findings are sufficiently similar to their own situations. A determination of sufficient similarity would warrant testing for the viability of local application—that is, for localization, not for generalization. *Dependability,* which is roughly equivalent to reliability, is established through the use of audits with the assistance of an external auditor, who examines the record of inquiry much as a fiscal auditor examines fiscal records, to determine the methodological decisions made and to understand the reasons for them. *Confirmability,* roughly parallel to objectivity, is established by an external auditor who examines and determines the extent to which constructions, assertions, facts, and data can be traced to their sources. The "raw products" and "processes used to compress them" are examined and confirmed as appropriate.

Authenticity criteria include *fairness, ontological authenticity, educative authenticity, catalytic authenticity,* and *tactical authenticity* (Guba & Lincoln, 2001). *Fairness* is determined by an assessment of the extent to which all competing constructions have been accessed, exposed, and taken into account in the evaluation report—that is, in the negotiated emergent construction. *Ontological authenticity* is determined by an assessment of the extent to which individual constructions, including those of the evaluator, have become more informed or sophisticated. *Educative authenticity* is determined by an assessment of the extent to which individuals, including the evaluator, have become more understanding, even if not tolerant, of the understandings of others. *Catalytic authenticity* is determined by an assessment of the extent to which action (clarifying the focus at issue, moving to eliminate or address problems, sharpening values) is stimulated and facilitated by the evaluation. *Tactical authenticity* is determined by an assessment of the extent to which individuals are empowered to take action that the evaluation implies or proposes.

Values-Prioritizing Evaluations

Major foci of **values-prioritizing evaluations** include decision focused or accountability oriented evaluation, utilization focused or pragmatic evaluation, and stakeholder interest focused on deliberative democratic evaluation. *Values-prioritizing evaluations* are guided by many of the concerns and conceptualizations endemic to fourth generation evaluations (as highlighted above when discussing *values-relativistic evaluation).* Incorporating stakeholders' perspectives and judgments into the evaluation process is important for both types of values-related evaluations. The aim of such evaluations, however, differ. Where *values-relativistic evaluation* focuses on issues and uses an iterative dialogue process to identify and clarify issues and values held by stakeholders, *values-prioritizing evaluation* relies on stakeholder input for purposes of pragmatic assessments about day-to-day program functioning or policy implementation and making specific decisions based on a continuous reassessment of priorities as circumstances warrant. As noted above when discussing *values-relativistic evaluation,* one of the evaluator's roles is to make possible and facilitate a deliberative democratic process of decision making, but the aim here is to get clarity and consensus about priorities among stakeholders.

Values-Positioned Evaluations

A major focus of **values-positioned evaluations** includes organization or empowerment evaluation, whose multiple roots have been traced in part to emancipatory or transformative research practices associated with liberation pedagogy (Freire, 1970), feminist inquiry (Harding, 1987), critical theory (Forester, 1985), and communicative action (Habermas, 1984, 1987), and to evaluation research practices associated with participatory action research (King, 1995; Stern, 2009; Whyte, 1993) and collaboration research (Cousins & Earl, 1992, 1995). Other attributed roots of empowerment evaluation, stemming primarily from Fetterman (1982, 1988, 2002), include community psychology, action anthropology, the social reform movement, and grassroots community development (Patton, 2005). As advocated by Fetterman (1994), fostering self-determination is one of the defining features of empowerment evaluation, serving as "the heart of its explicit political and social change agenda" (Patton, 1997, pp. 148–149). Other defining features that it shares with "participatory evaluation" include its localized focus—that is, its responsiveness to local needs, and collaboration of trained evaluation personnel (research specialists) and practice-based decision makers working in partnership (Smith, 1999).

Sechrest (1997) characterizes empowerment evaluation more as a movement than as a set of tools and techniques, contending that it is "frankly ideological" with its focus on disadvantaged groups and its advocacy efforts to enhance their power. The role of advocacy in evaluation remains controversial. Chelimsky (1998), the former director of the Program Evaluation and Methodology Division (PEMD) of the General Accounting Office (GAO), contended that advocacy destroys evaluators' credibility and therefore has no place in evaluation. When speaking at the annual meeting of the American Evaluation Association about congressional or legislative policymakers, Chelimsky (1998) put the issue this way:

> The need in a political environment is not for still another voice to be raised in advocacy, but rather for information to be offered for public use that is sound, honest, and without bias toward any cause. Policy makers in the Congress *expect* evaluators to play precisely such a role and provide precisely this kind of information. (p. 39)

On the other hand, House and Howe (1998) argue that advocacy can be properly tempered by a process they refer to as the "deliberative democracy approach" to evaluation, guided by three criteria: (1) evaluations or studies should be inclusive, representing all relevant views, interests, values, and stakeholders; (2) there should be sufficient dialogue between groups so that views are "properly and authentically" represented; and (3) there should be sufficient deliberation to arrive at proper findings. In House and Howe's formulation, evaluators must embrace *some* conception of the public interest, such as democracy or an egalitarian concept of justice, and they "*should be advocates* for democracy and the public interest" (pp. 235–236). House and Howe (1998) put the issue of the proper place for advocacy in evaluation this way:

> Our notion of the public interest in evaluation is one of deliberative democracy in which the evaluation informs public opinion objectively by including views and interests, promoting dialogue, and fostering deliberation directed towards reaching valid conclusions. Objectivity is supplied by inclusion, dialogue, and deliberation, and by the evaluation expertise the professional evaluator brings to bear. Evaluators cannot escape being committed to some notion of democracy and the public interest. The question is how explicit and defensible is it. (p. 236)

N.L. Smith (2007) also contends that empowerment evaluation is "primarily an ideology" since it is defined less as by its methods and more by the collaborative manner in which methods are applied in accord with its principles, particularly that of self-determination. Empowerment evaluation practices that foster a concept of self-determination compatible with several advocacy-related and social justice dimensions of social work practice include (1) training program or policy participants to conduct their own evaluation (capacity building), (2) the role of evaluators as facilitators and coaches rather than as judges, (3) evaluators advocating on behalf of groups that are disempowered in advocating for themselves, (4) illumination, and (5) liberation for those involved.

Given that empowerment and self-determination are integral components of social work practice (Cleek/Wofsky, Boyd-Franklin, Mundy, & Howell, 2012; Conway et al., 2012; Hawkins & Kim, 2012), social workers of all stripes might be readily inclined to adopt aims, tools, and techniques associated with empowerment evaluation whole cloth, perhaps at the expense or to the exclusion of other approaches to evaluation. A caution, however, is warranted, given the limitations of and concerns about any evaluation approach that relies so heavily on self-assessments and that has a transformative agenda as an integral component of its own practices—even if a noble one, such as promoting democracy, achieving social justice, or empowering program participants (King, 2007). Nothing precludes rigor in self-evaluations, particularly within the confines of producing local or context-specific, improvement-oriented learning—that is, evaluation by participants and/or staff for participants, and/or for staff (Patton, 1997). Evaluations based entirely on self-assessments invariably raise credibility concerns with external audiences, even when carefully done. Nor does anything preclude incorporating the concept of empowerment and operationalizing it in the design stage of the policy-making process that takes into account how a policy will be implemented and how and by what criteria it will be evaluated. For this to be meaningful, it would need to be done in such a way that consensus is reached about the desirability of empowerment as an integral component of implementation and as a policy objective, and so a common understanding is obtained about what would distinguish a successful policy outcome from an unsuccessful one. Clements (2012), for example, shows how empowerment can be used as a criterion derived from Rawls's normative theory of social justice to help assess the merits of microfinance programs run by Grameen Bank of Bangladesh for predominantly rural poor women.

THE ROLE OF THEORY IN PROGRAM EVALUATION AND POLICY ANALYSIS

At the outset, it is important to distinguish between two main uses of theory in the world of policy analysis—namely, those that explain and those that justify (Geuss, 1981; S.R. Smith, 2007). Theories as explanation and justification are to be distinguished from models or frameworks that show relationships among concepts and that often form the basis of reconstructing chains of assumptions in evaluations of policies and programs. A discussion of theory-oriented evaluations and reconstructing chains of assumptions follows.

Explanatory and Justificatory (Normative) Theories

Theories as explanations account for an observed relationship between a policy or program and outcomes and might be morally neutral in that a moral position is not necessarily explicitly promoted. **Normative justifications**, on the other hand, involve a defense or critique of moral and ethical positions in relation to a policy or program—for example, questions about the desirability of ends or appropriateness of means to achieve those ends. Both explanatory and normative theories assume that empirical data collection is insufficient for analyzing policy and practice. As such, normative or ethical analysis is viewed as a particular form of theory, given the premise that an interpretation of facts is required when analyzing policy and practice. This in turn involves theoretical analysis that might (or might not) be philosophical and normative in character, especially in regard to the "ends" or purposes of policies. Theories about "the good" (i.e., the nature of and justification for doing good—e.g., policies tying vouchers for food benefits for low-income parents with young children to labor force participation activity) and "the right" (i.e., the nature of and justification of doing right—e.g., policies aimed at redistributing income from more affluent to economically needy individuals and families) are used as the basis for arguments about what ought to be the general nature and structure (institutional forms of) social welfare provisioning (Clements, 2012; Nichols, 2012).

Social scientists use theories to formulate and test hypotheses about relationships between attributes or characteristics of individuals, groups, or events germane to their discipline, and they modify the explanatory accounts based on findings of their studies. Political philosophers use normative theories to justify—for example, as do Rawls (1971) and Clements (2012)—a particular arrangement of institutions that could be considered as a basis for social justice—or as does Goodin (1988)—to understand why on normative grounds one policy proposal might be preferred over another.

Explanatory theories and normative theories are meant to be viewed as complementary essential and legitimate domains of policy analysis, rather than as competing, adversarial, or mutually exclusive. Emancipatory theories, such as those falling under the umbrella of critical theory, promulgated by the Frankfurt School and its intellectual heirs, most notably Jürgen Habermas (1973; Geuss, 1981; Therborn, 1970), are normative insofar as they are critical of social conditions and explicitly aim to eliminate domination, exploitation, oppression, and repression, whether by raising individual or group-level consciousness or promoting institutional or structural change (Fuhrman & Snizek, 1979–1980). Emancipatory theories in general and critical theory in particular are moral political philosophy theories and as such they are not open to empirical refutation or, for that matter, Marxist assertions of failure (Fuhrman, 1979).

Case in Point 11.1: Inequality Explained and Justified

Income and wealth inequality have long been thought about as byproducts of economic growth, particularly in market-based economies. Adam Smith posited this relationship in the eighteenth century and contemporary theorists have retained the central tenet in their explanatory accounts of and explorations of dynamics, distributional effects, and mechanisms that result in increasing inequality (DiPrete & Eirich, 2006; Korzeniewicz & Moran, 2005; Leicht, 2008). Such explanatory accounts of inequality, which are subject to further testing, differ from normative accounts that justify inequality. Political philosopher John Rawls (1971) took inequality for granted when theorizing about justice as fairness. Rawls's Difference Principle posited that inequality could be deemed a justified or fair outcome of social processes, when unequal outcomes were to the advantage of those who were the worst off.

Policy analysts are well advised to bring critical skills to bear on both the explanatory and normative uses of theory, and to avoid conflating the two or taking extreme or exclusive stands about one or the other. Doing so may result in intellectual paralysis or ideological rigidity, precluding the use of social scientific theories about human behavior and the social environment in policy analysis, or nullifying the merits of undertaking policy analysis from any vantage point other than that to which only the analyst or policymakers adhere, whether for emancipatory purposes or political expediency. Policy analysts are also well advised to clarify their purpose and role when analyzing policy and to specify upfront how or in what ways they will use theory. Feminist scholar and political philosopher Iris Marion Young (1990) is exemplary in this regard: drawing on critical theory but treating epistemological and methodological issues as background; focusing on the substantive normative and social issues at hand regarding social justice; and urging that normative theory and public policy should undermine group-based oppression by affirming social group difference. Whether policies affirming social group differences lead to better or more just social outcomes, such as reducing income inequality within and between classes, ethnic groups, and genders can be subject to empirical investigation and in principle be shown to be correct or false.

Caputo (2007) has argued that much of contemporary social theory has lost its moorings in regard to resolving social problems, in large part because in principle they defy ways of bringing empirical data to bear on determinations of whether or not they can be found to be incorrect. As Popper (1961, 1965, 1968) would have it, many emancipatory theories in the Marxist and Frankfurt School traditions cannot be truly tested or shown to be false and as a result are less useful for purposes of policy analysis and policy change. This is not to jettison normative theories from policy analysis. As Caputo (2002a) and others (e.g., Clements, 2012; Daniels, Kennedy, & Kawachi, 1999; Nichols, 2012) have demonstrated, moral and political philosophy, such as those theories proposed by Rawls (1971) and by Goodin (1988), provide criteria about what is good and about what is right that policy analysts and policymakers can use to justify the merits of policies and programs designed to meet human need in the public interest. These criteria can be used in conjunction with other theories providing more practical criteria, such as efficiency, political feasibility, and technical feasibility.

Theory-Oriented Evaluations

The **theory-oriented tradition** of evaluation research is known by several names, including theory-based, theory-driven, or program evaluation theory (Vaesson & Leeuw, 2010). It is considered a relatively recent theory of evaluation practice that attempts to build upon knowledge acquired from the practice of program evaluation over the past several decades (Donaldson, 2003). Interventions are treated as theories in the sense that they are based on a hypothesis that postulates, "If we deliver a programme in this way or manage services like so, then it will bring about some improved outcome" (Pawson, 2006, p. 26). Such conjectures are grounded in assumptions about what gives rise to poor performance, inappropriate behavior, and the like, and then move to speculate how changes may be made to these patterns. Inserted into existing social systems that are thought to underpin and account for a present problem or public concern, interventions signify fresh inputs thought to generate improvements in those social conditions. Theory-oriented evaluators are concerned primarily with questions of why particular interventions work in certain circumstances by looking inside the "black box" of implementation (a topic discussed in Chapter 9). They seek to develop valid and reliable ways of reconstructing chains of assumptions about how specific interventions work (Leeuw, 1991, 2003).

These chains of assumptions often go by the names of policy theories (e.g., Hoogerwerf, 1990), intervention theories (e.g., Vedung, 1997), program theories (e.g., Bickman, 1987a, 1987b), or theories of change (e.g., Weiss, 1997). The word *intervention* generically signifies policies, programs, and projects— including so-called tools of government, such as subsidies, levies, information campaigns, inspections, loans—and the term *intervention theory* refers to the assumptions underlying interventions. Program theory, for example, is not meant to be construed as equivalent to social science theory but is used in a much more restrictive sense, to refer to rather small and specific models of how social programs, treatments, or interventions are supposed to work (Bickman, 1987a; Donaldson, 2003). For the most part, unlike many of those working with social science theories, theory-oriented evaluators are less concerned with optimizing the internal (and external) validity of established causal links between interventions and effects or outcomes and with developing or using methods and tools for this purpose. Instead, theory-oriented evaluators construct plausible models of how a program is supposed to work, construct sets of propositions regarding what goes on inside the "black box" during the transformation of program or policy inputs to outputs, and identify processes through which program or policy components are presumed to affect outcomes and the conditions under which these processes are believed to operate. They contend that different types of assumptions upon which the program or policy model is based call for particular types of evidence in order to test them, implying in turn divergent methods of data collection and analysis. Such flexibility about methods and tools and the resulting heterogeneity make it difficult to provide clear or unequivocal practical guidelines. The main sources of the resulting heterogeneity are a function of the defining characteristics of theory-oriented evaluation work: the nature of intervention theories (the sources, focus, and nature of assumptions behind the interventions) and the sheer multiplicity of methods used to construct and test them (with varying levels of confidence to draw valid and reliable inferences and conclusions based on them).

As Vaesson and Leeuw (2010) suggest, the major sources of assumptions about interventions include (1) politicians, decision makers, and intervention staff, all of whom have their own beliefs and expectations about how an intervention should work; (2) other groups of stakeholders; and (3) social science research about intervention-specific topics as well as more generic theories about human behavior and the social environment. Assumptions are contested, leading to divergent practices across policy or program implementation sites as well as over time. Most contemporary theory-oriented work adheres to an integrative view of theory reconstruction, with both stakeholder theory and insights from the social sciences used to make sense of interventions.

The focus of assumptions reflects the noted "performance paradox"—that is, the observation that high positive scores on process criteria (e.g., audibility of interventions, or how interventions were carried out) do not necessarily correlate with high positive scores on final impact and effectiveness, thereby raising questions about the merits or appropriateness of using outcome performance measures for public policies and programs (Van Thiel & Leeuw, 2002). The continuing national and local level controversies about the use of standardized performance testing to determine whether public schools are progressing sufficiently along the guidelines established under the No Child Left Behind Act (NCLB, P.L. 107–110), signed into law in 2001, for example (Brigham, Gustashaw, Wiley, &. Brigham, 2004; Seifman, 2012; Skinner, 2009).

The nature of assumptions is the third source of heterogeneity about theory-driven evaluation (Vaesson & Leeuw, 2010). Descriptive theory concerns the set of assumptions about the underlying causal relationships between an intervention's activities/outputs and the alleviation of a social problem. As noted above, such assumptions can be those of politicians, decision makers, and intervention staff, sometimes gleaned from social science research. The same applies to prescriptive theory, which captures the assumptions about what should be done in terms of objectives, activities, and outputs in order to achieve a desired result. One of the current approaches to theory-driven evaluation that has drawn the attention of social workers and health professionals, known as realist evaluation (Kazi, 2003), adheres to the principle of *generative causality*. Rather than treat interventions in a temporal ordering or *successive causality* manner as independent variables, as is common among evaluators who adopt social science theories and methodologies, realist evaluators view interventions as opportunities that may or may not be acted upon in certain circumstances. That is, interventions, embedded as they are in complex processes of human interaction, entail processes of human agency that can make seemingly identical programs work in one place and fail in another (Pawson & Tilley, 1997; Vaesson & Leeuw, 2010).

The fourth source of heterogeneity of theory-oriented evaluation concerns the methodologies for reconstructing and assessing assumptions or theories behind strategies, policies, and program interventions. Leeuw (2003) describes three such methods or approaches that can be used when underlying assumptions or theories are not well-specified by stakeholders, policymakers, or producers of programs: (1) a policy-scientific approach (e.g., see Leeuw & van Gils, 1999); (2) a strategic-assessment approach (e.g., see Mason & Mitroff, 1981); and (3) an elicitation-of-mental-models approach (e.g., see Daniels, De Chernatony, & Johnson, 1995). Table 11.4 highlights the steps or processes and major strengths/weaknesses associated with each of these three approaches.

Table 11.4	Approaches for Restructuring Program Theories	
Approach	**Steps or Processes**	**Strengths and Weaknesses**
Policy-Scientific	Identify specific mechanisms expected to solve the problem	Focus on documents as well as interview data which stimulate use of multiple methods
	Use the following types of statements to get at mechanisms:	
	"In our opinion, the best way to go about this problem is to . . ."	Use of argumentation analysis helps validate reconstruction process
	"Our institution's *x* years of experiences tells us that . . ."	Diagrammatic presentation of underlying theory helps dialogues with stakeholders and others
	Compile a survey of such statements and link them to program goals	
	Reformulate these statement in "if-then" propositions or propositions of similar structure ("the more *x*, the less *y*")	Use of research reviews reduces likelihood of ideology or politically correct statements about the content of the program theory
	Search for warrants to identify missing links in or between propositions through argumentation	

Table 11.4	(Continued)	
Approach	**Steps or Processes**	**Strengths and Weaknesses**
	Reformulate the warrants in "if-then" (similar) propositions and draw chart of causal links Evaluate the validity of propositions by looking into: The logical consistency of the propositions The empirical content: the extent to which the theory & assumed impact of behavioral mechanisms correspond with state of the art within the social sciences The extent to which variables can be manipulated or steered through the policy programs	Little attention is paid to social & behavioral dynamics involved in articulation and evaluation of theory Cumbersome and time consuming Little attention paid to power differential among stakeholders
Strategic-Assessment	*Group formation:* Assemble wide cross section of persons with interest or stake in the policy; arrange in groups maximizing convergence of viewpoints within groups and maximizing divergence of perspectives between groups *Assumption surfacing:* Obtain the most significant assumptions that underpin preferred policies and programs; use following techniques among the different groups: Stakeholder analysis: Ask each group to identify key individuals or groups upon whom success or failure of their preferred strategy would depend; then list assumptions they are making about each of them in believing that the preferred strategy would succeed Assumption rating: Rank each assumption according to degree of certainty about and importance to success Most-least certain Least-most important *Dialectical debate:* Bring the groups together and have them make the best case for their respective preferred strategies; ensure that each fully understands the perspectives and rationales or warrants of the other groups	Focus on group formation and dynamics encourages sharing knowledge and perspectives Openly addresses declared conflicts Promotes democratic decision making Criteria used for assessing the validity of assumptions remain largely unspecified Group-think, yeah-saying, and similar social-psychological artifacts of group dynamics are not adequately considered Too little attention paid to power positions of participants and their consequences for group behavior

(Continued)

Table 11.4	(Continued)	
Approach	**Steps or Processes**	**Strengths and Weaknesses**
	Synthesis: Negotiate assumptions and modify key assumptions to reach an agreed-upon synthesis if possible; if no agreement is reached, highlight areas of disagreement and discuss what might be done to resolve the differences	
Elicitation-of-Mental-Models	Examine concrete record of strategic intentions through a study of the documentation designed to direct behavior	Highlights the importance of observing managerial behavior in critical circumstances, not only when things are going well
	Get involved in the program in order to observe decision makers in action and listen to their stories	The "anthropological" orientation is useful in unraveling the ways in which managers work with mental models
	Work with managers on strategic "breakdown" or critical situations; become immersed in the related thinking and social processes	
	Use well-designed trigger questions in interview situations so "theories-in-use" can be gleaned; follow interviews with feedback to individuals and teams; use the following techniques to encourage an iterative open-ended dialogue:	Unclear about the knowledge bases used and criteria
	Create an open-ended atmosphere in the interview	Untrue assumptions may go undetected
	Omit formal language and create a "playful" atmosphere to make deviations from formal phraseology and official scripts relatively easy	Low-level specificity about how to create and sustain an "open-atmosphere"
	Create dialectical or critical tension by having interviewees adopt unusual roles	
	Listen carefully for inconsistencies	
	Use content or text analysis programs on data obtained from interviews, reports, documents	
	Compare the results with relevant social science research	

Source: Adapted from Leeuw, F.L. (2003). Reconstructing program theories: Methods available and problems to be solved. *American Journal of Evaluation, 24,* 5–20.

Skill Building Exercises

1. What responsibilities and tasks are associated with an evaluator's role as scientist, assistant, judge, and educator?

2. Discuss ways evaluators can set the framework for valuing, guide the valuing process, and/or serve as an active co-contributor to the determination of merit or worth of a policy or program when establishing relationships with stakeholders.

3. Discuss the relationship between each of the following evaluation models and liberal political philosophy: systems analysis, decision making, and behavioral objectives.

4. What distinguishes values-distant, values-salient, and values-positioned evaluations?

5. What distinguishes values-relativistic evaluations from values-prioritizing evaluations?

6. Discuss the role of theories in evaluation.

    a. What distinguishes explanatory from normative theories?
    b. Identify the steps or processes and strengths/limitations of taking each of the following approaches to restructuring program theories: policy scientific, strategic assessment, and elicitation-of-mental-models

Epilogue

A Holistic Framework
for Policy Analysis

The Epilogue provides some general guidelines and an overarching framework for program evaluation and policy analysis. It draws on many of the concepts, themes, tools, and techniques presented throughout this volume. Upon completion of the epilogue, students will be able to (1) identify and apply general guidelines for conducting program and policy evaluations while retaining professional integrity and keeping social justice in mind, and (2) conduct program and policy evaluations at the appropriate level.

Upon successful completion of the skill building exercises, students will have mastered the following Council on Social Work Education (CSWE) Competencies and Practice Behaviors:

Epilogue	CSWE Core Competencies
#	Description
2.1.1	**Identify as a Professional Social Worker and Conduct Oneself Accordingly**
	Advocate for client access to the services of a social worker
	Practice personal reflection and self-correction to ensure continual professional development
	Attend to professional roles and boundaries
	Demonstrate professional demeanor in behavior, appearance, and communication
	Engage in career-long learning
	Use supervision and consultation
2.1.2	**Apply Social Work Ethical Principles to Guide Professional Practice**
	Recognize and manage personal values in a way that allows professional values to guide practice

(Continued)

Epilogue	(Continued)
#	**Description**
	Make ethical decisions by applying standards of the NASW Code of Ethics
	Tolerate ambiguity in resolving ethical conflicts
	Apply strategies of ethical reasoning to arrive at principled decisions
2.1.3	**Apply Critical Thinking to Inform and Communicate Professional Judgments**
	Distinguish, appraise, and integrate multiple sources of knowledge, including research-based knowledge and practice wisdom
	Analyze models of assessment, prevention, intervention, and evaluation
	Demonstrate effective oral and written communication in working with individuals, families, groups, organizations, communities, and colleagues
2.1.4	**Engage Diversity and Difference in Practice**
	Recognize the extent to which a culture's structures and values may oppress, marginalize, alienate, or create or enhance privilege and power
	Gain sufficient self-awareness to eliminate the influence of personal biases and values in working with diverse groups
	Recognize and communicate their understanding of the importance of difference in shaping life experiences
2.1.5	**Advance Human Rights and Social and Economic Justice**
	Understand the forms and mechanisms of oppression and discrimination
	Advocate for human rights and social and economic justice
	Engage in practices that advance social and economic justice
2.1.6	**Engage in Research-Informed Practice and Practice-Informed Research**
	Use practice experience to inform scientific inquiry
	Use research evidence to inform practice
2.1.7	**Apply Knowledge of Human Behavior and the Social Environment**
	Utilize conceptual frameworks to guide the processes of assessment, intervention, and evaluation
	Critique and apply knowledge to understand person and environment
2.1.8	**Engage in Policy Practice to Advance Social and Economic Well-Being and to Deliver Effective Social Work Services**
	Analyze, formulate, and advocate for policies that advance social well-being

Epilogue	(Continued)
#	**Description**
2.1.9	**Respond to Contexts That Shape Practice**
	Continuously discover, appraise, and attend to changing locales, populations, scientific and technological development, and emerging societal trends to provide relevant services
2.1.10	**Engage, Assess, Intervene, and Evaluate With Individuals, Families, Groups, Organizations, and Communities**
2.1.10(a)	*Engagement*
	Substantively and affectively prepare for action with individuals, families, groups, organizations, and communities
2.1.10(b)	*Assessment*
	Collect, organize, and interpret client data
	Assess client strengths and limitations
2.1.10(c)	*Intervention*
	Implement prevention interventions that enhance client capacities
2.1.10(d)	*Evaluation*
	Analyze, monitor, and evaluate interventions

Source: Adapted from Council on Social Work Education (2012). *Educational policy and accreditation standards.* Washington, DC: Author. Retrieved from http://www.cswe.org/file.aspx?id=13780

GENERAL PRINCIPLES, GUIDELINES, AND STANDARDS OF EVALUATION PRACTICE

Evaluators who rely on theories, whether of the social scientific, normative, or "program-theory" variety, when conducting evaluations should keep in mind a primary non-variant goal of evaluation—namely, the evaluator's obligation to assess merit or worth in a professionally objective way. This essential value-determination function should not be subordinated under the banner of empowerment evaluation or emancipation theory to other activities that are not necessarily involved in evaluation work, such as providing evaluation training to clients, helping them institutionalize systematic evaluation, and informing public relations reports (Stufflebeam, 1994). Instead, when doing evaluation work, social workers, program evaluators, and other professionals would be well advised to uphold basic principles and standards of evaluation practice, such as those delineated in Table Ep.1.

Table Ep.1	Basic Principles and Standards of Evaluation
Basic Principles	**Standards/Values**
Utility	Ground evaluation in stakeholder interests and articulated values—that is, they should be credible, informative, timely, and influential
Propriety	Evaluations should be ethical and fair to affected parties, including service providers and clients
Feasibility	Evaluation procedures and level of effort are appropriate, affordable, politically viable, and reasonably easy to implement
Accuracy	Evaluations should reveal and convey technically adequate information and justified inferences about the features of the program or policy that determine its merit or worth

Source: Stufflebeam, D.L. (1994). Empowerment evaluation, objectivist evaluation, and evaluation standards: Where the future of evaluation should not go and where it needs to go. *Evaluation Practice, 15,* 322–323.

In addition to satisfying basic principles and standards of utility, propriety, feasibility, and accuracy, Stufflebeam (1994) provides other general guidelines for conducting evaluations that retain professional (impartial) integrity while, for our purposes and by extension, keeping in mind the social work commitment to social justice. These general guidelines are enumerated and summarized in Table Ep.2.

Table Ep.2	General Guidelines for Evaluations

1. Examine programs for their service to citizens of a democratic society and to effects on non-citizens, whether legal or illegal

2. Assess programs and policies for their merit (intrinsic value, e.g., appropriateness and adequacy of benefits or services) and worth (extrinsic value, e.g., meeting clients' needs)

3. Assess the extent administrators and staff are professionally accountable—that is, publicly and creditably responsible in fulfilling their professional responsibilities or duties

4. Provide direction for policy or program improvement based in part of ongoing assessment of performance and on relevant up-to-date studies and state of the art theoretical developments—that is, by conducting formative and summative evaluations

5. Conduct ongoing or *prospective assessments* of need, opportunities, and problems within a service area to help ensure consistency with institutional mission or goals and to reassess priorities accordingly

6. Conduct retrospective evaluations linking changes in clients' needs to program or policy effects

| Table Ep.2 | (Continued) |

7. Identify and assess the merit and worth of alternative policies and programs

8. Ground evaluation in ongoing communications among stakeholders about the key questions, criteria, findings, and implications of evaluation to promote their acceptance, use, and impact, making sure to avoid concealing later findings that may show the policy or program in less than a desirable light

9. Use the multiple perspectives of stakeholders, multiple outcome measures, and both quantitative and qualitative methods for data collection and analysis

Source: Adapted from Stufflebeam, D.L. (1994). Empowerment evaluation, objectivist evaluation, and evaluation standards: Where the future of evaluation should not go and where it needs to go. *Evaluation Practice, 15,* 330–333.

AN OVERARCHING FRAMEWORK FOR PROGRAM EVALUATION AND POLICY ANALYSIS

For purposes here, policy analysts are well advised to maintain an analytical distinction between facts and values when their primary role is to conduct an analysis rather than advocating for a particular aim or goal such as social justice. Informed by practical logic, policy analysts can integrate facts and values when evaluating social policies and programs. Drawing on Fischer (1980), Caputo (1989) provides a conceptual framework that integrates facts and values in evaluation while maintaining a distinction between them. The framework, which encapsulates in summary form many of the issues discussed throughout the book, delineates four phases containing both normative and empirical components. Table Ep.3 illustrates the framework.

| Table Ep.3 | Framework of Policy Evaluation Components | | |

Probe	Inference	Reasons	Criticism
Technical Verification of Policy Objectives			
Policy Objectives			
Empirical Consequences			
Unanticipated Effects			
Alternative Means			

(Continued)

Table Ep.3 (Continued)			
Probe	**Inference**	**Reasons**	**Criticism**
Validation of Policy Goals			
Relevance			
Situational Context			
Multiple Goals			
Precedence			
Vindication of Policy Choices			
System Consequences			
Equity			
Ideological Conflicts			
Rational Choice			
Alternative Social Orders			

Source: Adapted from Fischer, F. (1980). *Politics, values, and public policy.* Boulder, CO: Westview Press, p. 206.

The first two phases or components, verification and validation, involve decision making based on principles endemic to the value systems that govern the particular decision-making process in question (Caputo, 1989). In verification, evaluation focuses on the empirical demonstration of whether the program or policy being evaluated fulfills the requirements of the norms introduced by decision makers and other stakeholders. The program evaluator or policy analyst examines program or policy objectives, likely or actual empirical consequences of the policy or program, unanticipated effects, and alternative means. In validation, evaluation asks whether the goal itself is compatible with the basic value systems that provide competing criteria in the judgment process. Program evaluators or policy analysts assess questions of relevance, examine the situational context, delineate multiple goals, and account for precedence. The vindication and rational choice components of the framework entail choosing value systems by making decisions on principle. In vindication, evaluation seeks to determine whether the value system is instrumental or contributive to the adopted way of life or culture. Program evaluators and policy analysts examine and assess system consequences, equity, and ideological conflicts. In rational choice, program evaluators and policy analysts examine alternative ways of life and seek to show the extent to which a particular choice about a way of life is governed by rational processes in free and open deliberation. Each component is guided by different methodologies, which are highlighted in Table Ep.4.

Table Ep.4	The Levels of Evaluation as Social Science Methodology		
Levels of Evaluative Logic	**Social Science Methodology**	**The Role of Empirical Science**	**Mode of Inference**
Verification	Evaluation Research	Emphasis on research design and controlled experiment Reliability through statistical analysis Knowledge of secondary consequences	Causal explanation Knowledge of facts sufficient Formal inference
Validation	Phenomenological Analysis	Descriptive facts of the situation Application of causal knowledge about consequences of following a rule	Interpretive understanding Knowledge of facts necessary, but not sufficient
Vindication	Behavioral Systems Approach	Descriptive knowledge of *de facto* individual and group values Empirical data about instrumental and contributive consequences	Causal explanation Knowledge of facts sufficient Formal inference
Rational	Political Philosophy	Experiential knowledge about alternative ways of life Knowledge of human nature	Interpretive speculation Vision, speculation Knowledge of facts necessary, but not sufficient

Source: Adapted from Fischer, F. (1980). *Politics, values, and public policy.* Boulder, CO: Westview Press, p. 175.

As can be seen in Table Ep.4, verification and vindication rely on empirical modes of inquiry, while validation and rational choice use more interpretive modes of inference. Ideally, there would be sufficient time and resources to employ all four phases to assess the merit or worth of a policy or program, thereby encouraging more systematic and thorough integration of empirical inquiry and normative discourse (Caputo, 1989). Verification and validation would do so within a given set of acceptable, identifiable, and commonly held values, and each of these two phases of evaluation proceed to justify judgments based on these normative criteria. Vindication and rational choice occur when there are no more acceptable normative criteria within the set of values commonly held to which an appeal can be made.

Much of the program and policy evaluation literature falls into the verification and to a lesser although increasingly more extensive extent, given the greater acceptance of qualitative approaches to social inquiry, the validation categories. Many MDRC studies of welfare-to-work and educational training programs, several of which were noted above, are examples of these approaches. As Caputo (1989) has noted,

Wilson (1987) and Callahan (1987), respectively, are examples of the vindication and rational choice phases of evaluation. In *The Truly Disadvantaged* and in much subsequent work (e.g., Wilson, 2009, 2011; see Caputo & Deprez, 2012, for a summary), Wilson relies on a massive amount of data to challenge liberal (e.g., Duncan, 1984) and conservative (Mead, 1986; Murray, 1984) orthodoxy in analyzing inner-city problems (verification and validation phases), and to argue for moving beyond primary reliance on race-specific policies to address social conditions to policies that in part address broader structural problems of social organization and in part redress past injustices, such as discrimination. When discussing what accounts for "the underclass" in urban America, Wilson (1987) challenged "decisions of principle"—that is, those guides for subsequent decision making and political action. Whereas the more conservative analysts such as Murray (1984) and Mead (1986), who provided much intellectual and ideological fodder that shaped the1996 legislation reforming welfare (Caputo, 2011), based their policy recommendations on individualistic values and behaviors, Wilson focuses on macro-historical and structural factors associated with a changing economy, thereby challenging the extent to which a value system based on individual effort and merit is instrumental or contributes to the plight of inner-city, low-income residents.

Despite efforts to provide an alternative set of criteria to judge the merits of government action, Wilson nonetheless remains well within the rather elastic vision of American capitalism (Caputo, 1989). Although a self-proclaimed Social Democrat, Wilson never calls for major shifts in the capitalistic public-private partnership and thereby bypasses the rational choice phase of the framework, that phase that calls for a critical examination of alternative ways of life. This is not to say that Wilson eschews a rational approach to economic development and social reform. Quite the contrary: he is a solid advocate for activist government in the economy and general welfare of the country, particularly on behalf of economically vulnerable groups. He relies on empirical analysis to assess the merits of existing programs and policies (verification), then challenges them on the basis of their consequences for society in general and low-income urban families and individuals in particular (validation). Wilson goes on to challenge the criteria by which existing programs are assumed to benefit the citizenry, and he offers a range of alternative policies based more on active government in the economy and society rather than on the more restrictive role of government as primary regulator or umpire of the economy and welfare (vindication). On the whole, however, capitalism as the engine of the economy remains for Wilson normatively intact.

In a more recent work, political scientist, self-identified libertarian, and American Enterprise Institute resident scholar Murray (2006, 2012), relying on national level data, also challenged the criteria by which existing welfare state programs are assumed to benefit the citizenry (vindication). As an alternative to the welfare state, which Murray proposed to dismantle, he offered a basic income plan to eliminate poverty. He called on the U.S. government to provide individuals 21 years of age and older an intermittently adjusted amount of $10,000 a year, of which $3,000 would go to health care coverage. Unlike Wilson, Murray preferred less federal level government involvement in social welfare provisioning beyond a guaranteed unconditional annual cash nexus. Murray's basic income plan found no political traction, of which he was aware, admitting, "Today's politicians would not build it" (2006, p. xv). Despite a flurry of reviews in popular outlets such as *The New Republic* (Klein, 2006; Noah, 2012), the *National Review* (Ponnure, 2006), the *University of Pittsburgh Law Review* (Delgado, 2007), and *The New York Times* (Douthat, 2012), Murray's challenge was largely ignored (Caputo, 2012). For purposes, here, however, the works of Wilson and Murray explicitly integrate normative concerns in their empirical assessments of social welfare provisioning policies.

Unlike Wilson and Murray, both of whom eschewed the rational choice phase (of the framework in Table Ep.4), Callahan (1987) argues primarily from within it, and to a lesser extent within the vindication component (Caputo, 1989). He develops a rationale for limiting health resources to the elderly, given that those aged 65 years and older account for increasing shares of health care expenditures: from about 31 percent in 1984 to nearly half (about 43 percent) by 2002 (Stanton & Rutherford, 2006); and projected increases in the financial burden for those 65 years age and over from the median percentage of household income spent on health care costs rising from 10 percent in 2010 to 19 percent by 2040, and the percentage of those individuals spending more than 20 percent of their income on health care going from 18 percent in 2010 to 45 percent in 2040 (Johnson & Mommaerts, 2010). About one-quarter of Medicare expenditures are for care of beneficiaries in the last year of their life and one-tenth for care in the last 30 days, even though only about 5 percent of Medicare recipients die in any given year (McKeown, 2011).

Callahan (1987) traces changing conceptions of medicine, health, and family life, and then challenges contemporary criteria of what constitutes the good life, at least for aging persons. Technological advances that have transformed the nature of medicine from caring to curing have also moved the idea of health from a nebulous hope to a fundamental and social requirement: what can be done medically ought to be done and what ought to be done ought to be available to all, and what ought to be available to all becomes the moral responsibility of all. Advances in biomedical technologies, Callahan argues, alter perceptions about the capacity to control life—in effect strengthening the belief that medical destiny is in one's hands and posing new moral and ethical dilemmas that were inconceivable prior to such advances. Think, for example, about how ultrasound scanning and DNA tests expand parents' knowledge about the health of a fetus and the range of conditions under which they may deliberate about the option of abortion at varying stages of pregnancy, contingent upon test results (for a more extended discussion of this and related issues about how technology mediates morally related individual and collective or policy decision making see Verbeek, 2011).

Callahan (1987) asks if the aforementioned trends are prudent, sensible, or fair. Should they be allowed to continue unabated? Callahan thinks not, and he advises medicine to give up its relentless drive to extend the life of the aged and to attend instead to the relief of their suffering and an improvement in their physical and mental quality of life. This call for a restructuring of the health care research and financing policies, from extending life to improving its quality, occurs primarily within the rational choice component of the framework in Table Ep.4. Callahan offers an alternative resource allocation model to guide decisions about using life-extending technologies on the elderly. His model concomitantly limits macro- and micro-environmental medical options for the elderly. At the macro level, public policy would emphasize preventive rather than acute or chronic treatment; provision of equitable security or receipt of adequate income to ensure that impoverishment would not occur; priorities for care, especially primary care; fully subsidized home care; and institutional programs for the elderly; and perhaps most controversial, an end to the blind pursuit of technological advances aimed at the indefinite extending of life without regard to quality of life. At the institutional or micro-environmental level, Callahan proposes criteria for terminating those treatments that are unable to relieve pain and suffering when a patient has lived a "full life span," those that create burdens such as pain, loss of function, and disfigurement, as patients on renal dialysis after surgery and those unable to restore or maintain their quality of life, or a sense of personhood that can be sustained. What constitutes "full life span" and "sustained personhood" would be subjects of deliberation, the former reached in part when life's possibilities have been achieved and after which death may be understood as a sad, but nonetheless acceptable event, and the latter including at least the capacity to reason, to have emotions, and to enter into relations with others.

Government has a definite but limited role in Callihan's scheme. Government has a duty to help people live out a natural life span but not actively help extend life medically beyond that point. Government is obliged to develop, employ, and pay only for that kind and degree of life-extending technology necessary for medicine to achieve and serve the end of a natural life span. Finally, beyond the point of a natural life span, government should provide only the means necessary for the relief of suffering, not life-extending technology. In Callahan's scheme, age replaces need as a principle for the allocation of resources. Combined with an ideal of old age that focuses on its quality rather than its indefinite extension, age can be understood at the level of common sense or practical reason and can be made relatively clear and subject to policy analysis (Caputo, 1989).

Skill Building Exercises

1. Discuss the merits of the general guidelines that Stufflebeam (1994) provided for conducting evaluations in light of the likelihood of retaining professional (impartial) integrity, while keeping social justice in mind.

2. What is meant by levels of evaluation logic?

   a. Identify four such levels.
   b. What distinguishes each of the four levels from one another, accounting for appropriate social science methodology, the role of empirical research, and mode of inference?

3. Given what you know now, how would you go about analyzing H.R. 45, which appears in the Introduction to this volume?

4. Thinking globally, how would you go about assessing the merits of a policy permitting individuals to move freely across borders in pursuit of personal projects or for economic betterment?

Council on Social Work Education (CSWE) Core Competencies

#	Description	In Chapters
2.1.1	**Identify as a Professional Social Worker and Conduct Oneself Accordingly**	
	Advocate for client access to the services of a social worker	Epilogue
	Practice personal reflection and self-correction to ensure continual professional development	3, Epilogue
	Attend to professional roles and boundaries	1, 3, Epilogue
	Demonstrate professional demeanor in behavior, appearance, and communication	
	Engage in career-long learning	Epilogue
	Use supervision and consultation	Epilogue
2.1.2	**Apply Social Work Ethical Principles to Guide Professional Practice**	
	Recognize and manage personal values in a way that allows professional values to guide practice	5, 11, Epilogue
	Make ethical decisions by applying standards of the National Association of Social Work (NASW) Code of Ethics	3, 4, 5, 11, Epilogue
	Tolerate ambiguity in resolving ethical conflicts	3, 4, 5, 9, 11, Epilogue
	Apply strategies of ethical reasoning to arrive at principled decisions	4, 9, 11, Epilogue
2.1.3	**Apply Critical Thinking to Inform and Communicate Professional Judgments**	
	Distinguish, appraise, and integrate multiple sources of knowledge, including research-based knowledge and practice wisdom	6, 7, 8, 9, 10, 11, Epilogue

(Continued)

#	Description	In Chapters
	Analyze models of assessment, prevention, intervention, and evaluation	6, 7, 8, 9, 10, 11, Epilogue
	Demonstrate effective oral and written communication in working with individuals, families, groups, organizations, communities, and colleagues	1, 2, 3, 4, 5, 6, 7, 8, 9, 10, 11, Epilogue
2.1.4	**Engage Diversity and Difference in Practice**	
	Recognize the extent to which a culture's structures and values may oppress, marginalize, alienate, or create or enhance privilege and power	6, 8, Epilogue
	Gain sufficient self-awareness to eliminate the influence of personal biases and values in working with diverse groups	Epilogue
	Recognize and communicate their understanding of the importance of difference in shaping life experiences	Epilogue
	View themselves as learners and engage those with whom they work as informants	9, 11
2.1.5	**Advance Human Rights and Social and Economic Justice**	
	Understand the forms and mechanisms of oppression and discrimination	4, 6, 8, 9, 11, Epilogue
	Advocate for human rights and social and economic justice	Epilogue
	Engage in practices that advance social and economic justice	Epilogue
2.1.6	**Engage in Research-Informed Practice and Practice-Informed Research**	
	Use practice experience to inform scientific inquiry	Epilogue
	Use research evidence to inform practice	6, 7, Epilogue
2.1.7	**Apply Knowledge of Human Behavior and the Social Environment**	
	Utilize conceptual frameworks to guide the processes of assessment, intervention, and evaluation	2, 4, 5, 6, 7, 8, 9, 10, 11, Epilogue
	Critique and apply knowledge to understand person and environment	2, 4, 5, 6, 7, 8, 9, 10, 11, Epilogue
2.1.8	**Engage in Policy Practice to Advance Social and Economic Well-Being and to Deliver Effective Social Work Services**	
	Analyze, formulate, and advocate for policies that advance social well-being	4, 5, 6, 7, 8, 9, 11, Epilogue
	Collaborate with colleagues and clients for effective policy action	2

#	Description	In Chapters
2.1.9	**Respond to Contexts That Shape Practice**	
	Continuously discover, appraise, and attend to changing locales, populations, scientific and technological development, and emerging societal trends to provide relevant services	1, 4, 5, 8, 9, 10, 11, Epilogue
	Provide leadership in promoting sustainable changes in service delivery and practice to improve the quality of social services	1
2.1.10	**Engage, Assess, Intervene, and Evaluate With Individuals, Families, Groups, Organizations, and Communities**	
2.1.10 (a)	*Engagement*	
	Substantively and affectively prepare for action with individuals, families, groups, organizations, and communities	Epilogue
	Use empathy and other interpersonal skills	
	Develop a mutually agreed-on focus of work and desired outcomes	
2.1.10 (b)	*Assessment*	
	Collect, organize, and interpret client data	Epilogue
	Assess client strengths and limitations	Epilogue
	Develop mutually agreed-on intervention goals and objectives	
	Select appropriate intervention strategies	10, 11
2.1.10 (c)	*Intervention*	
	Initiate actions to achieve organizational goals	
	Implement prevention interventions that enhance client capacities	10, 11, Epilogue
	Help clients resolve problems	
	Negotiate, mediate, and advocate for clients	10, 11
	Facilitate transitions and endings	
2.1.10 (d)	*Evaluation*	
	Analyze, monitor, and evaluate interventions	10, 11, Epilogue

Source: Adapted from Council on Social Work Education (2012). *Educational policy and accreditation standards.* Washington, DC: Author. Retrieved from http://www.cswe.org/file.aspx?id=13780

APPENDIX B

Historical Overview of Policy Analysis and Policy Studies

Policy analysts may be found in many different settings and, by training, possess conceptual skills and methodological tools, along with varied levels and types of technical proficiency and expertise. Organizational settings where policy analysts work include the executive and legislative branches of the federal and state governments, local level executive agencies, think tanks and policy-research organizations (of which, according to *NIRA's World Directory of Think Tanks* [http://www.nira.or.jp/past/ice/nwdtt/2005/index.html], there are about one hundred in the United States), and profit-seeking firms in industries affected by government action. In addition, faculty at many universities and colleges with departments or programs offering advanced degrees from professional schools such as business, government, law, medicine, nursing, public administration, public policy, and social work, and from academic disciplines such as economics, international studies, political science, sociology, and perhaps to a lesser extent philosophy also incorporate policy analysis as part of their respective research agendas (Ascher, 1986; Medvetz, 2012, 2007; Radin, 1997; Watson, 1983; Weimer & Vining, 2011).

This appendix provides a historical overview of the professionalization of the social sciences and of social work and the roles they play in the formation of policy analysts/experts. It discusses the relation between advocates' and reformers' efforts to speak authoritatively about the causes and remedies of social problems; the ascendency of universities to provide the institutional settings for carrying out policy analysis that had the paradoxical effect of legitimating the authority of social science faculty while concomitantly narrowing their focus, as faculty became increasingly specialized experts; and the emergence and proliferation of **think tanks**, those hybrid organizations that traverse the social worlds of politics, academics, business, and journalism to address social problems and influence policy debates (Medvetz, 2007).

Upon completion of Appendix B, students will have learned that (1) policy analysis has a formidable history with roots in the reform efforts of the eighteenth century, and (2) social work is only one among several disciplines and professions seeking to assess and influence social welfare policy. Upon successful completion of the skill building exercises of Appendix B, students will have mastered the following Council on Social Work Education (CSWE) Core Competencies and Practice Behaviors:

Appendix B	CSWE Core Competencies
#	Description
2.1.1	**Identify as a Professional Social Worker and Conduct Oneself Accordingly**
	Attend to professional roles and boundaries
2.1.3	**Apply Critical Thinking to Inform and Communicate Professional Judgments**
	Demonstrate effective oral and written communication in working with individuals, families, groups, organizations, communities, and colleagues
2.1.7	**Apply Knowledge of Human Behavior and the Social Environment**
	Critique and apply knowledge to understand person and environment
2.1.9	**Respond to Contexts That Shape Practice**
	Continuously discover, appraise, and attend to changing locales, populations, scientific and technological development, and emerging societal trends to provide relevant services
	Provide leadership in promoting sustainable changes in service delivery and practice to improve the quality of social services

Source: Adapted from Council on Social Work Education (2012). *Educational policy and accreditation standards*. Washington, DC: Author. Retrieved from http://www.cswe.org/file.aspx?id=13780

HISTORICAL ROOTS

The contemporary configuration of policy analysis in the United States has its roots in social reform efforts dating back to the end of the Civil War with the formation of the American Social Science Association (ASSA) in 1865, the professionalization of the social sciences (particularly the academic disciplines of economics, political science, and sociology) in the latter part of the nineteenth century and the Progressive Era in the twentieth century, and both World Wars, which increased the demand, among other things, for human science experts working in government agencies and in private foundations to address social problems (Furner, 2011; Smith, 1994). In addition, since World War II the contemporary configuration of policy analysis has been shaped by the proliferation of issue-oriented think tanks and foundations that seek to influence economic and social public policies at all levels of government, by financially supporting policy-related research of scholars whose work supports their views, by promoting the publication of related books, policy briefs, and position papers targeting policymakers, and by nurturing a cadre of policy analysts/experts to serve as staff to and on committees of government officials (Feinberg, 2007; Fischer, 1991; Stahl, 2008; Stefancic & Delgado, 1996; Tevelow, 2005).

The earlier social reform efforts fused natural law moralism with scientific methodology, especially the empirical inductive approach espoused by Francis Bacon (1620/2012; Snyder, 2011) and advanced by natural and social philosophers on both sides of the Atlantic. These included Frank B. Sanborn, who became secretary to the first State Board of Charities in 1863 and an organizer of the first "Conference of Boards of Public Charities," which had initially met in New York in 1874 as a section of the American Social Science Association (ASSA) (Haskell, 2000; Mann, 1954; Sanborn & Ayers, 1931), and Richard Jones in England (Snyder, 2011). Natural law moralism entailed a set of unverifiable, universally binding and knowable precepts of practical reason that would serve as ethical guides to human action, helping to determine what constitutes right reason about what one ought to do in conformity with nature. Some philosophical and religious traditions regard this as a reflection of *a priori* divine law, while others accept nature as a limit and its own precondition as self-evident practical truths (Lee, 1928; McAniff, 1953; George, 1999; O'Scannlain, 2011). Bacon's method demanded three steps in problem solving—namely, collection, classification, and interpretation of facts—and it required no consciously articulated theory of causation and no theoretical questions to guide research, not even hypotheses (Furner, 2011).

Not coincidentally, social work, which had strong roots in social reform, particularly among the settlement house workers, also developed during this period (Bricker-Jenkins & Joseph, 2008). As professionally emergent social workers and social scientists attempted to ground their efforts in less moralistic and more objective ways of thinking and practices (Bryson, 1932; Franklin, 1986), they became increasingly ensconced in university settings, distanced themselves from reform efforts and applied work, and narrowed their advocacy to areas within their expertise (Bannister, 1987). At the time, however, there was no contradiction between Bacon's approach and social reformers' intentions; this made it convenient for the largely upper class amateurs or generalists who attended meetings of the Conference of Boards of Public Charities and filled the ranks of the ASSA. As Daniels (1963) noted, for Bacon, knowledge was power and application of his then revolutionary inductive science provided hope for human progress, an attitude pervasive among the philanthropists, bureaucrats, reformers, and educators who joined the ASSA and sought to make a social revolution by developing a social science (Furner, 2011).

The ASSA served as the institutional focal point to establish and defend authority in an increasingly interdependent world, which presented formidable challenges to commonsense thinking about causality and human behavior among a discordant hodgepodge of gentry-class practitioners as they organized into professions, including the eclectic mix of law, medicine, divinity, history, education, business, arts, and letters, under the rubric of "social science." Social science, which was to emerge gradually from the cocoon of moral philosophy (Bryson, 1932), referred to the whole realm of problematic relationships in human affairs, descriptions and explanations of which were becoming less familiar to common sense and more alien to common knowledge as the United States increasingly industrialized and urbanized between the Civil War and World War I. ASSA's departmental structure—that is, its Departments of Education, Health, Finance, and Jurisprudence—was designed to accommodate the classic professions in an enterprise devoted as much to practical reform as to social investigation (Haskell, 2000; Ross, 1991). Many of these gentry-class practitioners clung to the fiction that piling up enough data would lead to the discovery of self-evident truths, which in turn would show people how they should live (Furner, 2011). Although its model of social inquiry was eclipsed but not annihilated by university-based disciplines, the ASSA was instrumental in legitimating the authoritative pronouncements of social problems and remedies by increasingly specialized social science professionals, a process consistent with the development of the professionalization of science in the United States that had begun in the first half of the eighteenth century (Daniels, 1967).

Seeking to create a more "scientific" philanthropy as a corrective to indiscriminate almsgiving to poor and destitute individuals and to introduce more objective attitudes to the study of social welfare (Bremner, 1956; Franklin, 1986; Gettelman 1969/1970), forerunners of professional social work had organized the National Conference of Charities and Correction (NCCC) and its predecessors in conjunction with the ASSA—the organizations held annual meetings together from 1874 to 1878. In its efforts to transcend a class-based or self-interest basis of authority and to create a more impartial basis, the ASSA sowed the seeds of its own demise by 1909. It inadvertently spawned the American Historical Association (AHA) in 1884, from which the American Economic Association (AEA) splintered off in 1885, and the American Political Science Association (APSA) in 1904. The American Sociology Society (ASS) separated from the American Economic Association in 1905. Speaking at the National Conference of Charities and Correction in 1915, educator Abraham Flexner had raised doubts about the professional standing of social work, in part due to its lack of discipline-specific knowledge. Impersonal neutrality and discipline-specific knowledge became hallmarks of professional development, as evidenced by the development of university-based academic disciplines, professional organizations, and credentialing bodies. Reflecting these developments, the National Social Workers Exchange (later the American Association of Social Workers) was organized in 1917, the same year Mary Richmond's *Social Diagnosis,* a basic methodological text for social work education, was published.

As atheoretical and reformist as it was, the ASSA had nonetheless become too abstract for the National Conference of Charities and Correction, which began meeting separately in 1879. The splintering of the American Historical Association, begun in 1894, signified the perceived inadequacy of ASSA as a viable organizational entity for the pursuit of social inquiry. This inadequacy was also exemplified by the failed attempt of ASSA to become a part of Johns Hopkins University, an attempt initiated in 1878 when Johns Hopkins was only two years old (Haskell, 2000; Lengermann & Niebrugge, 2007). Universities were deemed more viable institutions within which to carry out more authoritative and legitimate social inquiry by scholars and professionals, including social workers. These academics and professionals could devote themselves full time to their investigations and thereby be better equipped to replace the "social science amateurs," reflecting ASSA's open membership, and to denounce charlatans and quacks. Cornell University's co-founder and first president, Andrew Dickson White (1896), had made this clear when writing about the rationale for Cornell's founding in 1865 (Goode, 1960). Edward L. Youmans (1874), editor of *Popular Science Monthly* and proponent of Herbert Spencer's social evolutionary theory, considered the ASSA "an organization for public action," whose members were "hot with the impulses of philanthropy . . . [and] full of projects of social relief, amelioration, and improvement," but "of pure investigation, of the strict and passionless study of society from a scientific point of view, we hear very little" (p. 368). In Youmans's estimation, ASSA meetings advanced social science about as much as political conventions. A year later Youmans (1875), for whom the development of social science meant uncovering "the natural laws of the social state" (p. 366), accused the ASSA of deceiving the public. In short, by having "social science" in its name, ASSA—whose membership advanced the "heterogeneous and discordant opinions of unscientific men" (p. 367)—merely cloaked reformist schemes in the dignity of science.

At issue in the failure of ASSA to join Johns Hopkins University, in part, was the distinction between agitation and investigation. In the late nineteenth century, agitation and advocacy were correlated with a relativistic view of human affairs that precluded "sound opinion," the formation of which required support of organized communities of inquiry. Implicit in organized communities of competence was a consensus about the criteria of competence. Universities as they were developing during the late nineteenth and early twentieth centuries were deemed the place where members of such communities viewed even their bitterest rivals inside the community as fundamentally competent. They thereby provided an institutional framework better suited to investigate and interpret facts among competent peers, even if rivals. Since practical reform was inherently controversial, precluding the formation of consensual communities about competency, those dedicated to social reform were deemed less fit if not unfit for professionalization. The true person of science, admonished astronomer and mathematician turned political economist Simon Newcomb (1886b) in the opening address of the International Congress of Arts and Science, Universal Exposition in St. Louis in 1904, "has no such expression in his vocabulary as 'useful knowledge'" (Newcomb, 1904, p. 3).

By 1909 when ASSA ceased, the inquiry and reform mission had become sufficiently frayed, with universities providing the institutional framework within which to organize professional communities of competent inquirers. The fraying was helped by several academic freedom cases that were embarrassing to universities during the 1890s, including the economist Edward Bemis at the University of Chicago and political economist Edward Ross at Stanford University, resulting in faculty dismissals (Furner, 2011; Mohr, 1970). Bemis incorporated socializing essential public services into his economic philosophy and was forced to resign after launching a crusade for municipal control of Chicago's gas supply. A proponent of free silver and supporter of William Jennings Bryan for president, Ross openly attacked continued importation of "Oriental" labor into the United States and proposed that public ownership of municipal utilities was the wave of the future, two policy-related positions that enraged Mrs. Jane Lathrop Stanford, the sole trustee of the university, who demanded and eventually succeeded in getting Ross dismissed.

The American Social Science Association's departments of education, health, social economics, finance, and jurisprudence constituted operational fields of action for the diagnosis and cure of society's ills, whereas disciplinary boundaries that professional associations such as the American Historical Association and the American Economic Association sought to promote as their memberships increasingly became university based focused less on social problems per se. Instead, they served to allocate the materials of scholarship by assigning to each group of specialists a field of factual data, developing knowledge bases and methodological tools of their respective disciplinary trades. These specialists enjoyed first rights of exploring such data—a division of labor among investigators, not agitators (Cravens, 1971; Dunbar, 1891; Haskell, 2000).

TWENTIETH CENTURY: FIRST HALF—THE QUEST FOR OBJECTIVITY

It is important to keep in mind that this transition took decades, well into the twentieth century, and was never totally complete. On the eve of the Progressive Era in the early twentieth century, American Economic Association (AEA) membership was open to anyone willing to pay dues, and its chief organizer, Richard T. Ely, retained ASSA's commitment to social reforms by crusading against laissez-faire economics. This was to the dismay of Newcomb (1886a, 1894) and others (e.g., see Farnam, 1886), who questioned his science, pro-labor bias, and by extension his professionalism, setting off a debate among political economists of all stripes (Furner, 2011, pp. 81–106; also see *Science, 7* and *8,* 1886 for lively exchanges about related issues between Ely and Newcomb and other major participants, a "discussion" considered the high point of conflict, while disclosing areas of compromise, between what was at the time deemed the old [classic laissez-faire] and new [morally infused interventionists] schools of economics vying for authoritative control of the emerging profession). Ely nonetheless stressed the need to encourage research, publish monographs, and facilitate communication among members.

AEA, other offshoots of ASSA, and forums such as the National Conference of Charities and Correction (NCCC) served as the crucible or laboratories for the development of the cadre of experts who could air their views about matters of policy. Rather than concerning themselves exclusively with theoretical or discipline-bound questions, AEA and other splinter groups afforded their members a viable forum in which to air their views about policy. They created committees to examine such contemporary questions about trade and tariff policies and labor conditions, and their members also served as the first group of policy experts serving state and local governments, as well as increasingly the federal government. Ely, for example, not only was a major figure in establishing AEA but also, while assistant professor at Johns Hopkins University, served on the Maryland and Baltimore tax commissions (Smith, 1991). Likewise, in its formative years prior to World War II, American sociology and social work had a fair share of practically minded social reformers, including the likes of Jane Addams, Charles Ellwood, Graham Taylor, Mary Richmond, Robert Woods, Paul V. Kellogg, and Robert MacIver (Mills, 1943; Turner, 2007).

ASSA's organizational splintering was nonetheless important given the dominance of positivism in the social sciences and the quest for objectivity through the first half of the twentieth century (Bannister, 1987; Manicas, 1987), as well as the influx of academics into government agencies and departments during World War I and World War II (Smith, 1991). In one respect, whether social science practitioners were academics or not, the tension between knowledge and reform remained and universities invariably sought to jettison faculty who were deemed "politically incorrect" at the time (e.g., see Gruber, 1972). Academic social scientists, however, were able to wrap their reform intentions in the mantle of professional prerogative, shielding them from consequences of advocacy that otherwise would expose them to severe risk. Columbia University's John Bates Clark (1897), who articulated the role of political scientists as properly trained to look beneath the surface of industrial society and inform the public of their findings, was an example of such. As emerging professionals in the early decades of twentieth century America, social scientists increasingly tempered both the form and substance of their advocacy, and the tension between reform and knowledge reappeared as a conflict between advocacy and objectivity (Furner, 2011).

Prior to World War I, objectivity in what was then the emerging professionalization of the social sciences was thought about in several ways: first, as deriving from the nature of the subject matter, as in Ward's notion that "pure" sociology dealt exclusively with the consequences of non-purposive human behavior; second, as the methods used by trained observers, as in Giddings's increased emphasis on statistics; and finally, as the attitude of the unbiased observer, the most common use of the term (Bannister, 1987). The formation of professional associations such as the American Economic Association (AEA), the American Political Science Association (APSA), and the like dampened but did not extinguish the reformist ethos characteristic of ASSA from which they sprang. Economics, political science, and sociology had applied sides aimed at improving social functioning.

Between the Civil War and World War I, a particular strain of positivism with references to precisely measurable, deterministic physical processes had come to characterize scientific accounts of human conduct, pitting the likes of Herbert Spencer against William James. As a social Darwinist, Spencer had promoted an environmental determinism that had little room for individual influence on events, whereas the philosopher and psychologist William James had posited more proximate causes of human conduct and attributed to the will the power of attending to particular aspects of one's environment rather than others (Cooley, 1920; James, 1897; Spencer, 1881). Social reformers moved away from alleviating hardship through individual charity and increasingly to eliminating collective ills through sustained research that attended to broad structural and environmental causes of these collective ills. New institutional forms that brought together larger groups of researchers for long-term investigation took shape, with the backing of new general-purpose philanthropic foundations. The Carnegie Corporation, founded in 1911, and the Rockefeller Foundation, founded in 1913, brought unparalleled resources to social research. The Russell Sage Foundation, set up in 1907, served as a bridge from the former amateur social investigators to the emerging social scientists, who served in the traditional sphere of state and local policy while helping to create a national policy elite that increasingly looked to the federal government for solutions to the nation's social problems (Bulmer & Bulmer, 1981; Camic, 2007; Karl & Katz, 1981; Mafinezam, 2003; Smith, 1991).

Along a slightly different vein, under a congressional charter signed by President Abraham Lincoln in 1863, the National Research Council (NRC) was created in 1916 to coordinate the work of U.S. scientists during World War I. The National Research Council (NRC) was reorganized in 1919 on a permanent basis, with funding totally from the private sector, including $5 million from the Carnegie Foundation to provide a building in Washington and maintain its administration. Throughout the 1920s, the National Research Council (NRC) served primarily as an administrative agency for the distribution and management of scientific research funds for foundations and other funding sources supporting scientific research, along with having a group of national experts to make decisions and exercise control over the expenditure of grants (Feuer & Maratano, 2010; Karl, 1969; National Research Council, 1933). The Social Service Research Council (SSRC), established in 1923 and funded by the Laura Spelman Rockefeller Trust, drew researchers from across the country and fostered interdisciplinary research aimed at addressing contemporary social problems and public policy (Bryson, 2009; Laski, 1928; Solovey, 2004; Worcester, 2001). Although different from many policy studies of today, these early research enterprises brought together technical experts with private citizens and officials of municipal governments across the country (Camic, 2007; Karl & Katz, 1981; Mafinezam, 2003; Smith, 1991).

The emergence and development of these foundations, particularly the Russell Sage Foundation, nurtured a "faculty of experts" who did original social scientific research in a setting different from discipline-based faculties in the universities (Mafinezam, 2003). Although committed to educational and sometimes advocacy work—social-survey, statistical research and analysis of social conditions were viewed as means of raising awareness of social problems, of rousing the public to intelligent action— these researchers thought of themselves as nonetheless neutral scientific investigators. Between 1900 and 1928 about 2,700 such surveys were undertaken in the United States, including the Pittsburgh Survey, funded by the Russell Sage Foundation and directed by Paul V. Kellogg (1912), which by means of team research was the first to examine the effects of industrialization on the social life of one city (Greenwald & Anderson, 1996), resulting in a six-volume study of Pittsburgh's housing, sanitation, and working conditions, and whose final volume was published in 1914.

In addition to such prominent figures in the history of the social work profession as Hull House's Jane Addams (1909, 1910; Addams & De Forest, 1902) and the Franklin Delano Roosevelt New Deal administrator Harry Hopkins (1934), another leading example was Mary van Kleeck, a graduate of Smith College in 1904, who began her career working for a settlement house in New York, where she surveyed the conditions of working women. She joined the Russell Sage Foundation and in 1909 became head of its Department of Industrial Studies. Her work and that of colleagues at the foundation (e.g., see van Kleeck, 1910, 1913, 1915, 1919) paved the way for her participation in government research projects in the Department of Labor during and after World War I, projects that in part led to the creation of the U.S. Women's Bureau (Smith, 1991).

The early social scientists such as Mary van Kleeck were committed to the idea of public education, yet as their investigatory work became increasingly systematic and specialized, the relation between the expert and the public shifted, in a sense, from acting as doctors seeking to prevent and cure social ills to scientists of efficiency, experts in the techniques and methods of institutional management (Smith, 1991). By about 1910 the quest for efficiency had gained wide political currency, spurred in part by Frederick Taylor (1915), who had toiled since the 1880s to uncover scientific principles of management. Experts began to carve out permanent places within the bureaucratic domain of government; they set up bureaus of municipal research to advance the cause of efficient government. Henry Bruere, a student of economist and sociologist Thorstein Veblen at the University of Chicago, a student of political science at Columbia University, and a law degree recipient from Harvard University, helped organize the New York Bureau of Municipal Government, one of the best known of the new agencies, in 1907. By 1910 the bureau had 46 staff and by 1911 it ran the Training School for Public Service, the first in the United States dedicated to public administration. This was the linear ancestor of the Maxwell School of Syracuse University, which was the first university in the nation to offer graduate professional education in public administration, beginning in 1924. Also in 1910, seeking greater executive control of the budgetary process, President William Howard Taft set up the Commission on Economy and Efficiency, naming Frederick Cleveland of the New York Bureau chairman. Although the committee's work—which was reported in 1912 and went nowhere under the newly elected President Woodrow Wilson, who had little interest in budgetary reform—the proponents retreated to the New York Bureau. With financial assistance from the Rockefeller Foundation, these budget reformers kept their ideas alive in Washington by establishing in 1916 the private Institute for Government Research, which expanded and was renamed the Brookings Institution in 1927.

Robert S. Brookings was a retired St. Louis businessman who at the time of his initial appointment to the institute's board was then president of the Board of Trustees of Washington University. The institute chair was Frank Goodnow, a scholar of public administration—having held the first American chair in the field at Columbia University—and president of Johns Hopkins University (Smith, 1991). The institute's first director, William Willoughby, a Johns Hopkins graduate, had been a statistician for the Labor Department and worked for both the U.S. Bureau of the Census and the Taft Commission on Economy and Efficiency. In 1919, Willoughby helped organize congressional hearings on budgetary reform, drafted a bill for the House Appropriations Committee, and lobbied to get the bill passed. President Wilson vetoed the bill, but it found favor with President Warren G. Harding who signed the Budget and Accounting Act in 1921. Budgetary reform was viewed by the institute's staff as nonpartisan administrative reform separate from political domains, adhering to the distinction between politics and administration that President Wilson (1887) had advanced as an academic—Wilson had completed the PhD in history and political science from Johns Hopkins University in 1886 and held academic appointments at Bryn Mawr College and Wesleyan University before going to Princeton University in 1890, where he served as president from 1902 to 1910 (Smith, 1991).

In 1923 Brookings endowed a graduate department of government and economics at Washington University, St. Louis, whose curriculum reflected practical problems of government. Due to problems with Missouri tax law, the graduate program was reincorporated as a separate entity in the District of Columbia. In this innovative program, there were no formal courses, credits, or majors. Students were expected to work on practical projects with members of the staff at the Institute for Government Research and the Institute of Economics, with the aim of teaching students to solve contemporary problems. Friction developed between specialists in public administration, the economists, and teachers in the graduate program. At issue was the role of the expert in government and the intellectual tools that would influence policy. With a disdain for partisan politics, public administration experts wanted students to master accounting and finance, expressing continued faith in scientific methods and nonpartisan expertise. They criticized the graduate school for its focus on history and theory and its neglect of applied government. The economists explored broader issues including tariff and trade policies, agricultural policy, and the disposition of international war debts. They published books designed to guide policymakers through these complex topics. The graduate school's dean, Walter Hamilton, challenged the view that nonpartisan experts could determine the public interest and contended that unacknowledged choices among values lurked beneath the surface of policies. In Hamilton's view, policymakers needed broader training in the liberal arts to learn what values were at issue and how to think about ordering them. The graduate school closed; the Institute for Government Research and the Institute of Economics merged and formed the present-day Brookings Institution in 1927. What began as an effort to make federal agencies more efficient, the Brookings Institution continued to address budgetary and tax policies, international trade and economic issues, and agencies for international cooperation while retaining its language of efficiency (Smith, 1991).

Between World War I and II, objectivists in general took a more extreme position about the premises that human volition and subjective consciousness have no place in social science. Objectivity meant more than lack of bias; it lay in the elimination of the psychological dimensions of experience and of the willing, feeling self. Further, neutrality in matters of ethics and public policy—that is, refraining from passing judgments or setting up ethical standards for human conduct—was more strictly observed across the social sciences academic disciplines. Such "objectivism" took various forms depending on the academic discipline: in philosophy, the referent linguistics of Charles K. Ogden and I.A. Richards (1923), and later logical positivism; in jurisprudence, the legal realism of Karl Llewellyn (1930/2008) and Jerome Frank (1930/2009); in psychology, the behaviorism of John B. Watson (1930), and the push for educational testing; in political science, the public opinion surveys and other empirical work of Harold Lasswell (1935/1990) and Charles Merriam (1924); in economics, the institutionalism of Wesley C. Mitchell (1925, 1927), who was also one of the main organizers of the National Bureau of Economic Research (NBER) set up in 1920; and in sociology, in the works of William F. Ogburn (1922), F. Stuart Chapin (1920/2009), and Luther Lee Bernard (1911) (Backhouse & Fontaine, 2010; Bannister, 1987).

Among other things that detracted from the need for and use of social scientists during World War I, such as some anthropologists being used as spies (Boas, 1919), the war effort also showed the vast productive capacities of the United States while exposing a dearth of knowledge about the national economy and how essential statistical data were for sound planning and efficient economic management. Such concerns prompted Mitchell to organize the National Bureau of Economic Research (NBER), a new type of research institute that would collect data the government did not have at hand and whose empirical investigations would yield both theoretical insights about the economy and practical, tentative guidelines for policy-making (Mitchell, 1922, 1927). For example, Mitchell contended that forecasting of economic events, however tentative, nonetheless had a sound scientific basis and was a valuable phase of economic study—even erroneous forecasts enable researchers, policymakers, and businesspeople to learn from such mistakes and make adjustments (Mitchell & van Kleeck, 1923).

It was Herbert Hoover, however, who made a decade-long experiment with ways of connecting research and policy (Critchlow, 1986; Himmelberg, 1975; Karl, 1969; Metcalf, 1975; Smith, 1991; Tobin, 1995). As secretary of the Commerce Department from 1921 to 1929—who had also chaired the President's Conference on Unemployment in 1923 and worked with the National Research Council (NRC)—as president, Hoover's views reflected a basic consensus among "enlightened" business leaders, economists, and philanthropists, who saw the business cycle and irregular employment not as inevitable features of capitalism, the former a result of natural processes of overproduction and the latter necessary for a pool of surplus labor, but rather as aberrations, as signs of economic waste and inefficiency. Funded in part by the Rockefeller Foundation and drawing social scientists from the National Bureau of Economic Research (NBER), the Russell Sage Foundation, and elsewhere, Hoover fully expected his Research Committee on Social Trends to produce a thorough statement of social fact as a guide to social policy. The 1933 two-volume 1,500 page report, *Recent Social Trends in the United States,* however, was primarily descriptive, evaded the Depression, lacked agreement about diagnosis of the state of the economy, and, despite its comprehensive, analytic, and unbiased attributes, had little impact as a serviceable tool in guiding policy. Instead, the report exposed the gap between knowledge and its applications to policy: it offered neither clear remedies nor a framework for discussing whether the economic system needed repair or restructuring—something more than mere inefficiencies seemed to be at work. The value of social science knowledge as a contributing factor in policy deliberations and political action was severely questioned (Smith, 1991).

The economic crisis of the 1930s provided policy experts an unparalleled opportunity to promote solutions. During his campaign for president, Franklin D. Roosevelt amassed a "Brain Trust" of academics to hammer out many of the initiatives that were eventually incorporated into the New Deal legislation. Unlike Hoover, the engineer deeply committed to scientific methods of fact-finding and deliberation, Roosevelt reached out to experts for something to try, to take action that met exigencies of the unprecedented national crisis. The rhetoric of economic and social experimentation, which was cast in terms of assessing the merits of proposed adjustments to and planning of programs and legislation, became commonplace among social scientists and politicians. During the legislative rush of 1933, the demand for knowledgeable researchers was insatiable as social science researchers from the Russell Sage Foundation, the National Bureau of Economic Research (NBER), and the Social Service Research Council (SSRC) in New York were lured to Washington to serve emergency agencies, such as the Federal Emergency Relief Administration and the Works Progress Administration. Brookings researchers were also enlisted, but broke with the administration over price-setting provisions in the version of the National Industrial Recovery Act that was finally passed (Smith, 1991).

By 1938, with most of the New Deal programs in place, roughly 7,800 social scientists were working in the federal government, with over 5,000 of them economists. The newly launched Social Security Administration housed economists, demographers, and statisticians who did research that private agencies could not do, collecting social and economic data on a huge scale, analyzing programs, and looking at long-term needs of the elderly, children, and the disabled. Research in older federal agencies like the Bureau of Agricultural Economics, the Children's Bureau, and the Women's Bureau got an additional impetus. Scholarly disagreements and political controversies ensued. Economic planners, such as Rexford G. Tugwell from Columbia University and Simon Patten from the University of Pennsylvania, comfortable with a degree of corporate concentration, clashed with those who cursed bigness and wanted to restore free-market competition, such as Benjamin Cohen from Harvard University, and Harvard law school graduates David Lilienthal and Charles Wyzanski (Smith, 1991).

A different type of research organization, the Twentieth Century Fund (TCF), also came into its own during this period, founded and funded by Edward A. Filene, the onetime department store magnate who devoted a portion of his fortune in 1911 to establishing a research organization interested in workers' cooperatives, the Cooperative League. Broadening its scope in 1919, the League was renamed the Twentieth Century Fund. Operating from Boston and New York, the Twentieth Century Fund adapted more quickly than the National Bureau of Economic Research and the Russell Sage Foundation to the fast-paced policymaking in the 1930s, in part because it focused on useable knowledge, a combination of laboratory research and practical experience, and was generally amenable to federal intervention. The Twentieth Century Fund assembled large committees of prominent scholars, businesspeople, and public officials to oversee teams of researchers and writers who produced compendia of expert opinions on policy issues rather than original research, a sharp contrast to the National Bureau of Economic Research. It served as a broker of ideas, discussing the merits of policy proposals to address issues related to the stock market, labor relations, and problems of the elderly, health, and international debt structure and disseminating related distilled expert recommendations primarily to the president and officials in the executive branch of government and occasionally to members of Congress. The Twentieth Century Fund provided a forum for winnowing proposals and, along with research institutes such as Brookings and the Rockefeller Foundation, supported the National Bureau of Economic Research and the Social Service Research Council, and functioned as an instrument for building an elite consensus on policy (Karl & Katz, 1981; Smith, 1991).

By the end of the 1930s, federal activism had transformed the wider public arena for debates about policies. As Karl and Katz (1981) note, this was a substantive cultural and institutional shift given the traditional unwillingness of Americans to give the national government the authority to set national standards of social well-being. The national focus moved from states and localities to Washington, with the executive branch of government accumulating considerable intellectual resources and organized interest groups building their own cadres of researchers, analysts, and public relations experts to be better able to engage governmental economists and lawyers. Long-time head of the Rockefeller Foundation's social science division J.H. Willits admonished that scholars drawn to Washington had sacrificed their independence, allying with patrician politicians, whether supporters or opponents of the New Deal and as advocates thinking less in terms of testable, amendable hypotheses and more of policy arguments with political consequences. Willits "decried the growing partisanship of the Washington intellectuals, their work as propagandists, and their resulting 'blindness to inconvenient facts'" (as cited in Smith, 1991, p. 81). Whatever credibility academic or foundation scholars had as disinterested "fact finders" was severely eroded as these experts increasingly occupied policy advisory positions, working as planners and administrators of government programs. Knowledge looked less like a form of higher intellectual counsel than another instrument of political power, prompting Robert Lynd, professor of sociology at Columbia University, to ask the question *"Knowledge for What?"* in a book of that title.

Knowledge for What? (Lynd, 1939) raised doubts about the scientific claims of social scientists and such claims usefulness for policy by asking whose interests were actually served by a discipline pursuing disinterested inquiry into social conditions. Lynd was highly critical of the strictly empirical studies undertaken by the National Bureau of Economic Research, given its tacit assumption that private enterprise and the profit incentive alone were sufficient to guide the application of technical skills to problems of production and supply. He also faulted the Brookings Institution for allowing business interests to define its research agenda, in selection of problems to address and policy options to assess. Lynd admonished social scientists' quest for scientific certainty, professionalism, and service to power, the combination of which removed them from genuine social concerns. Social scientists' concern with technique, whether about research methods or management practices, rendered social scientists irrelevant in discussions of social and political ends. He advised social scientists to go beyond their own culture as the natural source of values and to explore more basic values rooted in people's needs and longings (Smith, 1991).

TWENTIETH CENTURY: WORLD WAR II AND AFTERWARD

World War II provided a response to Lynd's inquiry about the purpose of knowledge, one that despite horrific uses to which science was put—such as eugenics (Kenny, 2002; Lombardo, 2002), systematic slaughter of innocents, and unimaginably destructive weapons—nonetheless restored faith in scientific approaches to problem solving, namely, the goals of defeating fascism and afterward sustaining employment and production, as well as the military and political aims of combatting communist advances during the Cold War of the 1950s and 1960s. Social scientists joined the physicists, mathematicians, chemists and others in the war effort. By mid-1942 some fifteen thousand historians, geographers, linguists, anthropologists, economists, sociologists, and psychologists served in the State Department, Office of War Information, War Production Board, Office of Strategic Services, Bureau of Naval Personnel, Army Information and Education Division, and countless other wartime boards and agencies. Their practical contributions included economic analyses, public opinion surveys, intelligence testing, examinations of stress in combat, and explorations of group dynamics. Among the social sciences, economics emerged from the wartime experience as exerting the most tangible influence on the thinking of government officials and businesspeople, giving rise to new research organizations in and out of government, such as the Committee for Economic Development (CED), and shaping policy in ways other advisory relationships could not (Backhouse & Fontaine, 2010; Lears, 2011; Smith, 1991).

The Great Depression and FDR's New Deal policies were only preludes to debates about the government's role in the economy (Caputo, 1994). Policy research groups such as Brookings, the Twentieth Century Fund, and the National Bureau of Economic Research, took different stances about how best to maintain employment and production after the war, about what tools the government might use to intervene in economic affairs, and about what the limits of such interventions should be. The choice of particular policy instruments shaped the role that economists might play, with the likes of British economist John Maynard Keynes, who argued for government deficit spending or fiscal stimulus to reduce unemployment, and Austrian economist Friedrich Hayek, who argued against such measures for fear of inflation and potential political tyranny (Wapshott, 2011). Brookings threw its lot with opponents of the New Deal, both in Congress and in the business community, and it resisted what became a consensus of Keynesian ideas about demand management. The Twentieth Century Fund identified most closely with formal planning schemes and liberal interpretations of Keynes. The Russell Sage Foundation, which was more heavily swayed by academic sociologists in the mid-1940s, said little about the postwar economy. Amid this alignment among the well-established policy research groups, the Committee for Economic Development (CED) emerged as a major contributor (Smith, 1991).

Founded in 1942, the Committee for Economic Development (CED) was run by businesspeople and funded directly by business rather than by endowed foundations. It established a pattern of publishing scholarly work of individual staff members, while reserving for the business membership the prerogative of issuing institutional policy statements. The Committee for Economic Development's directors created a forum that brought "business thinking" together with representatives of government agencies and the most eminent scholars from American universities. The Committee for Economic Development served as the businessperson's bridge to both professional economists and governmental policymaking. It struck a policy course between orthodox fiscal conservatives, who persistently called for annually balanced budgets and minimal governmental intervention, and the liberal interpreters of Keynes, who had concluded that the economy was so prone to stagnation that continual governmental spending was needed to keep it going. The Committee for Economic Development specifically linked private enterprise to the common good, and it acknowledged a role for government intervention when "the ability of private individuals to better serve the common good" reached its limits" (Benton, 1944, p. 5).

The Committee for Economic Development helped settle the debate on acceptable instruments of postwar economic policy—namely, the use of federal spending (fiscal policy), interest rates, and on occasion tax policy to stimulate and regulate demand. These tools in effect limited the scope of direct governmental involvement in the economy more narrowly than advocates of national planning had foreseen and set the boundaries for serious discussion of policies in the two decades after the war. Research results and policy recommendations that had relied on those scholars whose training had equipped them with tools and techniques of macroeconomics and aggregate economic analysis were given more weight in public policy debates. The economist's theory and analytic techniques were directly linked to policy measures that required the ongoing presence of economists in the government. By 1946 economic insights had become the basis of law—the Employment Act; and theory thereby determined where some economists would sit as governmental advisors, such as on the Council of Economic Advisors (CEA) in the executive branch of government and on the Joint Economic Committee in the legislative branch of government (Bernstein, 2004; Smith, 1991).

In the 1950s the behavioral sciences—which came to mean psychology, sociology, and anthropology—and those parts of economics and political science concerned with individual and group behavior rather than institutions and processes, got a boost from the Ford Foundation, which set up a separate division under the direction of sociologist Bernard Berelson (Lyons, 1969). Grants of some $38.5 million were made over five years, much of it to major universities to enable them to improve conditions and facilities for research in the behavioral sciences. In 1954 the Center for the Advanced Study in the Behavioral Sciences in Palo Alto, California, was established as an independent Ford-launched enterprise.

President John F. Kennedy expressed this optimism in the social sciences, discussing knowledge and political action in an address to Yale's graduates this way:

> What is at stake in our economic decisions today is not some grand warfare of rival ideologies which will sweep the country with passion but the practical management of a modern economy. What we need is not labels and clichés but more basic discussion of the sophisticated and technical questions involved in keeping a great economic machinery moving ahead. . . .

I am suggesting that the problems of fiscal and monetary policies in the sixties as opposed to the kinds of problems we faced in the thirties demand subtle challenges for which technical answers, not political answers, must be provided. These are matters upon which government and business may and in many cases will disagree. They are certainly matters that government and business should be discussing in the most dispassionate, and careful way if we [are] to maintain the kind of vigorous [*sic*] upon which our country depends. (Woolley & Peters, 1962)

As Lyons (1969) reported, in 1962 the president's Science Advisory Committee acknowledged the relevancy of the behavioral sciences and called for expansion of the National Academy of Sciences—National Research Council beyond anthropology and psychology. Shortly after the 1968 report of the National Academy's Advisory Committee on Government Programs in the Behavioral Sciences was submitted, calling for increased use of and support for the behavioral sciences, the National Research Council's Division of Anthropology and Psychology became the Division of Behavioral Sciences, which included anthropology, economics, political science, psychology, and sociology at that time, with history, geography, linguistics, and psychiatry added later.

As Halberstam (1972) chronicled, presidents Kennedy and Lyndon Baines Johnson actively sought academics allured by proximity to action, to seeing their ideas used in the shaping of policy. The assumption then was that policy analysis units would be established at the top of organizations, with top executives and senior line staff as the clients for analysis. These clients were expected to define the perspective, values, and agenda for the analytic activity. The completed analysis was to become an additional resource for decision makers and thereby improve policymaking. Over the next several decades policy sciences developed as a formal branch of study, and ideologically driven think tanks seeking to influence government policies proliferated.

Policy Studies

The policy sciences emerged as an amalgamation of "the philosophies, procedures, techniques, and tools of the management and decision sciences—operations research, systems analysis, simulation, 'war' gaming, game theory, policy analysis, program budgeting, and linear programing" that had become accepted in business, industry, and defense between World War II and the Kennedy and Johnson administrations (Quade, 1970, p. 1). Acknowledging the disparate origins of the policy sciences, Lasswell (1970) identified a converging outlook, particularly about problem orientation and technique synthesis. Problem orientation included the intellectual tasks of goal clarification, trend description, analysis of conditions, projection of future developments, and invention, evaluation, and selection of alternatives. Technique synthesis entailed principles of content (for example, searching for equivalency of reference among theorists or policy participants) and procedure (e.g., establishing "referents" employed in a particular situation). In addition, lest anyone fret about an overemphasis on technique, the policy sciences as then understood also emphasized cultivation of the "creative flash" essential to innovative and realistic problem solutions. Reflecting the heady optimism of the times, Dror (1970, p. 135) characterized this "revolutionary" burgeoning new comprehensive and integrative field of studies as follows:

Establishment of policy sciences as a new supradiscipline involves a scientific revolution, requiring fargoing innovations in basic paradigms. Particularly essential are: (1) Integration between various disciplines, and especially of social sciences with analytical decision approaches; (2) bridging of the "pure" vs. "applied" dichotomy; (3) acceptance of tacit knowledge as a scientific resource; (4) changes in interface between science and values; (5) broad time perspectives; (6) focus on metapolicies; (7) commitment to policymaking improvement; and (8) concern with extrarational and irrational processes, such as creativity.

Unique subjects of policy analysis, opened up by these paradigms, include, among others, (a) policy analysis, which involves critical changes in system analysis so as to permit application to complex policy issues; (b) policy strategies, involving determination of postures and main guidelines for specific policies, such as on degrees of incrementalism vs. innovation and on attitudes to risks; (c) policymaking system redesign, including evaluation and improvement of the policymaking system, e.g., through changes in one-person-centered high-level decision-making, development of politicians, and institutionalization of social experimentation.

Development of policy sciences requires many innovations in research, teaching, and professional activities. It constitutes a main effort to reconstruct the role of intellectualism and rationality in human affairs and, therefore, justifies intense efforts.

Such heady optimism occurred when universities were marked by New Left student protests demanding greater "relevance" to address social problems in light of the Civil Rights movement, the Vietnam War, as well as those issues associated with the increased pace of social change accompanying the technological and cybernetic revolutions of the time (Feuer, 1969; Glazer, 1969; Jerome, 1969; Kerr, 1964; Reagan, 1969; Truman, 1968). The Great Society of the Lyndon Baines Johnson administration fostered the growth of the public policy research industry, with Brookings Institution scholar Henry J. Aaron (1978) noting the infancy, limitations, and disutility of the social sciences, claiming that they "undercut the faith" (p. 159) that led to many of LBJ's programs, and with Princeton professor Richard P. Nathan (1985) taking a more optimistic view about their usefulness as theories and methodologies improved.

The policy sciences offered a way for universities to reverse what *Fortune* magazine editor Max Ways (1969) and others (Biderman, 1970) had claimed was the inward looking discipline approach to specialized knowledge that had become "independent from the direct demands of life" (as cited in Ericson, 1970, p. 434), despite (or perhaps in part because of) the proliferation of positivist-oriented social science research centers (Birnbaum, 1969; Rossi, 1964). Universities set up interdisciplinary centers for the study of public policy designed to produce hybrid doctoral or master's level professionals as research–scientists and practitioners. Those trained in these new programs would assume a variety of roles in policy-making organizations, such as policy analysts, evaluation researchers, knowledge brokers, research feedback disseminators, process monitors, and consultants. The Public Policy Program of the Kennedy School of Government at Harvard University, the Policy Sciences Program at the State University of New York, Buffalo, the Institute of Public Policy Studies at the University of Michigan, and the Graduate School of Industrial Administration at Carnegie-Mellon University were examples of these new graduate programs (Benker, 1971; Bunker, 1971; Crecine, 1971). The 1980s push in social work for research practitioners was quite consistent with this earlier development in the policy sciences (Tripodi, Layalayants, & Zlotnik, 2008).

In addition to finding a home within universities, freestanding or independent research institutes also provided opportunities for the development of the policy sciences. Building on its extensive links to faculty and research institutions in major metropolitan areas such as the University of California at Los Angeles and the New School for Social Research in New York City, the RAND Corporation developed its own graduate program in policy analysis (Wolf, 1971). The program consisted of nine academic quarters of ten weeks each, and the curriculum included:

> (a) an "on-the-job" training segment, comprising ongoing Rand research projects that students will work on, initially in an apprenticeship role, assuming increasing responsibility as training progresses; (b) a seminar workshop based on ongoing and prior Rand studies, conducted by the project leader and participants in the study; and (c) two core courses, one in *concepts and theory* and the other in *tools and techniques,* which would continue through the entire nine quarters. (Wolf, 1971, p. 5)

The apprenticeship/on-the-job segment was viewed as providing research organizations such as RAND a comparative advantage over universities, given immediate and continuous exposure to real policy problems from start to completion of requirements for a doctorate. Qualifying students had to have a master's degree and at least a modest degree of literacy in mathematics, the social sciences, and the physical sciences. As with policy studies in universities, the graduate program at RAND was comprehensive and inclusive, although some modes of contemporary discourse—particularly those associated more with qualitative or interpretive approaches to research—were noticeably absent. A typical course of study in the RAND program would nonetheless include how a problem was initially conceived, how it changed in the course of effort, methodological and data problems encountered in the process of carrying out the analysis and how they were resolved, results and implementation (if any) issuing from the study, and how it might be done differently in light of what was gleaned from participation in the project. The *concept and theory* courses included microeconomic theory, mathematical game theory, decision theory, and organization theory, as well as the politics of policymaking, and law and legal reasoning. *Tools and techniques* included computer software and hardware, multivariate analysis, operations research, linear and dynamic programming, program budgeting, cost-benefit and systems analysis, simulation, and forecasting through Delphi and other techniques (Wolf, 1971).

If anything were lacking in such burgeoning programs in the early 1970s, it was the "frank confrontation of the value issues in the teaching of policy sciences" (Dror, 1971, p. 84). Discussion of values was deemed important to lessen the possibility of "corruption of the policy sciences on the one hand and/or (these two dangers can go together) subordination of the policy sciences to any one particularistic advocacy approach on the other" (p. 84). Tribe (1972) echoed this sentiment when he identified the anesthetizing of moral sentiments or values as one of four main distorting effects of the policy sciences' adherence to the objectivist ideal. A second distorting effect, narrowing the role of rationality, precluded taking account of values in the process of choices associated with problem formation, desired ends or outcomes of policies to the exclusion of considering others, and weights given to assessing probabilities of likely outcomes.

The two remaining distorting effects, typical of economic reasoning and analysis, were collapsing processes into results—that is, treating process as exogenous, and collapsing results into an undifferentiated mass that presupposed a common metric of equivalency valuations when confronted with alternative courses of action. Tribe indicated that each of these distorting effects of adherence to the objectivist ideal were correctable. As the policy sciences developed over the next several decades, they addressed the concerns Tribe raised, and while doing so they had to confront postmodernist thinking, which also encouraged the field to grapple with value issues. Somewhat paradoxically, as the policy sciences adapted to incorporate values analysis as part of their core programming, throughout the 1980s and beyond proliferation of ideologically driven think tanks contributed to the very subordination of much policy analysis to advocacy efforts—about which hopeful proponents of policy studies such as Dror (1971) and of think tanks such as Dror (1984) had warned and not foreseen.

In addition to challenges from postmodernist thinkers, the policy sciences also faced challenges about their usefulness and relevancy by those within the social sciences. Political scientist Edward C. Banfield (1977) noted with alarm the proliferation of policy sciences in universities throughout the United States and in the various branches of the U.S. government. He contended that few social science theories or findings were of much assistance to policymakers, citing as evidence the lackluster results of the Ford Foundation's efforts to produce a handbook of behavioral sciences for policy making. Not only were the policy sciences theoretically bereft, their methods and techniques—steeped as they were in the computer sciences and operations research on one hand and in economic or mathematical modeling on the other—were inappropriate. "It will always be impossible to construct a formal model that will be of use to policymakers," Banfield quipped, "when, as is the case with 'important' problems, one cannot identify all of the crucial parameters or match them with adequate data" (p. 19). Further, political executives and lawmakers did not know enough or were unlikely to learn enough statistics to interpret analysts' reports. The short-term election cycle that framed lawmakers' interest in reelection worked against sustained systematic analysis. Banfield also noted that the policy sciences added to the complexity of social problem solving rather than further clarifying things: in particular, results were too often ambiguous and recommendations less than clear-cut, especially about alternative courses of action. In the final analysis, echoing the art versus science debates about social work practice (Powell, 2003), Banfield contended that policymakers required "not policy science, but good judgment, or better, the union of virtue and wisdom which the ancients called prudence" (p. 31).

By the mid-1980s, however, it was clearly evident that, regardless of institutional setting, whether in universities, in independent research institutes, or in think tanks, policy analyses that disregarded the policy process were inadequate, that politics mattered, and that case studies per se were limited and needed to incorporate the self-awareness of the analyst in the policy process (Ascher, 1987). Reflecting upon what it meant to do an analysis that way was deemed requisite to increasing understanding about issues in the policy process and the characteristics of that process, as well as to enhancing the ability to solve other problems. Despite some internal disciplinary critiques, for the most part social science and policy analysis had so fused theories and techniques that they invariably reflected applications of the same habit of mind, albeit in different settings and for different audiences (Mead, 1985). This is not to suggest that they completely overlapped, that policy analysts and social scientists were interchangeable, or that they did the same things. Behn (1985) insisted that having a client was a requisite for doing policy analysis. This criterion provided a basis for evaluating any piece of policy analysis, making possible an assessment of how demanding and rigorous the analysis would be. As will be seen below when discussing roles of policy analysts and again when discussing the proliferation of think tanks, having a client nonetheless poses challenges to policy analysts who worry about maintaining the integrity of their work while helping policymakers do their job.

The key standard for evaluating the merits of policy analysis, Behn (1985) contended, is policy relevance, helping a policy-making client do his or her job, vis-à-vis the social scientists' standard of contributing to advancing their respective disciplines by producing general theory. For Behn, "policy significance is more demanding than the standard of statistical significance, which dominates academic social science" (p. 430). Policymakers invariably juggle important concerns beyond the development of scientifically reproducible, statistically significant tests of propositions that relate policy actions to policy consequences, a prime concern for discipline-oriented social scientists. Other concerns of policymakers include more substantive matters such as managing conflicts between interests, obtaining general agreement on a particular course of action, working out how action on one issue affected other issues, even if apparently unrelated. The "good" policy analyst must be able to expose conflicting values that affect a policy choice, develop creative options, specify uncertainties about possible consequences of policy options, develop outcome measures so actions can be evaluated and modified accordingly, and design strategies for political adoption and organizational implementation. The professional standard that the policy analyst must be able to present all of this "clearly, concisely, and convincingly," Behn opined, "disqualifies most social scientists from the business" (p. 430). Testing relationships between variables over which policymakers had little or no control further reduces the policy relevancy of much social science research.

Also accenting differences between academic and nonacademic policy analysts, Cook and Vaupel (1985) suggested three styles of research that varied by audience: (1) policy analysts—decision-maker clients; (2) policy researchers—present and future policymakers, policy analysts, academics, the public; and (3) applied social science researchers—academics and policy analysts. Cook and Vaupel further commented that the type of products also varied: policy analysts were more likely to produce staff memos, summaries, and position papers that were neither prepared for nor expected to be published; policy researchers produced monographs, the research agendas of which were defined by a particular policy problem rather than the needs and interests of academic disciplines; and applied social science researchers produced technical articles, reflecting a primary concern with obtaining answers that were reasonable given available information rather than to use the most sophisticated available techniques or to confirm disciplinary preferences or prejudices.

Although the policy sciences met their interdisciplinary objectives, fending off challenges from single-discipline approaches and the general-law approach associated with "behavioralism," overreliance on instrumental reasoning, a technocratic orientation, and application of neoclassical economics to social science issues remained problematic (Ascher, 1987; deLeon, 1994). Neoclassical economists assumed a generalizable preference ordering to explain, for example, how people decide on family size, for nations, whether to wage war, or for politicians what platform issues to advance. For the policy sciences no *a priori* objective functions could be taken for granted: even Maslow's value hierarchy would be regarded as very unlikely to hold universally, stripped as it was of any contextually driven variation. Further, for the policy sciences maximization efforts of nongovernmental individuals were not assumed to be confined to oneself or one's family unit, as was the case in neoclassical economics. Value maximization, to the extent it occurred, did serve as a point of departure for the policy sciences, with many potential beneficiaries, yet unlike neoclassical economics posited little confidence that such pursuits yielded general laws in the aggregate (such as equilibrium) or even precise answers in particular instances. The policy sciences placed much more emphasis on conditions that affected the achievement of valued outcomes. Contextual conditions included recognizing the importance of and accounting for the intentions of policymakers and variations in other more subjective factors (Ascher, 1987).

Proliferation of Think Tanks

As an organizational form continually negotiating the institutional space it occupies as a significant contributor shaping policy debates and promoting public policies, think tanks are a late twentieth century phenomenon (Medvetz, 2012). They emerged as a distinct form of social organization from a proliferation of policy research centers after 1970, increasingly competing with each other for funding, media visibility, and political attention. Over time, despite ideological differences they became increasingly linked, for example, by sharing personnel, organizing conferences, and producing similar products, such as policy briefs, background reports, issue briefs, and the like. Think tanks came to occupy an intellectual niche between academia, politics, the media, and the market, with several cultural and institutional markers. For a more thorough treatment, see Medvetz (2012).

The idea of think tanks as currently understood had not developed in the 1960s when the Kennedy and Johnson administrations actively pursued scholars. By one estimate over two-thirds of think tanks that existed in the United States by the mid-1990s were founded after 1970 (Rich, 2000, pp. 64–65). At that time, the Brookings Institution and the RAND Corporation typified the role of policy analysts in and out of government service. RAND, which had its own programs with students earning doctorates, was launched in 1946 as a freestanding division within the Douglas Aircraft Company and became independent of Douglas in 1948 (Campbell, 2004; Fortune & Schweber, 1993; Specht, 1960). In particular, the contract research organization RAND and *think tank* became synonymous as a way of organizing and financing research, development, and technical evaluation that would be done at the behest of government agencies but was carried out by privately run nonprofit research centers. RAND also contributed to the development of new analytic methods characteristic of systems and strategic thinking, of which operations research (OR), Program Planning and Budgeting Systems (PPBS), game theory, and cost-benefit analyses were examples, adding to the existing array of policy serviceable tools and techniques such as survey research, institutional analysis, and aggregate statistical studies (Fischer, 1991; Hart, 1978; Mirowski, 2005; Sapolsky, 2004; Smith 1991).

Many of the paradoxes associated with the heady optimism of linking scientific knowledge in general and social scientific knowledge in particular to political action became increasingly apparent—pointed out by those on the left and right of the political spectrum throughout the 1960s (Biderman, 1970; Lyons, 1969; Medvetz, 2012). Reactions to the cancellation of Project Camelot, a military sponsored social science study of revolutionary processes highlighted connections between Cold War politics, military patronage, and American social science, helping to undermine mainstream scholarly epistemological commitments to objectivity and related ideals, such as value-neutrality and professional autonomy (Solovey, 2001). Similarly, the War on Poverty, urban and race-related strife, antiwar protests, and the emergent modern feminist movement challenged many operating assumptions about the relationship between the state and science. Horowitz (1970) showed how social scientists engaged in government, such as those in Project Camelot, were committed to advocacy models defined by politicians and how such social scientists did not establish or verify policy but rather legitimated it.

In particular, as scholars and policymakers alike highlighted the limitations of the social sciences in addressing social problems, policy experts and advocates first on the left of the political spectrum and then on the right became ascendant, (1) creating an ideological divide that made little pretense of objectivity, and (2) legitimating an organizational form labeled think tanks, as an alternative to universities, for nurturing and promoting policy analysts and commentators who sought to shape public policy and social action (Easterbrook, 1986; Fischer, 1991; Medvetz 2007). On the one hand, there was Daniel Patrick Moynihan (1970)—whose earlier report about the black family in America (U.S. Department of Labor, Office of Planning and Research, 1965) was part of the reason for the Office of Economic Opportunity (OEO) policies and programs designed to expand employment opportunities primarily for urban black

American males (Cravens, 2004; Horowitz, 1970), but who nonetheless indicted the War on Poverty. There were also Marris and Rein (1969), whose examination of community action programs highlighted the incompatibility between serious research that had to adhere to a definite course of action to allow for testing of theoretically driven hypotheses and policies and programs that were inevitably tentative, non-committal, and adaptive (Fischer, 1991; Smith, 1991).

On the other hand, situated on the political left compared to Brookings and RAND, was the Institute for Policy Studies (IPS), opened in 1963, and the Urban Institute, currently one of Washington's largest policy research organizations and founded in 1968. Funded primarily by a handful of wealthy families with liberal leanings such as Sears' heir Philip Stern, James Warbug (banking), and the Samuel Rubin Foundation (Fabergé perfumes), the public scholars at IPS were dismissive of objectivity and suspicious of claims of a value-free social science that could direct policy. IPS co-founder Marcus Raskin (1971), for example, criticized social science in general and operations research in particular for reinforcing hierarchical aspects or the "pyramidal structure" (p. xiii) of American society and government, contending that policy experts and their analytic tools were antithetical to ideals of participatory democracy (Smith, 1991). Retaining a faith in enlightened human action as self-perfecting, Raskin's "existential pragmatism rooted in experience and experiment" (p. xxv) called for reconstituting society based on a new kind of knowledge, with empathy and verification replacing the meaningless facts gathered by bureaucratic policy analysts as guides to social action (Lowi, 1971; Michelson, 1971).

On the political right, originally founded by businesspeople in 1943, the American Enterprise Association was renamed the American Enterprise Institute (AEI) for Public Policy Research in 1960 at the request of board member economist turned policy entrepreneur William J. Baroody. Labeling Brookings "liberal," AEI subsequently evolved into one of Washington's most prominent policy-research centers, with half its revenues from corporations, one-third from foundations (e.g., John M. Olin Foundation and the J. Howard Pew Freedom Trust, part of the Pew Charitable Trusts), and much of the remainder from individuals. Through part-time arrangements, visiting fellowships, consultancies, grant-funded research projects, and resident fellowships, AEI built an expanding network of conservative academics and politicians during the 1990s, including former president Gerald R. Ford, Melvin Laird, Arthur Burns, Herbert Stein, Jeane J. Kirkpatrick, Murray Weidenbaum, James Miller, Lawrence Korb, and Michael Novik. In addition, Irving Kristol, the founding editor of *The Public Interest* and professor of social thought at New York University, made AEI his Washington base of operations (Smith, 1991).

The Heritage Foundation was founded by a group of conservative legislative aides in 1973, with nearly half (about 44%) its financial resources coming from individual donors such as Colorado brewer Joseph Coors and Mellon heir John Scaife, and more than one-quarter (28%) from foundations (e.g., the John M. Olin Foundation and the oil and gas Noble Foundation of Oklahoma). Many of its domestic economic policy analysts focus on budget cutting and tax reform proposals and they advocate for free market approaches, especially about environmental issues. Members of Congress and their staffs comprise the primary clientele of Heritage, but its two hundred plus publications per year, from short policy briefs to full length books such as *Mandate for Leadership: Policy Management in a Conservative Administration,* edited by Charles L. Heatherly, enable it influence a broader market. Its long-standing president Edwin Feulner (1985) explicitly laid out Heritage's agenda to promote conservative ideas and shape the political agenda. In the 1980s, Heritage actively promoted the idea of supply side economics advanced by business economist Laffer (1981) to opinion leaders in Washington, by coauthoring *Essays in Supply Side Economics* with the Institute for Research on the Economics of Taxation and cohosting a conference that attracted 400 members of Congress, administration officials, professors, and media representatives. In its efforts to make conservative ideas mainstream, Heritage has come close to collapsing the legal boundary separating research and education from outright lobbying, and it explicitly dismisses any pretense to objectivity, elevating its advocacy role. Staff at Heritage marshal facts and ideas to serve their cause, as one staffer explained:

> We state upfront what our beliefs are and admit that we are combatants in the battle of ideas. . . . We are not just for better government and efficiency, we are for particular ideas . . . the staff uses its expertise to mobilize arguments. They are advocates. . . . We make it clear to them that they are not joining an academic organization but one committed to certain beliefs. We tell them that they will write papers with a format that is not for a professional peer group. (Smith, 1991, pp. 205–206)

The resignation of U.S. Senator Jim DeMint (R-SC) in December 2012 to become president of the Heritage Foundation is telling, suggesting continuity with the role of advocacy. DeMint helped ignite the anti–tax increase grassroots Tea Party Movement that had played a prominent role in securing a Republican majority in the U.S. House of Representatives in the 2010 mid-term elections and that opposed, albeit unsuccessfully, the reelection of Barack Obama in 2012 (Tea Party Movement, 2012). Upon resigning from the U.S. Senate, DeMint was reported to have stated "I've decided to join the Heritage Foundation at a time when the conservative movement needs strong leadership in the battle of ideas" (Steinhauer, 2012b). Elsewhere he stated, "We must take our case to the people themselves, and we must start where all good marketing starts: with research. . . .We need to test the market and our message to communicate more effectively" (DeMint, 2013; also cited in Silverstein, 2013).

For Heritage and other contemporary **policy institutes** such as RAND and Cato, political ideas have become commodities to be sold, experts are those who gain access to media, and the objective is for more immediate or short-term political gains (Fischer, 1991; McGann, 2007; Stahl, 2008). Such policy research centers have come to occupy the organizational space that became known more formally as "think tanks," in effect nullifying earlier contentions by Lane (1966) and Bell (1960), which were suspect even then (Hodges, 1967), that scientific knowledge had eclipsed ideology in the making of social policy (Segal, 2004). Based on a study of 410 think tanks, Minozzi (2006) reported a positive correlation between percentage increases in ideological statements within mission statements and percentage increases of total funding from private donors, in 2003, when controlling for a variety of other factors such as total expenses, age, and number of mentions in newspapers. The finding suggested market forces are contributing to contemporary partisanship among think tanks.

Access to information about such policy experts is readily available. Heritage, which has long published press handbooks and directories of experts such as *The Annual Guide to Public Policy Experts,* maintains an online (http://www.policyexperts.org/) listing of U.S. and international policy experts: such scholars can be searched by name, organization, country, state, region, and by issue, with links provided to their curricula vitae, résumés, and biographies, as well as indicating whether they testified before a state or federal legislative committee. RAND also has an online list of policy experts with links to their curricula vitae, publications, and commentaries, many of which are downloadable, in addition to a media resources icon indicating whether they are available for interviews and, if so, with information about how to contact them to do so (http://www.rand.org/media/experts.html).

Also, with seed money from the Fred C. Koch Trust, the self-proclaimed libertarian Cato Institute was founded in San Francisco in 1977 and moved to Washington, DC, in 1981 when it began to exert a significant intellectual influence on national policy debates (Smith, 1991). Cato also has an online list of policy exerts, although given its libertarian ethos, with a far more limited number than those of Heritage or RAND but also with additional links to curricula vitae and publications, speeches, and commentaries, many of which are also downloadable (http://www.cato.org/people/experts.html). As with the Heritage Foundation, Cato explicitly states advocacy as a major component of its mission to promote its brand of free-market ideas:

> The mission of the Cato Institute is to increase the understanding of public policies based on the principles of limited government, free markets, individual liberty, and peace. The Institute will use the most effective means to originate, advocate, promote, and disseminate applicable policy proposals that create free, open, and civil societies in the United States and throughout the world. (Cato Institute, 2011)

Given their antipathy to government sponsored initiatives and programs, other Cato-like libertarian think tanks such as Maine's Hannibal Hamlin Institute, Pennsylvania's Commonwealth Foundation, California's Claremont Institute, and Colorado's Independence Institute, the Dallas-based National Center for Policy Analysis, the Manhattan Institute for Policy Research, and Florida's James Madison Institute, focus on state and local level governments, many seeking to create free-market based policy models that are applicable elsewhere (Smith, 1991).

Case in Point Appendix B.1: Think Tanks and Welfare Reform

Think tanks were most influential in shaping the conceptual shift that established dependency and personal responsibility as the core problems of welfare reform efforts throughout the 1980s and 1990 (Medvetz, 2007, 2012). As Caputo (2011) notes, dependency on cash welfare payments, particularly those of the Aid to Families with Dependent Children (AFDC) program, eclipsed poverty as a social problem during this period. As the more socially and economically conservative think tanks that proliferated during this period advocated their positions in media debates leading up to the welfare reform legislation in 1996, the purported neutral or objective expertise of their fellows and scholars (e.g., political scientist Charles Murray who at different times was employed by three conservative think tanks: the Manhattan Institute for Policy Research, the Heritage Foundation, and the American Enterprise Institute where he is employed at the time of this writing) provided ample cover for policymakers to marginalize independently produced opposing views (e.g., sociologist William J. Wilson—University of Chicago and Harvard) in the public interest.

Medvetz's (2007, 2012) sociological explanatory account and historical overview of the development and contemporary understanding of the role of think tanks in the United States highlights the decided structural shift in the 1970s and thereafter when objective analysis was summarily rejected. The merits of think tanks' intellectual products were judged less by academic, scholarly, or objective standards and more by politics, business, and journalism. This was most evident in the welfare reform debates in the 1990s, the closing Case in Point of this volume.

Skill Building Exercises

1. Discuss how the historical tension between reform and knowledge, between advocacy and objectivity, informs and influences the contemporary professional mandate for policy practice by social workers.

2. Given the self-proclaimed partisan biases of many contemporary think tanks, discuss the merits of NASW's launching the Social Work Policy Initiative (SWPI).

3. What lessons about the integrity of policy analysis can social workers draw from the professionalization of the social sciences and social work and the development of the policy sciences?

Web Sites

Association for Policy Analysis and Management—http://www.appam.org/

Association for Research on Nonprofit Organizations and Voluntary Action—http://www.arnova.org/

Center for American Progress Experts—http://www.americanprogress.org/about/experts-alphabetical/

Council on Social Work Education—http://www.cswe.org/

Government Accountability Office (GAO – formerly, the General Accounting Office)—http://www.gao.gov/

Information for Practice—http://ifp.nyu.edu/

Institute for Policy Studies—http://www.ips-dc.org/

National Association of Social Workers—http://socialworkers.org/

NIRA's World Directory of Think Tanks—http://www.nira.or.jp/past/ice/nwdtt/2005/index.html

Rand policy experts—http://www.rand.org/media/experts.html

Social Entrepreneurs: Pioneering Social Change—YouTube video (9:04 minutes) http://www.youtube.com/watch?v=jk5LI_WcosQ

Social Work Policy Institute—http://www.socialworkpolicy.org/

The Annual Guide to Public Policy Experts—http://www.policyexperts.org/

The Digital Library at the University of North Texas [for Congressional Research Service Reports]—http://digital.library.unt.edu/explore/collections/CRSR/

The Library of Congress: THOMAS—http://thomas.loc.gov/home/thomas.php

Web Center for Social Research Methods—http://www.socialresearchmethods.net/

WWW Virtual Library: Evaluation—http://www.policy-evaluation.org/

Glossary

Administrative feasibility: the likelihood that a department or agency can implement the policy or deliver the program well.

Advocacy Coalition Framework: used to analyze processes associated with policymaking; assesses the learning that occurs by coalition members and its relationship to policy change within *policy subsystems* over time

Cost-benefit analysis: a widely used tool that summarizes both positive and negative consequences of a proposed policy or program, and then weighs these against each other. A common metric or unit of measure is determined, usually in dollars. Cost-benefit analysis relies on several monetization methods (e.g., *travel cost method, avoided cost method, contingent valuation methods*) to determine one's willingness to pay, the dollar amount, for one more unit of the good in question. Cost-benefit analysis also includes determination of *shadow prices* (intangible costs and benefits).

Critical thinking: mental processes of conceptualizing, synthesizing, and evaluating information that is clear, rational, open-minded, and informed by evidence.

Decision-theoretic evaluations: use descriptive methods to produce reliable and valid information about policy outcomes that are explicitly valued by multiple stakeholders.

Difference Principle: a social welfare function in which a reallocation of resources is justified to the extent that the reallocation is to the greatest benefit of the least advantaged members of society.

Disjointed incrementalism: a mode of policy analysis that relies on partisan mutual adjustments as an effective way of improving the political nature of the policy-making process, primarily by curbing the power dimension often associated with politics.

Effectiveness: the likelihood of achieving policy goals and objectives or demonstrated achievement of them.

Efficiency: an assessment of achieving program goals or providing benefits in relation to costs.

Elite theory: of public policy portrays policy as a function of a governing elite whose preferences and values influence how social problems and policy responses get formulated by virtue of their control over and leadership roles among large corporate and financial institutions.

Equity: fairness or justice in the distribution of a policy's cost, benefits, and risks across population subgroups.

Evaluability assessment: a set of procedures designed to analyze decision-making systems that benefit from performance information by clarifying the goals, objectives, and assumptions against which performance is to be measured.

Explanatory theories: usually meant to be viewed as complementary, essential, and legitimate domains of policy analysis, rather than as competing, adversarial, or mutually exclusive.

Feasible manipulations: approach to determining policy alternatives entails identifying policy-relevant variables the modifications of which form the basis for developing coherent strategies that can be subsequently revised as the problem the policies are meant to address is redefined and evaluation criteria shift.

Formal evaluations: use descriptive methods to produce reliable and valid information about policy outcomes that have been formally announced as policy program objectives.

Formative evaluations: monitor continuously the accomplishment of formal goals and objectives of policies and programs.

Interest group theory of politics: situations where both costs and benefits of political engagement are concentrated, providing the relevant actors with incentives to participate in policymaking and policy analysts with a way of readily identifying and predicting their reactions to policy proposals.

Levels of evaluative logic: include *verification, validation, vindication,* and *rational choice.* In *verification,* evaluation focuses on the empirical demonstration of whether the program or policy under evaluation fulfills the requirements of the norms introduced by decision makers and other stakeholders as appropriate. In *validation,* evaluation asks whether the goal itself is compatible with the basic value systems that provide competing criteria in the judgment process. In *vindication,* evaluation seeks to determine whether the value system is instrumental or contributive to the adopted way of life or culture. In *rational choice,* program evaluators and policy analysts examine alternative ways of life and seek to show the extent to which a particular choice about a way of life was governed by rational processes in free and open deliberation.

Lexicographic ordering: a policy where alternatives are ranked, one criterion at a time, starting with the most important first. If two or more alternatives occupy the highest ranking on the most important criterion, then they are compared on the second criterion. The surviving alternatives are compared on the third most important criterion, and so forth.

Liberty: or freedom; refers to the extent to which public policy extends or restricts privacy and individual rights and choices.

Logic of governance (LOG): framework used to analyze implementation of policies; rests on the notion that politics, policymaking, public management, and service delivery are hierarchically linked with one another in the determination of public policy outputs and outcomes. Logic of governance suggests that policy analysts are well advised to take into account management actions and processes as initiation of management structures, management tools, and values, as well as service delivery actions and processes such as fieldworker discretion and values and the carrying out of administrative rules and regulations.

Macroeconomists: focus on the economy as a whole and study the determinants of total output. Inflation, unemployment, growth, and changes in the level of business activity are the subject matters of macroeconomics.

Market failures: circumstances in which decentralized behavior—the respective maximizing actions of individuals (satisfaction) and firms (profits)—does not lead to *Pareto efficiency*—that is, a distribution of goods in such a way that no one could be better off without making anyone else worse off.

Means test: an investigation into the financial well-being of a person, family, or household to determine eligibility for social benefits.

Microeconomics: deals with studies of behavior of the individual participants (e.g., households, business firms) in the economy: how individual businesses behave in competitive environments, and how prices of individual commodities are determined.

Moral hazard: situations where the behavior of one party may change to the detriment of another—for example, insured drivers in no-fault states may become less cautious about speed limits, coming to a full stop at stop signs, or remaining a safe distance behind the vehicle in front of them because negative consequences of such actions are partially if not fully absorbed by the insurance company.

Multi-attribute utility analysis: a set of procedures designed to elicit from multiple stakeholders subjective judgments about the probability of occurrence and value of policy outcomes.

Normative justifications or theories: involve a defense or critique of moral and ethical positions in relation to a policy or program—for example, questions about the desirability of ends or appropriateness of means to achieve those ends. They are usually meant to be viewed as complementary, essential, and legitimate domains of policy analysis, rather than as competing, adversarial, or mutually exclusive.

Objectivity: in its most common usage refers to the attitude of the impartial or unbiased observer, often contrasted with social constructivists.

Opportunity costs: those associated with the loss of the next-best alternative. *Free goods* have *zero opportunity costs*—that is, users can have more, like air, without others having to give up some of the good. *Scarce goods* have *positive opportunity cost*—that is, in order to have more of a scarce good (e.g., electricity), an alternative must be sacrificed, so the billion tons of coal, seven trillion cubic meters of natural gas, and the 190 million barrels of petroleum used to produce electricity could have been used for other things, such as driving more miles or creating more petrochemical products.

Outcome equity, often used interchangeably with **social justice:** the fair distribution of societal goods such as wealth, income, or political power.

Path dependence theory: how past policy decisions affect the content and likely adoption of proposed policy alternatives.

Policy institutes: primarily nonprofit (tax exempt) organizations that perform research and advocacy functions for social policy purposes.

Political feasibility: the likelihood that a policy will be adopted—that is, the extent to which elected officials accept and support a policy proposal.

Positivism: an approach to understanding that includes the ontological belief in a deterministic universe and the epistemological beliefs that knowledge reflects external realities, the laws of the universe can be known, and science can be unified through a common methodology, one that favors deductive, inductive, and reductionist/analytical approaches and quantitative analyses.

Probative inference: a conclusion, drawn from the vocabulary of jurisprudence, that has been established such that those making the claim are prepared to support it as beyond reasonable doubt. It is contrasted to **statistical (probabilistic) inference**.

Process equity: decision-making procedures or processes—that is, the extent to which they are voluntary, open, and fair to all participants.

Pseudo-evaluations: use descriptive methods to produce reliable and valid information about policy outcomes.

Risk: the probability that an event or exposure will occur and the consequences that follow if it does.

Risk assessment: the use of different methods to identify, estimate, and evaluate the magnitude of the risk to citizens from exposure to various intermittent situations such as natural hazards (e.g., hurricanes and earthquakes), as well as to various daily life situations such as driving a car.

Risk evaluation: the determination of the acceptability of the risks or a decision about what level of safety is desired.

Satisficing: a rule-of-thumb way of making a satisfactory, but not necessarily the best choice among policy alternatives.

Scarcity: resources (land and natural resources, labor, and capital, which are called *factors of production*) in which the amount that economic agents would want free of charge exceeds the amount available.

Selective benefits: available on the basis of individual need, usually determined by a **means test**.

Sensitivity analysis: often used as a corrective to cost-benefit analysis; a technique used to determine how different values of a causal factor or an independent variable will impact a particular outcome or dependent variable under a given set of assumptions.

Social auditing: an approach to evaluation that explicitly monitors relations among inputs, processes, outputs, and impacts in an effort to trace policy inputs from the points of disbursement to the point at which they are experienced by the intended recipients of those resources.

Social construction framework: for analyzing processes associated with policymaking; relies on the notion that interpretive frameworks used to interpret our observations of the world can to some extent be altered by arguments, thereby providing an avenue for changing the political support for various policies. It applies this notion to the distribution of benefits and burdens among the groups that are targets of public policies, identifying four target groups in reference to their social construction and political power: advantaged, contenders, dependents, and outsiders.

Social constructivists: a proposition that all knowledge is value-laden, a by-product of social interactions reflecting cultural norms and values (weak sense) or inherently supportive of cultural norms and values (strong sense).

Social entrepreneurship: a contemporary global movement that links market-based principles and incentives with social purposes. It involves the innovative use and combination of resources to pursue opportunities to bring about social change and address social needs.

Social experimentation: an approach to evaluation that entails the systematic manipulation of policy actions in a way that permits more or less precise answers to questions about the sources of change in policy outcomes. It has many forms including laboratory, field, and quasi-experimentation.

Social welfare function: provides an alternative to *Pareto efficiency* as a way of allocating goods. Instead of defining efficiency as the inability to make someone better off without making someone else worse off (*Pareto efficiency*), efficiency is defined as the allocation of goods that maximizes the greatest good.

Stakeholders: those who have a concern in an evaluation and may include the presumptive or targeted beneficiaries for whom policies are made and programs implemented, as well as the policymakers and others with economic, pragmatic, moral, and/or ethical interests in programmatic outputs and outcomes.

State dependence: how current policies affect the content and likely adoption of proposed policy alternatives.

Street-level bureaucrats: include police, teachers, social workers, nurses, doctors, lawyers, and other service providers such as lower court judges, corrections officers, and prison guards, who occupy positions that have relatively high degrees of discretion and relative autonomy from organizational authority.

Summative evaluations: monitor the accomplishment of formal goals and objectives after a policy or program has been in place for some period of time.

Substitutability: the possibility that a public policy or program may be used in such a way so as not to produce desired effects. Food stamps, for example, whose recipients are meant to increase their food purchases and consumption, may instead hold such purchases and consumption and use the money "released" by their availability to purchase other commodities of choice.

Taxes: the main source of revenue for government, with varying distributional or "burden" effects depending on the type of tax (earned [wages, salaries, tips] or unearned [stocks, bonds]), level of income, and the tax-filing status of the taxpayer. *Payroll taxes,* used to fund Social Security, are *regressive:* that is, everyone pays the tax at the same rate regardless of their income up to the capped limit ($110,100 in 2012). *Consumption* or *sales* taxes are also *regressive,* as everyone pays the same tax on an item they purchase regardless of income level. Other taxes, such as the federal income tax, are *progressive* in the sense that individuals and families with higher incomes pay taxes at a higher rate than lower-wage workers.

Technical feasibility: the availability and reliability of technology needed for policy implementation.

Theories as explanations: account for an observed relationship between a policy or program and outcomes and might be morally neutral in that a moral position is not necessarily explicitly promoted.

Theory-oriented tradition: this tradition of evaluation research is known by several names, including **theory-based**, **theory-driven**, or **program evaluation theory**, whose aim is to build upon knowledge acquired from the practice of program evaluation.

Think tanks: organizations dedicated to problem-solving, interdisciplinary research, and to varying degrees advocacy, usually in such areas as technology, social or political strategy, or the military.

Universal benefits: available to an entire population as a basic right and for the most part not **means tested**—that is, they are provided regardless of income levels of recipients, their families, or households.

Value relevance: values that enter into the selection of problems investigators choose to examine.

Value neutrality: (1) the normative injunction that persons of science should be governed by the ethos of science in their role as scientists, but not at all necessary in their role as citizens, and (2) the disjunction between the world of facts and the world of values, the impossibility of deriving "ought statements" from "is statements."

Value-distant evaluations: objectives-focused, experimental design, quasi-experimental designs, cost-benefit analyses, realistic evaluation, and theory-driven evaluation that rely predominantly on quantitatively oriented methodologies and analysis. They tend to focus on goals and outcomes but not on processes. They are most appropriate for summative evaluations.

Values-relativistic evaluations: *issues focused* or *responsive evaluation* and *dialogue focused* or *constructivist evaluation.* These approaches, and *values-prioritizing evaluations* and *values-positioned evaluations* are incorporated in what is known as *fourth generation evaluation,* which emphasizes deliberation among stakeholders who have different values and perspectives about the nature and importance of the program, policy, and evaluation. They focus on issues and use an iterative dialogue process to identify and clarify issues and values stakeholders have about them.

Values-positioned evaluations: include **self-organization** or **empowerment evaluation**, whose multiple roots have been traced in part to emancipatory or transformative research practices associated with liberation pedagogy, feminist inquiry, critical theory, and communicative action, and to evaluation research practices associated with participatory action research and collaboration research. Fostering self-determination is a defining feature. Other defining features include responsiveness to local needs and collaboration of trained evaluation personnel and practice-based decision makers working in partnership.

Values-prioritizing evaluations: include decision focused or accountability oriented evaluation, utilization focused or pragmatic evaluation, and stakeholder interest focused or deliberative democratic evaluation. They rely on stakeholder input for purposes of pragmatic assessments about day-to-day program functioning or policy implementation and of making specific decisions based on a continuous reassessment of priorities as circumstances warrant.

Values-salient evaluations: grounded in what is deemed the practical philosophy approach to social inquiry, seeking to infuse moral discourse in evaluation practices. They encompass both descriptive and normative undertakings by analysts who engage and incorporate the perspectives and judgments of policy and program participants at all levels in the evaluation process.

Verstehen: the "interpretive understanding" of human behavior, often contrasted with positivism.

References

Aaron, H.J. (1978). *Politics and professors: The great society in perspective.* Washington, DC: Brookings Institution.

Action, J.P. (1975). Nonmonetary factors in the demand for medical services: Some empirical evidence. *Journal of Political Economy, 83,* 595–614.

Addams, J. (1909). *The spirit of youth and the city streets.* New York: Macmillan.

Addams, J. (1910). *Twenty years at Hull House.* New York: Macmillan.

Addams, J., & De Forest, R.W. (1902). The housing problem in Chicago. *Annals of the American Academy of Political and Social Science, 20,* 99–107.

Advisory Commission on Intergovernmental Relations. (1979). *Citizenship participation in the American federal system.* Washington, DC: Author. Retrieved from http://www.library.unt.edu/gpo/acir/Reports/brief/B-3.pdf

Agnarsson, S., & Carlson, P.S. (2002). Family background and the estimated return to schooling: Swedish evidence. *Journal of Human Resources, 37,* 680–692.

Agodoa, L., & Eggers, P. (2007). Racial and ethnic disparities in end-stage kidney failure—Survival paradoxes in African Americans. *Seminars in Dialysis, 20,* 577–585.

Ahl, A.S. (1999). *Comprehensive review of the Office of Risk Assessment and Cost Benefit Analysis.* McLean, VA: Society for Risk Analysis (SRA). Retrieved from http://www.sra.org/rplsg/docs/ORACBA%20Evaluation.pdf

Alderson, A.S., Beckfield, J., and Nielsen, F. (2005). *Exactly how has income inequality changed? Patterns of distributional change in core societies.* (Luxembourg Income Study Working Paper Series, No. 422). Retrieved from http://www.lisproject.org/publications/liswps/422.pdf

Aldrich, J.H., & Rohde, D.W. (2000). The Republican revolution and the House Appropriations Committee. *The Journal of Politics, 62,* 1–33.

Alexander, E.R. (1979). The design of alternatives in organizational contexts: A pilot study. *Administrative Science Quarterly, 24,* 382–404.

Alexander, E.R. (1982). Design in the decision-making process. *Policy Sciences, 14,* 279–292.

Alkin, M.C., Vo, A.T., & Christie, C.A. (2012). The evaluator's role in valuing: Who and with whom. *New Directions for Evaluation, 2012*(133), 29–41.

Amy, D.J. (1984). Why policy analysis and ethics are incompatible. *Journal of Policy Analysis and Management, 3,* 573–591.

Anderson, C.W. (1979). The place of principles in policy analysis. *The American Political Science Review, 73,* 711–723.

Aos, S., Lieb, R., Mayfield, J., Miller, M., & Penucci, A. (2004). *Benefits and costs of prevention and early intervention programs for youth.* Olympia: Washington State Institute for Public Policy. Retrieved from http://www.wsipp.wa.gov/rptfiles/04-07-3901.pdf

Aos, S., Miller, M., & Drake, E. (2006). *Evidenced-based public policy options to reduce future prison construction, criminal justice costs, and crime rates.* Olympia: Washington State Institute for Public Policy. Retrieved from http://www.wsipp.wa.gov/rptfiles/06–10–1201.pdf

Aos, S., Miller, M., & Mayfield, J. (2007). *Benefits and costs of K–12 educational policies: Evidence-based effects of class size reductions and full-day kindergarten.* Document 07-03-2201. Olympia: Washington State Institute for Public Policy. Retrieved from http://www.leg.wa.gov/Senate/Committees/EDU/Documents/BensCosts_EdPolicies.pdf

Arcs, G., & Loprest, P. (2007). *TANF caseloads composition and leavers synthesis report.* Washington, DC: U.S. Department of Health and Human Services. Retrieved from http://www.acf.hhs.gov/programs/opre/welfare_employ/tanf_caseload/index.html

Arizona Civil Rights Initiative, The (2011). *Historical overview of race preference and affirmative action policy in America*. Phoenix: Author. Retrieved from http://www.arizonacri.org/Home/HistoryofAffirmativeAction.aspx

Arrow, K.J. (1963). Uncertainty and the welfare economics of medical care. *American Economic Review, 53,* 941–973.

Arrow, K.J. (1968). The economics of moral hazard: Further comment. *American Economic Review, 58,* 537–539.

Ascher, W. (1986). The evolution of the policy sciences: Understanding the rise and avoiding the fall. *Journal of Policy Analysis and Management, 5,* 365–689.

Ascher, W. (1987). Editorial: Policy sciences and the economic approach in a "post-positivist" era. *Policy Sciences, 20,* 3–9.

Association for Public Policy and Management (1996). *APPAM membership directory*. Washington, DC: Author.

Axinn, J., & Stern, M.J. (2011). *Social welfare: A history of the American response to need* (8th ed.). Upper Saddle River, NJ: Prentice Hall.

Backhouse, R.E., & Fontaine, P. (2010). Toward a history of the social sciences. In R.E. Backhouse & P. Fontaine (Eds.), *The history of the social sciences since 1945* (pp. 184–223). Cambridge, UK: Cambridge University Press.

Bacon, F. (2012). *Novum Organum* (Classic Reprint Edition). Forgotten Books. Online. Retrieved from http://www.forgottenbooks.org/. (Original work published 1620)

Baert, P. (2005). *Philosophy of the social sciences: Towards pragmatism*. Cambridge, UK: Policy Press.

Bailin, S., Case, R., Coombs, J.R., & Daniels, L.B. (1999). Conceptualizing critical thinking. *Journal of Curriculum Studies, 31,* 285–302.

Baker, T. (1996). On the genealogy of moral hazard. *Texas Law Review, 75,* 237–292.

Ballard, C.L. (1988). The marginal efficiency cost of redistribution. *American Economic Review, 78,* 1019–1033.

Banerjee, A.V., & Duflo, E. (2011). *Poor economics: A radical rethinking of the way to fight global poverty*. New York: PublicAffairs.

Banfield, E.C. (1977). Policy science as metaphysical madness. In R.C. Goodwin (Ed.), *Statesmanship and bureaucracy* (pp. 1–35). Washington, DC: American Enterprise Institute. Retrieved from http://www.scribd.com/doc/49103698/Edward-C-Banfield-Policy-Science-as-Metaphysical-Madness

Bannister, R.C. (1987). *Sociology and scientism: The American quest for objectivity, 1880–1940*. Chapel Hill: University of North Carolina Press.

Bannon, G. (1980). Economic justice: Which way from here? *Social Thought, 6,* 4–5.

Bargman, J.M. (2007). Is there more to living than not dying? A reflection on survival studies in dialysis. *Seminars in Dialysis, 20,* 50–52.

Barrett, S. (2007). The smallpox eradication game. *Public Choice, 130*(1/2), 179–207.

Barnett, W.S., & Masse, L.N. (2007). Comparative benefit-cost analysis of the Abecedarian program and its policy implications. *Economics and Education Review, 26,* 113–125.

Bateman, I.J., Carson, R.T., Day, B., Hanemann, W.M., Hett, T., Jones-Lee, M.W., Loomes, G., Mourato, S., Özdemiroglu, E., Pearce, D.W., Sugden, R., & Swanson, J. (2002). *Economic valuation with stated preference techniques*. Northampton, MA: Edward Elgar.

Bazelton Center for Mental Health Law. (2009). *Lifelines: Linking federal benefits for people exiting corrections. Blueprint for action*. Washington, DC: Author. Retrieved from http://www.bazelon.org/LinkClick.aspx?fileticket=-_dbVoVTKis%3d&tabid=104

Beetham, D. (1977a). From socialism to fascism: The relation between theory and practice in the work of Robert Michels. I. From Marxist revolutionary to political sociologist. *Political Studies, 25,* 3–24.

Beetham, D. (1977b). From socialism to fascism: The relation between theory and practice in the work of Robert Michels. II. Fascist ideologue. *Political Studies, 25,* 161–181.

Behn, R.D. (1985). Policy analysts, clients, and social scientists. *Journal of Policy Analysis and Management, 4,* 428–432.

Belfield, C.R., Nores, M., Barnett, S., & Schweinhart, L. (2006). The High/Perry preschool program: Cost-benefit analysis using data from the age-40 follow-up. *Journal of Human Resources, 41,* 162–190.

Bell, D. (1960). *The end of ideology*. Glencoe, IL: Free Press.

Benker, R.W. (1971). The public policy program of the Kennedy School of Government: A student's view. *Policy Sciences, 2,* 67–81.

Bennett, S.E. (2002). "Perestroika" lost: Why the latest "reform" movement in political science should fail. *PS: Political Science and Politics, 35,* 177–179.

Bentham, J. (1781). *An introduction to the principles of morals and legislation.* Retrieved from http://www .utilitarianism.com/jeremy-bentham/index.html

Benton, W. (1944). *The economics of a free society: A declaration of American business policy.* New York: Committee for Economic Development.

Benveniste, G. (1984). On a code of ethics for policy experts. *Journal of Policy Analysis and Management, 3,* 561–572.

Bergmann, B. (2005). The current state of economics: Needs lots of work. *Annals of the American Academy of Political and Social Science, 600,* 52–67.

Bernard, L.L. (1911). *The transition to an objective standard of social control.* Chicago: University of Chicago Press.

Bernstein, M.A. (2004). Statecraft and its retainers: American economics and public purpose after depression and war. In H. Cravens (Ed.), *The social sciences go to Washington: The politics of knowledge in the postmodern age* (pp. 41–59). New Brunswick, NJ: Rutgers University Press.

Berzin, S.C. (2012). Where is social work in the social entrepreneurship movement? *Social Work, 57,* 185–188.

Besharov, D.J., & Cottingham, P.H. (Eds.). (2011). *The Workforce Investment Act: Implementation experiences and evaluation findings.* Kalamazoo, MI: W.E. Upjohn Institute for Employment Research.

Bhaskar, R. (1986). *Scientific realism and human emancipation.* London: Verso.

Bhaskar, R. (1989). *Reclaiming reality: A critical introduction to contemporary philosophy.* London: Verso.

Bickman, L. (1987a). The functions of program theory. *New Directions for Program Evaluation, 1987*(33), 5–18.

Bickman, L. (Ed.) (1987b). Using program theory in evaluation. [Special issue]. *New Directions for Program Evaluation, 1987*(33), 1–109.

Biderman, A.D. (1970, September 11). Self-portrayal. [Review of the books *The behavioral sciences and the federal government,* by The National Academy of Sciences, *The behavioral and social sciences,* by The National Academy of Sciences and The Social Science Research Council, *Knowledge into action,* by the National Science Foundation, *Politics of social research,* by R.L. Beals, and *The uneasy partnership,* by G.M. Lyons]. *Science, 169,* 1064–1067.

Billups, A. (2011, July 12). Campus affirmative action again may head to Supreme Court. *The Washington Times.* Retrieved from http://www.washingtontimes.com/news/2011/jul/12/campus-diversity-challenges-may-send-affirmative-a/?page=all

Birnbaum, N. (1969). The arbitrary disciplines. *Change in Higher Education, 1*(4), 10–21.

Blaug, M. (1967). The private and social returns on investment in education: Some results for Great Britain. *Journal of Human Resources, 2,* 330–346.

Bloom, D., & Winstead, D. (2002). *Sanctions and welfare reform. Policy Brief No. 12.* Washington, DC: Brookings Institution. Retrieved from http://www.mdrc.org/sites/default/files/sanctions_and_welfare_reform_fr.pdf

Bloom, H.S. (1999). *Building a convincing test of a public housing employment program using non-experimental methods.* New York: MDRC. Retrieved from http://www.mdrc.org/sites/default/files/full_32.pdf

Bloom, H.S. (2006). *The core analytics of randomized experiments for social research.* New York: MDRC. Retrieved from http://www.mdrc.org/sites/default/files/full_533.pdf

Bloom, H.S. (2010). *Nine lessons about doing evaluation research.* New York: MDRC. Retrieved from http://www.mdrc .org/sites/default/files/presentation.pdf

Bloom, H.S., Hill, C.J., & Riccio, J. (2001). *Modeling the performance of welfare-to-work programs: The effects of program management and services, economic environment, and client characteristics.* New York: MDRC. Retrieved from http://www.mdrc.org/sites/default/files/full_445.pdf

Bloom, H.S., Thompson, S.L., & Unterman, R. (2010). *Transforming the high school experience: Executive summary.* Washington, DC: MDRC. Retrieved from http://www.mdrc.org/sites/default/files/full_589.pdf

Bloom, M., Fischer, J., & Orme, J.G. (2009). *Practice evaluation: Guidelines for the accountable professional* (6th ed.). Needham Heights, MA: Allyn & Bacon.

Blum, F.H. (1944). Max Weber's postulate of "freedom" from value judgments. *American Journal of Sociology, 50,* 46–52.

Board of Governors of the Federal Reserve System. (2011). Government Performance and Results Act strategic planning document, 2008–2011. Retrieved from http://www.federalreserve.gov/boarddocs/RptCongress/gpra/gpra2008-2011.pdf

Boardman, A.E., Greenberg, D.H., Vining, A.R., & Weimer, D.L. (1997). "Plug-in" shadow estimates for policy analysis. *Annals of Regional Science, 31,* 299–324.

Boardman, A.E., Greenberg, D.H., Vining, A.R., & Weimer, D.L. (2010). *Cost-benefit analysis: Concepts and practice* (4th ed.). Upper Saddle River, NJ: Prentice Hall.

Boas, F. (1919, December 20). Scientists as spies. Letter to *The Nation,* p. 797.

Bordon, W.S. (2011). The challenges of measuring performance. In D.J. Besharov & P.H. Cottingham (Eds.), *The Workforce Investment Act: Implementation experiences and evaluation findings* (pp. 177–207). Kalamazoo, MI: W.E. Upjohn Institute for Employment Research.

Brager, G.A. (1968). Advocacy and political behavior. *Social Work, 13*(April), 5–15.

Braybrooke, D., & Lindblom, C.E. (1970). *A strategy of decision: Policy evaluation as a social process.* New York: Free Press.

Bremner, R.H. (1956). "Scientific philanthropy," 1863–1893. *Social Service Review, 30,* 168–173.

Bricker-Jenkins, M., & Joseph, B.H.R (2008). Progressive social work. In T. Mizrahi & L.E. Davis (Eds.), *Encyclopedia of social work,* (20th ed.). Washington, DC: National Association of Social Workers and Oxford: Oxford University Press (e-reference edition). Retrieved from http://www.oxford-naswsocialwork.com/entry?entry = t203.e312

Brigham, F.J., Gustashaw, W.E., Wiley, A.L., & Brigham, M. (2004). Research in the wake of the No Child Left Behind Act: Why the controversies will continue and some suggestions for controversial research. *Behavioral Disorders, 29,* 300–310.

Brigham, J., & Brown, D.W. (1980). Distinguishing penalties and incentives. *Law & Policy Quarterly, 2,* 5–10.

Brodkin, E.Z. (1997). Inside the welfare contract: Discretion and accountability in state welfare administration. *Social Service Review, 71,* 1–33.

Brookfield, S. (1987). Developing critical thinkers. Milton Keynes, UK: Open University Press.

Brown, L.J. (1984). Neoclassical economics and the sexual division of labor. *Eastern Economic Journal, 10,* 367–379.

Brown, K., & Rutter, L. (2006). *Critical thinking for social work.* Exeter, UK: Learning Matters, Ltd.

Brown, R.H. (1998). Modern science and its critics: Toward a post-positivist legitimation of science. *New Literary History, 29,* 521–550.

Brown, S.R. (2013). *The history and principles of Q methodology in psychology and the social sciences.* Retrieved from http://facstaff.uww.edu/cottlec/QArchive/Bps.htm

Browne, A., & Wildavsky, A. (1984a). Implementation as exploration (1983). In J.F. Pressman & A. Wildavsky (Eds.), *Implementation* (pp. 232–256) (3rd ed. expanded). Berkeley: University of California Press.

Browne, A., & Wildavsky, A. (1984b). Implementation as mutual adaptation (1983). In J.F. Pressman & A. Wildavsky (Eds.), *Implementation* (pp. 206–231) (3rd ed. expanded). Berkeley: University of California Press.

Browning, E.K., & Johnson, W.R. (1984). The trade-off between equality and efficiency. *Journal of Political Economy, 92,* 175–203.

Brownstein, M. (2010). Conceptuality and practical action: A critique of Charles Taylor's Verstehen social theory. *Philosophy of the Social Sciences, 40,* 59–83.

Bruce, C. (1996). What is a discount rate? *Expert Witness, 1*(1). Retrieved from http://www.economica.ca/ew01_1p3.htm

Bruce, C., Aldridge, D., Beesley, S., & Rathje, K. (2000). Selecting the discount rate. *Expert Witness, 5*(3). Retrieved from http://www.economica.ca/ew05_3p1.htm

Brunet, G., & Cox, K. (2009). *Federal tax burdens for most near their lowest levels in decades.* Washington, DC: Center on Budget and Policy Priorities. Retrieved from http://www.cbpp.org/cms/?fa=view&id=139

Brunner, R.D. (1991). The policy movement as a policy problem. *Policy Sciences, 24,* 65–98.

Bruun, H.H., & Whimster, S. (Eds.). (2012). *Max Weber: Collected methodological writings.* London: Routledge.

Bryan, K., & Martinez, L. (2008). On the evolution of income inequality in the United States. *Federal Reserve Bank of Richmond Economic Quarterly, 94*(2), 97–120. Retrieved from http://www.richmondfed.org/publications/research/economic_quarterly/2008/spring/pdf/bryan_martinez.pdf

Bryson, D. (2009). Personality and culture, the social science research council, and liberal social engineering: The Advisory Committee on Personality and Culture, 1930–1934. *Journal of the History of the Behavioral Sciences, 45,* 355–386.

Bryson, G. (1932). The emergence of the social sciences from moral philosophy. *International Journal of Ethics, 42,* 304–323.

Bucaria, J. (2013, February 9). Birth control and religious freedom: To the editor. *The New York Times,* A18.

Buettner, R. (2008, August 2). For some close to anthrax scare, unwelcome memories. *The New York Times.* Retrieved from http://www.nytimes.com/2008/08/02/washington/02families.html?_r=1#

Bukszar, E., & Knetsch, J.L. (1997). Fragile redistribution choices behind a veil of ignorance. *Journal of Risk and Uncertainty, 14,* 63–74.

Bulmer, M., & Bulmer, J. (1981). Philanthropy and social science in the 1920s: Beardsley Ruml and the Laura Spelman Rockefeller Memorial, 1922–1929. *Minerva, 19,* 437–407.

Bunker, D.R. (1971). A doctoral program in the policy sciences. *Policy Sciences, 2,* 33–42.

Buraway, M. (2005). For public sociology. *American Sociological Review, 70,* 6–28.

Burtless, G., & Hausman, J.A. (1978). The effect of taxation on labor supply: Evaluating the Gary negative income tax experiment. *The Journal of Political Economy, 86,* 1103–1130.

Bush, G.W. (2005, July 15). Remarks to the 16th annual Energy Efficiency Forum. Online by G. Peters & J.T. Woolley, *The American Presidency Project.* Retrieved from http://www.presidency.ucsb.edu/ws/index.php?pid=62834

Butler, D., Alson, J., Bloom, D., Deitch, V., Hill, A., Hsueh, S., Jacobs, E., Kim, S., McRoberts, R., & Redcross, C. (2012). *What strategies work for the hard-to-employ? Final results of the Hard-to-Employ Demonstration and Evaluation Project and selected sites from the Employment Retention and Advancement Project.* Washington, DC: Office of Planning, Research and Evaluation, U.S. Department of Health and Human Services. Retrieved from http://www.mdrc.org/publications/630/full.pdf

Cain, H. (1971). Lindblom: A partisan analyst of the policy process. [Review of the book *The policy-making process,* by C.E. Lindblom]. *Policy Sciences, 2,* 191–198.

Caldwell, M.F., Vitacco, M., & Van Rybroek, G.J. (2006). Are violent delinquents worth treating? A cost-benefit analysis. *Journal of Research in Crime and Delinquency, 43,* 148–168.

Calhoun, C. (1993). Postmodernism as pseudohistory. *Theory, Culture & Society, 10,* 75–96.

Calkins, C.A., & Millar, M. (1999). The effectiveness of court appointed special advocates to assist in permanency planning. *Child and Adolescent Social Work Journal, 16,* 37–45.

Callahan, D. (1987). *Setting limits: Medical goals in an aging society.* New York: Simon & Schuster.

Calmes, J., & Harris, G. (2011, December 9). Obama endorses decision to limit morning-after pill. *The New York Times,* A20.

Camic, C. (2007). On edge: Sociology during the Great Depression and New Deal. In C. Calhoun (Ed.), *Sociology in America: A history* (pp. 235–280). Chicago: University of Chicago Press.

Campbell, D.T. (1957). Factors relevant to the validity of experiments in social settings. *Psychological Bulletin, 54,* 297–312.

Campbell, D.T. (1969). Reforms as social experiments. *American Psychologist, 24,* 409–429.

Campbell, D.T., & Stanley, J. (1963). *Experimental and quasi-experimental designs for research.* Belmont, CA: Wadsworth.

Campbell, V. (2004). How RAND invented the postwar world. *Invention and Technology Magazine, 20*(1), 50–59. Retrieved from http://www.rand.org/content/dam/rand/pubs/reprints/2009/RAND_RP1396.pdf

Caputo, R.K (1989). Integrating values and norms in the evaluation of social policy: A conceptual framework. *Journal of Teaching in Social Work, 3*(2), 115–131.

Caputo, R.K. (1994). *Welfare and freedom American style II: The role of the federal government, 1941–1980.* Lanham, MD: University Press of America.

Caputo, R.K. (2000). Multiculturalism and social justice in the United States: An attempt to reconcile the irreconcilable within a pragmatic liberal framework. *Race, Gender & Class, 7*(4), 161–182.

Caputo, R.K. (2002a). Correlates of mortality in a U.S. cohort of youth: Implications for social justice. *Social Justice Research, 15,* 271–293.

Caputo, R.K. (2002b). FAP flops (USBIG Discussion Paper No. 31). Retrieved from www.usbig.net/papers/031-Caputo.doc

Caputo, R.K. (2003). Head Start, other preschool programs, & life success in a youth cohort. *Journal of Sociology & Social Welfare, 30*(2), 105–126.

Caputo, R.K. (2004). Head Start and school-to-work program participation. *Journal of Poverty, 8*(2), 25–42.

Caputo, R.K. (2005). Distribution of the federal tax burden, share of after-tax income, and after-tax income by presidential administration and household type, 1981–2000. *Journal of Sociology & Social Welfare, 32*(2), 3–18.

Caputo, R.K. (2006). The Earned Income Tax Credit: A study of eligible participants and nonparticipants. *Journal of Sociology & Social Welfare, 4*(1), 9–29.

Caputo, R.K. (2007). Social theory & its relation to social problems: An essay about theory and research with social justice in mind. *Journal of Sociology & Social Welfare, 34* (1), 43–61.

Caputo, R.K. (2009). EITC & TANF participation among young adult low-income families. *Northwestern Journal of Law and Social Policy, 4*(1), 136–149.

Caputo, R.K. (2010). Family characteristics, public program participation, and civic engagement. *Journal of Sociology & Social Welfare, 37*(2), 35–61.

Caputo, R.K. (2011). *U.S. social welfare reform: Policy transitions from 1981 to the present.* New York: Springer.

Caputo, R.K. (2012). United States of America: GAI almost in the 1970s but downhill thereafter. In R.K. Caputo (Ed.), *Basic income guarantee and politics: International experiences and perspectives on the viability of income guarantee* (pp. 265–281). New York: Palgrave Macmillan.

Caputo, R.K. (2013). Policy analysis. In M. Reisch (Ed.), *Social policy and social justice* (chap. 6). Thousand Oaks, CA: Sage.

Caputo, R.K., & Deprez, L.S. (2012). Editors' introduction: Revisiting William J. Wilson's *The Declining Significance of Race. Journal of Sociology & Social Welfare, 39*(1), 7–15.

Card, D. (2001). Estimating the return to schooling: Progress on some persistent econometric problems. *Econometrica, 69,* 1127–1160.

Carney, T. (1991). [Review of the book *Fourth generation evaluation,* by E.G. Guba & Y.S. Lincoln]. *Canadian Journal of Communication, 16,* 318–319.

Carson, R.T. (2012). *Contingent valuation: A comprehensive bibliography and history.* Northampton, MA: Edward Elgar.

Carson, R.T., & Hanemann, W.M. (2005). Contingent valuation. In K.-G. Mäler & J.R. Vincent (Eds.), *Handbook of environmental economics,* Vol. 2 (pp. 821–936). Amsterdam, The Netherlands: Elsevier B.V.

Caterino, B., & Schram, S.F. (2006). Introduction: Reframing the debate. In B. Caterino & S.F. Schram (Eds.), *Making political science matter: Debating knowledge, research, and method* (pp. 9–20). New York: New York University Press.

Catholic Charities USA. (2012). *Catholic Charities at a glance.* Alexandra, VA: Author. Retrieved from http://www .catholiccharitiesusa.org/Document.Doc?id = 1924

Cato Institute. (2011). Cato's mission. Retrieved from http://www.cato.org/about-mission.html

Center on Budget and Policy Priorities. (2011). *Where do our federal tax dollars go?* Washington, DC: Author. Retrieved from http://www.cbpp.org/files/4-14-08tax.pdf

Center on Budget Policy Priorities. (2013). *How many weeks of unemployment compensation are available.* Washington, DC: Author. Retrieved from http://www.cbpp.org/files/PolicyBasics_UI_Weeks.pdf

Center on Budget and Policy Priorities. (2012a). *Chart book: The legacy of the Great Depression.* Washington, DC: Author. Retrieved from http://www.cbpp.org/cms/index.cfm?fa = view&id = 3252

Center on Budget and Policy Priorities. (2012b). *Policy basics: Where do our federal tax dollars go?* Washington, DC: Author. Retrieved from http://www.cbpp.org/cms/index.cfm?fa = view&id = 1258

Chalip, L. (1985). Policy research as social science: Outflanking the values dilemma. *Policy Studies Review, 5,* 287–308.

Challenges to the Health Law. (2011). *The New York Times.* Retrieved from http://www.nytimes.com/interactive/2011/11/13/us/politics/challenges-to-the-health-law.html

Chambers, D.E. (1985). The Reagan administration's welfare retrenchment policy: Terminating Social Security benefits for the disabled. *Policy Studies Review, 5*(2), 230–240.

Chambers, D.E., & Wedel, K.R. (2005). *Social policy and social programs: A method for the practical public policy analyst* (4th ed.). Boston: Allyn & Bacon.

Chapin, F.S. (2009). *Field work and social research.* Ithaca: Cornell University Press. (Original work published 1920)

Chapin, F.S., & Kaiser, E.J. (1979). *Urban land use planning* (3rd ed.). Urbana: University of Illinois Press.

Chelimsky, E. (1998). The role of experience in formulating theories of evaluation practice. *American Journal of Evaluation, 19,* 35–55.

Chesson, H., Harrison, P., & Kassler, W. (2000). Sex under the influence: The effect of alcohol policy on sexually transmitted disease rates in the United States. *Journal of Law and Economics, 43,* 215–238.

Child Advocacy 360 Foundation. (2010). *Solutions storytelling: Messaging to mobilize support for children's issues.* Message Development Research Report. Retrieved from http://images.magnetmail.net/images/template/HershelSarbin/Childadvocacy/CA360FullReportMay18.pdf

Child development plan vetoed. (1972). *Social Service Review, 46,* 108–111.

Christiansen, Ø., & Anderssen, N. (2010). From concerned to convinced: Reaching decisions about out-of-home care in Norwegian child welfare services. *Child and Family Social Work, 15,* 31–40.

Christie, C.A., & Alkin, M.C. (2013). An evaluation theory tree. In M.C. Alkin (Ed.), *Evaluation roots: A wider perspective of theorists' views and influences* (2nd ed.) (pp. 11–57). Thousand Oaks, CA: Sage.

Clark, J.B. (1897). The scholar's political opportunity. *Political Science Quarterly, 12,* 589–602.

Clarke, P.M. (1998). Cost-benefit analysis and mammographic screening: A travel cost approach. *Journal of Health Economics, 17,* 767–787.

Cleek, E.N., Wofsky, M., Boyd-Franklin, N., Mundy, B., & Howell, T.J. (2012). The family empowerment program: An interdisciplinary approach to working with multi-stressed urban families. *Family Process, 51,* 207–217.

Clements, P. (2012). *Rawlsian political analysis: Rethinking the microfoundations of social science.* Notre Dame, IN: University of Notre Dame Press.

Clinton, W.J. (1995, October 30). *Remarks to the White House conference on travel and tourism.* Online by G. Peters & J.T. Woolley, *The American Presidency Project.* Retrieved from http://www.presidency.ucsb.edu/ws/?pid=50715

Clinton, W.J. (1996, January 23). *Address before a joint session of the Congress on the state of the union.* Online by G. Peters & J.T. Woolley, *The American Presidency Project.* Retrieved from http://www.presidency.ucsb.edu/ws/?pid=53091

CNN. (2012). *Role of government.* Retrieved from http://www.cnn.com/election/2012/campaign-issues.html

Coate, D., & Grossman, M. (1988). Effects of alcohol beverage prices and legal drinking ages on youth alcohol use. *Journal of Law and Economics, 31,* 145–171.

Cogan, J.F. (1983). Labor supply and negative income taxation: New evidence from the New Jersey-Pennsylvania experiment. *Economic Inquiry, 21,* 465–484.

Collins, H., & Evans, R. (2007). *Rethinking expertise.* Chicago: University of Chicago Press.

Committee on the Institutional Means for Assessment of Risks to Public Health. Commission on Life Sciences. National Research Council [NRS Committee]. (1983). *Risk assessment in the federal government: Managing the process.* Washington, DC: National Academy Press.

Confessore, N., Kocieniewski, D., & Parker, A. (2012, January 17). Romney shares some tax data; Critics pounce. *The New York Times,* p. A1. Retrieved from http://www.nytimes.com/2012/01/18/us/politics/facing-pointed-attacks-romney-urges-focus-on-obama.html?_r=1

Cohn, J. (2013, February 5). Not-so-universal health care: Slipping through the cracks of Obamacare. *The New Republic.* Retrieved from http://www.newrepublic.com/article/112327/obamacare-not-universal-you-thought

Collins, G. (2013, February 14). The state of the 4-year-olds. *The New York Times,* A27.

Congressional Budget Office. (2004). *Administrative costs of private accounts in Social Security.* Washington, DC: Author. Retrieved from http://www.cbo.gov/ftpdocs/52xx/doc5277/Report.pdf

Congressional Budget Office. (2013). *Refundable tax credits.* Washington, DC: Author. Retrieved from http://www .cbo.gov/sites/default/files/cbofiles/attachments/43767_RefundableTaxCredits_2012-01-24_1.pdf

Congressional Research Service. (1996). *Food Quality Protection Act of 1996. Bill summary and status 104th Congress (1995–1996). H.R.1627 CRS summary.* Retrieved from http://thomas.loc.gov/cgi-bin/ bdquery/z?d104:HR01627:@@@D&summ2=m&

Congressional Research Service. (2011). *The social security disability amendments of 1980. Bill summary and status 96th Congress (1979–1980). H.R.3236 CRS summary.* Retrieved from http://thomas.loc.gov/cgi-bin/bdquery/ z?d096:HR03236:@@@D&summ2=m& |TOM:/bss/d096query.html|

Conklin, G.H. (1977). [Review of the book *New rules of the sociological method: A positive critique of interpretive sociologies,* by A. Giddens.]. *Annals of the American Academy of Political and Social Science, 432,* 178.

Conner, T.S., Tennen, H., Fleeson, W., & Barrett, L.F. (2009). Experience sampling methods: A modern idiographic approach to personality research. *Social and Personality Psychology Compass, 3,* 1–22.

Conway, P., Cresswell, J., Harmon, D., Pospishil, C., Smith, K., Wages, J., & Weisz, L. (2012). Using empowerment evaluation to facilitate the development of intimate partner and sexual violence prevention programs. *Journal of Family Social Work, 13,* 343–361.

Cook, B., Dodds, C., & Mitchell, W. (2003). Social entrepreneurship—False premises and dangerous forebodings. *Australian Journal of Social Issues, 38,* 57–72.

Cook, P.J. (1997). *Paying the tab: The costs and benefits of alcohol control.* Princeton, NJ: Princeton University Press.

Cook, P.J., & Vaupel, J.W. (1985). What policy analysts do: Three research styles. *Journal of Policy Analysis and Management, 4,* 427–428.

Cook, T.D., & Campbell, D.T. (1979). *Quasi-experimentation: Design and analysis issues for field settings.* Boston: Houghton Mifflin.

Cooley, C.H. (1920). Reflections upon the sociology of Herbert Spencer. *American Journal of Sociology, 26,* 129–145.

Coontz, S. (2013, February 17). Why gender equality stalled. *The New York Times,* SR1, SR6–7.

Cooper, H. (2012, February 10). After outcry, Obama shifts in birth control fight. *The New York Times.* Retrieved from http://www.nytimes.com/2012/02/11/health/policy/obama-to-offer-accommodation-on-birth-control-rule- officials-say.html?hp

Cooper, H., & Goldstein, L. (2012, February 11). Obama adjusts a rule covering contraceptions. *The New York Times,* A1, A12.

Corrigan, P.W. (2007). How clinical diagnosis might exacerbate the stigma of mental illness. *Social Work, 51,* 31–39.

Corrigan, P.W., Watson, A.C., Byrne, P., & Davis, K.E. (2005). Mental illness stigma: Problem of public health or social justice? *Social Work, 50,* 363–368.

Coser, L.A. (1977). *Masters of sociological thought: Ideas in historical and social context* (2nd ed.). Fort Worth, TX: Harcourt Brace Jovanovich College Publishers.

Cottingham, P.H., & Besharov, D.J. (2011). Introduction. In D.J. Besharov & P.H. Cottingham (Eds.), *The Workforce Investment Act: Implementation experiences and evaluation findings* (pp. 1–46). Kalamazoo, MI: W.E. Upjohn Institute for Employment Research.

Cousins, J.B., & Earl, L.M. (1992). The case for participatory evaluation. *Educational Evaluation and Policy Analysis, 14,* 397–418.

Cousins, J.B., & Earl, L.M. (Eds.). (1995). *Participatory evaluation in education: Studies in evaluation use and organizational learning.* London: Falmer Press.

Cowhig, J.D. (1971). Federal grant-supported social research and "relevance": Some reservations. *The American Sociologist, 6*(Supplementary Issue), 65–69.

Cravens, H. (1971). The abandonment of evolutionary social theory in America: The impact of professionalization upon American sociological theory, 1890–1920. *American Studies, 12*(2), 5–20.

Cravens, H. (2004). American social science and the invention of affirmative action, 1920s–1970s. In H. Cravens (Ed.), *The social sciences go to Washington: The politics of knowledge in the postmodern age* (pp. 9–40). New Brunswick, NJ: Rutgers University Press.

Crecine, J.P. (1971). University centers for the study of public policy: Organizational viability. *Policy Sciences, 2,* 7–32.

Critchlow, D.T. (1986). [Review of the book *From new era to new deal: Herbert Hoover, the economists, and American economic policy, 1921–1933,* by W.J. Barber]. *Business History Review, 60,* 663–665.

Crouhy, M., Gailai, D., & Mark, R. (2006). *The essentials of risk management.* New York: McGraw-Hill.

Culhane, D.P., Metraux, S., & Hadley, T. (2002). Public service reductions associated with placement of homeless persons with severe mental illness in supportive housing. *Housing Policy Debate, 13,* 107–163.

Currie. J., & Thomas, D. (1995). Does Head Start make a difference? *The American Economic Review, 85,* 341–364.

Daley, M., Argeriou, M., McCarty, D., Callahan, J.J., Shephard, D.S., & Williams, C.N. (2000). The costs of crime and the benefits of substance abuse treatment for pregnant women. *Journal of Substance Abuse Treatment, 19,* 445–458.

Daniels, G.H. (1963). *Baconian science in America, 1815–1845* (Unpublished doctoral dissertation). University of Iowa, Iowa City.

Daniels, G.H. (1967). The process of professionalization of American science: The emergent period, 1820–1860. *Annals of the American Academy of Political and Social Science, 58*(2), 150–166.

Daniels, K., De Chernatony, L., & Johnson, G. (1995). Validating a method for mapping managers' mental models of competition. *Human Relations, 48,* 971–975.

Daniels, N., Kennedy, B.P., & Kawachi, I. (1999). Why justice is good for our health: The social determinants of health inequalities. *Daedalus, 128,* 215–251.

Davis, C. (1986). Public involvement in hazardous waste siting decisions. *Polity, 19,* 296–304.

DC Coalition Against Domestic Violence. (2012). Imposing TANF sanctions and additional compliance requirements will force victims of domestic violence to make difficult choices about their survival. Washington, DC: Author. Retrieved from dcfpi.org/wp-content/uploads/2009/07/7-27-09tanf-dv.pdf

De Wispelaere, J., & Noguera, A. (2012). On the political feasibility of universal basic income: An analytic framework. In R.K. Caputo (Ed.), *Basic income guarantee and politics: International experiences and perspectives on the viability of income guarantee* (pp. 17–38). New York: Palgrave Macmillan.

Dee, T.S. (2004). Are there civic returns to education? *Journal of Public Economics, 88*(9–10), 1607–1720.

Dees, J.G. (2001). *The meaning of "social entrepreneurship."* Stanford School of Business. Retrieved from http://www.caseatduke.org/documents/dees_sedef.pdf

Delgado, R. (2007). The myth of upward mobility. [Review of the book *In our hands: A plan to replace the welfare state,* by Charles Murray.] *University of Pittsburgh Law Review, 68,* 879–913.

deLeon, P. (1994). Reinventing the policy sciences: Three steps back to the future. *Policy Sciences, 27,* 77–95.

deLeon, P. (1997). *Democracy and the policy sciences.* Albany: State University of New York Press.

deLeon, P., & Weible, C.M. (2010). Policy process research for democracy: A commentary on Lasswell's vision. *International Journal of Policy Studies, 1*(2), 23–34.

de Meyrick, J. (2003). The Delphi technique in health research. *Health Education, 103,* 7–16.

DeMint, J. (2013, January 10). Conservative ideas need a new message. *The Washington Post.* Opinion. Retrieved from http://articles.washingtonpost.com/2013-01-10/opinions/36272177_1_welfare-reform-conservative-ideas-missile-defense

DeNavis-Walt, C., Semega, B.D., & Stringfellow, J.C. (2011). *Income, poverty, and health insurance coverage in the United States: 2011. Consumer Population Reports: Consumer Income,* P60–239. Washington, DC: U.S. Government Printing Office. Retrieved from http://www.census.gov/prod/www/abs/p60.html

Dennis, K. (1995). Charities on the dole. *Policy Review, 76*(March/April), 5–8.

Devaney, B., Bilheimer, L., & Score, J. (1992). Medicaid costs and birth outcomes: The effects of prenatal WIC participants and the use of prenatal care. *Journal of Policy Analysis and Management, 11,* 573–592.

Dewan, S. (2012, February 26). Moral hazard: A tempest-tossed idea. *The New York Times,* Business Day, BU1, BU7.

Dewey, J. (1954). *The public and its problems.* Athens, OH: Swallow Press/Ohio University Press. (Original work published 1927)

Diamond, P.A., & Hausman, J.A. (1994). Contingent valuation: Is some number better than no number? *Journal of Economic Perspectives, 8*(4), 45–64.

Dickie, M., & Messman, V.L. (2004). Parental altruism and the value of avoiding acute illness: Are kids worth more than parents? *Journal of Environmental Economics and Management 48,* 1146–1174.

Deising, P. (1966). Objectivism vs. subjectivism in the social sciences. *Philosophy of Science, 33,* 124–133.

Dinkel, C. (2011). Welfare family caps and the zero-grant situation. *Cornell Law Review, 96,* 365–396.

DiPrete, T.A., & Eirich, G.M. (2006). Cumulative advantage as a mechanism for inequality: A review of theoretical and empirical developments. *Annual Review of Sociology, 32,* 271–297.

Dolfsma, W., & Hoppe, H. (2003). On feminist economics. *Feminist Review, 75,* 118–128.

Dolinsky, A.L., Caputo, R.K., & O'Kane, P. (1989). Competing effects of culture and situation on welfare receipt. *Social Service Review, 63,* 359–371.

Domhoff, G.W. (1967). *Who rules America?* Englewood Cliffs, NJ: Prentice Hall.

Domhoff, G.W. (1974). Watergate: Conflict and antagonisms within the power elite. *Theory and Society, 1,* 99–102.

Domhoff, G.W. (1983). Guest editor's introduction. *Social Science History, 7* (*The American Corporate Network, 1815–1974*), 123–127.

Domhoff, G.W. (2007). C. Wright Mills, Floyd Hunter, and 50 years of power structure research. *Michigan Sociological Review, 21,* 1–54.

Donaldson, S.I. (2003). Theory-driven program evaluation in the new millennium. In S.I. Donaldson & M. Scriven (Eds.), *Evaluating social programs and problems: Visions for the new millennium* (pp. 109–141). Mahwah, NJ: Erlbaum.

Douglas, H. (2000). Inductive risk and values in science. *Philosophy of Science, 67,* 557–579.

Douthat, R. (2012, February 11). Can the working class be saved? *The New York Times Sunday Review,* SR11.

Dowd, K. (2009). Moral hazard and the financial crisis. *Cato Journal, 29*(1), 141–166.

Dror, Y. (1970). Prolegomena to policy sciences. *Policy Sciences, 1,* 135–150.

Dror, Y. (1971). Universities and the teaching of policy sciences. *Policy Sciences, 2,* 83–85.

Dror, Y. (1984). Required breakthroughs in think tanks. *Policy Sciences, 16,* 199–225.

Duclos, J.Y. (2006). *Innis Lecture: Equity and equality.* Canadian Journal of Economics, 39, 1073–1104.

Dudley, J.R. (2000). Confronting stigma within the services system. *Social Work, 45,* 449–455.

Dunbar, C.F. (1891). The academic study of economics. *The Quarterly Journal of Economics, 5,* 397–416.

Duncan, D.J. (1984). *Years of poverty, years of plenty: The changing economic fortunes of American workers and families.* Ann Arbor: Institute for Social Research, University of Michigan.

Duncan, O.D. (1978). Sociologists should reconsider nuclear energy. *Social Forces, 57,* 1–22.

Dunn, W.N. (2008). *Public policy analysis: An introduction* (4th ed.). Upper Saddle River, NJ: Pearson Education.

Durkheim, E. (1982). *The rules of sociological method and selected texts on sociology and its method* (S.Lukes, Ed., & W.D. Halls, Trans.). New York: Free Press.

Durning, D. (1999). The transition from traditional to postpositivist policy analysis: A role for Q-methodology. *Journal of Policy Analysis and Management, 18* (3), 389–410.

Durning, D., & Osuna, W. (1994). Policy analysts' roles and value orientations: An empirical investigation using Q methodology. *Journal of Policy Analysis and Management, 13,* 629–657.

Dusek, V. (1969). Falsifiability and power elite theory. *Administration & Society* [*Journal of Comparative Administration*], 1, 198–212.

Dye, T.R. (1978). Oligarchic tendencies in national policy-making: The role of the private policy-planning organizations. *The Journal of Politics, 40,* 309–331.

Dye, T.R. (2001). *Top down policymaking.* New York: Chatham House.

Dyer, W.T., & Fairlie, R.W. (2003). *Do family caps reduce out-of-wedlock births? Evidence from Arkansas, Georgia, Indiana, New Jersey and Virginia* (Center Discussion Paper No. 877). New Haven, CT: Yale University, Economic Growth Center. Retrieved from http://ssrn.com/abstract = 487488

Dworkin, R. (1996). Objectivity and truth: You'd better believe it. *Philosophy & Public Affairs, 25,* 87–139.

Dye, T.R. (1992). *Understanding public policy.* Englewood Cliffs, NJ: Prentice Hall.

Easterbrook, G. (1986). "Ideas move nations": How conservative think tanks have helped to transform the terms of political debate. *The Atlantic Monthly, 257*(1), 66–80.

Easton, D. (1950). Harold Lasswell: Policy scientist for a democratic society. *The Journal of Politics, 12,* 450–477.

Economic Report of the President. (2011). Washington, DC: U.S. Government Printing Office. Retrieved from http://www.gpo.gov/fdsys/browse/collection.action?collectionCode = ERP&browsePath = 2011&isCollapsed = false&leafLevelBrowse = false&isDocumentResults = true&ycord = 0

Edelman, P. (2011). *Affirmative action: Courts and the making of public policy.* Oxford, UK: The Foundation for Law, Justice and Society. Retrieved from http://www.fljs.org/uploads/documents/Edelman.pdf

Edmundson, M. (2012, April 1). Education's hungry hearts. *The New York Times,* p. SR8.

Ekelund, R.B., & Hébert, R.F. (2002). Retrospectives: The origins of neoclassical microeconomics. *Journal of Economic Perspectives, 16*(3), 197–215.

Eligon, J. (2012, March 8). Cuomo and G.O.P. quiet so far on tuition aid for illegal immigrants. *The New York Times,* p. A24.

Ell, K. (1996). Social work and health care practice and policy: A psychosocial research agenda. *Social Work, 41,* 583–592.

Ellwood, D.T., & Bane, M.J. (1985). The impact of AFDC on family structure and living arrangements. *Research in Labor Economics, 7,* 137–207.

Elmore, R.F. (1979–1980). Backward mapping: Implementation research and policy decisions. *Political Science Quarterly, 94,* 601–616.

Employee Benefit Research Institute. (2011). *EBRI databook on employee benefits. Chapter 2. Finances of the employee benefit system.* Retrieved from http://www.ebri.org/publications/books/?fa = databook

Entman, R.M. (1993). Framing: Toward clarification of a fractured paradigm. *Journal of Communication, 43*(4), 51–58.

Ericson, R.F. (1970). The policy analysis role of the contemporary university. *Policy Sciences, 1,* 429–442.

Etzioni, A. (1967). Mixed-scanning: A third approach to decision-making. *Public Administration Review, 27,* 385–392.

Etzioni-Halvey, E. (1990). Democratic elite theory. *European Journal of Sociology, 31,* 317–350.

Eurich, A.C. (1942). Evaluation of general education in colleges. *The Journal of Educational Research, 35,* 502–516.

Faith, J., Panzarella, C., Spencer R.C., Williams, C., Brewer, J., & Covone, M. (2010). Use of performance-based contracting to improve effective use of resources for publicly funded residential services. *The Journal of Behavioral Health Services and Research, 37,* 400–408.

Farnam, H. (1886). [Review of the book *The labor movement in America* by R.T. Ely]. *Political Science Quarterly, 1,* 682–687.

Farr, J., Hacker, J., & Kazee, N. (2006). The political scientist of democracy: The discipline of Harold D. Lasswell. *The American Political Science Review, 100,* 579–587.

Fass, S.M., & Pi, C.R. (2002). Getting tough on juvenile crime: An analysis of costs and benefits. *Journal of Research in Crime and Delinquency, 39,* 363–399.

Federal Regulations. (2012). *Title 45—Public welfare: Part 96 block grants.* Retrieved from http://ecfr.gpoaccess.gov/cgi/t/text/text-idx?c = ecfr&tpl = /ecfrbrowse/Title45/45cfr96_main_02.tpl

Feinberg, C. (2007). The knowledge traders: Psychological experts, political intellectuals, and the rise of the new right (Doctoral dissertation, University of California, Santa Barbara). Available from ProQuest Dissertations and Theses database. (UMI No. 3255183)

Ferber, M.A., & McMahon, W.W. (1979). Women's expected earnings and their investment in higher education. *Journal of Human Resources, 14,* 405–420.

Fetterman, D.M. (1981). Blaming the victim: The problem of evaluation design and federal involvement, and reinforcing world views in education. *Human Organization, 40,* 67–77.

Fetterman, D.M. (1982). Ethnography in educational research: The dynamics of diffusion. *Educational Researcher, 11*(3), 17–22 + 29.

Fetterman, D.M. (1988). Qualitative approaches to evaluating education. *Educational Researcher, 17*(8), 17–23.

Fetterman, D.M. (1994). Empowerment evaluation. *Evaluation Practice, 15*(1), 1–15.

Fetterman, D.M. (2002). Empowerment evaluation: Building communities of practice and a culture of learning. *American Journal of Community Psychology, 30*, 89–102.

Feuer, L.S. (1969). Berkeley and beyond. *Change in Higher Education, 1*(1), 47–51.

Feuer, M.J., & Maratano, C.J. (2010). Science advice as procedural rationality: Reflections on the National Research Council. *Minerva, 48*, 259–275.

Feulner, E.J. (1985). *Ideas, think tanks, and governments.* Washington, DC: The Heritage Foundation. Retrieved from http://thf_media.s3.amazonaws.com/1986/pdf/h151.pdf

Field, G.L., Higley, J., & Burton, M.G. (1990). A new elite framework for political sociology. *Revue européenne des sciences sociales, 28*(88), 149–182.

Figlio, D.N. (1995). The effect of drinking age laws and alcohol-related crashes: Time series evidence from Wisconsin. *Journal of Public Policy Analysis and Management, 14*, 555–566.

Fischer, F. (1980). *Politics, values, and social policy: The problem of methodology.* Boulder, CO: Westview Press.

Fischer, F. (1991). American think tanks: Policy elites and the politicization of expertise. *Governance, 4*, 332–353.

Fischer, F. (1993). Citizen participation and the democratization of policy expertise: From theoretical inquiry to practical cases. *Policy Sciences, 26*, 165–187.

Fischer, F. (1995). *Evaluating public policy.* Chicago: Nelson-Hall.

Fleming, M.F., Mundt, M.P., French, M.T., Manwell, L.B., Stauffacher, E.A., & Barry, K.L. (2002). Brief physician advice for problem drinkers: Long-term efficacy and benefit-cost analysis. *Alcoholism: Clinical and Experimental Research, 26*, 36–43.

Fletcher, M.A. (2011, October 13). Cain's "9-9-9" tax plan hits poor, helps wealthy, experts say. *The Washington Post.* Retrieved from http://www.washingtonpost.com/business/economy/cains-9-9-9-tax-plan-hits-poor-helps-wealthy-experts-say/2011/10/13/gIQAiE3UiL_story.html

Flynn, T.R. (1997). *Sartre, Foucault, and historical reason. Volume 1: Toward an existentialist theory of history.* Chicago: University of Chicago Press.

Flynn, T.R. (2005). *Sartre, Foucault, and historical reason. Volume 2: A poststructuralist mapping of history.* Chicago: University of Chicago Press.

Flyvbjerg, B. (2001). *Making social science matter: Why social inquiry fails and how it can succeed again.* Cambridge, UK: Cambridge University Press.

Flyvbjerg, B. (2004). A perestroikan straw man answers back: David Laitin and phronetic political science. *Politics & Society, 32*, 389–416.

Folbre, N. (2001). *The invisible heart: Economics and family values.* New York: The New Press.

Folbre, N., & Pujol, M. (1996). Explorations: Introduction. *Feminist Economics, 2*(3), 121.

Forester, J. (Ed.) (1985). *Critical theory and public life.* Cambridge, MA: MIT Press.

Fortune, M., & Schweber, S.S. (1993). Scientists and the legacy of World War II: The case of operations research (OS). *Social Studies of Science, 23*, 595–642.

Foundation Center. (2012). *Top 100 U.S. foundations by asset size.* New York: Author. Retrieved from http://foundationcenter.org/findfunders/topfunders/top100assets.html

Fox, C. (2009). [Review of the book *Illegal, alien, or immigrant: The politics of immigration reform,* by L. Newton.] *Contemporary Sociology, 38*, 558–559.

Frank, J. (2009). *Law and the modern mind.* Piscataway, NJ: Transaction Publishers. (Original work published 1930)

Franklin, D.L. (1986). Mary Richmond and Jane Addams: From moral certainty to rational inquiry in social work practice. *Social Service Review, 60*, 504–525.

Friedman, M. (1955). The role of government in education. In R.A. Solo (Ed.), *Economics and the public interest* (pp. 85-107). New Brunswick, NJ: Rutgers University Press. Retrieved from http://www.freerepublic.com/focus/f-news/1173402/posts

Friedman, M. (1962/1982). *Capitalism and freedom.* Chicago: University of Chicago Press.

Freire, P. (1970). *Pedagogy of the oppressed.* New York: Seabury Press.

French, M.T., McCollister, K.E., Sacks, S., McKendrick, K., & De Leon, G. (2002). Benefit cost analysis of a modified therapeutic community for mentally ill chemical abusers. *Evaluation and Program Planning, 25,* 137–148.

Friedman, B.M. (2005). *The moral consequences of economic growth.* New York: Alfred A. Knopf.

Friedman, H.S. (2012). *The measure of a nation: How to regain America's edge and boost our global standing.* Amherst, NY: Prometheus Books.

Friedman, L.S. (1977). An interim evaluation of the supported work experiment. *Policy Analysis, 3*(2), 147–170.

Fronlich, N., Oppenheimer, J., & Eavey, C.L. (1987). Choices of principles of distributive justice in experimental groups. *American Journal of Political Science, 31,* 606–636.

Fuhrman, E.R. (1979). The normative structure of critical theory. *Human Studies, 2,* 209–227.

Fuhrman, E.R., & Snizek, W.E. (1979/1980). Some observations on the nature and content of critical theory. *Humboldt Journal of Social Relations, 7*(1), 33–51.

Fulton, A.D., & Weimer, D.L. (1980). Regaining a lost policy option: Neighborhood parking stickers in San Francisco. *Policy Analysis, 6,* 335–348.

Furner, M.O. (2011). *Advocacy and objectivity: A crisis in the professionalization of American social science, 1865-1905.* New Brunswick, NJ: Transaction Publishers.

Garfield, L.Y. (2005). Back to Bakke: Defining the strict scrutiny test for affirmative action policies aimed at achieving diversity in the classroom. *Nebraska Law Review, 83,* 631–684.

Gardiner, S. (2011). *A perfect moral storm: The ethical tragedy of climate change.* New York: Oxford University Press.

Gardenhire, A., & Nelson, L. (2003). *Intensive qualitative research: Challenges, best uses, and opportunities.* New York: MDRC. Retrieved from http://www.mdrc.org/publications/339/full.pdf

Garza, H. (1999). *Objectivity, scholarship, and advocacy: The Chicano/Latino scholar in America.* (JSRI Occasional Paper #58). Julian Samora Research Institute. East Lansing: Michigan State University.

Gellner, E. (1973). *Cause and meaning in the social sciences.* London: Routledge.

George, R.P. (1999). *In defense of natural law.* Oxford: Oxford University Press.

Gettelman, M.E. (1969/1970). John H. Finley and the academic origins of American social work, 1887-1892. *Studies in History and Society, 2*(Fall/Spring), 13–26.

Geuss, R. (1981). *The idea of a critical theory: Habermas & the Frankfurt School.* Cambridge, UK: Cambridge University Press.

Ghiloni, B.W., & Domhoff, G.W. (1984). Power structure research in America and the promise of democracy. *Revue française d'études américaines, 21/22* (ÉCONOMIE ET POUVOIRS AUX ÉTATS-UNIS / THE ECONOMICS OF POWER IN THE UNITED STATES), 335–341.

Gibbons, J., & Gray, M. (2004). Critical thinking as integral to social work practice. *Journal of Teaching in Social Work, 24*(1/2), 19–38.

Gil, D. (1992). *Unraveling social policy: Theory, analysis, and political action towards social equality* (5th rev. enl. ed.). Rochester, VT: Schenkman.

Gilbert, N., & Specht, H. (1976). Advocacy and professional ethics. *Social Work, 21,* 288–293.

Gilbert, N., & Terrell, P. (2005). *Dimensions of social welfare policy* (6th ed.). Boston: Allyn and Bacon.

Giving USA Foundation. (2011). *Giving USA 2011: The annual report on philanthropy for the year 2010. Executive summary.* Chicago: Author. Retrieved from http://www.givingusareports.org/products/GivingUSA_2011_ExecSummary_Print.pdf

Gladwell, M. (2005, August 29). The moral hazard myth. *The New Yorker,* pp. 44–49. Retrieved from http://www.gladwell.com/pdf/hazard.pdf

Glass, B.L. (1990). Child support enforcement: An implementation analysis. *Social Service Review, 64,* 542–558.

Glassman, J.K. (2009). The hazard of moral hazard. *Commentary Magazine* (September). Retrieved from http://www .commentarymagazine.com/article/the-hazard-of-moral-hazard/

Glazer, N. (1969, July). Student politics and the university. *The Atlantic*. Retrieved from http://www.theatlantic.com/ magazine/archive/1969/07/student-politics-and-the-university/303378/

Goddard, D. (1973). Max Weber and the objectivity of social science. *History and Theory, 12,* 1–22.

Goldberg, H., & Schott, L. (2000). *A compliance-oriented approach to sanctions in state and county TANF programs.* Washington, DC: Center on Budget and Policy Priorities. Retrieved from http://www.cbpp.org/archiveSite/10-1-00sliip.pdf

Goldhill, D. (2009, September). How American health care killed my father. *The Atlantic*. Retrieved from http://www .theatlantic.com/magazine/archive/2009/09/how-american-health-care-killed-my-father/307617/

Goldhill, D. (2013a). *Catastrophic care: How American health care killed my father — and how we can fix it.* New York: Knopf.

Goldhill, D. (2013b, February 17). The health benefits that cut your pay. *The New York Times,* SR6.

Goldstein, L.J. (1964). [Review of the book *Phenomenology and the human sciences: A contribution to a new scientific ideal,* by S. Strasser.] *The Journal of Philosophy, 61,* 428–431.

Goode, W.J. (1960). Encroachment, charlatanism, and the emerging profession: Psychology, sociology, and medicine. *American Sociological Review, 25,* 902–965.

Goodin, R.E. (1988). *Reasons for welfare: The political theory of the welfare state.* Princeton, NJ: Princeton University Press.

Goodin, R.E. (1991). Permissible paternalism: In defense of the nanny state. *The Responsive Community, 1*(3), 42–51. Also in A. Etzioni (Ed.) (1998), *The essential communitarian reader* (pp. 125–134). Lanham, MD: Rowman & Littlefield.

Goodman, A. (2011, October 25). Details emerge on student loan plans. *Commentary Magazine*. Retrieved from http://www.commentarymagazine.com/2011/10/25/obama-student-loans-plan/

Goodstein, L. (2012, February 10). Bishops were prepared for battle over birth control coverage. *The New York Times,* A1, A16.

Gormley, W.T. (1987). Institutional policy analysis: A critical review. *Journal of Policy Analysis and Management, 6,* 153–169.

Gounden, A.M.N. (1967). Investment in education in India. *Journal of Human Resources, 2,* 347–358.

Government Programs. (2012). *Eligibility guidelines.* Retrieved from http://www.egyptianaaa.org/ EligibilityGuidelines.htm

Grafton, C., & Permaloff, A. (2001). Public policy for business and the economy: Ideological dissensus, change and consensus. *Policy Sciences, 34,* 403–434.

Gramlich, E.M. (1998). *A guide to benefit-cost analysis* (2nd ed.). Prospect Heights, IL: Waveland Press.

Gramm, W.S. (1987). Labor, work, and leisure: Human well-being and the optimal allocation of time. *Journal of Economic Issues, 21,* 167–188.

Grant. R.W. (2002). The ethics of incentives: Historical origins and contemporary understandings. *Economics and Philosophy, 18,* 111–139.

Grant. R.W. (2006). Ethics and incentives: A political approach. *American Political Science Review, 100,* 29–39.

Grant, R.W. (2011). *Strings attached: Untangling the ethics of incentives.* New York: Russell Sage Foundation.

Gray, D.J. (1983). Value-relevant sociology: The analysis of subjects of social consequence, including implications for human well-being. *American Journal of Economics and Sociology, 42,* 405–416.

Greenwald, B.C., & Stiglitz, J.E. (1990). Asymmetric information and the new theory of the firm: Financial restraints and risk behavior. *American Economic Review, 80*(2), Papers and proceedings of the hundred and second annual meeting of the American Economic Association, 160–165.

Gregory, P.R. (2004). *Essentials of economics* (6th ed.). Boston, MA: Addison-Wesley.

Greenstein, R. (1985, March 25). Losing faith in "Losing Ground." [Review of the book *Losing ground: American social policy, 1950–1980,* by C. Murray.] *The New Republic,* 12–17.

Greenwald, M.W., & Anderson, M. (Eds.) (1996). *Pittsburgh surveyed: Social science and social reform in the early twentieth century.* Pittsburgh, PA: University of Pittsburgh Press.

Grossman, M., Coate, D., & Arluck, G.M. (1987). Price sensitivity of alcoholic beverages in the United States. In H.D. Holder (Ed.), *Control issues in alcohol prevention: Strategies for states and communities* (pp. 169–198). Greenwich, CT: JAI Press.

Grossman, M., & Markowitz, S. (1998). Alcohol regulation and domestic violence toward children. *Contemporary Economic Policy, 16,* 309–320.

Grout, P. (1978). On minimax regret and welfare economics. *Journal of Public Economics, 9,* 405–410.

Grønbjerg, K.A. (2001). The U.S. nonprofit human service sector: A creeping revolution. *Nonprofit and Voluntary Sector Quarterly, 30,* 276–297.

Gruber, C.S. (1972). Academic freedom at Columbia University, 1917–1918: The case of James McKeen Cattell. *AAUP Bulletin, 58,* 297–305.

Guba, E.G., & Lincoln, Y.S. (1989). *Fourth generation evaluation.* Thousand Oaks, CA: Sage.

Guba, E.G., & Lincoln, Y.S. (2001). *Guidelines and checklist for constructivist (a.k.a. fourth generation) evaluation.* Retrieved from http://www.wmich.edu/evalctr/archive_checklists/constructivisteval.pdf

Gueron, J. (2000). *The politics of random assignment: Implementing studies and impacting policy.* New York: MDRC. Retrieved from http://www.mdrc.org/publications/45/full.pdf

Gunnell, J.G. (2009). Political inquiry and the metapractical voice: Weber and Oakeshott. *Political Research Quarterly, 62,* 3–15.

Gurwitsch, A. (1961). The problem of existence in constitutive phenomenology. *The Journal of Philosophy, 58,* 625–632.

Gutiérrez, D. (2005). John Rawls and policy formation. *Review of Policy Research, 22,* 737–742.

Habermas, J. (1973). *Theory and practice.* Boston, MA: Beacon Press.

Habermas, J. (1984). *The theory of communicative action.* Volume I. Boston, MA: Beacon Press.

Habermas, J. (1987). *The theory of communicative action.* Volume II. Boston, MA: Beacon Press.

Hacker, J.S. (2002). *The divided welfare state: The battle over public and private social benefits in the United States.* Cambridge, UK: Cambridge University Press.

Halberstam, D. (1972). *The best and the brightest.* New York: Random House.

Hall, P.A. (1993). Policy paradigms, social learning, and the state: The case of economic policymaking in Britain. *Comparative Politics, 25,* 275–296.

Hall, W. (2010). What are the policy lessons of national alcohol prohibition in the United States, 1920–1933? *Addiction, 105,* 1164–1173.

Hamburg, M. (2011, December 7). *Statement from FDA Commissioner Margaret Hamburg, M.D. on Plan B One-Step.* Washington, DC: FDA. Retrieved from http/www.hhs.gov/news/press/2011press/12/20111207a.html

Hampton, G. (2004). Enhancing public participation through narrative analysis. *Policy Sciences, 37,* 261–275.

Hannan, M.T., Tuma, N.B., & Groeneveld, L.P. (1977). Income and marital events: Evidence from an income-maintenance experiment. *American Journal of Sociology, 82,* 1186–1211.

Harberger, A.C. (1993). The search for relevance in economics. *The American Economic Review, 83* (2), Papers and Proceedings of the Hundred and Fifth Annual Meeting of the American Economic Association, 1–16.

Harding, S. (1978). Four contributions values can make to the objectivity of social science. *PSA: Proceedings of the Biennial Meeting of the Philosophy of Science Association, 1978,* 199–209.

Harding, S. (1986). *The science question in feminism.* Ithaca, NY: Cornell University Press.

Harding, S. (Ed.) (1987). *Feminism and methodology.* Milton Keynes, UK: Open University Press.

Harris, G. (2011, December 7). Plan to widen availability of morning-after pill is rejected. *The New York Times,* p. A1.

Harsanyi, J.C. (1977). Rule utilitarianism and decision theory. *Erkenntis, 11*(1), Social ethics, Part I, 25–53.

Hart, A.F. (1978). The policy sciences, social work, and the analysis of social policy. (Doctoral dissertation, Columbia University). Available from ProQuest Dissertations and Theses database. (UMI No. 7819350)

Hartzell,S.L. (2007). Managing welfare stigma from the other side of the desk: A look at rural TANF workers. (Doctoral dissertation, West Virginia University). Available from ProQuest Dissertations and Theses database. (UMI No. 1451635)

Harward, J. (2013, March 2). Deep philosophical divide underlies the impasse. *The New York Times,* A10.

Haskell, T.L. (2000). *The emergence of professional social science: The American Social Science Association and the nineteenth-century crisis of authority.* Baltimore, MD: Johns Hopkins University Press.

Hauptmann, E. (2005). Defining "theory" in postwar political science. In G. Steinmetz (Ed.), *The politics of method in the human sciences* (pp. 207–232). Durham, NC: Duke University Press.

Haveman, R. (1988). *Starting even: An equal opportunity program to combat the nation's new poverty.* New York: Simon & Schuster.

Hawkins, R.L., & Kim, E.J (2012). The socio-economic empowerment assessment: Addressing poverty and economic distress in clients. *Clinical Social Work Journal, 40,* 194–202.

Hayek, F.A. (1945). The use of knowledge in society. *American Economic Review, 35,* 519–530.

Haynes, K.S., & Mickelson, J.S. (2010). *Affecting change: Social workers in the political arena* (7th ed.). Boston, MA: Allyn & Bacon.

Haynes, L., Service, O., Goldacre, B., & Torerson, D. (2012). *Test, learn, adapt: Developing public policy with randomised controlled trials.* London: Cabinet Office Behavioural Insight Team. Retrieved from http://www .cabinetoffice.gov.uk/sites/default/files/resources/TLA-1906126.pdf

Health and Safety Executive. (2012). *Five steps to risk assessment.* Bootle Merseyside, UK: Author. Retrieved from http://www.hse.gov.uk/risk/fivesteps.htm

Health Care Reform. (2011, December 21). Times topics. *The New York Times.* Retrieved from http://topics.nytimes. com/top/news/health/diseasesconditionsandhealthtopics/health_insurance_and_managed_care/health_ care_reform/index.html

Heap, J.L. (1995). Constructionism in the rhetoric and practice of fourth generation evaluation. *Evaluation and Program Planning, 18,* 51–61.

Heinzerling, L., & Ackerman, F. (2002). *Pricing the priceless: Cost-benefit analysis of environmental protection.* Washington, DC: Georgetown Environmental Law and Policy Institute, Georgetown University Law Center.

Hellebust, L. (ed.) (1996). *Think tank directory: A guide to nonprofit public policy research organizations.* Topeka, KS: Government Research Service.

Hempel, C. (1942). The function of general laws in history. *The Journal of Philosophy, 39,* 35–48.

Hernandez, V.R. (2008). Generalist and advanced generalist practice. In T. Mizrahi & L.E. Davis (Eds.), *Encyclopedia of social work* (20th ed.). Retrieved from http://www.oxford-naswsocialwork.com/entry?entry = t203.e160

Higley, J. (2009). [Review of the book *Vilfredo Pareto's sociology: A framework for political psychology,* by A.J. Marshall.] *Contemporary Sociology, 38*(1), 66–67.

Hill, M. (1968). A goals-achievement matrix for evaluating alternative plans. *Journal of the American Institute of Planners, 34,* 19–29.

Himelfarb, R. (1995). *Catastrophic politics: The rise and fall of the Medicare Catastrophic Coverage Act of 1988.* University Park: Pennsylvania State University Press.

Himmelberg, R.F. (1975). [Review of the book *Herbert Hoover: Forgotten progressive,* by J.H. Wilson.] *Business History Review, 49,* 527–529.

Himmelweit, S. (2010). Making visible the hidden economy: The case for gender-impact analysis of economic policy. *Feminist Economics, 8*(1), 49–70.

Hirshleifer, J. (1958). On the theory of the optimal investment decision. *Journal of Political Economy, 66,* 329–352.

Hitlin, S., & Piliavin, J.A. (2004). Values: Reviving a dormant concept. *Annual Review of Sociology, 30,* 359–393.

Hjern, B. (1982). Implementation research: The link gone missing. *Journal of Public Policy, 2,* 301–308.

Hodder, A.L. (1892). Utilitarianism. *International Journal of Ethics, 3,* 90–112.

Hodge, D.R., & Roby, J.L. (2010). Sub-Sarahan African women living with HIV/AIDS: An exploration of general and spiritual coping strategies. *Social Work, 55,* 27–37.

Hodges, D.C. (1967). The end of "The end of ideology." *American Journal of Economics and Sociology, 26,* 135–146.

Holonen, J.S. (1995). Demystifying critical thinking. *Teaching of Psychology, 22,* 75–81.

Holtman, A.G. (1970). *Cost-benefit analysis in adult literacy programmes.* Paris: United Nations Educational, Scientific, and Cultural Organization. Retrieved from http://www.eric.ed.gov/PDFS/ED052437.pdf

Hoogerwerf, A. (1990). Reconstructing policy theory. *Evaluation and Program Planning, 13,* 285–291.

Hopkins, H. (1934). Unemployment relief and the Public Works Administration. *Proceedings of the Academy of Political Science, 15*(4), 81–83.

Horowitz, I.L. (1970). Social science mandarins: Policymaking as a political formula. *Policy Sciences, 1,* 339–360.

Horowitz, I.L. (1981). C. Wright Mills's power elite: A twenty-five year retrospective. *The Antioch Review, 39,* 373–382.

Houghton, R.W. (1958). A note on the early history of consumer's surplus. *Economica, 25*(97), 49–57.

House, E.R. (1978). Assumptions underlying evaluation models. *Educational Researcher, 7*(3), 4–12.

House, E.R., & Howe, K.R. (1998). The issue of advocacy in evaluations. *American Journal of Evaluation, 19,* 233–236.

Hrywna, M. (2011, November 1). The NPT 2011 Top 100: An in-depth study of America's largest nonprofits. *The NonProfit Times.* Retrieved from http://shop.nptimes.com/npttop100.aspx

Hu, W. (2013, February 18). When being jobless is a barrier to finding a job. *The New York Times,* A13. Retrieved from http://www.nytimes.com/2013/02/18/nyregion/for-many-being-out-of-work-is-chief-obstacle-to-finding-it .html?src=recg

Hughes, M.A. (1990). [Review of the books *Starting even: An equal opportunity program to combat the nation's new poverty,* by R. Haveman; *Welfare policies for the 1990s,* by P.H. Cottingham & D.T. Ellwood; *To promote the general welfare: Market processes vs. political transfers,* by R.E. Wagner.] *Journal of Policy Analysis and Management, 9,* 581–590.

Hurteau, M., Houle, S., & Mongiat, S. (2009). How legitimate and justified are judgments in program evaluation? *Evaluation, 15,* 307–319.

Ignatieff, M. (2012a). The price of everything. [Review of the book *What money can't buy: The moral limits of markets,* by M. J. Sandel.] *The New Republic, 243*(4,924), 23–26.

Ignatieff, M. (2012b). The return of sovereignty. [Review of the book *Sovereign equality and moral disagreement,* by B.R. Roth.] *The New Republic, 243*(4,917), 25–28.

Ingram, H., & Schneider, A. (1990). Improving implementation through framing smarter statutes. *Journal of Public Policy, 10,* 67–88.

Ingram, H., Schneider, A.L., & deLeon, P. (2007). Social construction and policy design. In P.A. Sabatier (Ed.), *Theories of the policy process* (2nd ed.) (pp. 93–126). Boulder, CO: Westview Press.

Institute for Innovation in Social Policy. (2012). *The index of social health.* Poughkeepsie, NY: Vassar College. Retrieved from http://iisp.vassar.edu/ish.html

Insurance Institute for Highway Safety. (1999). Deaths go up on interstate highways where higher speed limits are posted. *Status Report, 34*(1), 4. Retrieved from http://www.iihs.org/externaldata/srdata/docs/sr3401.pdf

Investopedia. (2012a). *Asymmetric information.* Retrieved from http://www.investopedia.com/terms/a/ asymmetricinformation.asp#axzz1nEXrh01Z

Investopedia. (2012b). *Deadweight loss.* Retrieved from http://www.investopedia.com/terms/d/deadweightloss .asp#axzz1tGQA5MDD

Investopedia. (2012c). *Monetary policy.* Retrieved from http://www.investopedia.com/terms/m/monetarypolicy .asp#axzz1ngtV4cs8

Investopedia. (2012d). *Natural monopoly.* Retrieved from http://www.investopedia.com/terms/n/natural_ monopoly.asp#axzz1n3RvePmj

Investopedia. (2012e). *Sensitivity analysis.* Retrieved from http://www.investopedia.com/terms/s/ sensitivityanalysis.asp#axzz1rIALuaoD

Jacobs, K., Graham-Squire, D., Roby, D.H., Kominsky, G.F., Kinane, C.M., Needleman, J., Watson, G., & Gans, G. (2011). *Proposed regulations could limit access to affordable health coverage for workers' children and family members. Policy Brief.* Berkeley: University of California, Center for Labor Research and Education / Los Angeles: University of California, Center for Health Policy Research. Retrieved from http://laborcenter.berkeley.edu/ healthcare/Proposed_Regulations11.pdf

James, W. (1897). *The will to believe and other essays in popular philosophy.* Norwood, MA: The Plimpton Press.

Janis, I.L., & Mann, L. (1977). *Decision making: A psychological analysis of conflict, choice, and commitment.* New York: Free Press.

Jarratt, K.P. (2005). The CAS and NEPSY as measures of cognitive processes: Examining the underlying constructs. (Doctoral dissertation, Texas A&M University.) Available from ProQuest Dissertations and Theses database. (UMI No. 3231539)

Jarvie, I.C. (1964). Explanation in social science. [Review of the book *Explanation in social science* by R. Brown.] *The British Journal for the Philosophy of Science, 15*(57), 62–72.

Jenkins, D. (1996). A reflecting team approach to family therapy: A Delphi study. *Journal of Marital and Family Therapy, 22,* 219–238.

Jenkins, J.C., & Eckert, E.M. (2000). The right turn in economic policy: Business elites and the new conservative economics. *Sociological Forum, 15,* 307–338.

Jenkins-Smith, H. (1982). Professional roles of policy analysts. *Journal of Policy Analysis and Management, 2,* 88–100.

Jenkins-Smith, H. (1990). *Democratic politics and policy analysis.* Pacific Grove, CA: Brooks/Cole.

Jennings, B. (1987). Policy analysis: Science, advocacy, or counsel? In S. Nagel (Ed.), *Research in public policy analysis and management: A research annual.* (Vol. 4, pp. 121–134). Greenwich, CT: JAI Press.

Jensen, H.E. (2001). John Stuart Mill's theories of wealth and income distribution. *Review of Social Economy, 59,* 491–507.

Jerome, J. (1969). The American academy 1970. *Change in Higher Education, 1*(5), 10–47.

Jervis, R. (2002). Politics, political science, and specialization. *PS: Political Science and Politics, 35,* 187–189.

Johansson, P.-O. (1997). On the use of market prices to evaluate medical treatments. *Journal of Health Economics, 16,* 609–615.

Johnson, D. (2013). *Do companies lay people off because of taxes or a minimum wage rise?* Washington, DC: Campaign for America's Future. Retrieved from http://blog.ourfuture.org/20130213/do-companies-lay-people-off-it-they-have-to-pay-taxes

Johnson, M.P., Ladd, H.F., & Ludwig, L. (2002). The benefits and costs of residential mobility programmes for the poor. *Housing Studies, 17,* 125–138.

Johnson, R.W., & Mommaerts, C. (2010). *Will health care costs bankrupt aging boomers?* Washington, DC: The Urban Institute. Retrieved from http://www.urban.org/uploadedpdf/412026_health_care_costs.pdf

Joint United Nations Programme on AIDS/HIV [UNAIDS]. (2008). *Report on the global AIDS epidemic: Executive summary.* Geneva, Switzerland: Author. Retrieved from http://data.unaids.org/pub/ . . . /jc1511_gr08_executive-summary _en.pdf

Jones, M.D., & McBeth, M.K. (2010). A narrative policy framework: Clear enough to be wrong? *Policy Studies Journal, 38,* 329–353.

Jost, T. (2013). Implementing health reform: Shared responsibility tax exemptions and family coverage affordability. *Health Affairs* [Web log post]. Retrieved from http://healthaffairs.org/blog/2013/01/31/ implementing-health-reform-shared-responsibility-tax-exemptions-and-family-coverage-affordability/

Kahlenberg, R. (2011). The amicus briefs on affirmative action. *The Chronicle of Higher Education.* Retrieved from http://chronicle.com/blogs/innovations/the-amicus-briefs-on-affirmative-action/30735

Kaiser Family Foundation, Health Research & Educational Trust, & NORC. (2011). *Employer health benefits: 2011 annual survey.* Menlo Park, CA: Kaiser Family Foundation and Chicago, IL: Health Research & Educational Trust. Retrieved from http://ehbs.kff.org/

Kaplan, T.J. (1986). The narrative structure of policy analysis. *Journal of Policy Analysis and Management, 5,* 761–778.

Karhunan, J.P., Jokinen, J.J., Raivio, P.M., & Salminen, U.-S. (2011). Long-term survival and quality of life after cardiac resuscitation following coronary artery bypass grafting. *European Journal of Cardio-Thoracic Surgery, 40,* 249–254.

Karl, B. (1969). Presidential planning and social science research. *Perspectives in American history, 3,* 347–409.

Karl, B., & Katz, S. (1981). The American private philanthropic foundation and the public sphere 1890–1930. *Minerva, 19,* 236–270.

Kazi, M.A.F. (2003). *Realist evaluation in practice: Health and social work.* Thousand Oaks, CA: Sage.

Kraft, M.E., & Furlong, S.R. (2010). *Public policy: Politics, analysis, and alternatives* (3rd ed.). Washington, DC: CQ Press.

Kauff, J., Brown, J., Altshuler, N., Denny-Brown, N., & Martin, E. (2009). Findings from a study of the SSI/SSDI Outreach, Access and Recovery (SOAR) initiative: Final report. Washington, DC: Mathematica Policy Research, Inc. Retrieved from http://www.usich.gov/usich_resources/research/findings_from_a_study_of_the_ssi_ssdi_outreach_access_and_recovery_initiati/

Keiser, L.R., & Meier, K.J. (1996). Policy design, bureaucratic incentives, and public management: The case of child support enforcement. *Journal of Public Administration Research and Theory: J-PART, 6,* 337–364.

Kellogg, P.U. (1912). The spread of the survey idea. *Proceedings of the Academy of Political Science in the City of New York, 2*(4), 1–17.

Kelly, M. (1994). Theories of justice and street-level discretion. *Journal of Public Administration Research and Theory: J-PART, 4,* 119–140.

Kelly, M., & Maynard-Moody, S. (1993). Policy analysis in the post-positivist era: Engaging stakeholders in evaluating the economic development district program. *Public Administration Review, 53,* 135–142.

Kemper, A.R., Davis, M.M., & Freed, G.L. (2002). Expected adverse events in a mass smallpox vaccination campaign. *Effective Clinical Practice, 5,* 84–90.

Kennedy, J.F. (1962, June 11). Commencement address at Yale University. In J.T. Woolley & G. Peters (compilers), *The American Presidency Project* [online]. Retrieved from http://www.presidency.ucsb.edu/ws/?pid=29661#axzz1NxYzMenl

Kenny, M.G. (2002). Toward a racial abyss: Eugenics, Wickliffe Draper, and the origins of the Pioneer Fund. *Journal of the History of the Behavioral Sciences, 38,* 259–283.

Keohane, G.L. (2013). *Social entrepreneurship for the 21st century: Innovation across the nonprofit, private, and public sectors.* New York: McGraw-Hill.

Kerbo, H.R., & Fave, R.D. (1979). The empirical side of the power elite debate: An assessment and critique of recent research. *The Sociological Quarterly, 20,* 5–22.

Kerlinger, F. (1973). *Foundations of behavioral research.* New York: Holt, Rinehart & Winston.

Kerr, C. (1964). The frantic race to remain contemporary. *Daedalus, 93,* 1051–1070.

Kiewiet, D.R., & McCubbins, M.D. (1985). Appropriations decisions as a bilateral bargaining game between president and Congress. *Legislative Studies Quarterly, 10,* 181–201.

Kim, D.H. (2009). Measuring street-level bureaucrats' use of behavioral discretion over information, transaction costs, and stigma in U.S. welfare policy implementation: A comparative analysis of public management in state and local government. (Doctoral dissertation, University at Albany, State University of New York). Available from ProQuest Dissertations and Theses database. (UMI No. 3354651)

Kim, R.Y. (2001). Welfare reform and "ineligibles": Issue of constitutionality and recent court rulings. *Social Work, 46,* 315–323.

Kim, J.-C. (1985). The "market" for lemons reconsidered: A model of the used car market with asymmetric information. *American Economic Review, 75,* 836–843.

King, D.M., & Mazzotta, M.J., with technical assistance of Markowitz, K.J. (2012). *Dollar-based ecosystem valuation methods.* Solomons Island, MD: University of Maryland Center for Environmental Science, Chesapeake Biological Laboratory. Retrieved from http://www.ecosystemvaluation.org/dollar_based.htm

King, J.A. (1995). Involving practitioners in education research. In J.B. Cousins & L.M. Earl (Eds.), *Participatory evaluation in education: Studies in evaluation use and organizational learning* (pp. 86–102). London: Falmer Press.

King, J.A. (2007). Making sense of participatory evaluation. *New Directions for Evaluation, 2007*(114), 83–86.

Kirsch, I.S., Jungeblut, A., Jenkins, L., & Kolstad, A. (2002). *Adult literacy in America: A first look at the findings of the National Adult Literacy Survey.* Washington, DC: National Center for Education Statistics. Retrieved from http://nces.ed.gov/pubs93/93275.pdf

Kitcher, P. (1993). *The advancement of science: Science without legend, objectivity without illusions.* New York: Oxford University Press.

Klein, E. (2006). Mr. Big: Charles Murray's nuttiest idea yet. [Review of the book *In our hands: A plan to replace the welfare state,* by Charles Murray.] *The New Republic, 234*(13), 12–13.

Kneebone, E., & Garr, E. (2011). *Responding to the new geography of poverty: Metropolitan trends in the Earned Income Tax Credit.* Washington, DC: Brookings. Retrieved from http://www.brookings.edu/~/media/Files/rc/papers/2011/0217_eitc_poverty_kneebone/0217_eitc_poverty_kneebone.pdf

Kolata, G. (2002, March 30). With vaccine available, smallpox debate shifts. *The New York Times,* p. A8. Retrieved from http://www.nytimes.com/2002/03/30/us/a-nation-challenged-vaccinations-with-vaccine-available-smallpox-debate-shifts.html

Korzeniewicz, R.P., & Moran, T.P. (2005). Theorizing the relationship between inequality and economic growth. *Theory and Society, 34,* 277–316.

Korzenik, D. (1977). On Robert Stake's responsive evaluation. *Journal of Aesthetic Education, 11*(1), 106–109.

Kozlowsky, R. (2011). *Corporate pension plan funding increases.* Retrieved from http://www.pionline.com/article/20110613/PRINTSUB/306139982

Kraft, M.E., & Clary, B.B. (1991). Citizenship participation and the Nimby syndrome: Public response to radioactive waste disposal. *The Western Political Quarterly, 44,* 299–328.

Kraft, M.E., & Furlong, S.R. (2010). *Public policy: Politics, analysis, and alternatives* (3rd ed.). Washington, DC: CQ Press.

Kristoff, N.D. (2011, May 19). Getting smart on aid. *The New York Times,* A27.

Krueger, A.O. (1972). Rates of return to Turkish higher education. *Journal of Human Resources, 7,* 482–499.

Kucinich, J. (2011, November 11). Is Herman Cain's 9-9-9 tax plan fair? *USA Today.* Retrieved from http://www.usatoday.com/money/perfi/taxes/story/2011-10-10/herman-cain-9-9-9-tax-plan/50723976/1

Kuitunen, J. (1993). Policy orientation and ethics: How incompatible and why? *Science Studies, 6,* 34–50.

Labonte, M. (2009). *The size and role of government.* Washington, DC: Congressional Research Service. Retrieved from http://digital.library.unt.edu/ark:/67531/metadc26213/m1/

Laffer, A.B. (1981). Government exactions and revenue deficiencies. *Cato Journal, 1,* 1–21.

Lai, L.L., & Sorkin, A.L. (1998). Cost benefit analysis of pharmaceutical care in a Medicaid population—from a budgetary perspective. *Journal of Managed Care Pharmacy, 4,* 303–308.

Laitin, D.D. (2003). The perestroikan challenge to social science. *Politics & Society, 31,* 163–184.

Lamontagne, M. (1947). Some French contributions to economic theory. *The Canadian Journal of Economics and Political Science, 13,* 514–532.

Landman, T. (2011, July 22). *Rebutting "Perestroika": Method and substance in political science.* Retrieved from http://privatewww.essex.ac.uk/~todd/rebutting%20perestroika.pdf

Lane, C. (1984, March 25). The Manhattan Project. *The New Republic,* 14–15.

Lane, R.E. (1966). The decline of politics and ideology in a knowledgeable society. *American Sociological Review, 31,* 649–652.

Laski, H.J. (1928). Foundations, universities, and research. *Harper's Monthly Magazine, 157*(June/November), 295–303.

Lasswell, H.D. (1951). The immediate future of research policy and method in political science. *The American Political Science Review, 45,* 133–142.

Lasswell, H.D. (1956). The political science of science: An inquiry into the possible reconciliation of mastery and freedom. *The American Political Science Review, 50,* 961–979.

Lasswell, H.D. (1957). The normative impact of the behavioral sciences. *Ethics, 67*(3, Part 2), 1–42.

Lasswell, H.D. (1970). The emerging conception of the policy sciences. *Policy Studies, 1,* 3–14.

Lasswell, H.D. (1990/1935). *Power: Who gets what, when, and how.* Gloucester, MA: Peter Smith Publishers.

Lasswell, H.D., Brunner, R.D., & Willard, A.R. (2003). On the policy sciences in 1943. *Policy Sciences, 34,* 71–98.

Lasswell, H.D., & McDougal, M.S. (1943). Legal education and public policy: Professional training in the public interest. *The Yale Law Journal, 52*(2), 203–295.

Lawler, E.F. (1996). [Review of the books *The argumentative turn in policy analysis and planning,* by F. Fischer & J. Forester; *Narrative policy analysis: Theory and practice* by E. Roe; and *Policy change and learning: An advocacy coalition approach* by P. Sabatier & H.C. Jenkins-Smith.] *Journal of Policy Analysis and Management, 15,* 110–121.

Lawrence, R.G. (2004). Framing obesity: The evolution of news discourse on a public health issue. *Harvard International Journal of Press/Politics, 9*(3), 56–75.

Lawrence, S.A. (2010). The impact of stigma on the child with obesity: Implications for social work practice and research. *Child Adolescence and Social Work Journal, 27,* 309–321.

Lears, J. (2011, May 16). Same old new atheism. [Review of the books *The end of faith,* by S. Harris; *Letter to a Christian nation,* by S. Harris; and *The moral landscape,* by S. Harris]. *The Nation, 292*(2), 27–34.

Lee, H.N. (1928). Morals, morality, and ethics: Suggested terminology. *International Journal of Ethics, 38,* 450–466.

Lee, M. (2010). Adverse reactions: Structure, philosophy, and outcomes of the Affordable Care Act. *Yale Law & Policy Review, 29,* 559–602.

Leeuw, F.L. (1991). Policy theories, knowledge utilization, and evaluation. *Knowledge & Policy, 4*(3), 73–92.

Leeuw, F.L. (2003). Reconstructing program theories: Methods available and problems to be solved. *American Journal of Evaluation, 24,* 5–20.

Leeuw, F.L., & van Gils, G.H.C. (1999). Evaluating anti-corruption initiatives: Underlying logic and mid-term impact of a World Bank program. *Evaluation, 5,* 194–219.

Lehmann, C. (2012, June 25). The higher Bealism. [Review of the books *Why some things should not be for sale,* by D. Satz; and *What money can't buy: The moral limits of markets,* by M.J. Sandel.] *The Nation,* 27–33.

Lemann, N. (1984, November 19). After the Great Society. [Review of the books *Losing ground: American social policy, 1950–1980,* by C. Murray; and *The new American poverty,* by M. Harrington.] *The New Republic,* 27–32.

Leicht, K.T. (2008). Broken down by race and gender? Sociological explanations of new sources of earnings inequality. *Annual Review of Sociology, 34,* 237–255.

Lengermann, P., & Niebrugge, G. (2007). Thrice told: Narratives of sociology's relation to social work. In C. Calhoun (Ed.), *Sociology in America* (pp. 63–114). Chicago: University of Chicago Press.

Lens, V. (2000). Welfare reform and the media: A content analysis of two newspapers. (Doctoral dissertation, Yeshiva University). Available from ProQuest Dissertations and Theses database. (UMI No. 9973140)

Lens, V. (2008). Welfare and work sanctions: Examining discretion on the front lines. *Social Service Review, 82,* 197–222.

Lens, V. (2010). RESPECT: The missing policy tool of welfare reform. *Social Work, 55,* 281–282.

Leonard, R. (2000). [Review of the book, *The secret origins of modern microeconomics: Dupuit and the engineers,* by R.B. Ekelund & R.F. Herbert.] *Isis, 91,* 791–792.

Leonhardt, D. (2011, February 8). What are social impact bonds? *The New York Times.* Retrieved from http://economix.blogs.nytimes.com/2011/02/08/what-are-social-impact-bonds/#h

Lerner, G. (1997). Rethinking the paradigm. In G. Lerner (Ed.), *Why history matters: Life and thought.* [Kindle version] New York: Oxford University Press.

Levin, H.M., Belfield, C., Muenning, P., & Rouse, C. (2007). The public returns to public educational investments in African-American males. *Economics and Education Review, 26,* 699–708.

Levin-Epstein, J. (2003). *Lifting the lid off the family cap: States revisit problematic policy for welfare mothers* (Policy Brief No. 1). Washington, DC: Center for Law and Social Policy. Retrieved from http://www.clasp.org/admin/site/publications/file/0166.pdf

Levy, C. (1974). Advocacy and the injustice of justice. *Social Service Review, 48,* 39–50.

Library of Congress, The. (2012). *List of bills introduced in the 111th Congress.* Retrieved from http://thomas.loc.gov/home/Browse.php?n=bills&c=111

Liebman, J.B. (2011). *Social impact bonds: A promising new financing model to accelerate social innovation and improve government performance.* Washington, DC: Center for American Progress. Retrieved from http://www.americanprogress.org/issues/2011/02/pdf/social_impact_bonds.pdf

Lindblom, C.E. (1958). Policy analysis. *The American Economic Review, 48,* 298–312.

Lindblom, C.E.(1959). The science of "muddling through." *Public Administration Review, 19,* 79–88.

Lindblom, C.E.(1968). *The policy-making process.* Englewood Cliffs, NJ: Prentice Hall.

Lindblom, C.E.(1972). Integration of economics and the other social sciences through policy analysis. In J.C. Charlesworth (Ed.), *Integration of the social sciences through policy analysis* (pp. 1–14). Philadelphia, PA: American Academy of Political and Social Science.

Lindblom, C.E.(1979). Still muddling, not yet through. *Public Administration Review, 39,* 517–526.

Lindblom, C.E.(1990). *Inquiry and change: The troubled attempt to understand and shape society.* New Haven: Yale University Press.

Lindblom, C.E., & Woodhouse, E.J. (1993). *The policy-making process* (3rd ed.). Englewood Cliffs, NJ: Prentice Hall.

Lincoln, Y.S. (2003). Fourth generation evaluation in the new millennium. In S.I Donaldson & M. Scriven (Eds.), *Evaluating social programs and social problems: Visions for the new millennium* (pp. 84–97). Mahwah, NJ: Erlbaum.

Lincoln, Y.S., & Guba, E.G. (2013). The roots of fourth generation evaluation: Theoretical and methodological origins. In M.C. Alkin (Ed.), *Evaluation roots: A wider perspective of theorists' views and influences* (2nd ed.) (pp. 218–228). Thousand Oaks, CA: Sage.

Lipsky, M. (1969). *Toward a theory of street-level bureaucracy* (Institute for Research on Poverty Discussion Paper No. 48–69). Madison: University of Wisconsin.

Lipsky, M. (2010). *Street-level bureaucracy: Dilemmas of the individual in public service* (30th anniversary expanded ed.). New York: Russell Sage Foundation.

Liptak, A. (2011a, November 14). Health law puts focus on limits of federal power. *The New York Times,* p. A1. Retrieved from http://www.nytimes.com/2011/11/14/us/politics/health-law-debate-puts-focus-on-limit-of-federal-power.html?ref=us

Liptak, A. (2011b, November 15). Justices to hear health care case as race heats up. *The New York Times,* p. A1. Retrieved from http://www.nytimes.com/2011/11/15/us/supreme-court-to-hear-case-challenging-health-law.html

Liptak, A. (2012a, June 28). Justices, by 5–4, uphold health care law; Roberts in majority; Victory for Obama. *The New York Times,* p. A1. Retrieved from http://www.nytimes.com/2012/06/29/us/supreme-court-lets-health-law-largely-stand.html

Liptak, A. (2012b, October 9). Race and college admissions, facing a new test by Justices. *The New York Times,* p. A1. Retrieved from http://www.nytimes.com/2012/10/09/us/supreme-court-to-hear-case-on-affirmative-action.html?pagewanted=all

Llewellyn, K. (2008) (Original work published 1930). *The bramble bush: The classic lectures on the law and the law school.* New York: Oxford University Press.

Logan, T.K., Hoyt, W.H., McCollister, K.E., French, M.T., Leukfeld, C., & Minton, L. (2004). Economic evaluation of drug court: Methodology, results, and policy implications. *Evaluation and Program Planning, 27,* 381–396.

Lombardo, P.A. (2002). "The American breed": Nazi eugenics and the origins of The Pioneer Fund. *Albany Law Review, 65,* 743–830.

Long, D.A., Mallar, C.D., & Thornton, C.V.D. (1981). Evaluating the benefits and costs of the Job Corps. *Journal of Policy Analysis and Management, 1,* 55–76.

Lovett, R.M (1927, August 24). A real public. [Review of the book *The public and its problems,* by J. Dewey.] *The New Republic, 52*(664), 22–23.

Lowi, T.J. (1971, August 8). The citizens are exploited and made to like it. [Review of the book *Being and doing*, by M.G. Raskin.] *The New York Times Book Review*, pp. 4, 14.

Lowi, T.J. (1972). Four systems of policy, politics, and choice. *Public Administration Review, 32*, 298–310.

Lu, M.C., Lin, Y.G., Prietto, N.M., & Garite, T.J. (2000). Elimination of public funding of prenatal care for undocumented immigrants in California. *American Journal of Obstetrics Gynecology, 182*, 233–239.

Lueck, S. (2010). *States should structure insurance exchanges to minimize adverse selection*. Washington, DC: Center on Budget and Policy Priorities. Retrieved from http://www.cbpp.org/files/8-17-10health.pdf

Lueck, S. (2011). *States should take additional steps to limit adverse selection among health plans in an exchange*. Washington, DC: Center on Budget and Policy Priorities. Retrieved from http://www.cbpp.org/files/6-28-11health.pdf

Lynd, R.S. (1939). *Knowledge for what? The place of social science in American culture*. New York: Grove Press.

Lynn, L.E. (1999). A place at the table: Policy analysis, its postpositive critics, and the future of practice. *Journal of Policy Analysis and Management, 18*, 411–424.

Lynn, L.E., Heinrich, C.J., & Hill, C.J. (2001). *Improving governance: A new logic for empirical research*. Washington, DC: Georgetown University Press.

Lyons, G.M. (1969). *The uneasy partnership: Social science and the federal government in the twentieth century*. New York: Russell Sage Foundation.

MacDonald, S. (1986). Theoretically sound: Practically useless? Government grants for industrial R&D in Australia. *Policy Research, 15*, 269–283.

MacRae, D. (1971). A dilemma of sociology: Science vs. policy. *American Sociologist, 6* (Supplementary Issue), 2–7.

MacRae, D. (1972). Commentary on Lindblom's paper. In J.C. Chalresworth (Ed.), *Integration of the social sciences through policy analysis* (pp. 20–29). Philadelphia, PA: American Academy of Political and Social Science.

MacRae, D., & Wilde, J.A. (1985). *Policy analysis for public decisions*. Lanham, MD: University Press of America.

Machamer, P., & Douglas, H. (1998). How values are in science. *Critical Quarterly, 40*(2), 29–43.

Mafinezam, A. (2003). For inquiry and reform: Think tanks of the Progressive Era (Doctoral dissertation, Rutgers, The State University of New Jersey). Available from ProQuest Dissertations and Theses database. (UMI No. 3077113)

Mahoney, J. (2000). Path dependence in historical sociology. *Theory and Society, 29*, 507–548.

Maine Equal Justice. (2011). *The impact of "sanctions" in the Temporary Assistance for Needy Families Program (TANF)*. Augusta, ME: Author. Retrieved from http://www.mejp.org/PDF/sanctions.pdf

Mair, J., & Marty, J. (2006). Entrepreneurship in and around institutional voids: A case study from Bangladesh. *Journal of World Business, 41*, 36–44.

Malos, S.B. (2011). *Legal issues in affirmative action: Recent developments on executive, judicial, and legislative fronts*. Bowling Green, OH: Society for Industrial & Organizational Psychology, Inc. Retrieved from http://www.siop.org/tip/backissues/tipapr96/malos.aspx

Manicas, P.T. (1987). *A history & philosophy of the social sciences*. New York: Basil Blackwell.

Mann, A. (1954). *Yankee reformers in the urban age: Social reform in Boston, 1880–1900*. Chicago: University of Chicago Press.

Manski, C.F. (2013). *Public policy in an uncertain world: Analysis and decisions*. Cambridge, MA: Harvard University Press.

Marmor, T. (1986). Policy analysis. [Review of the books *Policy analysis for public decision*, by D. MacRae & J.A. Wilde; *Policy analysis in social science research*, by S.S. Nagel & M. Neef; and *The aims and outcomes of social policy research*, by P. Thomas.] *Journal of Policy Analysis and Management, 6*, 112–114.

Marr, C., & Brunet, G. (2011). *Federal income taxes on middle income families at historically low levels*. Washington, DC: Center on Budget and Policy Priorities. Retrieved from http://www.cbpp.org/cms/index.cfm?fa=view&id=3151

Marris, P., & Rein, M. (1969). *Dilemmas of social reform: Poverty and community action in the United States*. New York: Atherton Press.

Marshall, J.M. (1976). Moral hazard. *American Economic Review, 66,* 880–890.

Martin, L. (2000). Performance contracting in the human services. *Administration in Social Work, 24*(2), 29–44.

Martin, L. (2004). Performance-based contracting for human services. *Administration in Social Work, 29*(1), 63–77.

Mason, I., & Mitroff, I. (1981). *Challenging strategic planning assumptions.* New York: Wiley.

Mason, S.E., & Caputo, R.K. (2006). Marriage and women's earnings from work: Perspectives on TANF. *Journal of Policy Practice, 5*(1), 31–47.

Massé, R., & Williams-Jones, B. (2012). Ethical dilemmas in health promotion practice. In I. Rootman, S. Dupéré, A. Pederson, & M. O'Neill (Eds.), *Health promotion in Canada* (pp. 241–253). Toronto, ON: Canadian Scholars Press.

Mathewman, S., & Hoey, D. (2006). What happened to postmodernism? *Sociology, 40,* 529–547.

May, P.J. (1981). Hints for crafting alternative policies. *Policy Analysis, 7,* 227–244.

May, P.J. (1991). Reconsidering policy design: Politics and publics. *Journal of Public Policy, 11,* 187–206.

May, P.J. (1993). Mandate design and implementation: Enhancing implementation efforts and shaping regulatory styles. *Journal of Policy Analysis and Management, 12,* 634–663.

May, P.J., & Winter, S.C. (2007). Politicians, managers, and street-level bureaucrats: Influences on policy implementation. *Journal of Public Administration Research and Theory: J-PART, 19,* 453–476.

May, T., Aulisio, M.P., & Silverman, R.D. (2003). The smallpox vaccination of health care workers: Professional obligations and defense against bioterrorism. *The Hastings Center Report, 33*(5), 26–33.

Mazmanian, D.A., & Sabatier, P.A. (1989). *Implementation and public policy.* Lanham, MD: University Press of America.

McAniff, J.E. (1953). The natural law—Its nature, scope and sanction. *Fordham Law Review, 22,* 246–253.

McBeath, B. (2006). Nonprofit adaptation to performance-based, managed-care contracting in Michigan's foster care system. *Administration in Social Work, 30*(2), 39–70.

McGann, J.G. (2007). *Think tanks and policy advice in the United States: Academics, advisors, and advocates.* New York: Routledge.

McKeown, K.D. (2011). Empowering patients as key decision makers in the face of rising health care costs. *Backgrounder,* No. 2636. Washington, DC: The Heritage Foundation. Retrieved from http://thf_media .s3.amazonaws.com/2011/pdf/bg2635.pdf

McNeill, T. (2006). Evidenced-based practice in an age of relativism: Toward a model for practice. *Social Work, 51,* 147–156.

Mead, L.M. (1985). Science versus analysis: A false dichotomy. *Journal of Policy Analysis and Management, 4,* 419–422.

Mead, L.M. (1986). *Beyond entitlement: The social obligations of citizenship.* New York: Free Press.

Medvetz, T. (2007). Think tanks and the production of policy-knowledge in America. (Doctoral dissertation, University of California, Berkeley). Available from ProQuest Dissertations and Theses database. (UMI No. 3306255).

Medvetz, T. (2012). *Think tanks in America.* Chicago: University of Chicago Press.

Meehaghan, T.M., Kilty, K.M., & NcNutt, J.G. (2004). *Social policy analysis and practice.* Chicago: Lyceum Books.

Meltsner, A. (1976). *Policy analysis in the bureaucracy.* Berkeley: University of California Press.

Mendez, J.P. (2006). The history of the Pillsbury Doughboy: The essential elements of the federal Pell Grant (Doctoral dissertation, Indiana University). Available from ProQuest Dissertations and Theses database. (UMI No. 3215185).

Merriam, C.E. (1924). *Non-voting: Causes and methods of control.* Chicago: University of Chicago Press.

Merton, R.K. (1942). A note on science and democracy. *Journal of Legal and Political Sociology, 1,* 115–126.

Merton, R.K. (1968). *Social theory and social structure* (enlarged ed.). New York: Free Press.

Metcalf, E.B. (1975). Secretary Hoover and the emergence of macroeconomic management. *Business History Review, 49,* 60–80.

Mettler, S. (2002). Bringing the state back in to civic engagement: Policy feedback effects of the G.I. Bill for World War II veterans. *American Political Science Review, 96,* 351–365.

Mettler, S., & Soss, J. (2004). The consequences of public policy for democratic citizenship: Bridging policy studies and mass politics. *Perspectives on Politics, 2,* 55–73.

Meyer, D. (2011). *Global broadband prices halved over last two years.* Retrieved from http://www.zdnet.co.uk/blogs/communication-breakdown-10000030/global-broadband-prices-halved-over-last-two-years-10022481/

Meyer, M. (2008). Political interventions. In T. Mizrahi & L.E. Davis (Eds.), *Encyclopedia of social work* (20th ed.). Retrieved from http://www.oxford-naswsocialwork.com/entry?entry = t203.e293

Meyers, M.K., Glaser, B., & Mac Donald, K. (1998). On the front lines of welfare delivery: Are workers implementing welfare reform? *Journal of Policy Analysis and Management, 17,* 1–22.

MHA of Minnesota v. Schweiker. (1982, December 22). Retrieved from http://mn.findacase.com/research/wfrmDocViewer.aspx/xq/fac.%2FFDCT%2FDMN%2F1982%2F19821222_0000057.DMN.htm/qx

Michelbach, P.A., Scott, J.T., Matland, R.E., & Bornstein, B.H. (2003). Doing Rawls justice: An experimental study of income distribution norms. *American Journal of Political Science, 43,* 523–539.

Michels, R. (1962). *Political parties: A sociological study of the oligarchical tendencies of democracy.* New York: Free Press. (Original work published 1917)

Michels, R. (1927). Some reflections on the sociological character of political parties. *American Political Science Review, 21,* 753–772.

Michelson, P. (1971, July 10). Reconstruction or revolution? [Review of the book *Being and doing,* by M.G. Raskin.] *The New Republic, 162*(2), 25–26.

Mill, J.S. (1863). *Utilitarianism.* Retrieved from http://www.utilitarianism.com/jsmill.htm

Miller, D. (1980). Project location analysis using the goals achievement method of evaluation. *Journal of the American Planning Association, 46,* 195–208.

Miller, S.M. (1985). Faith, hope, and charity—The public relations of poverty. *Contemporary Sociology, 14,* 684–687.

Mills, C.W. (1943). The professional ideology of social pathologists. *American Journal of Sociology, 49,* 165–180.

Mills, C.W. (1967). *The power elite.* New York: Oxford University Press (Original work published 1956).

Mills, F.B. (1996). The ideology of welfare reform: Deconstructing stigma. *Social Work, 41,* 391–395.

Mincer, J. (1962). On-the-job training: Costs, returns, and some implications. *Journal of Political Economy, 70* (5, Part 2: Investment in human beings), 50–79.

Minozzi, W. (2006). Ideas for sale (Doctoral dissertation, Stanford University). Available from ProQuest Dissertations and Theses database. (UMI No. 3235293)

Miringoff, M.-L., & Opdycke, S. (2007). *America's social health: Putting social issues back on the public agenda.* Armonk, NY: M.E. Sharpe.

Mirowski, P. (2005). Economics/philosophy of science: How positivism made a pact with the postwar social sciences in the United States. In G. Steinmetz (Ed.), *The politics of method in the human sciences* (pp. 142–172). Durham, NC: Duke University Press.

Mintz, B., Freittag, P., Hendricks, C., & Schwartz, M. (1976). Problems of proof in elite research. *Social Problems, 23,* 314–324.

Mitchell, C.W. (1922). The crisis of 1920 and the problem of controlling the business cycle. *American Economic Review, 12*(1, Supplement), 20–32.

Mitchell, C.W. (1925). Quantitative analysis and economic theory. *American Economic Review, 15,* 1–12.

Mitchell, C.W. (1927). *The business cycle: The problem and its setting.* New York: National Bureau of Economic Research, Inc.

Mitchell, C.W., & van Kleeck, M. (1923). The outlook for 1923—Discussion. *American Economic Review, 13*(1, Supplement), 45–49.

Mitchell, R.C., & Carlson, R.T. (1989). *Using surveys to value public goods: The contingent valuation method.* Baltimore, MD: Johns Hopkins University Press.

Mkandawire, T. (2005). *Targeting and universalism in poverty reduction*. Geneva, Switzerland: United Nations Research Institute for Social Development. Retrieved from http://www.unrisd.org/80256B3C005BCCF9/(httpPublications)/955FB8A594EEA0B0C12570FF00493EAA?OpenDocument

Mohr, J.C. (1970). Academic turmoil and public opinion: The Ross case at Stanford. *Pacific Historical Review, 39*, 39–61.

Molenaar, P.C.M. (2004). A manifesto on psychology as an idiographic science: Bringing the person back into scientific psychology, this time forever. *Measurement: Interdisciplinary Research and Perspectives, 2*, 201–218.

Mone, L.J. (2002, May 29). *How think tanks achieve public policy breakthrough* [Event Transcript]. New York: Manhattan Institute for Policy Research. Retrieved from http://www.manhattan-institute.org/html/lm_pr_address.htm

MoneyChimp. (2012). *Federal tax brackets*. Retrieved from http://moneychimp.com/features/tax_brackets.htm

Morçöl, G. (2001). Positivist beliefs among policy professionals: An empirical investigation. *Policy Sciences, 34*, 381–401.

Moynihan, D.P. (1965). The professionalization of reform. *The Public Interest, 1*(Fall), 6–16.

Moynihan, D.P. (1970). *Maximum feasible misunderstanding: Community action in the war on poverty*. New York: Free Press.

Mullahy, J., & Sindelar, J. (1996). Employment, unemployment, and problem drinking. *Journal of Health Economics, 15*, 409–434.

Munger, M.C. (2000). *Policy analysis: Choices, conflicts, and practices*. New York: W.W. Norton & Company.

Muro, M., Rothwell, J., & Saha. D. (2011). *Sizing the clean economy: A national and regional green jobs assessment*. Washington, DC: Brookings Institution. Retrieved from http://www.brookings.edu/research/reports/2011/7/13-clean-economy

Murphy, J.W. (1986). Phenomenological social science: Research in the public interest. *The Social Science Journal, 23*, 327–343.

Murray, C. (1984). *Losing ground: American social policy, 1950–1980*. New York: Basic Books, Inc.

Murray, C. (2006). *In our hands: A plan to replace the welfare state*. Washington, DC: American Enterprise Institute.

Murray, C. (2012). *Coming apart: The state of white America, 1960–2010*. New York: Crown.

Mussa, M. (1994). U.S. monetary policy in the 1980s. In M. Feldstein (Ed.), *American economic policy in the 1980s* (pp. 81–145). Chicago: University of Chicago Press.

Nagel, S., & Quant, K. (Eds.). (1996). *Policy studies personnel directory*. Urbana-Champaign, IL: Policy Studies Organization.

Nankin, J., Umansky, E., Kjellman, K., & Klein, S. (2009). *History of U.S. gov't bailouts*. New York: ProPublica. Retrieved from http://www.propublica.org/special/government-bailouts

NASW Foundation. (2010). *Connecting social work research & practice to inform policy decisions: First anniversary report*. Washington, DC: Author. Retrieved from http://www.socialworkpolicy.org/publications/swpi-annual-report.pdf

Nathan, R.P. (1985). Research lessons from the Great Society. *Journal of Policy Analysis and Management, 4*, 422–426.

Nathanson, S. (1998). *Economic justice*. Upper Saddle River, NJ: Prentice Hall.

National Association for the Repeal of Abortion Laws (NARAL) Pro-Choice America. (2012a). *Discriminatory restrictions on abortion funding threaten women's health*. Retrieved from http://www.naral.org/assets/files/abortion-access-to-abortion-women-government-discriminatory-restrictions.pdf

National Association for the Repeal of Abortion Laws (NARAL) Pro-Choice America. (2012b). *Who decides? The status of women's reproductive rights in the United States*. Retrieved from http://www.prochoiceamerica.org/assets/download-files/2011-who-decides.pdf

National Association of Social Workers. (2011). *Code of ethics*. Washington, DC: Author. Retrieved from http://www.socialworkers.org/pubs/code/code.asp

National Association of State Budget Officers. (2011). *Fiscal year 2010 state expenditure report: Examining fiscal 2009–2011 state spending*. Washington, DC: Author. Retrieved from http://nasbo.org/LinkClick.aspx?fileticket=5VMZ59stp1w%3d&tabid=38

National Bureau of Economic Research. (2010). *Business Cycle Dating Committee* [September 20, 2012 Meeting Summary Report]. Cambridge, MA: Author. Retrieved from http://www.nber.org/cycles/sept2010.html

National Bureau of Economic Research. (2012). *U.S. business cycle expansions and contractions.* Cambridge, MA: Author. Retrieved from http://www.nber.org/cycles.html

National Council on Teacher Quality. (2011). Student teaching in the United States: Executive summary. Washington, DC: Author. Retrieved from http://www.nctq.org/edschoolreports/studentteaching/executiveSummary.jsp

National Law Center on Homelessness and Poverty. (2008). *Helping your clients access SSI benefits* [NLCHP Audio Training]. Washington, DC: Author. Retrieved from http://www.nlchp.org/content/pubs/SSI_Audio_Training. pdf

National Research Council. (1933). *A history of the National Research Council, 1919–1933.* Washington, DC: Author.

National Research Council. (2012). *Improving adult literacy instruction: Options for practice and research.* Washington, DC: The National Academies Press. Retrieved from http://www.nap.edu/catalog .php?record_id=13242

Newcomb, S. (1886a). Dr. Ely on the labor movement. [Review of the book *The labor movement in America,* by R.T. Ely.] *Nation, 43,* 293–294.

Newcomb, S. (1886b). *Principles of political economy.* New York: Harper & Brothers.

Newcomb, S. (1894). [Review of the books *An introduction to political economy,* by R.T. Ely; and *Outlines of economics,* by R.T. Ely.] *Journal of Political Economy, 3,* 106–111.

Newcomb, S. (1904). *The evolution of the scientific investigator.* St. Louis, MO: Universal Exposition.

Newton, L. (2002). Constructing the immigrant ideal: Political rhetoric and the social construction of target groups in the 1986 Immigration Reform and Control Act and the 1996 Illegal Immigration Reform and Immigrant Responsibility Act (Doctoral dissertation, University of California, Irvine). Available from ProQuest Dissertations and Theses database. (UMI No. 3048061)

Newton, L. (2005). "It is not a question of being anti-immigration": Categories of deservedness in immigration policy making. In A.L Schneider & H.M. Ingram (Eds.), *Deserving and entitled: Social construction of public policy* (pp. 35–62). Albany: State University of New York Press.

Nichols, J.L. (2012). *Reason, tradition, and the good: MacIntyre's tradition-constituted reason and the Frankfurt School of Critical Theory.* Notre Dame, IN: Notre Dame University Press.

Nixon, R. (1971, December 9). *Veto of the Economic Opportunity Amendments of 1971.* Online by Gerhard Peters & John T. Woolley, *The American Presidency Project.* Retrieved from http://www.presidency.ucsb.edu/ ws/?pid=3251

Noah, T. (2012, February 20). The two Americas. [Review of the book *Coming apart: The state of white America, 1960–2010,* by Charles Murray.] Online review at *The New Republic.* Retrieved from http://www.tnr.com/book/review/ charles-murray-white-america

Noble, H.B. (2006). Milton Friedman, free market theorist, dies at 94. *The New York Times.* Retrieved from http:// www.nytimes.com/2006/11/16/business/17friedmancnd.html?_r=0

Norris, C. (1995). Truth, science, and the growth of knowledge. *New Left Review, 210,* 105–123.

Nozick, R. (1974). *Anarchy, state, and utopia.* New York: Basic Books.

Nussbaum, M.C. (2004). Mill between Aristotle and Bentham. *Daedalus, 133*(2), 60–68.

O'Hara, J., & McNamara, G. (1999). Evaluation: Business or vocation? *Evaluation, 5,* 497–502.

Obama, B. (2011a, October 26). Remarks at the University of Colorado-Denver in Denver, Colorado. Online by Gerhard Peters & John T. Woolley, *The American Presidency Project.* Retrieved from http://www .presidency.ucsb.edu/ws/?pid=96953

Obama, B. (2011b, December 8). *Statement by the president.* Washington, DC: The White House. Retrieved from http://www.whitehouse.gov/the-press-office/2011/12/08/statement-president

Obama, B. (2013). *State of the union address.* Retrieved from http://www.nytimes.com/2013/02/13/us/politics/ obamas-2013-state-of-the-union-address.html

Office of Income and Security Policy. (1983). *Overview of the final report of the Seattle-Denver income maintenance experiment.* Washington, DC: Office of the Assistant Secretary for Planning and Evaluation, U.S. Department of Health and Human Services. Retrieved from http://aspe.hhs.gov/hsp/SIME-DIME83/index.htm

Office of Management and Budget. (2012). *Analytical perspectives: Fiscal year 2012 budget of the U.S. government.* Washington, DC: Author. Retrieved from http://www.whitehouse.gov/sites/default/files/omb/budget/fy2012/assets/spec.pdf

Ogburn, W.F. (1922). *Social change with respect to culture and original nature.* New York: B.W. Huebsch.

Ogden, C.K., & Richards, I.A. (1923). *The meaning of meaning.* London: Kegan Paul.

Oleszek, W.J. (1996). *Congressional procedures and the policy process* (4th ed.). Washington, DC: CQ Press.

Oliver, T.R., Lee, P.R., & Lipton, H.L. (2004). A political history of Medicare and prescription drug coverage. *The Milbank Quarterly, 82,* 283–354.

Olkowski, D.E. (2012). *Postmodern philosophy and the scientific turn.* Bloomington: Indiana University Press.

Oreskes, N., & Conway, E.M. (2010). *The merchants of doubt: How a handful of scientists obscured the truth on issues from tobacco smoke to global warming.* New York: Bloomsbury Press.

Organisation for Economic Co-operation and Development. (2011). Social expenditure. *OECD factbook 2011.* Paris: Author. Retrieved from http://www.oecd-ilibrary.org/sites/factbook-2011-en/11/03/01/index.html?contentType=/ns/Book,/ns/StatisticalPublication&itemId=/content/book/factbook-2011-en&containerItemId=/content/serial/18147364&accessItemIds=mimeType=text/html

Ornstein, E.D., & Ganzer, C. (2005). Relational social work: A model for the future. *Families in Society, 86,* 565–572.

Orphanides, A. (2006). *The road to price stability.* Washington, DC: Board of Governors of the Federal Reserve System. Retrieved from http://www.federalreserve.gov/pubs/feds/2006/200605/200605pap.pdf

Osborn, A.F. (1957). *Applied imagination: Principles and procedures of creative problem-solving* (Rev. ed.). New York: Scribner's.

Ostrom, E. (2007). Institutional rational choice: An assessment of the institutional analysis and development framework. In P.A. Sabatier (Ed.), *Theories of the policy process* (2nd ed.) (pp. 21–64). Boulder, CO: Westview Press.

O'Scannlain, D.F. (2011). The natural law in the American tradition. *Fordham Law Review, 79,* 1513–1528.

Outhwaite, W. (1999). The myth of modernist method. *European Journal of Social Theory, 2,* 5–25.

Overview: 2012–2013 Term. (2013, January 9). *The New York Times.* Retrieved from http://topics.nytimes.com/top/reference/timestopics/organizations/s/supreme_court/index.html?inline=nyt-org

Padgett, D.K. (2008). *Qualitative methods in social work research.* Thousand Oaks, CA: Sage.

Page, E.B., & Stake, R.E. (1979). Should educational evaluation be more objective or subjective? *Educational Evaluation and Policy Analysis, 1*(1), 45–47.

Papineau, D. (1993, July 25). How to think about science. [Review of the book *The advancement of science: Science without legend, objectivity without illusions,* by P. Kitcher.] *The New York Times Book Review,* pp. 14–15.

Parker, A. (2012, January 17). Romney says his effective tax rate is about 15 percent. *The New York Times.* Retrieved from http://thecaucus.blogs.nytimes.com/2012/01/17/romney-says-his-effective-tax-rate-is-about-15-percent/

Parsons, T. (1939). The professions and social structure. *Social Forces, 17,* 457–467.

Parsons, T. (1968). *The structure of social action: Vol. 2. Weber.* New York: Free Press. (Original work published 1937)

Pascal, G. (1986). *Social policy: A feminist analysis.* New York: Tavistock Books.

Patashnik, E.M. (2001). Budgeting more, deciding less. In M.A. Levin, M.K. Landy, & M. Shapiro (Eds.), *Seeking the center: Politics and policymaking at the new century* (pp. 35–53). Washington, DC: Georgetown University Press.

Patashnik, E.M. (2008). *Reforms at risk: What happens after major policy changes are enacted?* Princeton, NJ: Princeton University Press.

Patton, C.V. (1975). A seven-day project: Early faculty retirement alternatives. *Policy Analysis, 1,* 731–753.

Patton, C.V. (1979). *Academia in transition: Early retirement or mid-career change.* Cambridge, MA: Abt Books.

Patton, C.V., & Sawicki, D.S. (1993). *Basic methods of policy analysis and planning* (2nd ed.). Englewood Cliffs, NJ: Prentice Hall.

Patton, M.Q. (1997). Toward distinguishing empowerment evaluation and placing it in a larger context. *Evaluation Practice, 18,* 147–163.

Patton, M.Q. (2002). *Qualitative research & evaluation methods* (3rd ed.). Thousand Oaks, CA: Sage.

Patton, M.Q. (2005). [Review of the book *Empowerment evaluation principles in practice,* by D.M. Fetterman & A. Wandersman (Eds.).] *American Journal of Evaluation, 26,* 408–414.

Pauly, M.V. (1968). The economics of moral hazard: Comment. *American Economic Review, 58,* 531–537.

Pawson, R. (2006). *Evidence-based policy: A realist perspective.* Thousand Oaks, CA: Sage.

Pawson, R., & Tilley, N. (1997). *Realistic evaluation.* Thousand Oaks, CA: Sage.

Pear, R. (2012, January 20). Obama reaffirms insurers must cover contraception. *The New York Times,* A17.

Pear, R. (2013, February 7). Bishops reject birth control compromise. *The New York Times,* A14.

Penna, S., & O'Brien, M. (1996). Postmodernism and social policy: A small step forward? *Journal of Social Policy, 25,* 39–61.

Perlman, R. (1966). Observations on overtime and moonlighting. *Southern Economic Journal, 33,* 237–244.

Persky, J. (2001). Retrospective: Cost-benefit analysis and the classical creed. *Journal of Economic Perspectives, 15*(4), 199–208.

Peterson, P.L., Hawkins, J., Abbott, R.D., & Catalano, R.F. (1994). Disentangling the effects of parental drinking, family management, and parental alcohol norms on current drinking by black and white adolescents. *Journal of Research on Adolescence, 4,* 203–227.

Phelps, C.E. (1988). Death and taxes: An opportunity for substitution. *Journal of Health Economics, 7,* 1–24.

Pierson, P. (1993). When effect becomes cause: Policy feedback and political change. [Review of the books *The three worlds of welfare capitalism,* by G. Esping-Anderson; *The political power of economic ideas: Keynesianism across countries,* by P. Hall; *Institutions, institutional change and economic performance,* by D.C. North; and *Protecting mothers and soldiers: The political origins of social policy in the United States,* by T. Skocpol.] *World Politics, 45,* 595–628.

Pierson, P. (2001). From expansion to austerity: The new politics of taxing and spending. In M.A. Levin, M.K. Landy, & M. Shapiro (Eds.), *Seeking the center: Politics and policymaking at the new century* (pp. 54–80). Washington, DC: Georgetown University Press.

Pizzigati, S., & Collins, C. (2013, February 25). The great regression. *The Nation,* pp. 25–26.

Pizzo, P.D. (1998). *Does Head Start help parents? A critical review of longitudinal studies of Head Start children and families.* New York: Carnegie Corp. Retrieved from http://www.eric.ed.gov/PDFS/ED425868.pdf

Pless, N.M. (2012). Social entrepreneurship in theory and practice—An introduction. *Journal of Business Ethics, 111,* 317–320.

Politics and the morning after pill. (2011, December 7). *The New York Times* [Editorial]. The Opinion Pages, p. A 38.

Polsby, N.W. (1968). [Review of the book *Who rules America?,* by G.W. Domhoff.] *American Sociological Review, 33,* 476–477.

Ponnure, R. (2006). A better deal. [Review of the book *In our hands: A plan to replace the welfare state,* by Charles Murray.] *National Review, 58*(6), 46–48.

Porter, E. (2012, September 5). G.O.P shift moves center far to right. *The New York Times,* B1, B4.

Porter, T.M. (1995). *Trust in numbers: The pursuit of objectivity in science and public life.* Princeton, NJ: Princeton University Press.

Popper, K.R. (1961). *The poverty of historicism.* New York: Harper & Row. (Original work published 1957)

Popper, K.R. (1965). *Conjectures and refutations: The growth of scientific knowledge.* New York: Harper & Row.

Popper, K.R. (1968). *The logic of scientific discovery.* New York: Harper & Row. (Original work published 1959)

Poterba, J.M. (1994). Federal budget policy in the 1980s. In M. Feldstein (Ed.), *American economic policy in the 1980s* (pp. 235–270). Chicago: University of Chicago Press.

Portney, P.R. (1994). The contingent valuation debate: Why economists should care. *Journal of Economic Perspectives, 8*(4), 3–17.

Powell, W. (2003). Doing it, artfully. *Families in Society, 84*, 457–459.

Presidential/Congressional Commission on Risk Assessment and Management. (1997). *Framework for environmental health risk management. Final report.* Washington, DC: Environmental Protection Agency. Retrieved from http://cfpub.epa.gov/ncea/cfm/recordisplay.cfm?deid=55006

Quadagno, J. (2007). Who are the deciders now? The legacy of C. Wright Mills. [Review of the books *Radical nomad: C. Wright Mills and his times,* by T. Hayden; and *Diversity in the power elite: How it happened, why it matters,* by R.L Zweigenhaft & G.W. Domhoff.] *Contemporary Sociology, 36,* 422–425.

Quade, E.S. (1970). Why policy sciences? *Policy Sciences, 1,* 1–2.

Radin, B.A. (1997). The evolution of the policy analysis field: From conversation to conversations. *Journal of Policy Analysis and Management, 16,* 204–218.

Rampell, C. (2011a, July 26). The help-wanted sign comes with a frustrating asterisk. *The New York Times,* B1. Retrieved from http://www.nytimes.com/2011/07/26/business/help-wanted-ads-exclude-the-long-term-jobless.html

Rampell, C. (2011b, September 1). Obama backs bill barring discrimination against jobless. *The New York Times.* Retrieved from http://economix.blogs.nytimes.com/2011/09/01/obama-backs-bill-barring-discrimination-against-jobless/

Raskin, M.G. (1971). *Being and doing.* Boston: Beacon Press.

Raspberry, W. (1984, September 17). Welfare and work. *The Washington Post,* A15.

Ratner, L. (2012, January 2). Food stamps vs. poverty. *The Nation, 294*(1), 12, 14–15, 17.

Rawls, J. (1971). *A theory of justice.* Cambridge, MA: The Belknap Press of Harvard University Press.

Rawls, J. (1985). Justice as fairness: Political not metaphysical. *Philosophy & Public Affairs, 14,* 223–250.

Rawls, J. (2001). *Justice as fairness: A restatement.* Cambridge, MA: The Belknap Press of Harvard University Press.

Reading, H.F. (1977). *A dictionary of the social sciences.* London: Routledge & Kegan Paul.

Reagan, R. (1969). Academic freedom and academic order. *Change in Higher Education, 1*(4), 33–36.

Reed, I., & Alexander, J. (2009). Social science as reading and performance: A cultural-sociological understanding of epistemology. *European Journal of Social Theory, 12,* 21–41.

Reich, R. (2008, March 25). Moral hazard. *The American Prospect.* Retrieved from http://prospect.org/article/moral-hazard-0

Rein, M. (1976). *Social science and public policy.* New York: Penguin Books.

Rein, M., & Rainwater, L. (1978). Patterns of welfare use. *Social Service Review, 52,* 511–534.

Reisch, M. (2002). Defining social justice in a socially unjust world. *Families in Society, 84,* 343–354.

Reisch, M. (Ed.). (2013). *Social policy and social justice.* Thousand Oaks, CA: Sage.

Remler, D.K., & Glied, S.A. (2003). What other programs can teach us: Increasing participation in health insurance programs. *American Journal of Public Health, 93,* 67–74.

Riccio, J., Friedlander, D., & Freedman, S. (1994). *GAIN: Benefits, costs, and three-year impacts on a welfare-to-work program.* New York: MDRC. Retrieved from http://www.mdrc.org/publications/175/full.pdf

Riccucci, N.A. (2005). Street-level bureaucrats and intrastate variation in the implementation of Temporary Assistance for Needy Families policies. *Journal of Public Administration Research and Theory: J-PART, 15,* 89–111.

Rich, A. (2000). Think tanks, public policy, and the politics of expertise (Doctoral dissertation, Yale University). Available from ProQuest Dissertations and Theses database. (UMI No. 9954357)

Ringer, F. (1997). *Max Weber's methodology: The unification of the cultural and social sciences.* Cambridge, MA: Harvard University Press.

Robichau, R.W., & Lynn, L.E. (2009). The implementation of public policy: Still the missing link. *The Policy Studies Journal, 37,* 21–36.

Robins, P.K., & West, R.W. (1980). Program participation and labor supply response. *The Journal of Human Resources, 15,* The Seattle and Denver Income Maintenance Experiments, 449–523.

Robinson, O.C. (2011). The idiopathic/nomothetic dichotomy: Tracing historical origins of contemporary confusions. *History & Philosophy of Psychology, 13*(2), 32–39.

Rodgers, D.T. (2011). *Age of fracture.* Cambridge, MA: The Belknap Press of Harvard University Press.

Rodham, H. (1977). [Review of the book *The children's cause,* by G.Y. Steiner.] *The Yale Law Journal, 86,* 1522–1531.

Roman, J., Brooks, L., Lagerson, E., Chalfin, A., & Tereshchenko, B. (2007). *Impact and cost-benefit analysis of the Maryland Reentry Partnership Initiative.* Washington, DC: Urban Institute Press. Retrieved from http://www.urban.org/UploadedPDF/311421_Maryland_Reentry.pdf

Romer, C. (2013, March 3). The business of the minimum wage. *The New York Times,* BU8.

Rorty, R. (1981). Method, social science, and social hope. *Canadian Journal of Philosophy, 11,* 569–588.

Rosenau, P.M. (1992). *Post-modernism and the social sciences: Insights, inroads, and intrusions.* Princeton, NJ: Princeton University Press.

Rosenberg, T. (2012, June 20). The promise of social impact bonds. *The New York Times.* Retrieved from http://opinionator.blogs.nytimes.com/2012/06/20/the-promise-of-social-impact-bonds/

Ross, D. (1991). *The origins of American social science.* New York: Cambridge University Press.

Rossi, P.H. (1964). Researchers, scholars and policy makers: The politics of large scale research. *Daedalus, 93,* 1142–1161.

Rossi, P.H., & Wright, S.R. (1977). Evaluation research: An assessment of theory, practice, and politics. *Evaluation Quarterly, 1,* 5–52.

Rothman, J. (1974). *Planning and organizing for social change: Action principles from social science research.* New York: Columbia University Press.

Rubin, A., & Babbie, E.R. (2008). *Research methods for social work* (6th ed.). Belmont, CA: Wadsworth.

Rubio, M. (2013). *Marco Rubio's response to Obama's State of the Union.* Retrieved from http://www.businessinsider.com/marco-rubio-state-of-the-union-response-2013-2

Sabatier, P.A. (1988). An advocacy coalition framework of policy change and the role of policy-oriented learning therein. *Policy Sciences, 21,* 129–168.

Sabatier, P.A. (Ed.). (1999). *Theories of the policy process.* Boulder, CO: Westview Press.

Sabatier, P.A. (Ed.). (2007). *Theories of the policy process* (2nd ed.). Boulder, CO: Westview Press.

Sabatier, P.A., & Jenkins-Smith, H.C. (1999). The advocacy coalition framework: An assessment. In P.A. Sabatier (Ed.), *Theories of the policy process* (pp. 117–166). Boulder, CO: Westview Press.

Sabatier, P.A., & Weible, C.M (2007). The advocacy coalition framework: Innovations and clarifications. In P.A. Sabatier (Ed.), *Theories of the policy process* (2nd ed.) (pp. 189–220). Boulder, CO: Westview Press.

Sabia, J.J., & Burkhauser, R.V. (2008). *Minimum wages and poverty: Will the Obama proposal help the working poor?* Washington, DC: Employment Policies Institute. Retrieved from http://epionline.org/studies/sabia_burkhauser_09-2008.pdf

Saisana, M., Saltelli, A., & Tarantola, S. (2005). Uncertainty and sensitivity analysis techniques as tools for the quality assessment of composite indicators. *Journal of the Royal Statistical Society. Series A (Statistics in Society), 168,* Part 2, 307–323.

Saltelli, A., Tarantola, S., & Camplongo, F. (2000). Sensitivity analysis as an ingredient of modeling. *Statistical Science, 15,* 377–395.

Same-sex marriage, Civil unions, and domestic partnerships. (2013, May 15). *The New York Times.* Retrieved from http://topics.nytimes.com/top/reference/timestopics/subjects/s/same_sex_marriage/index.html

Samuelson, R.J. (1984, September 10). Escaping the poverty trap. *Newsweek, 60.*

Sanborn, F.B., & Ayers, J. (1931). The first public welfare association. *Social Service Review, 5,* 468–477.

Sandel, M.J. (2012). *What money can't buy: The moral limits of markets.* New York: Farrar, Straus and Giroux.

Sanders, D. (1991). Collective rights. *Human Rights Quarterly, 13,* 368–386.

Sandmo, A. (1971). Investment and the rate of interest. *Journal of Political Economy, 79,* 1335–1345.

Santoni, G.J. (1986). *The employment act of 1946: Some history notes.* St. Louis, MO: Federal Reserve Bank of St. Louis. Retrieved from http://research.stlouisfed.org/publications/review/86/11/Employment_Nov1986.pdf

Sapolsky, H.M. (2004). The science and politics of defense analysis. In H. Cravens (Ed.), *The social sciences go to Washington: The politics of knowledge in the postmodern age* (pp. 67–77). New Brunswick, NJ: Rutgers University Press.

Schatzki, T. (2005). On interpretive social inquiry. *Philosophy of the Social Sciences, 35,* 231–249.

Schensul, J.J., & LeCompte, M.D. (1999). *Ethnographer's toolkit* (Vols. 1-7). Walnut Creek, CA: Altamira.

Scheufele, D.A. (1999). Framing as a theory of media effects. *Journal of Communication, 49*(1), 103–122.

Schmicking, D. (2005). Is there imaginary loudness? Reconsidering phenomenological method. *Phenomenology and the Cognitive Sciences, 4,* 169–182.

Schmidt, E. (2012). Pay businesses to keep people out of prison. *Harvard Business Review, 90* (1/2), 64.

Schmidt, M. J. (2012). Cost benefit analysis (CBA). *Encyclopedia of business terms and methods.* Retrieved from http://www.solutionmatrix.com/cost-benefit-analysis.html

Schmitz, H., Müllan, R.O., & Slaby, J (2011). Emotions outside the box—The new phenomenology of feeling and corporeality. *Phenomenology and the Cognitive Sciences, 10,* 241–259.

Schneider, A., & Ingram, H. (1993). The social construction of target populations. *American Political Science Review, 87,* 334–346.

Schneider, G., & Shackelford, J. (2012). *Ten principles of feminist economics: A modestly proposed antidote.* Lewisburg, PA: Bucknell University, Department of Economics. Retrieved from http://www.facstaff.bucknell .edu/gschnedr/FemPrcpls.htm

Schochet, P.Z., McConnell, S., & Burghardt, J. (2003). *National Job Corps study: Findings using administrative earnings records data* (Report 8140-840). Princeton, NJ: Mathematica Policy Research, Inc. Retrieved from http://www. mathematica-mpr.com/publications/pdfs/jobcorpsadmin.pdf

Scholz, R.W., & Tietje, O. (2002). *Embedded case study methods: Integrating quantitative and qualitative knowledge.* Thousand Oaks, CA: Sage.

Schram, S.F. (1993). Postmodern policy analysis: Discourse and identity in welfare policy. *Policy Sciences, 26,* 249–270.

Schram, S.F. (1995). *Words or welfare: The poverty of social science and the social science of poverty.* Minneapolis: University of Minnesota Press.

Schram, S.F. (2000). *After welfare: The culture of postindustrial social policy.* New York: New York University Press.

Schram, S.F. (2003). Return to politics: Perestroika and postparadigmatic political science. *Political Theory, 31,* 835–851.

Schuck, P.H. (1975, December 20). [Review of the book *Thinking about crime,* by J.Q. Wilson.] *The New Republic, 173*(25), 26–27.

Schultze, C.L. (1968). *The politics and economics of public spending.* Washington, DC: Brookings Institution.

Schwabish, J., & Griffiths, C. (2012). *The U.S. federal budget, fiscal year 2011.* Washington, DC: Congressional Budget Office. Retrieved from http://www.cbo.gov/ftpdocs/125xx/doc12577/budgetinfographic.pdf

Schweigert, F.J. (2007). The priority of justice: A framework approach to ethics in program evaluation. *Evaluation and Program Planning, 30,* 394–399.

Schwandt, T.A. (1989). Recapturing moral discourse in evaluation. *Educational Researcher, 18*(8), 11–16 + 35.

Schwandt, T.A. (1996). Farewell to criteriology. *Qualitative Inquiry, 2*(1), 58–72.

Scitovsky, T. (1951). The state of welfare economics. *American Economic Review, 51,* 301–315.

Scriven, M. (1960). The philosophy of science in educational research. *Review of Educational Research, 30,* 422–429.

Scriven, M. (1967). *The methodology of evaluation.* In R.E. Stake (Ed.), Curriculum evaluation (American Educational Research Association Monograph Series on Evaluation No. 1). Chicago: Rand McNally.

Scriven, M. (1971-1972). Evaluation: Noble profession and pedestrian practice. *Curriculum Theory Network, 8/9* (Monograph Supplement: Curriculum Evaluation: Potentiality and Reality), 132–139.

Scriven, M. (2012). The logic of valuing. *New Directions for Evaluation, 2012*(133), 17–28.

Seafield Research and Development Services. (2012). *Fourth generation evaluation*. Retrieved from http://www .toonloon.bizland.com/nutshell/4th.htm

Sebelius, K. (2011, December 7). *A statement by U.S. Department of Health and Human Services Secretary Kathleen Sebelius*. Washington, DC: HHS. Retrieved from http//www.hhs.gov/news/press/2011pres/20111207a.html

Sechrest, L.E. (1997). [Review of the book *Empowerment evaluation: Knowledge and tools for self-assessment and accountability,* by D.M. Fetterman, S.J. Kaftarian, & A. Wandersman.] *Environment and Behavior, 29,* 422–426.

Seifman, D. (2012, February 10). Bloomberg slams Obama for allowing states to opt out of federal "No Child" law. *New York Post.* Retrieved from http://www.nypost.com/p/news/local/bloomberg_slams_obama_for_allowing_ fTRDC7B10t70fFeDX8aoVN

Segal, H.P. (2004). Progress and its discontent: Postwar science and technology policy. In H. Cravens (Ed.), *The social sciences go to Washington: The politics of knowledge in the postmodern age* (pp. 110–128). New Brunswick, NJ: Rutgers University Press.

Seligson, L.V. (2004). Beyond technique: Performance and the art of social work practice. *Families in Society, 85,* 531–537.

Selinger, E. (2008). Does microcredit "empower"? Reflections on the Grameen Bank debate. *Human Studies, 31,* 27–41.

Sen, A.K. (1966). Education, vintage, and learning by doing. *Journal of Human Resources, 1,* 3–21.

Sen, A.K (1972). Utilitarianism and inequality. *Economic and Political Weekly, 7,* 343–344.

Sen, A.K (1988). *On ethics and economics.* New York: Blackwell Publishing.

Shadish, W.R., Cook, T.D., & Campbell, D.T. (2001). *Experimental and quasi-experimental designs for generalized causal inference.* Belmont, CA: Wadsworth.

Shadish, W.R., & Luellen, J.K. (2013). Donald Campbell: The accidental evaluator. In M.C. Alkin (Ed.), *Evaluation roots: A wider perspective of theorists' views and influences* (2nd ed.) (pp. 61–65). Thousand Oaks, CA: Sage

Shallat, T. (1989). Engineering policy: The U.S. Army Corps of Engineers and the historical foundation of power. *The Public Historian, 11*(3), 6–27.

Shdaimah, C.S. (2009a). "CPS is not a housing agency"; Housing is a CPS problem: Towards a definition and typology of housing problems in child welfare cases. *Children and Youth Services Review, 31,* 211–218.

Shdaimah, C.S. (2009b). Rescuing children and punishing poor families: Housing related decisions. *Journal of Sociology & Social Welfare, 36,* 33–57.

Shdaimah, C.S., & Stahl, R.W. (2006). Reflections on doing phronetic social science: A case study. In B. Caterino & S.F. Schram (Eds.), *Making political science matter: Debating knowledge, research, and method* (pp. 100–113). New York: New York University Press.

Sherk, J. (2007). Raising the minimum wage will not reduce poverty. *Backgrounder, No. 1994.* Washington, DC: The Heritage Foundation. Retrieved from http://www.heritage.org/research/reports/2007/01/ raising-the-minimum-wage-will-not-reduce-poverty

Sherwood, K. (1999). *Designing and administering a wage-paying community service employment program under TANF: Some considerations and choices.* New York: MDRC. Retrieved from http://www.mdrc.org/publications/96/ print.html

Shoemaker, D.W. (2006). [Review of the book *Satisficing and maximizing: Moral theorists on practical reason,* by M. Byron.] *Mind, 115,* 129–135.

Silverstein, K. (2013, February 19). The great think tank bubble. *The New Republic.* Retrieved from http://www .newrepublic.com/article/112381/salary-inflation-beltway-think-tanks

Simon, H.A. (1955). A behavioral model of rational choice. *Quarterly Journal of Economics, 69,* 99–118.

Simon, H.A. (1957). *Models of man.* New York: Wiley.

Simon, H.A. (1976). *Administrative behavior: A study of decision-making processes in administrative organization* (3rd ed.). New York: Free Press.

Simon, H.A. (1979). Rational decision making in business organizations. *American Economic Review, 69,* 493–513.

Skinner, R.R. (2009). *The No Child Left Behind Act: An overview of reauthorization issues for the 111th Congress.* Washington, DC: Congressional Research Service. Retrieved from http://www.leahy.senate.gov/imo/media/doc/The%20No%20Child%20Left%20Behind%20Act%20-%20An%20overview%20of%20Reauthorization%20Issues%20for%20the%20111th%20Congress.pdf

Slann, M. (1988). [Review of the book *Power elites and organizations,* by G.W. Domhoff & T.R. Dye.] *The Journal of Politics, 50,* 1104–1107.

Smith, J. (2006). Justifying and applying moral principles. *The Journal of Value Inquiry, 40,* 393–411.

Smith, J.A. (1991). *The idea brokers: Think tanks and the rise of the new policy elite.* New York: Free Press.

Smith, J.P., & Ingham, L.H. (2005). Mother's milk and measures of economic output. *Feminist Economics, 11*(1), 41–62.

Smith, M.C. (1994). *Social science in the crucible: The American debate over objectivity and purpose, 1918–1941.* Durham, NC: Duke University Press.

Smith, M.F. (1999). Participatory evaluation: Not working or not tested? *American Journal of Evaluation, 20,* 295–308.

Smith, N.L. (2007). Empowerment evaluation as evaluation ideology. *American Journal of Evaluation, 28,* 169–178.

Smith, S.R. (2007). Applying theory to policy and practice: Methodological problems and issues. In S.R. Smith (Ed.), *Applying theory to policy and practice: Issues for critical reflection* (pp. 1–18). Burlington, VT: Ashgate Publishing Company.

Snyder, L. J. (2011). *The philosophical breakfast club: Four remarkable friends who transformed science and changed the world.* New York: Random House.

Social Security Administration. (2003). *Annual statistical supplement to the Social Security Bulletin.* Baltimore, MD: Author. Retrieved from https://www.socialsecurity.gov/policy/docs/statcomps/supplement/2003/supplement03.pdf

Social Security Administration. (2011). *Annual report of the Supplemental Income Security program.* Baltimore, MD: Author. Retrieved from http://www.ssa.gov/oact/ssir/SSI11/ssi2011.pdf

Social surplus. (2012). [Definition]. Retrieved from http://market.subwiki.org/wiki/Social_surplus

Social Work Congress. (2005). Social work imperatives for the next decade. Retrieved from SocialWorkers.org/congress/imperatives0605.pdf.

Solovey, M. (2001). Project Camelot and the 1960s epistemological revolution: Rethinking the politics-patronage-social science nexus. *Social Studies of Science, 31,* 171–206.

Solovey, M. (2004). Riding natural scientists' coattails onto the endless frontier: The SSRC and the quest for scientific legitimacy. *Journal of the History of the Behavioral Sciences, 40,* 393–422.

Somers, M.-A., Zhu, P., & Wong, E. (2011). *Whether and how to use state tests to measure student achievement in a multi-state randomized experiment: An empirical assessment based on four recent evaluations.* New York: MDRC. Retrieved from http://www.mdrc.org/sites/default/files/whether-and-how-use-state-tests-measure-FR.pdf

Soper, N.E. (1979). The stigma of public assistance programs. (Doctoral dissertation, Carleton University). Available from ProQuest Dissertations and Theses database. (UMI No. NK49545)

Sorkin, A.R., & Thomas, L. (2008, March 16). JPMorgan acts to buy ailing Bear Stearns at huge discount. *The New York Times.* Retrieved from http://www.nytimes.com/2008/03/16/business/16cnd-bear.html

Soss, J., & Schram, S.F. (2007). A public transformed: Welfare reform as policy feedback. *American Political Science Review, 101,* 111–127.

Specht, R.D. (1960). RAND—A personal view of its history. *Journal of the Operations Research Society of America, 8*(6), 825–839.

Spector, M., & Kitsuse, J.I. (1987). *Constructing social problems.* New York: Aldine de Gruyter.

Speer, S. (2010). Economics and evaluation. In J. Vaessen & F.L. Leeuuw (Eds.), *Mind the gap: Perspectives on policy evaluation and the social sciences* (pp. 69–88). New Brusnwick, NJ: Transaction Publishers.

Spencer, H. (1881). *The principles of sociology.* New York: D. Appleton and Company.

Sprinker, M. (1987). [Review of the book *Scientific realism and human emancipation*, by R. Bashkar.] *MLN, 102,* 1225–1227.

Stahl, J.M. (2008). Selling conservatism: Think tanks, conservative ideology, and the undermining of liberalism, 1945-present (Doctoral dissertation, University of Minnesota). Available from ProQuest Dissertations and Theses database. (UMI No. 3318033)

Stake, R.E. (1967). The countenance of educational evaluation. *Teachers College Record, 68,* 523–540.

Stake, R.E. (1970). Objectives, priorities, and other judgment data. *Review of Educational Research, 40,* 181–212.

Stake, R.E. (1975). *Program evaluation, particularly responsive evaluation.* Keynote presentation at "New Trends in Evaluation" conference at the Institute of Education, Göteborg University. Retrieved from http://education .illinois.edu/circe/Publications/Responsive_Eval.pdf

Stake, R.E. (1976). To evaluate an arts program. *Journal of Aesthetic Education, 10*(3/4), 115–133.

Stake, R.E. (1981a). Interview with Robert E. Stake. *Educational Evaluation and Policy Analysis, 3*(3), 91–94.

Stake, R.E. (1981b). Persuasions, not models. *Educational Evaluation and Policy Analysis, 3*(1), 83–84.

Stake, R.E., & Schwandt, T.A. (2006). On discerning quality in evaluation. In I.F. Shaw, J.C. Greene, & M.M. Marks (Eds.), *The Sage handbook of evaluation* (pp. 404–418). Thousand Oaks, CA: Sage.

Stanton, M.W., & Rutherford, M. (2006). The high concentration of U.S. health care expenditures. Rockville, MD: Agency for Health Care Research and Quality. *Research in Action Issue 19.* AHRQ Pub. No. 06–0060. Retrieved from http://www.ahrq.gov/research/ria19/expendria.pdf

Starkman, S., Butkovich, C., & Murray, T. (1976). The relationship among measures of cognitive development, learning proficiency, academic achievement, and IQ for seventh grade, low socioeconomic status black males. *Journal of Experimental Education, 45*(2), 52–56.

Steiner, G.Y., with the assistance of Milius, P.H. (1976). *The children's cause.* Washington, DC: The Brookings Institution.

Stefancic, J., & Delgado, R. (1996). *No mercy: How conservative think tanks and foundations changed America's social agenda.* Philadelphia, PA: Temple University Press.

Steinhauer, J. (2011, May 11). Senate Democrats reintroduce dream act. *The New York Times.* Retrieved from http:// thecaucus.blogs.nytimes.com/2011/05/11/senate-democrats-reintroduce-dream-act/

Steinhauer, J. (2012a, February 8). Birth control is covered, and G.O.P vows a fight. *The New York Times,* A12.

Steinhauer, J. (2012b, December 7). Tea Party hero is leaving the Senate for a new pulpit. *The New York Times,* A1, A25. Retrieved from http://www.nytimes.com/2012/12/07/us/politics/jim-demint-to-leave-senate-to-run-heritage-foundation.html

Stephan, A.S. (1935). Prospects and possibilities: The New Deal and the new social research. *Social Forces, 13,* 515–521.

Sterba, J.P. (1999). *Justice: Alternative political perspectives* (3rd ed.). Belmont, CA: Wadsworth Publishing Company.

Sterba, J.P. (2001). *Three challenges to ethics: Environmentalism, feminism, and multiculturalism.* Oxford: Oxford University Press.

Stern, D., Dayton, C., Paik, I-W., & Weisberg, A. (1989). Benefits and costs of dropout prevention in a high school program combining academic and vocational education. *Educational Evaluation and Policy Analysis, 11,* 405–416.

Stern, E. (2009). Editorial. *Evaluation, 15,* 259–262.

Stevenson, R.W. (2013, February 27). Fight over spending cuts a prelude to budget battles ahead. *The New York Times.* Retrieved from http://thecaucus.blogs.nytimes.com/2013/02/27/fight-over-spending-cuts-a-prelude-to-budget-battles-ahead/?hp

Stiglitz, J.E. (2002). Information and the change in the paradigm in economics. *American Economic Review, 92,* 460–501.

Stone, D. (1997). *Policy paradox: The art of political decision making.* New York: W.W. Norton & Company..

Stone, D. (2011). *Policy paradox: The art of political decision making* (3rd ed.). New York: W.W. Norton.

Strand, V.C. (1994). Clinical social work and the family court: A new role in child sexual abuse cases. *Child and Adolescent Social Work Journal, 11,* 107–122.

Stuber, J.P. (2003). Stigma and means-tested programs: A broader perspective on participation. (Doctoral dissertation, Yale University). Available from ProQuest Dissertations and Theses database. (UMI No. 3068360)

StudentLoanNetwork. (2011). *Federal student loans overview.* Quincy, MA: Author. Retrieved from http://www.studentloannetwork.com/federal-student-loans/

Stufflebeam, D.L. (1983). The CIPP model for program evaluation. In G.F. Madaus, M.S. Scriven, & D.L. Stufflebeam (Eds.), *Evaluation models: Viewpoints on educational and human services evaluation* (pp. 117–141). Boston: Kluwer-Nijhoff.

Stufflebeam, D.L. (1994). Empowerment evaluation, objectivist evaluation, and evaluation standards: Where the future of evaluation should not go and where it needs to go. *Evaluation Practice, 15,* 321–338.

Sugden, R., & Williams, A. (1978). *The principles of cost-benefit analysis.* Oxford: Oxford University Press.

Taeuber, C. (1978). Preface. *Annals of the American Academy of Political and Social Science, 435,* vii-viii.

Tanner, M. (2013). The Patient Protection and Affordable Care Act: A dissenting opinion. *Journal of Family and Economic Issues, 34*(1), 3–15.

Tauberer, J. (2011). *Kill bill: How many bills are there: How many are enacted?* Retrieved from http://www.govtrack.us/blog/2011/08/04/kill-bill-how-many-bills-are-there-how-many-are-enacted/

Taylor, B. (2006). *Positive externality.* Retrieved from http://economics.fundamentalfinance.com/positive-externality.php

Taylor, C. (1985). *Philosophy and the human sciences. Philosophical papers 2.* New York: Cambridge University Press.

Taylor, F.W. (1915). *The principles of scientific management.* New York: Harper & Brothers.

Taylor-Gooby, P. (1994). Postmodernism and social policy: A great leap backwards? *Journal of Social Policy, 23,* 385–404.

Tea Party movement. (2012). *The New York Times.* Retrieved from http://topics.nytimes.com/top/reference/timestopics/subjects/t/tea_party_movement/index.html

Teles, S.M. (2001). The politics of rights retraction: Welfare reform from entitlement to block grant. In M.A. Levin, M.K. Landy, & Shapiro, M. (Eds.), *Seeking the center: Policy and policymaking in the new century* (pp. 215–238). Washington, DC: Georgetown University Press.

Temple, J.A., & Reynolds, A.J. (2007). Benefits and costs of investments in preschool education: Evidence from the child-parent centers and related programs. *Economics of Education Review, 26,* 126–144.

Tevelow, A.A. (2005). From corporate liberalism to neoliberalism: A history of American think tanks. (Doctoral dissertation, University of Pittsburgh). Retrieved from http://etd.library.pitt.edu/ETD/available/etd-08192005-162045/unrestricted/FinalTevelowETD.pdf

Thaler, R.H. (2012, July 8). Watching behavior before writing the rules. *The New York Times,* BU 4.

Thaler, R.H., & Rosen, S. (1976). The value of saving a life: Evidence from the labor market. In N.E. Terleckyj (Ed.), *Household production and consumption* (pp. 265–302). New York: National Bureau of Economic Research (NBER). Retrieved from http://www.nber.org/chapters/c3964

Thaler, R.H., & Sunstein, C.R. (2008). *Nudge: Improving decisions about health, wealth, and happiness.* New Haven, CT: Yale University Press.

The unemployed need not apply. (2011, February 20). *The New York Times,* Editorial, WK9. Retrieved from http://www.nytimes.com/2011/02/20/opinion/20sun2.html

Therborn, G. (1970). The Frankfurt school. *New Left Review, 163,* 65–96.

Thompson, W.B. (2001). Policy making through thick and thin: Thick description as a methodology for communications and democracy. *Policy Sciences, 34,* 63–77.

Titmuss, R.M. (1976). *Commitment to welfare.* London: George Allen & Unwin.

Tobin, W.A. (1995). Studying society: The making of "Recent social trends in the United States, 1929–1933." *Theory and Society, 24,* 537–565.

Togerson, D. (1986). Between knowledge and power: Three faces of policy analysis. *Policy Sciences, 19,* 33–59.

Towle, C. (1944). Common human needs in public assistance programs. *Social Service Review, 18,* 469–477.

Towle, C. (1965). *Common human needs*. Washington, DC: National Association of Social Workers. (Original work published 1945)

Tribe, L.H. (1972). Policy science: Analysis or ideology? *Philosophy & Public Affairs, 2*, 66–110.

Tripodi, T., Layalayants, M., & Zlotnik, J.L (2008). Research. In T. Mizrahi & L.E. Davis (Eds.), *Encyclopedia of social work*, 20th ed. Washington, DC: National Association of Social Workers and Oxford: Oxford University Press (e-reference edition). Retrieved from http://www.oxford-naswsocialwork.com/entry?entry = t203.e343-s2.

Truman, D.B. (1968, May 3). The social sciences and public policy. *Science, 160*, 508–512.

Trumbull, W.N. (1990). Who has standing in cost-benefit analysis? *Journal of Policy Analysis and Management, 9*, 201–218.

Turner, B., & Malpezzi, S. (2003). A review of the empirical evidence of the costs and benefits of rent control. *Swedish Economic Policy Review, 10*(2003), 11–56.

Turner, S. (2007). A life in the first half-century of sociology: Charles Ellwood and the division of sociology. In C. Calhoun (Ed.), *Sociology in America* (pp. 115–154). Chicago: University of Chicago Press.

Tyler, R.W. (1942). General statement on evaluation. *The Journal of Educational Research, 35*, 492–501.

United Nations Development Programme [UNDP]. (2011). *Human development report 2011: Sustainability and equity: A better future for all*. New York: Author. Retrieved from http://hdr.undp.org/en/reports/global/hdr2011/download/

United Nations Population Fund [UNFPA]. (2011a). Addressing low fertility in a world of 7 billion: Macedonians try financial incentives. *UNFPA News*, October 13. Retrieved from http://www.unfpa.org/public/home/news/pid/8591

United Nations Population Fund [UNFPA]. (2011b). *State of the world population 2011: People and possibilities in a world of 7 billion*. New York: United Nations Population Fund. Retrieved from http://www.unfpa.org/webdav/site/global/shared/documents/publications/2011/EN-SWOP2011-FINAL.pdf

University of Michigan School of Social Work. (2009). Addressing poverty through personal services. *ONGOING*, Winter/Spring. Retrieved from http://ssw.umich.edu/Ongoing/OngoingWS2009.pdf

U.S. Department of Agriculture. (2012). *Supplemental Nutrition Assistance Program: Eligibility*. Retrieved from http://www.fns.usda.gov/snap/applicant_recipients/eligibility.htm

U.S. Department of Education. (2003). *FSA handbook federal Pell Grant Program*. Washington, DC: Author. Retrieved from http://ifap.ed.gov/sfahandbooks/0304V013PellGrant.html

U.S. Department of Education. (2009). *Race to the top program: Executive summary*. Washington, DC: Author. Retrieved from www2.ed.gov/programs/racetothetop/executive-summary.pdf

U.S. Department of Health and Human Services. (1983). *Overview of the final report of the Seattle-Denver income maintenance experiment*. Washington, DC: Office of Income Security Policy. Retrieved from http://aspe.hhs.gov/hsp/SIME-DIME83/report.htm

U.S. Department of Health and Human Services. (2010). *Head Start impact study final report: Executive summary*. Washington, DC: Author. Retrieved from http://www.acf.hhs.gov/programs/opre/ ... /executive_summary _final.pdf

U.S. Department of Labor, Employment and Training Administration. (2012a). *Average employer contribution rates by state*. Retrieved from http://workforcesecurity.doleta.gov/unemploy/avg_employ.asp

U.S. Department of Labor, Employment and Training Administration. (2012b). *State unemployment insurance benefits*. Retrieved from http://workforcesecurity.doleta.gov/unemploy/uifactsheet.asp

U.S. Department of Labor, Office of Policy Planning and Research. (1965). *The Negro family: The case for national action*. Washington, DC: Government Printing Office. Retrieved minus tables and graphs from http://www.dol.gov/oasam/programs/history/webid-meynihan.htm

U.S. Department of Labor, Secretary's Office. (2012). *Retirement plans, benefits & savings*. Retrieved from http://www.dol.gov/dol/topic/retirement/typesofplans.htm

U.S. General Accounting Office. (1991). *Designing evaluations*. GAO/PEMD-10.1.4. Washington, DC: Author.

U.S. General Accounting Office. (1999). *Combating terrorism: Need for comprehensive threat and risk assessments of chemical and biological attacks.* GAO/NSIAD-99-163. Washington, DC: Author.

U.S. General Accounting Office. (2003). *Smallpox vaccination: Implementation of national program faces challenges.* GAO-03-578. Washington, DC: Author.

U.S. House of Representatives. (2007). *How our laws are made.* H.Doc. 110-49, 110th Cong. (H. Cong. Res. 190 by Mr. Sullivan). Washington, DC: Government Printing Office.

U.S. Senate. (2013). *Committees.* Retrieved from http://www.senate.gov/pagelayout/committees/d_three_sections_with_teasers/committees_home.htm

U.S. Small Business Administration. (2012a). *Providing employee benefits.* Retrieved from http://www.sba.gov/content/providing-employee-benefits

U.S. Small Business Administration. (2012b). *What is workers' compensation insurance?* Retrieved from http://www.sba.gov/content/what-workers-compensation-insurance

U.S. Social Security Administration. (2012). *Fact sheet: 2012 Social Security changes: Cost-of-Living Adjustment (COLA).* Retrieved from http://www.ssa.gov/pressoffice/factsheets/colafacts2012.htm

Urban Institute. (2008). *The case for evidence-based policy.* Washington, DC: Author. Retrieved from http://www.urban.org/uploadedPDF/900636_EvidenceBasedPolicy.pdf

Urist, J. (2012, June 9). Bloomberg soda bans win few fans, but fat tax may be better. *Newsweek. The Daily Beast.* Retrieved from http://www.thedailybeast.com/articles/2012/06/09/bloomberg-soda-ban-wins-few-fans-but-fat-tax-may-fare-better.html

Vaesson, J., & Leeuw, F.L. (2010). Interventions as theory: Closing the gap between evaluation and the disciplines? In J. Vaesson & F.L. Leeuw (Eds.), *Mind the gap: Perspectives on policy evaluation and the social sciences* (pp. 141–170). New Brunswick, NJ: Transaction Publishers.

Van Dyke, V. (1980). The cultural rights of peoples. *Universal Human Rights, 2*(2), 1–21.

van Kleeck, M. (1910). Child labor in home industries. *Annals of the American Academy of Political and Social Science, 35*(March, Supplement), 145–149.

van Kleeck, M. (1913). *Women in the binding trade.* New York: Russell Sage Foundation.

van Kleeck, M. (1915). The effect of unemployment on the wage scale. *Annals of the American Academy of Political and Social Science, 61*(September), 90–102.

van Kleeck, M. (1919). Federal policies for women in industry. *Annals of the American Academy of Political and Social Science, 81*(January), 87–94.

Van Thiel, S., & Leeuw, F.L. (2002). The performance paradox in the public sector. *Public Performance & Management Review, 25,* 267–281.

Vedung, E. (1997). *Public policy and program evaluation.* New Brunswick, NJ: Transaction Publishers.

Velicer, W.F., Hoeppner, B., & Palumbo, R. (2012, August 29). *Idiographic methods: Individual behavior change over time.* Paper presented at the 12th International Congress of Behavioral Medicine, August 29–September 1, 2012, Budapest Hilton, Hungry. Retrieved from http://www.icbm2012.com/pdf/Factsheet_ICBM2012Workshop_8.pdf

Verbeek, P-P. (2011). *Moralizing technology: Understanding and designing the morality of things.* Chicago: University of Chicago Press.

Vijverberg, W.P.M. (1993). Educational investments and returns for women and men in Côte d'Ivoire. *Journal of Human Resources, 28,* 993–974.

Vining, A.R., & Weimer, D.L. (2009). Overview of state-of-the-art of CBA in social policy. In D.L. Weimer & A.R. Vining (Eds.), *Investing in the disadvantaged: Assessing the benefits and costs of social policies* (pp. 282–314). Washington, DC: Georgetown University Press.

Viscusi, W.K. (1983). Alternative approaches to valuing the health impacts of accidents: Liability law and prospective evaluations. *Law and Contemporary Problems, 46*(4), 49–68.

Viscusi, W.K. (1992). *Fatal tradeoffs: Public and private responsibilities for risk.* New York: Oxford University Press.

Viscusi, W.K., & Aldy, J.E. (2003). The value of a statistical life: A critical review of market estimates throughout the world. *Journal of Risk and Uncertainty, 27,* 5–76.

Vogel, C.A., Xue, Y., Moiduddin, E.M., Kisker, E.E., & Carlson, B.L. (2010). *Early Head Start children in Grade 5: Long-term follow-up of the early Head Start research and evaluation study sample* (OPRE Report # 2011-8). Washington, DC: Office of Planning, Research, and Evaluation, Administration for Children and Families, U.S. Department of Health and Human Services.

Wagner, H.M. (1995). Global sensitivity analysis. *Operations Research, 42,* 948–969.

Walker, W.E. (1988). Generating and screening alternatives. In H.J. Miser & E.S. Quade (Eds.), *Handbook of systems analysis: Craft issues and procedural choices* (pp. 217–246). New York: North-Holland.

Wallace, S.W. (2000). Decision making under uncertainty: Is sensitivity analysis of any use? *Operations Research, 48,* 20–25.

Wapshott, N. (2011). *Keynes Hayak: The clash that defined modern economics.* New York: W.W. Norton.

Watson, D. (1983). Making reality intelligible: The relation between philosophical analysis and the study of social policies. *Journal of Social Policy, 12,* 491–513.

Watson, J.B. (1930). *Behaviorism.* Chicago: University of Chicago Press.

Ways, M. (1969, January). The faculty is the heart of the trouble. *Fortune,* p. 95.

Weber, M. (1946). Science as a vocation. In H.H. Gerth & C.W. Mills (Trans. & Eds.), *From Max Weber* (pp. 129–156). New York: Oxford University Press.

Weber, M. (1949). *The methodology of the social sciences.* In E.A. Shils & H.A. Finch (Trans. & Eds.). New York: Free Press.

Weber, M. (1962). *Basic concepts in sociology* (H.P. Secher, Trans.). Secaucus, NJ: Citadel Press.

Weber, M. (2012a). The meaning of value freedom in the sociological and economic sciences. In H.H. Bruun & S. Whimster (Eds.) & H.H. Bruun (Trans.), *Max Weber: Collected methodological writings* (pp. 304–334). London: Routledge.

Weber, M. (2012b). The "objectivity" of knowledge in social science and social policy. In H.H. Bruun & S. Whimster (Eds.) & H.H. Bruun (Trans.), *Max Weber: Collected methodological writings* (pp. 100–138). London: Routledge.

Weber, M. (2012c). Science as a profession and vocation. In H.H. Bruun and S. Whimster (Eds.) & H.H. Bruun (Trans.), *Max Weber: Collected methodological writings* (pp. 335–354). London: Routledge.

Wedel, K.R. (1991). Designing and implementing performance contracting. In R.L. Edwards & J.A. Yankey (Eds.), *Skills for effective service management* (pp. 335–351). Silver Springs, MD: NASW Press.

Wedel, K.R., & Colston, S.W. (1988). Performance contracting for human services: Issues and suggestions. *Administration in Social Work, 12*(1), 73–87.

Weimer, D.L. (1993). The current state of design craft: Borrowing, tinkering, and problem solving. *Public Administration Review, 53,* 110–120.

Weimer, D.L. (1995). *Institutional design.* Boston: Kluwer Academic.

Weimer, D.L. (1999). Comment: Q-method and the isms. *Journal of Policy Analysis and Management, 18,* 426–429.

Weimer, D.L., & Vining, A.R. (1999). *Policy analysis: Concepts and practice* (3rd ed.). Upper Saddle River, NJ: Prentice Hall.

Weimer, D.L., & Vining, A.R. (1999). *Policy analysis* (4th ed.). Boston, MA: Longman.

Weimer, D.L., & Vining, A.R. (2009). *Investing in the disadvantaged: Assessing the benefits and costs of social policies.* Washington, DC: Georgetown University Press.

Weimer, D.L., & Vining, A.R. (2011). *Policy analysis* (5th ed.). Boston, MA: Longman.

Weir, D. (2008). Fiscal policy. *The concise encyclopedia of economics.* Retrieved from http://www.econlib.org/library/Enc/FiscalPolicy.html

Weisbrod, B.A. (1962). Education and investment in human capital. *Journal of Political Economy, 70* (5, Part 2: Investment in human beings), 106–123.

Weisbrod, B.A. (1981). Benefit-cost analysis of a controlled experiment: Testing the mentally ill. *Journal of Human Resources, 16,* 523–548.

Weiss, C.H. (1991). Policy research as advocacy: Pro and con. *Knowledge & Policy, 4*(1/2), 37–55.

Weiss, C.H. (1997). Theory-based evaluation: Past, present, and future. *New Directions for Evaluation, 1997*(76), 41–55.

Weiss, R.S., & Rein, M. (1969). The evaluation of broad-aim programs: A cautionary tale and a moral. *Annals of the American Academy of Political and Social Science, 385,* 133–142.

Weissert, C.S. (1994). Beyond the organization: The influence of community and personal values on street-level bureaucrats' responsiveness. *Journal of Public Administration Research and Theory: J-PART, 4,* 225–254.

Westbrook, R.B. (1991). *John Dewey and American democracy.* Ithaca, NY: Cornell University Press.

White, A.D. (1896). *A history of the warfare of science with theology in Christendom.* New York: D. Appleton and Company.

White, S.K. (2002). [Review of the book *Making social science matter: Why social inquiry fails and how it can succeed again,* by B. Flyvbjerg.] *American Political Science Review, 96,* 179–180.

Wise, R.I. (1980). The role of evaluator as educator. *New Directions for Program Evaluation, 5,* 11–18.

Whyte, W.F. (Ed.). (1993). *Participatory action research.* Newbury Park, CA: Sage.

Wiedmann, D., Bernhard, D., Laufer, G., & Kocher, A. (2010). The elderly patient and cardiac surgery—A mini-review. *Gerontology, 56,* 241–249.

William, D. (2011, November 13). Cost, need questioned in $433 million smallpox drug deal. *Los Angeles Times.* Retrieved from http://articles.latimes.com/2011/nov/13/nation/la-na-smallpox-20111113

Williams, A. (1972). Cost-benefit analysis: Bastard science? And/or insidious poison in the body politick? *Journal of Public Economics, 1,* 199–225.

Wilson, J.Q. (1975). *Thinking about crime.* New York: Basic Books.

Wilson, J.Q. (1980). *The politics of regulation.* New York: Basic Books.

Wilson, W. (1887). The study of administration. *Political Science Quarterly, 2,* 197–222.

Wilson, W.J. (1987). *The truly disadvantaged: The inner city, the underclass, and public policy.* Chicago: University of Chicago Press.

Wilson, W.J. (2002). Expanding the domain of policy-relevant scholarship in the social sciences. *PS: Political Science and Politics, 35* (1), 1–4.

Wilson, W.J. (2009). *More than just race: Being black and poor in the inner city.* New York: W.W. Norton.

Wilson, W.J. (2011). The declining significance of race: Revisited and revised. *Daedalus, 140*(2), 55–69.

Winter, H. (2005). *Trade-offs: An introduction to economic reasoning and social issues.* Chicago: University of Chicago Press.

Wolf, C. (1971). Policy sciences and policy research organizations. *Policy Sciences, 2,* 1–6.

Wolfe, B.L. (2002). Incentives, challenges, and dilemmas of TANF: A case study. *Journal of Policy Analysis and Management, 21,* 577–586.

Wolfgang, M.E. (1975, July 20). [Review of the book *Thinking about crime,* by J.Q. Wilson]. *The New York Times,* p. BR5. http://query.nytimes.com/mem/archive/pdf

Wood, C.A. (1997). The first world/third party criterion: A feminist critique of production boundaries in economics. *Feminist Economics, 3*(3), 47–68.

Woody, C. (1942). Nature of evaluation. *The Journal of Educational Research, 35,* 481–491.

Woolley, J.T., & Peters, G. (1962, June 11). Commencement address at Yale University. *The American Presidency Project* [online]. Santa Barbara, CA. Retrieved from http://www.presidency.ucsb.edu/ws/?pid=29661.

Worcester, K.W. (2001). *Social Science Research Council, 1923–1988.* New York: SSRC. Retrieved from http://www.ssrc.org/workspace/images/crm/new_publication_3/%7B1f20c6e1-565f-de11-bd80-001cc477ec70%7D.pdf

Wrightstone, J.W. (1942). Techniques for measuring newer values in education. *The Journal of Educational Research, 35,* 517–524.

Yan, M.C., & Wong, Y.-L. R. (2005). Rethinking self-awareness in cultural competence: Toward a dialogic self in cross-cultural social work. *Families in Society, 86,* 181–188.

Yoshikawa, H., & Seidman, E. (2001). Multidimensional profiles of welfare and work dynamics: Development, validation, and associations with cognitive and mental health outcomes. *American Journal of Community Psychiatry, 29,* 907–936.

Youmans, E.L. (1874). The Social Science Association. *Popular Science Monthly, 5*(July), 367–369.

Youmans, E.L (1875). Under false colors. *Popular Science Monthly, 7*(July), 365–366.

Young, I.M. (1990). *Justice and the politics of difference.* Princeton, NJ: Princeton University Press.

Yin, R.K. (2003). *Case study research: Design and methods* (3rd ed.). Thousand Oaks, CA: Sage.

Yin, R.K., & Heald, K. (1975). Using the case survey method to analyze policy studies. *Administrative Science Quarterly, 20,* 371–381.

Zepeda, E., McDonald, S., Panda, M., & Kumar, G. (2013). *Employing India: Guaranteeing jobs for the rural poor.* Washington, DC: Carnegie Endowment for International Peace. Retrieved from http://carnegieendowment.org/files/india_rural_employment.pdf

Ziderman, A. (1973). Rates of return on investment in education: Recent results from Great Britain. *Journal of Human Resources, 8,* 85–97.

Index

About the Author

Richard K. Caputo is professor of social policy and research at Yeshiva University's Wurzweiler School of Social Work in New York City. He has authored five books, including most recently *U.S. Social Welfare Reform: Policy Transitions From 1981 to the Present* (2011), and has edited two books, including most recently *Basic Income Guarantee and Politics: International Experiences and Perspectives on the Viability of Income Guarantee* (2012). He also serves as an associate editor of the *Journal of Family and Economic Issues* and is on the editorial board of *Families in Society, Journal of Sociology & Social Welfare, Marriage & Family Review, Journal of Poverty,* and *Race, Gender & Class.* He has many peer-reviewed articles and book chapters, including "Policy Analysis" in *Social Policy & Social Justice* (Sage, 2014). Between June of 2005 and May of 2013, he served as the director of the doctoral program in Social Welfare at Yeshiva University's Wurzweiler School of Social Work.

⑤SAGE research**methods**

The essential online tool for researchers from the world's leading methods publisher

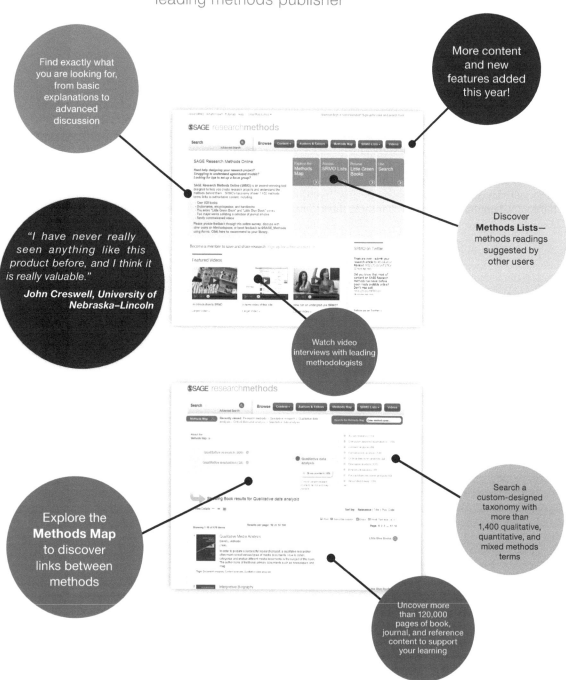

Find exactly what you are looking for, from basic explanations to advanced discussion

More content and new features added this year!

"I have never really seen anything like this product before, and I think it is really valuable."

John Creswell, University of Nebraska–Lincoln

Discover **Methods Lists**— methods readings suggested by other users

Watch video interviews with leading methodologists

Explore the **Methods Map** to discover links between methods

Search a custom-designed taxonomy with more than 1,400 qualitative, quantitative, and mixed methods terms

Uncover more than 120,000 pages of book, journal, and reference content to support your learning

Find out more at
www.sageresearchmethods.com